D0887012

FAITH AND POLITICAL PHILOSOPHY

FAITH AND POLITICAL PHILOSOPHY

The Correspondence Between Leo Strauss and Eric Voegelin, 1934–1964

Translated and edited by Peter Emberley and Barry Cooper

The Pennsylvania State University Press
University Park, Pennsylvania

Library of Congress Cataloging-in-Publication Data

Strauss, Leo.
[Correspondence. English]
Faith and political philosophy : the correspondence between Leo Strauss and Eric Voegelin, 1934–1964 / translated and edited by Peter Emberley and Barry Cooper.
p. cm.
Includes bibliographical references and index.
ISBN 0-271-00883-0 (alk. paper)
1. Political science—Philosophy. 2. Religion and politics. 3. Strauss, Leo, 1899–1973—Correspondence. 4. Voegelin, Eric, 1901–1985—Correspondence. 5. Political scientists—Correspondence. I. Voegelin, Eric, 1901–1985. II. Emberley, Peter. III. Cooper, Barry. IV. Title.
JA71.S793413 1993
320'.092'243—dc20 92-9181
CIP

Printed in the United States of America

Published by The Pennsylvania State University Press,
Suite C, Barbara Building, University Park, PA 16802-1003

It is the policy of The Pennsylvania State University Press to use acid-free paper for the first printing of all clothbound books. Publications on uncoated stock satisfy the minimum requirements of American National Standard for Information Sciences—Permanence of Paper for Printed Library Materials, ANSI Z39.48–1984.

Contents

Acknowledgments

Many individuals patiently and unstintingly gave of their time to correct our decipherment of Strauss's handwriting, to offer suggestions regarding our translations, and to track down sources. Of these, we are particularly indebted to Daniela Kopp, Elke Schmidt, Jennifer Strauss-Clay, Thomas Pangle, and Thomas Heilke, whose combined labors contributed considerably to the text. Professors Dante Germino, Jürgen Gebhardt, Ernest Fortin, Brendan Purcell, Ken Dorter, Zdravko Planinc, Richard Palmer, and Hans-Georg Gadamer also saved us from many errors. In addition, we are grateful to Carleton University, to the Earhart Foundation, and to the Social Sciences and Humanities Council of Canada for providing funds to support our research in the Voegelin archives at the Hoover Institution, Stanford. Finally, we are grateful to the estate of Leo Strauss and to Lissy Voegelin for permission to publish the correspondence and to the journals *Commentary, The Review of Politics, The Independent Journal of Philosophy, Harvard Theological Review, American Political Science Review,* and *Pickwick Publications* for permission to reprint the articles that first appeared in their pages.

Introduction

Political science was founded by Plato in the midst of the crisis of Hellenic society. A breakdown of consensus regarding the ordering principles of the political world and recurring intellectual and social dissension occasioned by the extreme polarities of dogmatism and skepticism provided Plato with a direct sense of political and spiritual instability. Characteristically the fundamental problems of political order become issues of widespread concern during times of instability. During quiet times, political science is apt to contract into a descriptive enterprise, perhaps into an apology for the principles that animate venerable institutions and traditional practices. On the other hand, periods of revolutionary turmoil and political upheaval, what Toynbee called the "time[s] of troubles," usually coincide with the expansion of political science to a comprehensive account of human society and history and of the fundamental principles of order. Again and again in the history of mankind, profound analyses have emerged from grave political crises.

To use conventional language, these analyses constitute the canon of political philosophy. Whether one confines one's focus to Western phenomena or expands it to consider the great political thinkers of India and China, the association of political crises with the formulation of principles of political science retains its validity. Moreover, this empirical generalization is theoretically intelligible insofar as the actual experience of political disorder is apt to elicit from spiritually sensitive thinkers a response that aims to restore an awareness of the principles of political, social, and individual order initially in the mind of the individual thinker and then, perhaps, in the minds and actions of others. The legacy of these efforts is contained in a number of paradigmatic texts that testify to the search for order and that permit subsequent readers to recollect or reconstitute the experiential and reflective origins of this process of consciousness.

There are no guarantees of success. The quest for an awareness of principles can lead down any number of false trails. One may search, for instance, for a precision that is to be found only in mathematics. One may value doctrine as the account of truth rather than an index of movement within the meditative process. On the other hand, antinomian temptations may lead a thinker to renounce common sense altogether. There are, in short, a myriad of ways to contract one's horizon and diminish the amplitude of experience. One thing, however, seems clear, at least so far as the evidence allows us to judge; it is that all the great thinkers have begun their quest by reflecting on the concrete situation of their own troubled times. Often an intense experience of disorder leads people to reflect first on its concrete meaning for them and then to begin the search for principles of order. Moreover, the tensions and ambiguities visible in immediate and concrete events usually reflect a complexity that must be entered into the equation when the order of reality is symbolized by the philosophic consciousness. The concrete, one may say, has a stabilizing effect on that symbolization.

The lives and work of both Leo Strauss and Eric Voegelin conform to the pattern just sketched. Both men developed comprehensive accounts of contemporary political disorders and did so, moreover, on the basis of similar concrete experiences, namely the National Socialist revolution, which made of them both refugees in America. One factor that unites their thought is that neither avoided the effort to come to grips with the complexities and ambiguities inherent in the concrete situation. Both attempted to retrieve the kind of direct encounter with political things that characterized the political science of Plato and Aristotle.

Since the deaths of Strauss (1973) and of Voegelin (1985), a considerable amount of scholarly publication has been devoted to the explication of their work. Moreover, posthumous publication of scattered essays and hitherto unpublished material has provided scholars with fresh material for exegesis, analysis, and, of course, with occasions to express their critical opinions of the two men and of other or rival interpreters of their work.

This doxographic material is of considerable interest in itself, not least of all because it illustrates to contemporary scholars the age-old problem of succession. The generation of the founders has now been succeeded by rival camps of diadochi as well as by their common barbaric enemies, mesmerized by doctrinal sectarianism and the joy of polemic. Much of this polemical material, no doubt, would have benefited from a close study of the correspondence presented here, an exchange that displays little of the doctrinal rigidity nowadays so much in the ascendant. What is significant about the present collection, however, is not simply that it provides a historical window on the early development of the Straussian and Voegelinian "positions" regarding the several topics that the two men discussed. Rather, the Strauss-Voegelin correspondence illustrates how two philosophers (or political scientists in the large sense) were able to carry on an intense discussion over a period of many years, committed not to victory over one another but to the cooperative exegesis of political reality. Both Strauss and Voegelin agreed that clarity regarding the most important and most fundamental questions was more important than agreement regarding any answers to those questions. These letters illuminate at least part of the process of critical clarification.

Agreement as regards the purpose of political science—namely, clarification of the fundamental issues—served, without paradox or contradiction, as the basis upon which Strauss and Voegelin could disagree with each other. Moreover, because their disagreements in detail as well as their agreement in principle aimed at clarifying the structure of political reality, the exchange of views was initially insightful for both the authors and remains so for us. Their agreement in detail, on the question of so-called behavioralism or on the significance of the celebrated intellectual, Sir Karl Popper, will come as no surprise, for both Strauss and Voegelin were serious thinkers for whom disregard of the fundamental questions was an abnegation of philosophical responsibility. The epistolary medium is clearly advantageous to later readers because it enables both men to express their views on the current degenerate state of social science with a demotic frankness that necessarily would have been expunged from scholarly publication.

The exchange in Letters 3 and 4 is a fine example of their common effort to attain clarity concerning the relevant issues. There they discussed some of the problems that arose during the course of Voegelin's critical review of *The Theory of Legal Science,* written by Huntington Cairns. Strauss began by observing that Cairns's position, which Voegelin had criticized, "is not worth discussing." It was characterized by Strauss as "the last remnant of the science established by Plato and Aristotle." Strauss then described the Platonic-Aristotelian science and added that Voegelin's criticism of Cairns's position was based not upon a recovery of original Platonic-Aristotelian science but upon Christianity. Here Strauss and Voegelin were in agreement regarding the scientific or intellectual value of Cairns's work, but they apparently had different reasons.

According to Strauss, Cairns's legal science was a defective remnant of Platonic-Aristotelian science. Cairns's legal science did not explicitly reject Platonic-Aristotelian science, though it did explicitly reject Christianity, which Strauss saw as the basis of Voegelin's criticism. For Strauss, then, the superficiality of Cairns's legal science was accounted for by the relationship between Platonic-Aristotelian science and this degenerate remnant. The criticism raised by Voegelin in light of Christianity accordingly lay outside this question. Hence Strauss observed to Voegelin: "Now, you will say . . . that the Platonic-Aristotelian concept of science was put to rest through Christianity and the discovery of history. I am not quite persuaded of that." For Strauss, then, it was sufficient to look at the critique by modern science of Platonic-Aristotelian science; when Strauss undertook to do so, the question remained open as to superiority of one over the other.

Strauss closed his letter by raising a related issue. He could not agree with Voegelin when the latter had spoken of Plato's attempt to create a myth of the Socratic soul: Plato's "effort was directed toward grounding science anew and especially the science of the soul and of the state." By implication the effort of Plato was independent of mythopoesis.

Strauss's far-ranging argument may be summarized as follows: (1) there is such a thing as Platonic-Aristotelian science; (2) Huntington Cairns's book *The Theory of Legal Science* is an example of a degenerate Platonic-Aristotelian science; (3) Voegelin's criticism is grounded less on that original science than on Christianity; (4) Plato did not ground his science on myth.

Voegelin's response addressed these topics directly. The starting point was not Platonic-Aristotelian science but "the Platonic-Aristotelian problem," at the center of which lay, at least for Plato, a complex of fundamental experiences focused on the personality and death of Socrates. Plato's soul, Voegelin said, was ordered in consequence of his real, immediate, concrete encounter with Socrates; this experience enabled him both to make sense of the surrounding disorder and to resist it, at least in his own soul. The evidence for such an assertion lay in the theoretical achievement of political science, on the one hand, and in Plato's communication of the meaning of his encounter with the ordered Socratic soul, on the other. According to Voegelin, Plato conveyed the basic, or fundamental, experiences of his encounter with Socrates by means of the discursive, linguistic form of the myth.

In addition, however, Plato employed the discursive form of science. Moreover, he used this form of discourse to discuss both "person-peripheral" topics (so called by Max Scheler) and substantive matters of human order. Subsequently in Western history this ambiguous usage led to the great confusion identified here by Voegelin as "scientism." In light of the confusions in the modern day occasioned by an overly rigid conception of what is to be counted as science, one might say that the difficulty was simply that Plato did not differentiate between the two kinds of scientific discourse; the central point Voegelin wished to make, therefore, was that Platonic political science was scientific because the Platonic myth of the order of the Socratic soul established the fundamental criteria by which evidence regarding political reality was judged to be relevant for scientific discussion. In that sense alone, according to Voegelin, Plato grounded his science in myth.

Voegelin followed these remarks with an account of Aristotle's political science and its foundation. According to Voegelin, not the myth of the Socratic soul but the theoretical life of the intellectual mystic was the experiential center of Aristotelian political science. However, that political science was possible only because of Plato's achievement, which Aristotle took as given. Accordingly, Aristotle accepted the criteria of relevance achieved by the Platonic myth and, in Voegelin's term, "conceptualized" it.

Finally, Voegelin turned to the matter of Christianity and of its relationship to Platonic-Aristotelian science. He disagreed with Strauss's interpretation of his own position, that Platonic-Aristotelian science was put to rest or put to an end or superseded by Christianity and the discovery of history. Rather, Voegelin said, Christianity and history changed the significance of the myth of the Socratic soul in one decisive respect: the Platonic-Aristotelian account of human being was that of a polis-being, a being tied to the divine cosmos by way of the Delphic *omphalos*. Accordingly, there was no direct communication between the individual person and God. And correlatively, according to Voegelin, the Platonic-Aristotelian science of man was particularly Hellenic and not, therefore, universal. Christianity and history had expanded the relevant criteria of the Platonic-Aristotelian achievement.

It is clear from this summary of two letters that Strauss and Voegelin were not in agreement about the importance of such fundamental issues as the basis and character of Platonic-Aristotelian science and of the relationship between that science and Christianity. Strauss's response, in Letter 5, illustrated well the point made earlier regarding their common concern for clarification of the fundamental issues. Strauss denied emphatically Voegelin's point that the political science of Plato and Aristotle was by intention particularistically Hellenic; accordingly, by his account, Christianity was not required to universalize the insights of Plato and Aristotle. Nonetheless, while he said flatly that he did not consider Voegelin's interpretation to be correct, he wrote that it was "toweringly superior" to nearly everything else available.

To use conventional and somewhat opaque language, the topic of "reason and revelation" remained implicit in much of their subsequent correspondence, most of which antedated the publication of the mature work of both men. Readers will notice that the longest and most philosophically sustained letters were written prior to and during the time they delivered their lectures at the University of Chicago as part of the series sponsored by the Charles R. Walgreen Foundation for the Study of American Institutions. Strauss gave his first series of lectures in 1949; the published results were *Natural Right and History* (1953). Voegelin's lectures of 1951 led to *The New Science of Politics* (1952) and Strauss's second series, in 1953, found their way into print as *Thoughts on Machiavelli* (1958). Moreover, in 1956 Voegelin published the first volume of his magnum opus, *Order and History* (5 vols., 1956–87). This present volume does not presume to be an introduction to the work of Voegelin and Strauss. This has been done with considerable success already, at least as regards Voegelin.[1] Apart from a splendid *Festschrift*, Strauss has not received the same scholarly attention, though, as was alluded to earlier, interpretation of his work has been the

1. See, in particular, Ellis Sandoz, *The Voegelinian Revolution* (Baton Rouge: Louisiana State University Press, 1981); Eugene Webb, *Eric Voegelin, Philosopher of History* (Seattle: University of Washington Press, 1981); Barry Cooper, *The Political Theory of Eric Voegelin* (Toronto: Edwin Mellen, 1986); Thomas W. Heilke, *Voegelin on the Idea of Race: An Analysis of Modern European Racism* (Baton Rouge: Louisiana State University Press, 1990). All of these books contain extensive bibliographies.

occasion for acerbic and polemical controversy from both within and without the so-called "Straussian" school.[2]

At the risk of imposing too rigid a scheme, one may say that the chief topics of the correspondence were focused upon the themes indicated in the title to this volume. The question of political philosophy was raised in Voegelin's review of Cairns's *Theory of Legal Science*. Cairns's book dealt with what might be called ordinary constitutional and liberal-democratic politics. The inadequacy of his treatment illustrated the current and still-unresolved crisis of modern social science. Voegelin's review of Strauss's edition of *On Tyranny*, which was, incidentally, the only public review either man made of the other's work, illustrated that same crisis in the more strenuous context of constitutional breakdown and tyranny. Both reviews were published during the most intense period of their correspondence.

The pieces in Part Two deal explicitly with the question of "reason and revelation," or of faith and political philosophy. However, unlike the material included in Voegelin's review and Strauss's response, and unlike the topics covered for the most part in the correspondence, these essays were all written from the perspectives and arguments developed by both men in their maturity. Readers will, therefore, be able to trace the late and more fully considered remarks of Strauss and Voegelin on these grave matters back to earlier formulations developed during the course of their epistolary conversation.

A number of issues emerge in such a comparison that are of assistance in understanding the nature of the agreement and disagreement between Strauss and Voegelin. The most immediate of these concerns the American intellectual environment in which they found themselves after fleeing National Socialism. It was a peculiar amalgam of pragmatism and common sense, but also of positivism, phenomenalism, historicism, and behavior-

2. See Joseph Cropsey, ed., *Ancients and Moderns: Essays on the Tradition of Political Philosophy in Honor of Leo Strauss* (New York: Basic Books, 1964). A more extensive bibliography of Strauss's writings can be found in Joseph Cropsey, "Leo Strauss: A Bibliography and Memorial, 1899–1973," *Interpretation: A Journal of Political Philosophy* 5/2 (1975): 133–47. Shadia B. Drury's bizarre splenetic, *The Political Ideas of Leo Strauss* (New York: St. Martin's, 1988), no longer stands alone. *Leo Strauss's Thought: Toward a Critical Engagement*, ed. Alan Udoff (Boulder, Colo.: Lynne Rienner, 1991) is a serious introduction to Strauss's work. See also the special edition on Strauss in *The Review of Politics* 53 (1991): i–x, 3–245. In addition, numerous scholarly articles have been written on both Voegelin and Strauss.

alism, the last named of which were bound together in great part by the desire to emulate the achievement of natural science. What concerned both thinkers about these intellectual movements was the absence of philosophical substance at their core. This hollowness was most evident in the inability of contemporary social science to analyze critically the manifest disorder of political life during the 1930s.

Strauss devoted much of his writing to explaining how the manifold crises of the day were symptomatic of a more fundamental intellectual crisis. The social sciences, he stated, are unable to justify the claim that their inquiries constitute a rational enterprise concerned with the truth. Indeed, the social sciences now avoid the question of analyzing or validating the rationality or justice of political purposes. The reason for this state of affairs is that the dominant interpretive instruments of the social sciences, positivism and historicism, do not recognize the distinctiveness of the political realm and consider undiscernible the grounds that once made an assessment of politics possible. Politics, for modern social science, has no higher dignity than other social pursuits; political philosophy has accordingly been degraded into merely another ideology. Positivism elevates scientific knowledge, based on the model of natural science, to the status of genuine knowledge, thus invalidating those judgments that do not display the universality, certainty, and precision of mathematical form. Historicism deprives principles of understanding and action of any ground other than "groundless decision" or "fateful dispensation." In its most radical, but at the same time inevitable, form, historicism demands total revaluation of all values and continual new beginnings. Heidegger's radical historicism, for instance, demands a wholesale repudiation of all previous types of human interaction and human thought, including the traditional forms of political work and action, and presumes, by standing at an "absolute moment" of insight into the structure of all history, to open up to a wholly new, but unspecifiable existence. This "eschatological prospect," Strauss points out, obviously spurns the naturally restraining and limiting features of politics and political philosophy alike.[3] The danger of such immoderation is best understood, he suggests, by examining Nietzsche's predictive comments on this century's wars, on planetary rule, and on other cataclysmic transformations. If the constructs of reality dominating current intellectual circles continue to prevail, according to Strauss, most

3. "Philosophy as Rigorous Science and Political Philosophy," *Interpretation: A Journal of Political Philosophy* 2/1 (1971): 5–7.

men and women will find it increasingly difficult simply to lead safe and decent lives.

Many of Strauss's assertions concerning the simplemindedness of the dominant models in the social sciences and the dangerous implications of that simplicity emerge in his analyses of classic texts. In Plato's and Aristotle's artful creations, positions are often presented only to show how politically volatile abbreviated accounts of reality can be. The arguments of Polymarchus, Adeimantus, Polus, Eryximachus, Aristophanes, Hippodamus, Phaedrus, or even Socrates himself, in these texts, are fragments abstracted from that whole toward which a comprehensive philosophy aspires. Neglecting man's synthetic nature or the essential conflict between politics and philosophy as a consequence of that nature, or failing to root inquiry in the elementary truths of prescientific understanding, or failing to balance awe with practicality, or demanding of human things an exactitude that the subject matter cannot bear, these acts are first and foremost intellectual errors. But in this century the expectations they advance have also come to nourish ideological activism and mass political movements. Abstracting from the whole leads not only to a lowered capacity for thought but also to "hyper-perfectionist" expectations along with cowardly cynicism regarding the possibility of political action. A survey of the major fields and streams within the social sciences reveals a pattern of persistent and repeated abstraction from the essential features of human existence. Only the restoration of a comprehensive political philosophy, Strauss contended, could reintegrate the fragments of human life, currently appropriated under separate and independent social science disciplines, into an adequate account of human existence.

Voegelin too questioned the reigning orthodoxy in terms of how it determined the criteria of theoretical relevance. Three factors in particular, he said, dominated social science orthodoxy. One was the scientism that proceeded on the assumption that all human phenomena could be studied in terms of physics; the second was the centrality of epistemology in intellectual inquiry; the third was the predominant focus on methodology. What all three produce, Voegelin suggested, is a transfiguration of the way that reality is known by humans and a debarring of crucial components of that reality from consideration. First, by stipulating that what can be scientifically known, that is, known to be true, about human existence is confined to what can manifest itself in the mathematical form of the laws of physics, the social scientist eventually annuls the singularity of man in relation to the rest of nature. Presuming that no decisive difference distinguishes human existence from other organic or vegetative nature condemns the study of humans to assessment of behavioral regularities emanating from their biological structure. It denies that human being is "the spiritually creative center of society and history."[4] It denies as well that human beings are responsible for the diverse understandings of order that they in fact entertain. Second, by assuming that philosophic inquiry can be exhausted by accounts of how and under what conditions the knowing subject apprehends the knowable object, one neglects the comprehensive context within which the subject seeks to know, namely, his consciousness of participation in a reality that transcends his own cognitive talents. Such consciousness, Voegelin proposes, if it is to be an expression of true responsiveness to reality in its entirety, will of necessity have to acknowledge that cognition is one part of the human response to the world-transcendent ground of being. Finally, the subordination of theoretical relevance to method makes it difficult, if not impossible, to recognize that there are different realms of being that require different methods to be analyzed adequately. The choice of the appropriate method depends on its usefulness to the purpose of the inquiry, not the other way round. The inversion of method and purpose simply means that even though the different disciplines of the social sciences are linked together by an identical "scientific" method, no frame of reference based on a comprehensive purpose composes those disciplines into a unity of meaning. Each discipline could assert its meaningfulness, but such an assertion does not establish meaning. Moreover, making the use of method the sole criterion of science would deny that the "elementary verities" of prescientific understanding had any bearing on the nature or purpose of the method used to come to a theoretical understanding of those verities. The result, Voegelin stated, could only be the loss of the meaning of science as "a truthful account of the structure of reality," because significant elements of reality would simply be ignored.[5]

By narrowing the scope and losing the substantive purpose of social scientific inquiry, the result is a closure of the psyche and a loss of responsiveness to reality to which science aspires. And this denial and imaginative reinvention of reality, Voegelin said, is the intellectual condition that contributes to the construction of political ideologies and finally to mass political action. An examination of the "race idea," of

4. Voegelin, "The Theory of Legal Science," *Louisiana Law Review* 4 (1942): 564.
5. *The New Science of Politics* (Chicago: University of Chicago Press, 1952), 5.

propaganda, of the destruction of language, and the construction of political religions and civil theologies shows, Voegelin demonstrated in his early work, how phenomena can be imaginatively distorted with the intention of re-creating the substance of existence. Later he would direct his attention to the imaginary transfiguration of world-transcendent symbols into world-immanent social projects. Despite the imaginary or "magical" aspect of these actions, they are nevertheless capable of mobilizing support for revolutionary transformations of human existence by promises of "the war to end all wars," "the liberation of mankind," or "the cessation of injustice." These dreams of a pragmatic and historical actualization of perfection and purity proceed by a conception of an intramundane personality for whom the ontological ambiguities implied by the combination of the symbols body/soul, perfection/imperfection, finite/infinite, life/death have been condensed into psychological or social, that is manipulable, variables that can be adjusted into harmony with one another by the application of sufficient technical force. What these "ideas" have in common is their negligible link to a frame of reference drawn from the common experience of primary reality. They share the assumption that human existence is simpler than the integrated compound of body and soul, than the ambiguities and pragmatic compromises of the historical situation, than the tensions of our spiritual existence in its movement toward the reality of the divine ground of being. They have "reality" only because they have been situated within a "system" and have had social effects by virtue of political mobilization and agitation. But there is in fact a "second reality" because the ontological ambiguities of human existence do not lend themselves to system. The "ideas" of perfection and purity contract reality, denying the ambiguities to which common sense and ordinary language still pay tribute. Such "contraction" of existence, Voegelin said, is not simply a scientific error, it is a manifestation of spiritual disorder, a resistance to reality. And the restrictions of consciousness played themselves out in the restrictive deformations of human existence that sustained the political ideologies and mass political movements of this century.

Strauss and Voegelin agree, then, that the political deformations of the twentieth century were anticipated by intellectual constructs of reality that depart from reality and restrict the horizon of human existence. In turn, these intellectual movements are preparation for political action. Such imaginary constructs arise from an incapacity to determine what is relevant or irrelevant to political science. "Abstracting" or "contracting" reality has provided effective but imaginary "ideas" for the murderous wars of ideology that may be waged in the name of science, progress, and a new humanism. The events of the twentieth century have demonstrated how deadly this seemingly "intellectual" error could be, how the dreamworld of intellectuals could translate into the horrors of political domination. And both Strauss and Voegelin realized that exposing the distortions of reality underlying these phenomena would require a restoration of the whole human being as the focus of political science, a renewal of a philosophy that again considered man's essential being. For both men, this resumption of philosophical anthropology would take its bearings from classical philosophy, from the clarity Plato and Aristotle brought, as Strauss says, to "what the fundamental questions are and how they should be approached."

Both thinkers shared the conviction that the internal unraveling of modern philosophy had made possible a renewal of the experience of thinking and a direct encounter with reality, unmediated by centuries of preoccupation with formulaic manifestations of that philosophic quest. But what was meant by renewing the philosophic enterprise on "the Platonic-Aristotelian level of questioning"? What shape would that renewal have?

Voegelin grounds the search for political order in human responsiveness to the order of being. Making sense of that order means symbolizing the experience of participation in it. But the experience of participation is always "a disturbing in-between of ignorance and knowledge, of time and timelessness, of imperfection and perfection, of hope and fulfillment, and ultimately of life and death."[6] The process of reality in which man participates contains a historical dimension whose most obvious aspect is experienced as unrest, disquiet, or "tension." What gives symbols their particular persuasive power is their proximity to this tension of and within reality. However, the intimacy of symbol and the experience of tension are easily disturbed, especially when the symbol is abstracted from the originating experience and turned into a constituent of doctrine. Transforming symbols into doctrines treats them as instruments of cognition, rather than as condensations of participation in a diffuse field of reality. Reality, Voegelin writes, is not external to consciousness and so not an object of cognition. It is a process within which humans are situated and that is illuminated from within.

6. "The Gospel and Culture" (1971), reprinted in *The Collected Works of Eric Voegelin*, vol. 12, *Published Essays, 1966–1985*, ed. E. Sandoz (Baton Rouge: Louisiana State University Press, 1990), 176.

Voegelin considers dogmatism, which colors all the modern crises, as a greater problem than lack of finality. The philosophizing consciousness cannot stand outside of the process of reality, beyond the experience of existential tension, and discern its meaning as a whole. This means that "truth" is less a possession than a dimension of "existence in tension." The symbolization of this "tensional truth" or "existential truth" is how the mystery of reality is made meaningful. "Existential truth" is not therefore a representation of reality in an image of achievement, completeness, and perfection. But neither should the term "existential" evoke the sense of a merely transient meaning somehow situationally grasped within infinite temporality. Under either case, Voegelin comments, "the symbols may cease altogether to be translucent for reality."[7] At this point reason ceases to be the faculty for illuminating the context within which personal existence is situated.

But Strauss is not content with this formulation; he objected, for example, to Voegelin's use of the word "existential." Behind the usage, he charges, lies the specter of Heidegger's separation of thinking and metaphysics, and the attachment of the former to Being, understood now as the indeterminate, generative process of emergence and withdrawal. The existentialist longing for a primordial "belongingness" to Being, which antedates subjectivism and objectivism, does not, Strauss objects, contribute to the human need for moral and political principles. "Existential," Strauss writes, "is opposed to the 'objective', 'theoretical', and thus betrays [an] anti-Platonic origin . . . insofar as I am serious and there are questions, I look for the objective truth." And such "objectivity" necessarily excludes the "infinitely unimportant" historical. "'History'," Strauss makes clear, "belongs in the practical dimension, in the dimension which is subordinated to the theoretical." Is this a difference over linguistic formulas or is it a difference in principle?

It is true that Voegelin does resist the demand for "objectivity," at least as it is commonly used, because he sees in the enterprise to achieve it a contraction and reduction of the range of relevant elements constituting the philosophizing consciousness. "The idea of man," he argued, "is not a datum in the external world but a creation of the human spirit, undergoing historical changes, and it has to be recreated every generation and by every single person." Moreover, again to Strauss's dismay, he is unwilling to make the strong statement that the aim of a recollective history of philosophy is

7. "Immortality: Experience and Symbol" (1967), in *Collected Works* 12:54.

truth, preferring to confine the task to the more modest aim of accounting for "existential transformations" in which "truth" becomes socially effective or is hindered in such effectiveness. For Voegelin this implies no negation or relativization of ontology, as should be clear from his list of "existential" themes: "theogony . . . destruction of the knowledge of truth through the *pleonexia* of intellectuals . . . the effectiveness of authority through existential readiness to reproduce the known truth imaginatively." It is not clear, however, that this response would satisfy Strauss's objection.

Voegelin, it seems, restricts himself to symbolizing the process of the noetic experience of transcendent divine being, which by its very character cannot be definitive or complete. The decisive issue here is Voegelin's reliance on what by convention would be called a metaphysics of process: process, while it evidently has structure and substance, cannot be objectively fixed. Nor could a comprehensive depiction of the process of consciousness occlude the "historical dimension," which Voegelin denies is a mere stream of temporal events distinguishable from what is real; the "historical dimension," for Voegelin, is "the permanent presence of the process of reality in which man participates with his conscious existence."[8] It is thus more than the merely contingent "practical"; it is certainly other than Heidegger's parousiastic speculation on Being.[9]

In opposition to what he sees as an implicit "historicism," Strauss raises the specter of a regression into the indeterminacy of a fateful encounter with the boundless and limitless. What he sees lost by such an encounter are the standards by which political regimes and psyches can be judged. Neither defective regimes nor the ascent of the soul toward perfection and completeness could be assessed without the possibility of a fulfillment to the philosophic enterprise. The term "existential," for Strauss, abnegates "theory," that is, the possibility of a transcendence of existence toward an essential order that is prescriptive. For Strauss, the issues of context and effectiveness of known truth are matters that do not essentially condition the possibility of truth; instead, they are related to remediable flaws of the discussants in a philosophic conversation. The decisive philosophic issue for Strauss and one that is denied in the term "existential," is the possibility of transcendence of the merely "practical."

Now obviously Voegelin too aims at the renewal of the possibility of

8. "Remembrance of Things Past" (1977), in *Collected Works* 12:311.

9. See Voegelin, *Science, Politics, and Gnosticism*, trans. William J. Fitzpatrick (Chicago: Regnery, 1968), 46–49, and *Collected Works* 12:8–10.

transcendence as the formative component of the substance of a sound society. And, from his point of view, as he writes to Strauss "we are in agreement . . . on the question of ontology." Moreover, there is on Voegelin's part neither lack of aptitude for political judgment nor any abandonment of the measures of political order in the exercise of that judgment. Wherein, then, lie their differences?

Voegelin warns of twin dangers accompanying dogmatic adherence to doctrines. First, the object representation of experience as doctrine threatens to sever the connection of experience with reality, which leads to "belief" in a remnant of ideas that are lifeless, not to say meaningless. Second, such doctrines lend themselves to the purpose of ideological agitation, by means of terms such as "progress," "the liberation of mankind" and so forth. The complex of experiences constituting the openness of consciousness to divine reality cannot be rendered into univocal and precise terms. Abbreviating the full amplitude of that complex fundamentally distorts the experiences, leaving the symbols available as practical political instruments for mobilizing emotions and sentiments and thereby human beings as well.

But Strauss hardly ignores the erotic dynamic of philosophy, as is evident in his denunciation of Kierkegaard's concept of "existence" because it denied "the passion of revelation that moves the Platonic dialogue, this highest *mania*." Nor is it appropriate to see Strauss's concern for measure as the inspiration for ideological activism. Indeed, he accuses "existentialist philosophy" of transforming praxis into "existence," that is, of analyzing away the distinct compromises and ambivalences peculiar to political prudence and to political life. In place of prudence and political life, existentialists recognize only a generalized sphere of sheer happenings that must be responded to by a systematic project, authentically or inauthentically, "a praxis," he comments, "that is no longer intelligible as praxis." Disagreements over the use of the term "existence," it seems, point to a divergence about the nature of the philosophizing psyche.

To clarify this divergence, difference, or even disagreement, perhaps one should turn to Plato, whose account of the self-moved psyche and of its appropriate motion may offer an explanation. Plato sees the psyche's self-movement as arising from its being situated in a field of tension structured by forces tending on the one hand toward limit, proportionality, and unity and on the other hand toward transience, flux, and dispersion. These forces apparently emanate from two polar determinations, the unmoved One and the boundless infinite, or *apeiron*. The interplay of these forces constitutes the essence of the psyche as being-in-motion, but it also informs that motion. When the two forces are in balance, the tension, and hence free self-movement, of the psyche is preserved. Thought will display a rhythm that unites measure and dynamism. But when one pole is abstracted and the field of experience is no longer structured by tension, the psyche no longer moves itself and thus loses its distinctive capacity for thought. It will incline toward sophistry when exercising its ratiocinative power, and toward a love for tyranny when it becomes a political force. Depending on the dominant pull within the psyches of his interlocutors, Plato's Socrates is portrayed in one dialogue or another as being dramatically opposed to dogmatism or to radical skepticism, often abstracting from the complete experience of the philosophic quest to exaggerate the temptations and dangers of lack of balance. Books 8 and 9 of the *Republic*, to illustrate, are a comprehensive catalogue of the pathology into which the psyche can be derailed.

In light of Plato's account of the nature of thought and his concern for its pathological manifestations, one could suggest that the divergence of focus between Strauss and Voegelin should not be seen as an indication that their "positions" are opposed. Rather, these "positions" are warnings to others of the danger of destroying the balance of the psyche's self-motion. Each "position" is a resistance to untruth. In a way, each thinker stands in the relation of Plato to Socrates in the *Apology*, advancing a subtle charge concerning the implications of a degeneration of the teaching in the hands of lesser minds unable to maintain balance in the experience of thinking.

The reason for the divergence may be traced to the distinct problems that each man emphasized in focusing attention upon the formative moment of thought that prevents derailment. Voegelin finds in the language of process an adequate account of how consciousness attempts from its finite experiences to understand the "infinite" processes in which it participates. "Truth" is not a representation of a reality external to consciousness but rather an illumination from within, structured by the philosophizing consciousness experiencing reality as transcending itself. "Process," "unrest," and "tension" evoke the experiences of the questioning being. Strauss, on the other hand, is concerned with the measures that necessarily structure and inform that process of ascent; the Platonic-Aristotelian questioning, for Strauss, is a progressive disclosure of truth, the replacement of the randomness and fickleness of opinion, by a complete account of the whole that is implied from the beginning of longing. But neither thinker denies they are necessarily complementary moments of the event of philosophizing. The combination of Strauss's and

Voegelin's analyses of the formative event that structures the thinking process brings out the comprehensive experience that Plato defines as the essence of the psyche. Together their accounts may be understood as adequate to the whole of that process, as expressing the healthy tension and balance between motion and finality, or between genesis and order. The apparent disagreement in terminology and details, then, can be seen as a difference in focus rather than of substance. Each identifies the vulnerability of the thinking process to corruption slightly differently. This leads each to emphasize one pole over the other as a means to restore balance. It would be inappropriate to build upon this difference in emphasis an interpretation of doctrinal divergence. Indeed, doctrinalization of thinking is precisely what each attempted to prevent. And this is, for us, the legacy that this correspondence leaves behind.

In Part Three contemporary scholars were asked to respond to the issues raised in the correspondence and in the mature published work of Strauss and Voegelin. The contributors are themselves distinguished scholars and all have devoted considerable effort to mastering the complex arguments of one or of both correspondents. Their insights commended themselves to us particularly because what recurs in their assessments is a notion we believe to be central to understanding the relationship between Strauss and Voegelin. Simply put, this philosophical conversation never founders into dogmatism or skepticism. Refusing to reduce either thinker to a doctrinaire position, these interpreters reopen for us the openness of Strauss and Voegelin to primary reality.

We would like to conclude this introduction with a few technical editorial observations. The correspondence of Leo Strauss and Eric Voegelin is held chiefly in the Voegelin collection at the Hoover Institution, Stanford. A few letters exist only in the Strauss collection at the University of Chicago. Approximately fifty letters survive from a thirty-year period, 1934–64, most of which were written in German and many of these, especially those by Strauss, written by hand.

The handwriting of both men was notoriously difficult to decipher. Strauss handwrote nearly all his letters; Voegelin typed most of his, adding only small changes by hand. Both men wrote in the midst of heavy teaching and scholarly commitments and often apologized for unavoidable delays. At one point Strauss observed that he had had proper paper some weeks earlier, but no time to write. Now that he had time, the only paper was of very poor quality. Three months went by and proper writing paper had yet to be found, so his message was again sent off on occasional scrap.

Matters were made more difficult owing to Strauss's use of a personal shorthand. The first letter of a word might be clear, the next few not so clear, and the ending little more than a wiggled line.

The procedure we followed was first to transcribe the autograph into typescript and translate the typed rendering. Several German-speakers of an older generation whom we thought might be more familiar than ourselves with the script Strauss employed were consulted. Voegelin, however, had no such expert assistance, with the result that he occasionally misread Strauss fundamentally. Indeed, there exist a few sentences all the words of which could reasonably be rendered two or three different ways. This simply means that one cannot expect precision in a work of this type.

The heart of the correspondence, as we mentioned, was written between 1942 and 1953. During these years the two men became more familiar with one another's work, and the strict formality of the old world epistolary style was slightly relaxed from the highly formal *Sehr geherter Herr Doktor Voegelin/Strauss* to *Lieber Herr Strauss/Voegelin*. It never evolved into Lieber Freund or Dear Eric and Dear Leo. In short, Strauss and Voegelin retained a consistent respect for one another and an air of gravity throughout their conversation.

Finally, we would like to repeat the warning issued earlier: newcomers to political philosophy should by no means consider the texts collected here in any way a substitute for the longer and harder arguments published elsewhere. It remains true, however, that the Strauss-Voegelin correspondence is remarkable for being directed toward the enduring topics of political philosophy. One can see in these exchanges how two scholars of great intelligence and good will were able to converse. Both men were aware of differences in their approach to political reality and in their interpretations of texts. Both men agreed profoundly on the sources of political fanaticism and speculative fantasy even while expressing their arguments in distinctive language. To give but one last example: Strauss later wrote of the forgetting, or the oblivion, of eternity as characterizing the modern crisis, whereas Voegelin later described it in terms of the effort to bring about an imaginary collapse in the tension between man and God. Not a great deal of interpretative ingenuity is required to apprehend the existence of a family resemblance between these two formulations. In reading these letters and the major published work of these two great political philosophers one is given a splendid opportunity to undertake a meditative exegesis along the lines of meaning that so clearly underlie the exchanges presented here.

Part

1

The Strauss-Voegelin Correspondence

1934–1964

List of Letters

Letter 1

London, 2.X. 1934
18 Taviton St., W.C. 1
Museum 7914

Esteemed Mr. Strauss,

Mr. Kitteredge of the Rockefeller Foundation was kind enough to give me your address, as he thought that we would have some points of contact in our scientific work.[1] I am currently occupied with some studies on Renaissance philosophy and theories of the state. I will remain in London only for a few days and I would be very grateful if you could phone me as soon as possible, sometime in the morning before nine o'clock, so that we can make an appointment, if your time allows.

With the best wishes, I am,

Very respectfully yours,
Eric Voegelin

1. Both Strauss and Voegelin were at various times supported by the Rockefeller Foundation. Tracy Kitteredge was Assistant Director for the Social Sciences.

Letter 2

Social Research
An International Quarterly of
Political & Social Science
66 West 12 Street
New York City
January 19, 1942

Dr. Eric Voegelin
University of Alabama
Department of Political Science
University, Alabama

Dear Dr. Voegelin:

Thank you for your letter of January 14. I regret not having been able to see you while you were in New York.

We should be very grateful if you could find it possible to give us some definite information as to when we might expect your manuscript on the theory of the political myth, and also a more precise title, which we might list on our agenda.

Sincerely yours,
Leo Strauss

Letter 3

3900 Greystone Avenue
New York City
24.11.1942

Esteemed Dr. Voegelin,

Many thanks for sending me your critique of Cairns's book;[2] I read the critique immediately with great interest and considerable agreement. One so rarely reads such detailed, thorough, and precise critiques. The flourish

2. Voegelin, "The Theory of Legal Science: A Review," *Louisiana Law Review* 4 (1942): 554–71; under review was Huntington Cairns, *The Theory of Legal Science* (Chapel Hill: University of North Carolina Press, 1941).

and the clarity of your diction make reading a pleasure. If there was some need for external confirmation of the appropriateness of your critique, then it is the response to it [by Cairns].[3]

There remains though, for me, a question that is not resolved by the refutation of Cairns (or of Weber either). After all, the position you attack is only the last remnant of the science established by Plato and Aristotle: the postulate of an exact ethics and politics in Plato; Aristotle's adhering to the ideal of exactness despite the abandonment of its application to the human things; the necessarily higher ranking of physics over ethics and politics, at least for Aristotle and his successors; the opinion that held for the whole tradition until the nineteenth century, "that the question of *generality* does have a bearing on the legitimacy of [the] status [of a science]" (contrary to p. 561);[4] the impossibility of grounding science on religious faith. People like Cairns (perhaps without knowing it) arrived from the Platonic-Aristotelian concept of science—indeed, not at their position, which is not worth discussing—but at the rejection of, for example, your position. Now, you will say (p. 563) that the Platonic-Aristotelian concept of science was put to rest through Christianity and the discovery of history.[5] I am not quite persuaded of that. Based on countercriticism of the Cartesian tradition, and leaving other questions aside, we can no longer adopt the thesis of Descartes and all his successors that Plato and Aristotle are fundamentally inadequate; we would have to verify this thesis more directly, by a direct critique of Plato and Aristotle. A critique requires adequate understanding. What about us? The more I read the classics, the more I see how inadequate the assistance is that one has been offered, for example, from classical philology. In short—I consider the central question

3. Huntington Cairns, "Comment," *Louisiana Law Review* 4 (1942): 571–72.

4. P. 561, top, "Is there not a distinction between generality of *intention* and generality of *factual* understanding?" [Footnote by Strauss.] Voegelin wrote, "A proposition may be illegitimate in a system of social science for one of two reasons: (1) because it is unverifiable, or (2) because it is irrelevant in the system of reference that is determined by philosophical anthropology; the question of generality has no bearing on the legitimacy of its status."

5. Voegelin wrote (562–63), "The appearance of Christ has added to the idea of man the dimension of spiritual singularity of every human being, so that we can no longer build a science of social order, for instance on the anthropologies of Plato or Aristotle. Likewise, within the Christian Western World the idea of man is not static, but changes constantly; it has acquired, for instance, through and since the Renaissance the dimension of historic singularity."

[of Plato and Aristotle versus Descartes] entirely open. I can especially not agree with you when you speak of Plato's attempt "to create a new myth": his effort was directed toward grounding science anew and especially the science of the soul and of the state.

But these are, in the context of the critique of Cairns, small matters. I have often asked myself how one could, for example, push the view held by Cairns in an intelligible manner *ad absurdum*; I find that you have resolved this problem excellently.

Please excuse me that I use the opportunity of these lines to remind you of a half-promised essay for *Social Research*. You would oblige me greatly if you could let me know when we might have it and what the exact title will be.

By rumor, I have heard that Dr. Benno Strauss (no relative of mine), an expert in German literature, particularly of the eighteenth century, and a very nice man, is at Louisiana University. Perhaps you will meet him at some point. In case you meet him, please greet him warmly from me.

Respectfully yours,
Leo Strauss

Letter 4

December 9, 1942

Dear Dr. Strauss,

Warmest thanks for your dear letter of November 24. It is a true joy to receive an answer to a modest review that enters into the substantial problems, even though they can only be incidentally addressed.

Unfortunately, I must agree with your critical comments: Mr. Cairns's critique of positivism dissolves none of the problems of the counterposition. I believe, to be sure, to have seen a bit of light in these questions, thanks to work done on the *History of Political Ideas*,[6] which for myself at least has the function of clarifying the theoretically essential problems. If

6. *The History of Political Ideas* was a multivolume work written during the 1940s but not published at that time. It was recast several times. Part of it appeared as the first three volumes of *Order and History*; a fragment of the later materials was edited by John Hallowell as *From Enlightenment to Revolution* (Durham, N.C.: Duke University Press, 1975).

you allow, I will briefly indicate where I see, if not solutions, at least possibilities of clarification; you will certainly be able to supplement further my necessarily fragmentary lines.

The Platonic-Aristotelian problem seems to me as well to be the inevitable starting-point. I see it in the following way: at the center of Platonic *political* thinking stand the *fundamental experiences*, which are tied together with the person and death of Socrates—catharsis through consciousness of death and the enthusiasm of eros both pave the way for the right ordering of the soul (*Dike*). The *theoretical* political-ethical achievement seems secondary to these fundamental experiences. Only when the fundamental order of the soul is defined, can the field of social relations determined by it be systematically ordered. In this sense, I understand the theoretical-scientific achievement of Plato as founded in myth (which he conveys as the representation of the fundamental experiences in the *Phaedo, Symposium,* the *Republic* and the *Laws*). The problem is thereby complicated in that Plato orients his idea of science to the nonmythical, person-peripheral sphere of logic, mathematics, and dialectic. The problem of scientism in the science of man as spiritual being appears to me to have its roots in the fact that the idea of science that is ordered by the model of person-peripheral areas is transferred to the subject fields that have to substantiate their scientific meaning in the mythical order of the soul (in the case of Plato it has less to do with a transfer than with a neglect of differentiation; out of this problem then arises the difficulty that the "idea" of a triangle can also be of a biological genus or of the Good). The "scientific" treatment of political and ethical problems seems to me to be possible since and because of Plato, because a myth of man (Socrates-Plato) has become the stable point for the choice of the relevant materials. The myth of man is, by the way, not a constant in Plato; in my chapters on the *Republic* and the *Laws*, I worked through in detail the change in the image of man from the first to the second dialogue.

The Aristotelian science of politics seems to be somewhat differently founded than the Platonic one. The Aristotelian center is no longer the Socratic myth, but rather the *bios theōrētikos* of the intellectual mystic. Through this, the great transformations become possible, from the "idea" of the state (which is directly founded in the myth) to the "ideal," which becomes the measure of empirical generalizations; from the forms of the soul of states in the *Republic* to the scientific types of regimes. Only from the Aristotelian position is the completely scientific-theoretical treatment of the political possible; but it is possible because the Platonic form, grown from the myth, can now be assumed as datum and thus without the existential participation [of the philosopher] in the myth. The Aristotelian conception of an empirical-technical science of politics, which can give proposals for improving a given situation (the central part of the *Politics* on revolutions, their origins, and their prevention), is possible on the basis of adopting, albeit manifoldly changed, a soul-image of the [Platonic] states of the ideas. I see the specific meaning of Aristotle in that as an unmythical, intellectual mystic, he is able to operate easily with the system of relevance achieved by the myth and could subsume masses of empirical material under the now conceptualized mythical image.

I would not say, then, that the Platonic-Aristotelian idea of science (insofar as it has to do with the field of the political) was put to an end through Christianity and the discovery of history, but rather that the very possibilities of the Platonic-Aristotelian science already have their roots in myths and that Christianity and historical consciousness only changed them. They did not repeal them completely but only partially; but all the same, they did so in the not unimportant point, namely, that the Hellenocentric man has been replaced by the individual, the person in direct communication with God. The Platonic-Aristotelian man is the man of the polis and is, even for Aristotle, tied to the *omphalos* of Delphi; precisely from the Hellenic position, a universal political science is radically impossible. Christianity and historical consciousness seem rather to be steps in the direction of the universalization of the image of man, than steps that lead away from it. In my opinion that is the decisive reason for the superiority of the Christian anthropology over the Hellenic (obviously the Christian anthropology has its prehistory: in Cynic and Stoic Hellenism on the one hand, in the Israelite tradition since Deutero-Isaiah on the other). The belief in the universality of the Hellenic image of man seems to be a product of the Renaissance—a classicist's misunderstanding that is possible only in the atmosphere of the universality of man achieved by Christianity.

I will leave it at that. The form of a letter hardly allows one to enter into the particulars of theoretical problems.

Your admonition with regard to a manuscript finds me in the still unhappy situation that I am not finished with the *History*. I can hardly interrupt the work to write an article, but it would please me greatly if a publication of a chapter in *Social Research* were possible. Obviously such a chapter would show traces of the larger context from which it is taken. I am enclosing a relatively independent piece for you to look at.[7] If you do not think it to be suitable, send it back to me without hesitation—I completely understand your editorial problems. If you believe it can be used, I would be glad to take on the revisions, which are probably necessary for an independent publication. In that case I would very much count on your suggestions.

I have not been able to find Dr. Benno Strauss to date; he is not indicated in the directory and none of my colleagues has heard of his name; are you sure that he is at LSU and not perhaps at one of the Junior Colleges that are scattered around the state?

With warmest greetings,
Eric Voegelin

Letter 5

3900 Greystone Ave.
New York City
20.12.1942

Dear Dr. Voegelin,

Warmest thanks for your interesting letter of the ninth of this month.

Your essay (or chapter) is at this moment circulating among the members of our editorial board. The decision will be made at the end of January. Generally, *Social Research* does not print chapters out of books. Therefore, I cannot express to you any hope. Perhaps there will be a compromise, agreeable to both sides.

What you wrote about Plato and Aristotle naturally interested me quite directly. The broad outlines of the interpretation you advance were already known to me; but you have drawn out these outlines with unusual emphasis. I do not hold this interpretation to be correct. But it is so toweringly superior to nearly all that one gets to read about Plato and Aristotle, that I would greatly welcome its being presented to the American public.

One correction seems to me, in any case, indispensable. Assuming that

7. The chapter, "The People of God," was taken from the *History*. See below, Letter 7.

the Platonic-Aristotelian politics were really by their intention Greek, and not universalizable (which I decisively deny), even so, under no circumstances would the universalization of the Greek *politike epistēmē* have been first executed in the Renaissance: the reception of the same by the Muslims and the Christians (from the ninth century on) stands and falls with that generalization. Over this there cannot be a shadow of doubt.

As for the question of Plato's intention, this can only be decided on the basis of a radical, relentless interpretation of *every* Platonic dialogue on its own terms, or, whenever possible, of any Platonic dialogue on its own terms. For this reason, a discussion by letter is in fact impossible.

Perhaps we will see each other sometime.

With best wishes from us to you,

Yours,
Leo Strauss

Letter 6

3900 Greystone Ave.,
New York, N.Y.
13.2.43

My dear Dr. Voegelin,

Please excuse that I have not responded to your earlier letter of 28.12.42.[8] But it was impossible, even with the best will in the world.

Unfortunately, the fate of your essay has still not been decided. The session in which it will be decided takes place at the end of the month. I have discussed your essay with various members of the editorial board. Overall enthusiasm prevails regarding this very interesting, stimulating, indeed fascinating work. The objections are solely of a technical nature: there is a dislike, which has transformed itself into a rule, for printing chapters out of books; and twenty-five typed pages is the maximum. Whether these objections can be overcome I cannot say before matters are put to the test in the next editorial session. Would you be prepared to write an approximately twenty-five-page-long essay on "the sectarian mentality in politics"? Perhaps an understanding could be reached on this basis.

8. Letter lost or reference to Letter 4, 9 December 1942.

I share the enthusiasm about your essay. Above all, I completely agree that the radical doubt about the dogmas of the last three or four centuries is the beginning of every pursuit of wisdom. The frankness with which you address this preliminary question is praiseworthy in the highest degree. Only I am not certain if you proceed far enough: in your review of Cairns you said, against Cairns's thesis that we do not have a political science (or social science). We do have it, for example: in Max Weber's frame of thought. Can you really exempt Max Weber's sociology or, for that matter, any of today's existing (and not only desirable) research from the bracketing of modern thinking, which you claim? You will say that, after all, in modern times there was always a movement of opposition against modern thinking. But is not this movement of opposition always concentrated on itself, even when in opposition to modern thinking? Husserl is the only one who really sought a new beginning, *integre et ab integro*; the essay on the crisis in modern science is the clearest signpost—and it points to the beginning, or to the social sciences.

I read your essay on the Mongols with great interest and learned a great deal from it.[9] Many thanks. Do you know my article "Persecution and the Art of Writing" (*Social Research*, 1941)? In case it is not known or accessible to you, please let me know. Hula was telling me that you are interested in Arabic political philosophy.[10] That was once my speciality. In case you are interested, I am sending you a list of my publications in this area.[11]

I would very much like to see the table of contents of your *History*. In case I see something, or do not see something, that can be added in, I will obviously be glad to mention it to you.

With best wishes from us to you,

Yours,

Leo Strauss

9. Voegelin, "The Mongol Orders of Submission to the European Powers, 1245–1255," *Byzantion* 15 (1941): 378–413.

10. Eric Hula, New School for Social Research, editor of *Social Research*.

11. Strauss, "Quelques remarques sur la science politique de Maimonide et de Farabi," *Revue des etudes juives* 100 (1936): 1–37; "Eine vermißte Schrift Farabis," *Monatsschrift für Geschichte und Wissenschaft des Judentums* 80 (1936): 96–106; "Der Ort der Vorsehungslehre nach der Ansicht Maimunis," ibid. 81 (1937): 93–105.

Letter 7

February 20, 1943

Dear Dr. Strauss,

For today let me respond only regarding the manuscript—the rest of the contents of your letter must wait for next time.

It pleased me greatly to hear that you and the other members of the editorial board find favor with the work; I myself was a bit doubtful, as I see what I wrote against the background of a fantastic mass of material and I am not sufficiently distanced to be certain that an intelligible image emerges at all.

It would be a shame if you had to decline the manuscript for the technical reasons you mentioned, because unfortunately I cannot write an independent article at the moment. Nevertheless, I did look at the manuscript and I believe one could simply leave out the last section ("Methods of Conviction"); whoever doesn't know that it was there won't miss it. That reduces the manuscript by a fifth. I would be quite in agreement with this reduction. With regard to the number of manuscript pages, I would like to draw your attention to the fact that the copy in your hands was typed by my secretary on a large-type typewriter with a generous distribution of space. My own manuscript, written on the machine with which I type this letter, has without the last section only twenty-five pages, with it, thirty-one. About your rule, not to print any chapters from books, I have naturally nothing to say; that is solely your editorial concern. I can only plead that the book is nowhere near publication and that the chapter in question deals with such a self-contained subject that it could really easily stand alone.

With warmest greetings,

Yours,
Eric Voegelin

The People of God

1. The Problem
   a. The Two Planes of Western Civilization
   b. The Category of Reformation
   c. Difficulties of Approach
   d. The Range of the Undercurrent Movement—Edward Gibbon
2. Institution and Movement
   a. The Institutionalization of Church and Empire
   b. The Church as the Basis of Western Civilization
   c. The Reaction of the Movement
3. Effects of the Movement on the Institution
   a. Spiritual Reformation
   b. Civilizational Destruction—the Fragmentary Civilization
4. The Phases of Disintegration
   a. Dissolution of Charisma and Rulership
   b. The Bourgeois State and the Proletarian Movement
   c. Sectarian Ignorance
   d. The Disintegration in the Realm of Ideas
5. The Social Structure of the Movement
   a. Movement and Town—the Middle-Class Character
   b. Peasant, Feudal, and Bourgeois Support
6. The Structure of Sentiment of the Movement
   a. The Problem of Oriental Influence
   b. Cathars and Paulicians
   c. The Paulician Puritanism
   d. The Cathar Manichaeism
   e. Scotus Eriugena—the De Divisione Naturae
   f. Amaury of Chartres—the Third Dispensation
   g. The World of Darkness and Light—Extreme Cases
   h. Puritan Ideas, Hansard Knollys, Thomas Collier
   i. The Changing Content of the World of Light
7. Methods of Conviction
   a. The Münster Kingdom—Display of Luxury
   b. Sensual Conviction
   c. The Rival Speech
   d. Propaganda

Letter 8

Social Research
An International Quarterly of
Political and Social Science
66 West 12 Street
New York City
February 25, 1943

Dr. Eric Voegelin
Department of Government
Louisiana State University
Baton Rouge, Louisiana

Dear Dr. Voegelin:

Thank you very much for your letter of February 20. It was only today that the Editorial Board of *Social Research* was able to reach a decision concerning your article. As I wrote in my previous letter, everyone enjoyed your unusually interesting article very much, but for the reasons which I stated in that letter, the Board did not feel able to accept it for publication in *Social Research.*

In spite of your refusal of the suggestion I made in my letter, I would urge you to consider whether you could write an article on the sectarian mentality in politics. Please let me know your decision as soon as you have reached it.[12]

Sincerely,
Leo Strauss
Associate Editor

Enc.

12. Voegelin's response, if made in a letter, is missing. From Letter 9, however, it would appear that he was unable to recast "The People of God" into a form acceptable to the editors of *Social Research.*

Letter 9

3900 Greystone Ave.,
New York City
9 May 1943

My dear Dr. Voegelin,

I am very sorry that you cannot write the article for *SR*—but we will take you at your word: you promise an article for *SR* immediately after the completion of your major work.

I read the table of contents with great interest, indeed with excitement.[13] A great achievement! You certainly do not leave out anything relevant. What I would have to say deals only with minor matters. For example, as to religion and mysticism, you should without question consult Scholem, *Major Trends of Jewish Mysticism*, which just appeared. It goes incomparably deeper than Keiler, etc., etc., para. 5, 7. You speak of *Neo*platonism of the *falasifa.*[14] Within the history of political ideas (but also in the history of philosophy) it is to a certain extent misleading to do so, because the basis of their political doctrine is expressly Plato's own thoughts. I dealt with this in my small book *Philosophie und Gesetz* (Berlin, 1935)[15] and in several articles ("La science politique chez Maimonides et Farabi," *Revue des etudes juives*, 1936;[16] "On Abravanel's Philosophical Tendency and Political Teaching," *Isaac Abravanel, Six Lectures*, Cambridge, 1937). The mistaken view should really not be retained. As it concerns Marsilius, I have clarified—so I believe—his background somewhat in an essay, which should appear at the end of this year, and which I will gladly make available to you.[17] (Unfortunately, I do not have any

13. Presumably this refers to Voegelin's *History of Political Ideas*; see Letter 6, last paragraph.

14. On the Arab philosophers, compare Strauss, "Quelques remarques sur la science politique de Maimonide et de Farabi," *Revue des etudes juives* 100 (1936): 1–37; *Persecution and the Art of Writing* (Glencoe, Ill.: The Free Press, 1952), introduction; *What Is Political Philosophy?* (Glencoe, Ill.: The Free Press, 1959), ch. 5; and Voegelin, "Siger de Brabant," *Philosophy and Phenomenological Research* 4 (1944): 505–26.

15. Strauss, *Philosophy and Law*, trans. Fred Bauman (Philadelphia: Jewish Publication Society, 1987).

16. "Quelques remarques sur la science politique de Maimonide et de Farabi," *Revue des etudes juives* 100 (1936): 1–37.

17. No publication of this essay seems to have taken place. Strauss did, however,

spare copies of the earlier publications, but they are easy to come by from the Library of Congress or the Hebrew Union College, Cincinnati.)

A word concerning our philosophical difference of opinion. You say: "You see, of course, how the phenomenological analysis (Husserl's) . . . has ended," p. 11 of the egology and so on.[18] That is, however, only one problem and not an important one at that: Husserl's phenomenological analysis ended in the radical analysis of the whole development of modern science (the essay in *Philosophia* and the essay on geometric evidence, as well as the great fragment on space consciousness in the Husserl Memorial Volume[19])—I know nothing in the literature of our century that would be comparable to this analysis in rigor, depth, and breadth. Husserl has seen with incomparable clarity that the restoration of philosophy or science—because he denies that that which today passes as science is genuine science—presupposes the restoration of the Platonic-Aristotelian level of questioning. His egology can be understood only as an answer to the Platonic-Aristotelian question regarding the *Nous*—and only on the level of this question is that answer to be discussed adequately.

In this is contained my answer to your question with regard to today's social science. An authentic beginning in the social sciences is impossible before the fundamental concepts are clarified, which means an awareness that the fundamental concepts—the very term "political," for example—are of Greek, and in particular of Greek philosophic origin; all that must be done before the Platonic-Aristotelian philosophy is really understood again. I am quite of your opinion that both in Max Weber, as in your work, highly important insights are contained; but I would claim the same for Hobbes, Locke, and Rousseau, for example. The question concerns the *beginning*: clarity about the fundamental questions and how they should be

---

publish another essay, "Marsilius of Padua," in Strauss and J. Cropsey, eds., *History of Political Philosophy*, 3d ed. (Chicago: University of Chicago Press, 1987), 276–95.

18. The reference is probably to Husserl's *Ideas* (1913); this remark attributed by Strauss to Voegelin, "You see . . . ," seems to be a paraphrase of Voegelin's view, not a quotation.

19. In 1936 an international philosophical yearbook, *Philosophia*, edited in Belgrade, published the first two parts of Husserl's last work, *The Crisis of the European Sciences and Transcendental Phenomenology*; the work was first published in its entirety in 1954. The English translation is by David Carr (Evanston, Ill.: Northwestern University Press, 1970). The "Husserl Memorial Volume" probably refers to Marvin Farber, ed., *Philosophical Essays in Memory of Edmund Husserl* (Cambridge, Mass.: Harvard University Press, 1940).

approached. The answer Plato and Aristotle gave to *this* question has been rejected since Hobbes (in a certain manner already since Machiavelli)—the anti-Platonic and anti-Aristotelian answer of the Enlightenment is seen as unacceptable from Rousseau on—but what was done was (in all cases known to me at least): to *complete* the answer of the Enlightenment or subsequently to *correct* it. The historical school, indeed every form of historicism, Hegel's dialectic, positivism of all kinds, Bergson, etc., etc., have this in common. Neo-Thomism is *in its intent* more radical—in its implementation, of course, it is of a low level, and not worth considering.

Dixi—I must close. Tomorrow evening I am supposed to give a public lecture on Machiavelli and I must still complete it.

Keep well!

With best wishes from us to you,
Leo Strauss

Letter 10

September 26, 1943

Dear Doctor Strauss:

I beg to acknowledge the receipt of Farber's *Foundation of Phenomenology*;[20] I shall deliver the review before the end of the year, as agreed.

Felix Kaufmann[21] was kind enough to lend me his copy of Husserl's essay in *Philosophia*.[22] I have read it and feel now better fortified to tackle Farber's book. You will remember that you counseled me to read this essay in order to gain the proper perspective for Husserl's work, and I must say that, indeed, no other work of Husserl's has enlightened me so much on the motive of his thought. It is a grandiose piece of work, and you are probably right when you say that it is one of the most important, if not *the* most important, contribution of our time to philosophy. Nevertheless, I have some misgivings of a fundamental nature. Great importance can be

20. Marvin Farber, *The Foundation of Phenomenology: Edmund Husserl and the Quest for a Rigorous Science of Philosophy* (Cambridge, Mass.: Harvard University Press, 1943). Reviewed by Voegelin in *Social Research* 11 (1944): 384–87.

21. Kaufmann was a pupil of Husserl and friend of Voegelin from Vienna. Both Kaufmann and Voegelin were for a time associated with Hans Kelsen.

22. See above, n. 19.

attributed unqualifiedly to this work only if we assume the problem of epistemology to be the cardinal problem of philosophy. But is it? Certainly none of the great philosophers from Plato and Aristotle to Kant and Hegel would agree with this proposition. They all have treated epistemology as one of the most important, but after all only as *one*, of the philosophical complexes. What I find missing in the present article, as well as in the other published work of Husserl, is a foundation of his phenomenology in the larger context of a metaphysical system. The "egological sphere" is for him an ultimate sphere beyond which he permits no questions. Well—I like to ask a few questions beyond.

It is a pity I had not read this article before I came to New York; I should have liked very much to hear you explain your opinion on this point at greater length than is possible in correspondence. I have sent, however, an eleven-page critique of the article to Schütz;[23] if you are interested in it, he will certainly let you have the letter.

You would oblige me greatly if you could give me the titles of your books and articles typewritten; I am afraid I could not decipher them properly in handwriting.

With our best regards to you and Mrs. Strauss,

Yours very sincerely,
Eric Voegelin

Appendix to Letter 10

Letter from Voegelin to Alfred Schütz on Edmund Husserl

September 17, 1943

Dear Friend:

Let me thank you heartily for the beautiful evening we were able to spend with you and your wife. Unfortunately the time was so short that we were not able to speak about many things that interest us both very much.

23. Originally published in Voegelin, *Anamnesis* (Munich: R. Piper Verlag, 1966), 21–36. An English translation follows. Alfred Schütz and Voegelin were close friends from their university days. In 1943 Schütz taught at the New School. See Helmut Wagner, *Alfred Schütz* (Chicago: University of Chicago Press, 1983), chs. 6 and 12.

Just now I find it very painful that I cannot come to an understanding with you by means of a conversation. Kaufmann was so kind as to lend me Husserl's essay on the "Crisis of the European Sciences" from volume 1 of *Philosophia.*[24] I have just read it and would like very much to speak to you about it. Allow me at least a few brief comments—you will probably not have time to go into them in detail; but perhaps it may be possible for you to correct me if I have misunderstood Husserl.

Before everything: the general impression is of greatness—not only in comparison with other philosophical production of our time but also in comparison with many other works of Husserl. Husserl abstains in a most satisfactory manner from all studied foolery ("great" and "toilsome" investigations, etc.), which spoils many pages of the *Ideas*; and he exudes the sweat of "philosophical existence" only two or three times. Despite the dryness of the language, the essay lives in an Olympian atmosphere of the purest philosophical enthusiasm. The control of the material is masterly; the treatment of the problem of the Galilean worldview and the reductions that lead to physicalism are unsurpassably clear; and the problem of transcendental subjectivity as the theme of philosophy since Descartes has never become so clear to me as on this occasion. The criticism of the earlier attempts at putting the transcendental question seems completely right, and correspondingly, the elaboration of the "egological" sphere and the grounding of the objectivity of the world in the operations of the transcendental ego seem to have completely succeeded. You see that I am prepared to acknowledge this essay as the most significant epistemological performance of our time.

Nevertheless, this essay has disappointed me just as much as the other works of Husserl—for epistemology is an eminently important theme of philosophy, but it does not exhaust the area of the philosophical, and in this area it is neither a self-sufficient theme nor a sphere in which all other philosophical problems take their root, as if with the foundation of an epistemology, a philosophy is also founded. The essay is, just as the *Logical Investigations* and as the *Ideas*, a prolegomenon to a philosophy, but is not itself the undertaking of an established philosophy. Of course it is possible to argue against this with the objection that the great revelations are to be found in the as yet unpublished works of Husserl. But I have been hearing this argument for the last twenty years, and it would make me distrustful

24. References in the text are to the English translation by David Carr. See above, n. 19. The translation is altered slightly.

that a great thinker did not even once, to the end of his life, in the course of a widely published production, touch upon a single fundamental philosophical problem. On the basis of this argument regarding further publications from unpublished manuscripts, it seems to me that we can expect nothing that would enhance in any unexpected way what we already know of Husserl's circle of themes, however valuable the unpublished manuscripts may still be as logical and epistemological studies. I believe, however, that from the essay we have before us itself, grounds can be clearly made that there is nothing more to expect that would be fundamental in the philosophical sense.

(1) In this essay, Husserl develops an image of history—in its general lines not different from the image of history in the Vienna lecture, which I heard. This image is Victorian. The relevant history of mankind comes from Greek antiquity and from modern times since the Renaissance. The Hellenistic period, Christianity, the Middle Ages—an insignificant time period of no more than two thousand years—are a superfluous interlude; the Indians and the Chinese (placed in quotation marks by Husserl) are a slightly ridiculous curiosity on the periphery of the globe, in the center of which is Western man simply as Man. Man is rational being. "Philosophy and science would accordingly be the historical movement through which universal reason, 'only-begotten' in humanity as such, is revealed" (pp. 15–16). In Greek humanity, the entelechy of humanity has arrived at its breakthrough (p. 15). After the Greek original foundation of philosophy and the two-thousand-year interval, in which the entelechy obviously amused itself elsewhere, the new foundation was performed by Descartes. Because of certain imperfections, excellently analyzed by Husserl, the Cartesian new foundation took the wrong path; Kant made a good but partial start in bringing it back on the right track again; we leave out the philosophy of German Idealism and the Romantics; and then we come to the final foundation in Husserlian transcendentalism.

(2) I do not believe that much can be said in defense of this impoverished vision of the spiritual history of mankind; but it could be objected that it is the pardonable naïveté of a great systematic philosopher and that its essential achievement is untouched, that it is perhaps improper to dwell too explicitly on it. On the contrary, I would emphatically object that any German philosopher, who after Hegel knows no better than to take up the problem of the historicity of spirit is, on this basis alone, and as is evident from this essay, a philosopher of dubious quality. But I will

abstain from this argument. It seems more important to me, that, as the essay shows, this image of history is not a pardonable, systematically inessential derailment, but rather constitutes the immediate presupposition of the Husserlian thematic.

Section 15 (pp. 70ff.) contains the "Reflections on the method of our historical mode of investigation," which is rich in conclusions. The principles of this method are the following:

(a) The historical becoming of philosophy has a teleology.

(b) This teleology can be "extrapolated" from the historical forms of philosophizing.

(c) The teleology, which has been "extrapolated" and brought to clarity, makes it possible to formulate the telos itself and to make this the task of contemporary philosophy (Husserl's).

(d) This personal philosophical task opens up from the understanding of the telos into the history of the spirit of modern times.

(e) The task does not, however, become historically relative. It is not a matter of classification in a "merely causal succession." The telos is timeless and merely unfolds itself in historical becoming.

(f) The philosopher's existence receives through this a particularly dialectical character, revealed by Husserl in the following two theses:

(aa) "We are through and through nothing other than the result of historical-spiritual becoming.

"Such a kind of enlightening of history as a further inquiry with regard to the original foundation of goals that bind together the chain of future generations . . . is nothing other than the genuine self-reflection of the philosopher on what he is truly seeking, from which he authentically wills to set out what in him is will *from* the will and *as* the will of his spiritual forefathers. That means to make vital again in its hidden historical meaning the sedimented conceptuality that is taken for granted as the basis of his private and nonhistorical work."

(bb) "To every original foundation belongs essentially a final foundation assigned as a task by the historical process. This is accomplished when the task has arrived at perfect clarity, and with that, at an apodictic method, that at every step of the realization is the constant avenue to new steps, *which have the character of absolute success, that is the character of apodictic steps. At this point philosophy as an infinite task would consequently have arrived at its apodictic beginning, at its horizon of apodictic forward movement.*" (Underlined by me [—E.V.])

(g) The "final foundation" is to be distinguished from the self-reflection that is carried on by every historic philosopher in order to fix his place with his fellow philosophers in the past and the present. The self-interpretations of all other philosophers do not teach us where "it" comes in the history of philosophy. The telos of history reveals itself only in the final-foundational interpretation, which is performed by Husserl; and with his help the philosophers of the past can be understood better than they understood themselves.

(h) It follows from the privileged position of the final-foundational, teleological consideration of history, that it cannot be contradicted by historical arguments (of the kind, e.g., that a philosopher interpreted by Husserl had in fact, and provable philologically, intended something quite different to what Husserl imputed to him on the basis of his knowledge of the telos). In the evidence of the critical total view there flashes up behind the "historical facts" of the history of philosophy for the first time the meaningful harmony of the historical movement.

(3) The relation between the systematic task of the transcendental philosophy and the history of philosophy is summarized in the formula:

> "In *our* philosophizing, we are *functionaries of humanity*" (p. 17) and "We are just what we are, as functionaries of modern philosophical humanity, as heirs and bearers together of the direction of the will that pervades it, and we are that from an original foundation, which is however at the same time a subsequent foundation and modification of the Greek original foundation. In this lies the *teleological beginning*, the true birth of the European spirit" (p. 71).

There are only a few things to mention with regard to this formulation, along with the principles of Section 15. And I am anxious, as you can well imagine, to hold back any strong remarks I might be tempted to make, as, e.g., that I have a prejudice against functionaries in general, and so, I do not distinguish sufficiently between functionaries of the national socialist party and functionaries of humanity; or that the functionaries of the party slaughter humanity, while the functionaries of humanity do not see deep enough into the nature of evil in order to see at least one of its roots in the nature of the functionary—but Lissy says that it would be terribly mean to thank you for the wonderful meal on the Champs Elysées by sending a criticism of Husserl, and if I must in fact do this, then it should at least have no "humorous touches." So let us be serious.

However, a serious analysis of the Husserlian position has its difficulties, for the formulation of his position is indeed perfectly clear verbally, but in no way intellectually. Husserl was no radical philosopher in the sense that he became clear about the *radices* of his thinking; his radicalism, which he always emphasized, is not a radicalism of philosophical existence but the radicalism of the pursuit of a specific problem, that of transcendental philosophy. He seems to me now to have pursued this special question to its root (and as far as this goes, his pathos of radicalism is genuine); the question, however, which, as far as I can see, Husserl in his published works has not once even touched upon, is whether the advance toward the objectivity of knowledge of the world—to its root in the constituting subjectivity of the ego—is in fact an advance toward the basic problems of philosophy. With regard to this point, Husserl seems to me to be absolutely naive. The clarity of the linguistic formulation in the essay under consideration conceals a world of actual implications that must be fully unfolded in order to understand Husserl's own position adequately. In the space of a letter, such an unfolding is not now possible and, I am afraid, in another form, with the scope it would require, is not worth the trouble. I must, therefore, limit myself to clearing away just a few of the concealed layers with brief indications, and leave it to your imagination to expand the backgrounds and explanations.

(a) At the uppermost and most general level, there is Husserl's teleology of history, to be classified as an instance of Averroistic speculation. I have treated this theme in detail in my *Autoritären Staat*[25] in relation to the national socialistic and fascist speculation; and the article "Siger de Brabant,"[26] which you probably remember better, attempts to make clear what I mean by this. In Western philosophy we have to distinguish two basic positions with regard to the nature of man, which through the Christian-orthodox attitude of Thomas and the heterodoxy of Siger arrive at their clearest representation.

25. *Der autoritäre Staat* (Vienna: Springer, 1936).
26. "Siger de Brabant," *Philosophy and Phenomenological Research* 4 (1944): 505–26.

In the Thomistic position, the accent lies on the singularity of the human substance (*intellectus*); in Siger, on the world soul, of which the individual human substance is a particle. Both positions derive historically from Aristotle's teaching on the soul (*De Anima* III), where this question is left in suspense, so that in fact either position can be traced to *De Anima*.

I name in a summarizing way "Averroistic" the position that accepts the world soul and the corresponding character of the individual soul as a particle, because Averroës' commentary on Aristotle is the most important literary-historic source of the formation of this position in the West since the thirteenth century. I am, of course, quite aware that Averroës did not develop this position originally, but that the Zenonian philosophy of the world logos and the *apospasmata* in the individual soul contained it in principle. The Averroistic position in this sense has now gone through many different developments and derivations. The collective soul can be understood in relation to the individual souls, as in Zeno, or the collective can be transferred to the world itself, e.g., as the rational entelechy of human development toward perfection, which makes up an essential component in the Kantian philosophy of history; and it can emerge as a particular, intramundane collectivity, as in the collective speculations of communism, national socialism, and fascism.

Husserl's collectivist telos of philosophical reason should be qualified in the coordinative system of these Averroistic variations as follows: Insofar as the collective telos of Husserl is a rational or spiritual substance, it remains close to the Stoic logos or the Averroistic intellectus. The problem of philosophy becomes then simply the problem of the spirit, and insofar as the spirit is the nature of man, the problem becomes identified with the problem of man in its fully developed form. "The real spiritual struggles of European humanity take the form of *struggles between the philosophies*" (p. 5). Humanity, however, as these and other passages (see especially pp. 15–16) show, is narrowed to European humanity and distinguished from "merely empirical anthropological types" like the Chinese and the Indian (p. 16). The problem of humanity is consequently shifted from its Zenonian, Averroistic, or Kantian generality, into the historic, and "Man" becomes a finite historical phenomenon of certain periods of the history of mankind, namely, of antiquity and modern times. (Medieval man is also permitted, although this is not said explicitly, to appear as a "mere anthropological type" like that of the Chinese or the Indian). Through this contraction of mankind to the community of those who philosophize together in the Husserlian sense, the philosophic telos draws near to the particular intramundane collectivity of the type of the Marxian proletariat, the Hitlerian German *Volk*, or Mussolini's *Italianà*.

(b) Husserl's collectivistic-historical metaphysics has its consequences for his historical method. In the contradiction of the collective to the small section of genuine humanity, there is implied the historical irrelevance of the preponderant quantity of human history, under the rubric of the "merely anthropological." But also within the small relevant section there is a future differentiation of relevance. Among the various possibilities that remain open, Husserl chooses his own, motivated by the spectacle of the succession of philosophical systems that come and go without any of them becoming definitive. Is the history of philosophy (which is indeed identical with the history of the humanly relevant spirit) therefore meaningless? Or is there an order, and with that order, a meaning, in history? His answer is the *telos* that is originally founded and that unfolds itself ever more clearly to its apodictic final foundation through a variety of dramatic ways. Or translated from Husserlian language into a more vulgar one: Husserl is a philosopher of progress in the best style of the time at which the German Empire was set up and about which Nietzsche had some telling things to say. Every progress philosophy that starts from the supposition of a self-unfolding *telos* has an important problem of relevance to solve, which had already deeply troubled Kant. Kant had also come up against the problem of a reason that unfolded itself in history in an unending progress toward fulfillment. In his *Idea of a Universal History with a Cosmopolitan Purpose*[27] he thought out the notion of unfolding and expressed in a decisive passage his "distaste" [for the supposition] that the earlier generations of mankind are, so to say, steps on which the later, fulfilled generation ascends onward toward its goal. Does this supposition mean that man is historically

27. Trans. H. B. Nisbet, in H. Reiss, ed., *Kant's Political Writings* (Cambridge, Eng.: Cambridge University Press, 1970), 41–53.

only a means to a goal that only the last generation of mankind will attain? Kant lets the matter rest with his "distaste." He would wish to be indeed systematic, but he is, however, not emotionally impelled to confront this question decisively. For the Averroistic conception is only a component of his general system, and the meaning of the individual human life at every single moment of history is at all events resolved for him satisfactorily through the belief in the immortality of the soul and its status of fulfillment in the beyond. In addition, the privilege of the later generations did not impinge so crassly on Kant, since along with the supposition of unending progress toward fulfillment, there was also the fact that every empirical-historical generation shares with every other the fate of imperfection.

The problem is somewhat different for Husserl. Like Kant, he believes in the progress of reason in the sense of the unfolding of the telos in history. But he does not believe in unending progress. His final foundation does not lie in an unendingly distant point but is performed here and now in Husserl's phenomenology. Philosophy has arrived at its "apodictic beginning" (p. 71) with the establishment of phenomenology, and the unending task of philosophy (which is his also) takes place in the "horizon of apodictic continuation." As a result, we have to distinguish in Husserl's history of reason two phases: the first reaches from the Greeks, through Descartes's renewed, original foundation, to the Husserlian final foundation; the second begins with Husserl as the apodictic continuation of his apodictic final foundation. We can remind ourselves now that the entelechy "achieved its breakthrough for the first time among Greek humanity" (p. 15), so that history before the Greeks is a prehistory of genuine humanity. Thus we have altogether three phases, and the Husserlian philosophy of history appears as a typical three-phase philosophy, the Old Testament (pre-Greek), New Testament (since the Greek original foundation), and Evangelium Aeternum (beginning with the Husserlian final foundation). The final phase, of unending continuation of phenomenological philosophy in the horizon of apodictic final foundation, has the same structure in the history of philosophy as the Marxian final reign or the Hitlerian millennium.

Husserl's attitude toward the New Testament period (from original foundation on to final foundation) is worth more particular consideration. Kant had some uneasiness, a "distaste," that the generations before the final reign should be only points of transition for reason, helpful and perhaps necessary on the way toward fulfillment but without absolute value in themselves. This feature of Kantian humanity is lacking in Husserl. That the Greeks and modern philosophy since Descartes are only the historical manure for the soil from which the flower of the Husserlian final foundation blooms does not seem "distasteful" to him in the least; this relation is only as it should be. The raising of this question should, however, in no way be the preparation for contesting Husserl's humanity—the problem lies deeper than that. The lack of the Kantian humanitarian "distaste," the lack of inner protest against considering history as prehistory, and allowing, with the final foundation, a "real history" (Lenin) to begin—in Husserl's language: an "apodictic" history—places Husserl, on the contrary, beyond the progress-problematic of the eighteenth century, with its implications of humanity, and makes it necessary to place him among the messianic representations of a final age to be found in our time. Husserl's "apodictic" history, just as the "real" history of communism, is not a continuation of empirical history (see Husserl's passionate warding off of any attempt at allowing his teleological interpretation of history to be confronted by empirical-historical arguments) but a transposition of history onto a new level of the revelation of the spirit of man, with which a new apodicity begins. Along with the specific and problematic component of transcendental subjectivity, Husserl's radicalism has a messianic component by virtue of which the final foundation, with its apodicity in the area of the historical and social, becomes the establishment of a philosopher's sect in the final phase of history.

In order to give an account of the particular structure of the Husserlian metaphysics it was necessary to refer to its frequent parallel phenomena in the political sphere. Beyond its structural relationship with national socialism or communism, Husserl's metaphysics of history has, however, naturally no more to do with them than, for example, Joachim de Flora, whose phasing of history passes through a similar process. In another, methodological relationship, Husserl's position is closely related to certain contemporary spiritual manifestations of the spirit—I mean, to the historical methodology of the Southwest German school, and even more to the historical works that are oriented toward this methodology. The works of political history are less relevant in this connection than a classic of history of the spirit, such as Gierke's *Law of Partnership*.[28] The *ratio* of this work is Gierke's supposition that the nature of a political society is its character as a "real person," and the history of political and legal ideas must therefore be selected so that the historical facts will be ordered as a chain of development leading to the unfolding of the idea of the "real person." Gierke therefore chooses those crumbs from an enormous amount of historical material, which more or less happily allow themselves to be ordered in this series—it does not matter what these crumbs have meant in the context of the author, or what material must consequently fall under the table. That is Husserl's method, even though Gierke lacked the terminological apparatus of entelechy, original foundation, and final foundation. As a result Gierke ran into difficulties when Dunning was sufficiently tactless to examine his fantastic treatment of Bodin more closely. As a result Gierke found himself compelled to publish an embarrassed *retractatio* in the third edition of his *Althusius*.[29] What Dunning did in Bodin's case could be carried out on almost every one of the authors treated by Gierke. Husserl would not suffer this malheur, because from the very beginning he rejected empirical-historical arguments against his telos. I would, therefore, say that the demonic obsession of Gierke's time, for treating world history as a preparatory work for the glory of the respective present, in this case, Gierke's, has been surpassed by Husserl's messianic position, which refuses any correction from the empirical material. Gierke could still be criticized by referring to the material he interpreted; Husserl cannot be criticized, since his interpretation of history *ex definitione* cannot be false. I speak of a "demonic" writing of history because the historian absolutizes his own spiritual position with its historical limitedness and "really" does not write history but misuses the material of history as historical supports for his own position. The task of a non-misusing the history of spirit is to penetrate every historical spiritual position to its own point of rest, i.e., to where it is deeply rooted in the experiences of transcendence of the thinker

28. *Das deutsche Genossenschaftsrecht* is a four-volume monument of German scholarship. It has been translated in parts under separate titles.

29. *Johannes Althusius und die Entwicklung der naturrechtlichen Staatstheorien* (Breslau: Winkle, 1913).

in question. Only when the history of spirit is carried on with this methodological aim can it attain its philosophical aim, which is to understand the spirit in its historicity or, formulated in another way, to understand the historical forms of the spirit as variations on the theme of experience of transcendence. These variations succeed one another in an empirical and factual way, not arbitrarily; they do not constitute an anarchic series; they permit the recognition of sequences of order, even though the order is somewhat more complicated than the progress metaphysicians would wish it to be. (It is obvious that I cannot go into the actual orders here.) A genuine historical reflection does not have the task that Gierke in his historiographic action and Husserl in his theory ascribe to it, which is to explain one's own precious position as the sediment of history (even though this self-interpretation is a valuable consequence of historical reflection). Rather, the primary task of genuine historical reflection is to penetrate the spiritual-historical form of the other to its experience of transcendence, and in such penetration to train and clarify one's own formation of transcendent experience. Spiritual-historical understanding is a catharsis, a *purificatio* in the mystical sense, with the personal goal of *illuminatio* and *unio mystica*; in fact, if it deals systematically with great chains of material, it can lead to the working out of sequences of order in the historical revelation of spirit; finally it can in this way in fact produce a philosophy of history. The guides to this understanding, however, which cannot allow any moment to be abandoned, are the "self-testimonies" of the thinker—those very self-testimonies that Husserl not only believes to have no rights but that he systematically avoided as disturbing his teleology.

(4) The most important implications of the Husserlian position have now been explained, and I can now in a few words approach the fundamental material question: the relation between Husserl and Descartes. Husserl is of the opinion that modern philosophy has been originally founded by Descartes and finally founded by himself. The final foundation brings the original foundation to its full unfolding. To prove this thesis, Husserl interprets the Cartesian *Meditations* as an imperfect form of the phenomenological reduction, the goal of which is an epoche of the world content in order to reconstitute the world as objective from the egological sphere. This interpretation is partially correct. The methodological elimination of

the world content and the suspension of judgment in order to find the Archimedean point from which the world can build up again is in fact the theme of the *Meditations*. Husserl's critique is also correct: that the epistemological epoche is not carried out radically and that the psychological "I" is made the point of departure for the reconstitution of the world instead of the transcendental ego. However, the assertion that Husserl makes, in reference to the historical telos, that the Cartesian reduction has no other positive meaning beyond the epistemological, which must later lead to the grounding of a transcendental philosophy, is false; and further, the assertion—that the attainment of certainty regarding the objectivity of the world by the roundabout route of the certainty of the existence of God collapses because the Cartesian proof of God is untenable—is also false.

Husserl's misinterpretations are due to his substituting his own philosophical theme, of the epoche of the world in order to attain the transcendental sphere of the ego, for Descartes's own and exclusive theme, even if he intended this only unclearly and imperfectly. In fact, the Cartesian meditation has a far richer content, which incidentally raises the question whether it can even be applied to the unfolding of that problematic. For a start, the Cartesian meditation is not as shockingly new in its principal form as Husserl believes. Descartes's meditation is in principle a Christian meditation in the traditional style; it can even be further classified as a meditation of the Augustinian type, and has been made hundreds of times in the history of the human spirit since Augustine. The anonymous author of the *Cloud of Unknowing* (a meditation of the fourteenth century) has formulated the classic theme of the meditation in the following sentence: "It is needful for thee to bury in a cloud of forgetting all creatures that ever God made, that thou mayest direct thine intent to God Himself." The goal of the meditation is the gradual elimination of the world content, from the bodily world to the animate, in order to attain the point of transcendence, in which the soul can, in Augustinian language, turn itself in the *intentio* toward God. This meditation is primarily a process in the biography of the individual who performs it; and the keeping at the point of transcendence and the *intentio* are an experience of brief duration. Secondarily, the process can be expressed verbally, and this gives rise to the literary form of the meditation. Conversely, the reenactment of a meditation that has been put down in words makes possible again an originary meditation in the reader. The Cartesian meditation is the literary sediment of an ordinary meditation of this type, up to the point, indeed, where the momentary character of the lingering at the point of transcendence is employed in a literary way for articulation in most of the meditations. The first meditation ends with the complaint: "I fall back insensibly into my former opinions," namely, into his belief in the objectivity of the world content, although the very aim of the meditation was to become free of this content, since such liberation alone makes possible the experience of the *realissimum* in the *intentio*.

To be sure, there is something new in the Cartesian meditation—if there were nothing new, Husserl's interpretation would not be only partially, but totally false. The classical style of meditation begins from the *contemptus mundi*; the objectivity of the world is unfortunately so obvious that the meditation is needed as an instrument of liberation from it; through the meditation the Christian thinker assures himself, if not of the unreality, at least of the irrelevance of the world content. The classic Christian thinker *wills in the meditation not to know the world*, and therefore its objectivity is not an epistemological problem for him. Descartes finds himself in the position in the history of the spirit where he *wants* to know the world, without ceasing at the same time to be a Christian thinker. Therefore, on the one hand, he can perform the Christian meditation, and on the other hand, he can *use* this meditation with its epoche of the world to assure himself again, from the "Archimedean point" of the experience of transcendence, of the reality of the world he has previously annihilated in the meditation. The Christian experience of transcendence has for Descartes the same significance, as indispensible presupposition of the objectivity of the world, as had Plato's mystical view of ideas, as the indispensible presupposition of his idealist epistemology. I would therefore formulate as being new in Descartes: that the sentiment of *contemptus mundi* gives way to the sentiment of interest in the world, and that from the care about *epistēmē*, the transcendent experience becomes in the meditation the instrument for making certain the objectivity of the world.

Husserl misunderstands this problematic fundamentally because he stumbles over the proof for God and does not see, beyond the proof for God, the experiential content of the experience of transcendence. It is a well-known fact in the history of philosophy, even if obviously not to Husserl, that the scholastic proofs for God, including the Cartesian, do not have the aim of assuring the thinker who employs this proof of the existence of God. The existence of God for the Christian thinkers from Anselm of Canterbury to Descartes is known from other sources. The proof is, however, the stylistic form of scholastic thinking, and the *demonstratio* in this style is extended to problems that are not susceptible of a *demonstratio*, and in no way need one. Certainly all the proofs of God are logically untenable—but none of the proofs of God were quite as stupid as they must appear after a reading of Kant. In the proof for God, there can of course be found, even in Descartes, the purely descriptive nondemonstrative report of the experience of transcendence, on which alone it meditatively depends. In the *Third Meditation* there can be read: "In some way I have the notion of the infinite before that of the finite, that is to say, of God before that of myself; for how could it be possible that I could know that I doubt and that I desire, that is to say, that something is lacking to me and that I am not wholly perfect, if I did not have in me any ideas of a being more perfect than my own, by comparison with which I knew the deficiencies of my nature?" The existence of God is therefore not conclusion, but, in the experience of the finitude of human nature, the infinite is given. God cannot be in doubt, for in the experience of doubt and of imperfection, God is implied. In the limit-experience of being finite there is given, along with this side of the limit, the beyond.

Descartes's *ego cogitans* is thus truly significant. Husserl saw two of these meanings correctly. He saw (1) the transcendental ego, which, turned toward the world content, has in its *cogitationes* the *intentio* toward the *cogitata*; (2) the psychological ego, the soul as world content, which Descartes, as Husserl correctly criticizes, allowed to slide into the transcendental ego. What Husserl did not see is the third meaning of the ego, which grounds the first two, the ego as the *anima animi* in the Augustinian sense, whose *intentio* does not turn toward the *cogitata* but toward transcendence. It is in the third meaning that the process of meditation has its primary sense; in the transcendence of the Augustinian *intentio*, that "I" is simultaneously certain of itself and of God (not in a dogmatic sense, but in a mystical sense of transcendence in the Ground). And only from *this* assurance can the egological sphere in Husserl's sense be founded, with its *intentio* going in the opposed direction toward the *cogitata*—whatever form this assurance may then receive in metaphysical speculation. (It is also important to compare the derivation of Hegel's dialectic as one of the possible constructions of the founding, from the mystic Jakob Böhme, and explicitated by Hegel in the *History of Philosophy*.)

So Husserl has isolated the egological problem from the Cartesian meditative complex, developing it in a masterly way in his theory of transcendentality. And this relation to Descartes seems to me to be at the root of the peculiarity of the Husserlian position. Husserl never performed an originary meditation in Descartes's sense—despite his pretended radicalism and his postulate of [being] the new beginning for every [subsequent] philosopher. He has *historically adopted* the reduction of the world from the cogitating ego and cannot therefore ground his own transcendental philosophical position from an originary bestowing metaphysics. The limit he never gets beyond is the founding subjectivity of the ego: where the ego gets its function of founding the objectivity of the world from subjectivity remains not only unexplained but inevitably is hardly touched on. Instead of the higher founding in the experience of transcendence, there enters the founding in the intramundane particularity of one of the epistemological problematics established by Descartes. Whether Husserl was unresponsive with regard to experiences of transcendence, whether he shrank back from them, whether it is a matter of a biographical problem (that he had withdrawn from Jewish religiousness and did not wish to enter into the Christian)—I do not know. At all events, to found his position, he has taken the way out in the immanence of a historical problematic and with the greatest care blocked himself off from the philosophical problem of transcendence—the decisive problem of philosophy. For this reason, then, there come from a philosopher of rank what appear to be the curiosities of interpretations of history through the telos revealed in him; for this reason the justification of his position as functionary of this telos; for this reason the inability to find the Archimedean point, which he could not find for himself, in the philosophy of others; for this reason the apparent inhumanity in the humiliation of his predecessors; and for this reason—I would also believe—the constantly preparatory character of his work.

Despite all this, I will not in the least—I hope I do not have to say in a more detailed way—contest Husserl's brilliant philosophical talents. He has certainly in a most successful way done all that a thinker can do within the context of a historically fixed problematic, without rising in an originary way to the level of the fundamental problem of philosophizing.

I have come to the end. As I said at the start, I am afraid that you will hardly have the time to go into these questions in detail. Even if you do not, this critique can provide the basis for a conversation when we see each other again—and in the meantime it was a cathartic exercise for me.

With many thanks for all the love that you and your wife showed us, and with the sincerest greetings,

Yours,

Eric Voegelin

(Concluded on 20 September 1943)

Letter 11

Social Research
66 West 12 Street
New York City
October 11, 1943

Dr. Eric Voegelin
Louisiana State University
Baton Rouge, Louisiana

Dear Dr. Voegelin:

Thank you very much for your letter of September 26. I look forward to seeing your review of Farber's book by Christmas or so. I am sure it will be a very interesting and worthwhile review.

On your advice I asked Dr. Schütz for your critique of Husserl. It is, of course, a very interesting piece of work; I admire the quickness and the energy of your reaction. You thoroughly succeed in showing the inadequacy of certain aspects or views that deform the surface of Husserl's thesis. I believe, however, that you do not do full justice to Husserl's fundamental intention and the important thread of his argument. You certainly overestimated the significance of the "epistemological" and "*geschichtlich-philosophischen*" *Eierschalen* owing to the situation from which Husserl started.[30] The decisive point in Husserl is the critique of modern science in the light of genuine science, that is to say, Platonic-Aristotelian [science]. His work can only be understood in the light of the enormous difficulties in which Platonic-Aristotelian science culminated, [namely,] the problem of the *nous*. Considering the enormous difficulties of understanding *De Anima* III, 5ff., Husserl's egological foundation of the ontologies is at least excusable. Incidentally, I think it is impossible to call Husserl's procedure Averroistical; there is no "ego" of fundamental significance in Averroës. And so I could go on and on. I disagree with your interpretation of the meaning of demonstrations of the existence of God, which to my mind had a much more serious and crucial meaning than you seem to assign to them. But we must reserve a proper discussion of these grave issues to a personal meeting.

30. This letter was written in English. Strauss's meaning is that Voegelin overestimated the significance of Husserl's dubious historical-philosophical starting point. *Eierschalen* means eggshells, as in the expression "to walk on eggshells"; using a similar metaphor, one could say that in Voegelin's opinion Husserl started out on thin ice, whereas in Strauss's opinion that ice was thicker.

As regards my medieval studies, I can mention: *Philosophie und Gesetz*, Berlin, 1935; "Quelques remarques sur la science politique de Maimonide et de Farabi," *Revue des etudes juives*, 1936; "The Literary Character of the Guide of the Perplexed," *Maimonides Memorial Volume*, Columbia, 1941; "The Law of Reason in the *Kuzari*" (to appear this year—I shall send you a reprint)[31]—My wife and I send you and Mrs. Voegelin our very best regards.

Yours very sincerely,

Leo Strauss

Letter 12

June 7, 1944

Dear Mr. Strauss,

Excuse me that I only thank you today for your fine essay on "The Law of Reason in the *Kuzari*." A colleague of mine was ill and I had a double teaching load, only now at the end of the semester do I have some breathing space.

I can say nothing critical about your essay. It concerns what is for me a foreign world, and I can only learn. But what there is to learn highly interests me. Above all the form of religious discourse. Unfortunately I know too little of the eastern literature; but religious discourses come to my mind, that were reported by Rubrouck[32] (at the court of the Mongol Khans). Do you know perhaps more about it, whether this form occurs more often? I have the impression that this type of discourse, which actually happened, as well as the ones that were fictional, at the intersection of Islam, Judaism, and Christianity, etc., is the prototype of the later Western discourses on tolerance—sociologically very interesting is also the position of Johnson, that only through religion is social order possible[33]—and I am especially grateful for the fact that your essay does not again remind me of Goethe's statement on belief and nonbelief as the main theme of world history. The whole part on Israel in the desert—in the notes to the *Divan*—is a fine specimen.

31. The Literary Character of *The Guide for the Perplexed*," in S. W. Baron, ed., *Essays on Maimonides* (New York: Columbia University Press, 1941); "The Law of Reason in the *Kuzari*," *Proceedings of the American Academy for Jewish Research* 13 (1943): 47–96. Both are reprinted in *Persecution and the Art of Writing*.

32. William of Rubruquis or Rubrouck was a thirteenth-century papal envoy to the Mongol court.

33. Alvin Johnson of the New School for Social Research.

In about two weeks I will pass through New York on my way to Cambridge; maybe we can see each other at this occasion. In any case, I will phone you.

In the meantime, warmest greetings from both of us to you and your dear wife.

Yours,
Eric Voegelin

Letter 13

3202 Oxford Ave.,
New York 63, N.Y.
21.4.45

My dear Mr. Voegelin,

Just a hastily dashed down word of thanks for your kind lines. You pleased me all the more, as I believed that, especially with regard to the classics, a radical opposition of views stood between us.

It would be very nice if we could discuss this and other things in June. We now live directly next to Hula—maybe you could arrange this time to visit me.

With best wishes from us to you,

Yours,
Leo Strauss

Letter 14

October 16, 1946

My dear Mr. Voegelin,

Warmest thanks for your letter of the eleventh of this month. I was very pleased with your reaction to my critique of Wild.[34] One must proceed with these public castigations from time to time. Perhaps here and there they have their uses.

I made immediate efforts to look at your critique of Schumann.[35]

34. Strauss, "On a New Interpretation of Plato's Political Philosophy," *Social Research* 13 (1946): 326–67.

35. Voegelin, review of *Soviet Politics, at Home and Abroad,* by Fred L. Schuman, *Journal of Politics* 8 (1946): 212–20.

Unfortunately, we do not have it (that is, the journal) in our library, and I cannot use other libraries. Could you lend me a copy for twenty-four hours? I would send it back immediately.

In case I see you, I would very much like to confer with you about a small investigation I completed for over a year ago but have not been able to place over here. It is the first attempt to interpret Xenophon's dialogue on tyrants (the *Hiero*).[36] It leads to results that are not very interesting for the man in the street but about which I am not so indifferent: ancient political theory appears in a different light. It seemed for a moment as if *Traditio* would publish the work (130 typed pages); the editors turned it down but without very persuasive reasons. And with completely American publishers and so on I have no connections. Could you be of help? The matter is not urgent: I write to you about it merely because by chance you might just now be aware of something.

Warm greetings,

Yours,
Leo Strauss

Letter 15

The Graduate Faculty of
Political & Social Science
66 West 12th Street
New York 11
Gramercy 7-8464
November 11, 1947

Professor Eric Voegelin
741 Canal Street
Baton Rouge, Louisiana

Dear Dr. Voegelin:

You have obliged me very much by letting me have your article,[37] which I read at once and found very interesting. I am in full agreement with the thesis developed by you on page 311. On the other hand, I have difficulties

36. Strauss, *On Tyranny: An Interpretation of Xenophon's "Hiero,"* Foreword by Alvin Johnson (New York: Political Science Classics, 1948).
37. Voegelin, "Plato's Egyptian Myth," *Journal of Politics* 9 (1947): 307–24.

in following you in what you suggest in the latter part of the article. I intend to let you have my very detailed criticism some time in spring when I am studying again the *Republic*. Permit me for the moment some very general and rather unsubstantiated remarks. I think that the quarrel between philosophy and poetry may be understood on Plato's terms, philosophy meaning *the* quest for *the* truth (a quest that, for everyone who understands what that means, is an erotic affair), and poetry meaning something else, i.e., at best the quest for a particular kind of truth. I wonder whether one can say, as you do, that *Rep.* 607B "can hardly mean anything but a reference to the attacks of Heraclitus and Xenophanes on Homer and Hesiod." At least as important is the attack of Aristophanes on Socrates; in fact the central theme of Aristophanes can be said to be, not only in the *Clouds*, the question of the superiority of philosophy or of poetry. Also what you say page 318, bottom, "since the Egyptian myth is Plato's invention, Solon is Plato himself," appears to be a *non sequitur*.[38]

I am so crowded with my schedule that I cannot even touch on the questions of principles involved in my scanty remarks.

Repeating my thanks for your stimulating study, I remain

Sincerely yours,

Leo Strauss

LS:ES

Letter 16

March 18, 1948

Dear Mr. Strauss,

Many thanks for your article on "The Intention of Rousseau."[39] I immediately read the *First Discourse* again, and I believe that you have indeed formulated the problem absolutely correctly. Particularly valuable seems to me to be the careful distinction between goodness and virtue, and the further division of goodness into that of the primitive man and that of the philosopher. To that which you yourself indicate, I have hardly anything critical to note; I can only agree. In the rereading of the *Discourse*, certain relations nevertheless came to mind, which were earlier not so clear to me and which perhaps might be acceptable as supplements.

38. Compare Voegelin, *Order and History*, vol. 3, *Plato and Aristotle* (Baton Rouge: Louisiana State University Press, 1957), 179–80.

39. Strauss, "On the Intention of Rousseau," *Social Research* 14 (1947): 455–87.

I mean the noticeable parallel between Rousseau's critique of civilization and Vico. There is little chance of any literary influence. Highly interesting to me is the apparent parallel between Rousseau's appraisal of science and Vico's "Barbarism of Reflection," as also the parallel between Rousseau's virtue and Vico's unbrokenness of "myth." Rousseau's efforts on behalf of a civil religion appear to me substantially an exposition concerning the problem of myth (in Vico's meaning) and its decomposition through reflection.—But details of this parallel would extend too far for a letter.

As I am writing to you, I do not want to let the opportunity pass, again to send you a manuscript with the question if you think it to be fit for publication in *Social Research.*[40] Were it not for this letter, I would not have sent it; do not then take the submission too seriously; if it doesn't appear appropriate to you (especially because it is perhaps too long), send it back without ceremony or apologies. It is a piece of the large work, but complete in itself. If it appears generally usable, I would take on the following changes:

1) The present first two pages would be replaced with an introduction, which would make the article self-sufficient.

2) All references to other parts of the large manuscript would be replaced simply by footnotes.

With many thanks and warmest greetings,
Eric Voegelin

Letter 17

Social Research
An International Quarterly of
Political & Social Science
66 West 12 Street 11
New York City
May 27, 1948

Dear Dr. Voegelin:

I regret that the Editorial Board took such a long time to arrive at a decision regarding your article "The Origins of Scientism."

The Board would be prepared to publish your article provided it is made

40. Voegelin, "The Origins of Scientism," *Social Research* 15 (1948): 462–94.

fully intelligible by itself and somewhat shortened (the normal maximum length of our articles is twenty-five typewritten pages).

Quite a few members of the Board felt that your argument is based on assumptions which are not clarified in this particular chapter of your work. This would apply especially to your distinction between "the realm of phenomena" and the "realm of substance," which, while being suggestive, is felt to be rather vague. I personally believe that this criticism, which refers only to this chapter, is well taken.

I venture to attach a copy of the suggestions made by one of the gentlemen who has read your paper. You are, of course, perfectly free as to what use you want to make of these observations. It is conceivable that one or the other of the points made might be of interest to you.

The chief point which you make is, of course, of the greatest importance, but I am not so certain that it suffices as an explanation of what you call "scientism." But this is too long a topic to allow a discussion in an official letter.

With kindest regards.

Sincerely,
Leo Strauss
Associate Editor

ls/dgs

Dr. Eric Voegelin
Louisiana State University
Baton Rouge, La.

Comments on Voegelin's "The Origins of Scientism"[41]

The author should state at the very outset in unambiguous terms what he considers to be the unwarranted claim of scientism. This might best be done by briefly contrasting scientific problems and methods with philosophical problems and methods. In this context, it should be made unmistakably clear, whether the word "scientism" is meant to apply to all doctrines which are "positivistic" (refuse to admit that there are genuine metaphysical problems), or only to those positivist doctrines which postulate the unity of the natural sciences, humanities, and social sciences under the hegemony of physics. (F. A. Hayek in his papers on scientism in

41. Enclosure with Letter 17.

Economica uses the term in the more restricted use;[42] Voegelin seems to use it in the broader sense.) The difference between philosophical and scientific approaches could then be exemplified by an analysis of the nature of space, with Berkeley and Leibniz representing the philosophical approach.

The great influence of the ancient (and particularly of the treatment of the problem of space in Aristotle's *Physics*) on pertinent seventeenth-century thinking could be emphasized. Voegelin's statement that the problem of absolute and relative space begins with Copernicus is untenable.

It should be pointed out that the thesis of absolute space was supposed to be strongly supported by the generally accepted view that the axioms of Euclidean geometry are descriptive of the structure of physical space, and unaffected by the constellations of material things in space.

The size of the paper could be substantially reduced by leaving out or cutting down a number of observations which are not needed for the presentation of the argument, i.e., the discussion of Galileo's trial and of Henry More's influence on Newton.

Some footnotes for the guidance of the readers of *SR* should be added. Not all of them can be expected to be familiar, e.g., with the meaning of Whitehead's fallacy of misplaced concreteness.

Letter 18

June 12, 1943

Dear Dr. Strauss:

I am sorry that only today I can acknowledge your letter of May 27 as well as the return of the manuscript.

I am quite happy that on the whole you seem to consider the problem of some importance. And I shall cut down the article and round it out so that it will be publishable as an independent piece.

With regard to the size, I should say offhand that I can cut off seven pages, which will leave about thirty pages. Whether I can reduce further five to come down to twenty-five pages I do not know, but I shall try. I am doubtful upon this point because due regard to the advice that you attached

42. The articles were published originally by *Economica* between 1942 and 1944 and reprinted in Hayek, *The Counter-Revolution of Science* (Glencoe, Ill.: The Free Press, 1955).

to your letter will make a few qualifications and explanations necessary, which will take space.

You have sensed quite rightly that the distinction between substance and phenomena presupposes analyses that are not included in the present manuscript. There is, indeed, in the book a whole extensive chapter on phenomenalism.[43] I mention that because I do not want to create the impression that the present manuscript is intended as an even faintly exhaustive treatment of the problem of scientism. The principal sections that in the book, deal with this problem are the chapters on the Encyclopedists, on Condorcet, and on Comte.[44]

We are leaving tomorrow for Cambridge. And I shall rewrite and send you the manuscript as soon as we get settled there.

With kindest regards,

Yours very sincerely,

Eric Voegelin

PS. I was agreeably surprised that the political interpretation proper seems to be acceptable to you and your friends. I had expected some resistance against the sections on spiritual eunuchism.

Letter 19

October 11, 1948

Dear Doctor Strauss:

At last I have found time to bring the article on "Origins of Scientism" into shape.

I have followed your suggestions and made certain cuts. In the aggregate, seven and a half pages have been removed. I could not do more without impairing the coherence of the argument.

With my best regards, I am,

Sincerely yours,

Eric Voegelin

43. This chapter appears in the *History of Political Ideas.*
44. Published in *From Enlightenment to Revolution.*

Letter 20

January 14, 1949

Dear Dr. Strauss,

Your publisher sent me a copy of your new book *On Tyranny*.[45] I take it that it is meant as a gift from you and thank you warmly for sending it.

I immediately read the book and find it to be excellent. It is a model of careful analysis of the inner relations of a work; and the systematic problem you unravel is of greatest importance. I can only heartily congratulate you on the completion of this work.

At the same time as your book arrived, I was requested by Gurian[46] to write a review for the *Review of Politics*.[47] I did that immediately, and I have enclosed a copy of it. I do not yet know if Gurian will bring it out in this form; maybe he will find it too long. But at least you see from it what I have to say in more detail to your problem.

All best wishes for your professorship in Chicago.[48] And again many thanks for the book.

With warmest greetings,
Eric Voegelin

Appendix to Letter 20

Voegelin's Review of Strauss's On Tyranny

The book *On Tyranny* by Professor Strauss has for its nucleus an analysis of the Xenophontic dialogue *Hiero*; here it is a contribution to the history of political thought. In addition, especially in the introductory chapter, it contains a number of reflections on the problem of tyranny in ancient and modern times, on differences between ancient and modern political

45. Strauss, *On Tyranny: An Interpretation of Xenophon's "Hiero,"* Foreword by Alvin Johnson (New York: Political Science Classics, 1948).

46. Waldemar Gurian, professor of political science at Notre Dame University and editor of the *Review of Politics*.

47. Voegelin, review of *On Tyranny*, by Leo Strauss, *Review of Politics* 11 (1949): 241–44.

48. Strauss moved to Chicago in 1949; he retired as Robert M. Hutchins Distinguished Service Professor of Political Science in 1967.

science, and on the relation between *Hiero* and Machiavelli's *Prince* as points of closest contact between the ancient and modern approaches to the problem of tyranny—thus justifying the more general title which the author has chosen for his book.

An interpretation of the *Hiero* is a very valuable undertaking. The dialogue, though the only work of antiquity dealing specifically with the subject of tyranny, is much neglected, sharing this neglect with the other works of Xenophon in the shadow of the greater Plato. While Professor Strauss's analysis will hardly affect the judgment that Xenophon was not a profound thinker, it certainly will compel a revision of judgment with regard to his psychological subtlety and his skill of composition as an artist. The *Hiero* is a conversation between the tyrant Hiero and the poet Simonides on the relative merits of the tyrannical and private life. As distinguished from the distribution of roles in the Platonic dialogues, the tyrant is charged with the indictment of tyranny, while the sage comforts the unhappy tyrant and suggests means for making his tyranny a beneficent rule and his person beloved by the subjects. Professor Strauss excels in his exposition of the dramatic qualities of the conversation. The interpretation as such, resting on the solid basis of impeccable erudition, is a model of careful analysis.

As for Professor Strauss's reflections of a systematic nature, they range widely, but are formulated so tersely, and sometimes esoterically, that the danger of misunderstanding is great. With all due apologies for mistakes which may arise from this source, I should say that the problem of most interest to the author was that of freedom of intellectual criticism under a tyrannical government. We are living in an age of tyranny; and therefore, what the ancients had to say on the subject is of importance; but perhaps of even more importance is how they managed to say it so frequently without getting killed in the process. The *Hiero* is full of instructive details; and Professor Strauss does not fail to point the lessons. Tyranny is considered, in the Socratic circle, a defective form of government; in the *Hiero*, the sage tenders advice about the practical improvement of this form; he "collaborates" with tyranny. In his careful and interesting exploration of this problem, Professor Strauss sheds light on the relation of the sage to civic freedom as well as on the potential conflict between freedom and virtue in government.

Yet in the exposition we miss a proper valuation of the point that for Xenophon, as well as for Plato, the problem of tyranny had already become one of historical necessity, not merely of theoretical discussion. The

Socratic circle might well define tyranny as a defective form of government; that, however, did not change the fact that the polis democracy had degenerated to the point where "tyranny" became the inevitable alternative to a democracy which had ceased to function effectively. A good many of the enigmas of the *Hiero* may derive from the fact that a new political situation is discussed in terms of "tyranny" because a vocabulary more suitable to the new problems had not yet been developed. Professor Strauss notes that, in the second part of the *Hiero*, the terminology quietly changes. Simonides no longer speaks of the tyrant but uses the term "ruler." This change in terminology seems not a mere matter of persuasive prudence; it seems to indicate the genuine necessity of dropping an inadequate term.

Professor Strauss opposes the *Cyropaedia* as a mirror of the perfect king to the *Hiero* as a mirror of the tyrant that has influenced the Machiavellian *Prince*. The opposition does not seem to me to exhaust the problem. Under another aspect, both *Cyropaedia* and *Hiero* are on the same side; for the very motivation of the *Cyropaedia* is the search for a stable rule that will make an end to the dreamy overturning of democracies and tyrannies in the Hellenic polis; and what makes the many tribes and nations obey Cyrus is not all sweetness and reason but the "fear and terror" which he inspires. Both works fundamentally face the same historical problem of the new rulership; and it is again perhaps only the lack of an adequate vocabulary that makes the two solutions of the perfect king and the improved tyrant look more opposed to each other than they really are.

This suggestion gains in plausibility if we take a closer look at the parallel with Machiavelli's problem, which Professor Strauss stresses. If I understand him rightly, he sees the *tertium comparationis* between *Hiero* and *Prince* in the tendency of both works to obliterate the distinction of king and tyrant. In this tendency of the *Prince* he recognizes its specifically "modern" character, and even one of the "deepest roots of modern political thought"; precisely for the understanding of this aspect of modern political thought, he finds some attention to the *Hiero* "very useful, not to say indispensable." The comparison is decisive for the understanding of both Xenophon and Machiavelli, but it will need some reformulation in detail. It seems insufficient to state that in *Hiero* and *Prince* we have a point of the closest contact between "ancient" and "modern" political thought. The contact certainly is there; but it is due to the fact that both Xenophon and Machiavelli are in the position of "moderns" in their respective civilizations; the parallel between the two thinkers is due to the parallel between their historical situations. The distinction between king and tyrant is obliterated in the *Prince*, because Machiavelli, like Xenophon, was faced with the problem of a stabilizing and regenerating rulership after the breakdown of constitutional forms in the city-state; it is obliterated because Machiavelli, too, was in search of a type of ruler beyond the distinction of king and tyrant that is politically significant only *before* the final breakdown of the republican constitutional order.

Luckier than Xenophon, however, Machiavelli was able to find a name for the new type of ruler which he envisaged. He called it the *profeta armato*, the prophet in arms; and for his paternity he claimed (besides Romulus, Moses, and Theseus) precisely the Xenophontic Cyrus whom, as the perfect king, Professor Strauss would rather put in opposition to the Hiero. The figure of the Sicilian tyrant would have been too weak to bear the burden of the savior prince that Machiavelli wanted to put on his shoulders; the composite figure of the *profeta armato* resembles rather Plato's royal ruler in the *Statesman* than any of the Xenophontic types. The obliteration of the old distinctions, we should say, is rather due to the attempt to create a new type. Within this new type, however, Machiavelli lets the good royal and bad tyrannical variants reappear; for he distinguishes between the "princes" whose actions are inspired by the *virtù ordinata*, tending toward the necessary public order, and those whose *sceleratezze* are motivated by the lust for personal power. Machiavelli, thus, has actually achieved the theoretical creation of a concept of rulership in the post-constitutional situation; and he has also achieved the theoretical distinction of the good and bad variants within the new type, corresponding to the distinction of king and tyrant in the constitutional situation. Xenophon, on the other hand, has in this respect achieved no more than the shift from the term *tyrannos* in the first part, to the term *archōn* in the second part of the *Hiero*.

It may be worthwhile to recall that the influence of Xenophon on Machiavelli's *Prince* makes itself felt in a roundabout way which Professor Strauss does not mention. Machiavelli's image of the prince is not quite original in its time; it must be seen against the background of the new genus of a "mirror of the prince" that developed in the second half of the fifteenth century in connection with events in the Near East, that is, against the background of the *Vita Tamerlani* as created by Poggio Bracciolini and standardized by Aeneas Silvio. Machiavelli's complete drawing of the savior prince in the *Vita di Castruccio Castracani* is hardly thinkable without the standardized model of the *Life of Timur*. This *Vita* of the Timur class uses for its pattern—besides the youth of Moses and the youth of Cyrus as reported by Herodotus—the Xenophontic Cyrus, in particular the ruthlessly conquering Cyrus of *Cyropaedia* 1.4–5, who compels obedience by fear and terror. This line of Xenophontic influence is of special import for Professor Strauss's study of the problem of tyranny: by way of the *Vita Tamerlani* there has entered into the classical post-constitutional conqueror and ruler the nonclassical conception of the new ruler as the avenger of the misdeeds of a corrupt people, that is, the idea of the ruler as the *ultor peccatorum*. This new factor, which has amalgamated with the Xenophontic elements, is also to be found in Machiavelli—in the *Castruccio* as well as in the apocalyptic aspects of the *profeta armato* in the *Prince*, in particular in the last chapter. The spiritual, apocalyptic aspect of the new ruler, however, is neither "ancient" nor "modern"; it is Western-Christian as opposed to Hellenic-Pagan. The "modernity" of Machiavelli's prince has a specific tone through the absorption of such medieval-Christian antecedents as the Joachitic *dux*, Dante's *veltro* and the realization of these ideas in the savior-tribunate of Rienzo. "Modern tyranny" must remain unintelligible unless we have proper regard for the fact that it is a phenomenon in Western, not in Hellenic, society and that, consequently, it is burdened with the tradition that leads from medieval and Renaissance Paracletes to the secularized Supermen of the nineteenth century and after. No problem of this kind is to be found in Xenophon, or anywhere else in Hellenic civilization before Alexander, except again in the figuration of the royal ruler in Plato's *Statesman*.

Nevertheless, there is one sign of a specific influence of the *Hiero* on Machiavelli: the point of the *contemptus vulgi*. One of the finest parts of Professor Strauss's analysis concerns the subtle graduation of human ranks in the *Hiero*. The dialogue starts with the question of the relative merits of the life of the tyrant and the life of the private man. Then, in the conversation, emerge the nuances of the "gentleman," the "just man," the "brave man," the "real man," and the "sage." With the elimination of these various types and their possible attitudes toward the government of the tyrant, there remains as the socially relevant type which the tyrant must face in the mass a somewhat nondescript, washed-out creature. This creature can be handled by various enticements and fears, by prizes for good conduct and by persuasion. The tyrant's contempt for the herd, as Professor Strauss points out, is strikingly paralleled in the *Prince*; here, too, the mass-man is seen as incapable of self-government, and as making the new type of ruler historically necessary.

This book, finally, is a noteworthy contribution to the systematic problems of political theory. Every political scientist who tries to disentangle himself from the contemporary confusion over the problems of tyranny will be much indebted to this study and inevitably use it as a starting point.

The book is preceded by a charming foreword from the pen of Alvin Johnson. The distinguished scholar and educator stresses the affinities between Xenophon and America. Like an American, Xenophon "failed to see the things that aren't there. And, indeed, as a wide-awake young fellow, Xenophon managed to get into the presence of Socrates, but got little that was Socratic out of his encounters." Instead, he was gallant and resourceful. He speculated on true happiness, "but no more than an American did he break his head on it. He wanted pragmatic answers, not nebulous ultimacies."

—Eric Voegelin

Strauss's Response to Voegelin's Review

RESTATEMENT ON XENOPHON'S *HIERO*

A social science that cannot speak of tyranny with the same confidence with which medicine speaks, for example, of cancer, cannot understand social phenomena as what they are. It is therefore not scientific. Present-day social science finds itself in this condition. If it is true that present-day social science is the inevitable result of modern social science and of modern philosophy, one is forced to think of the restoration of classical social science. Once we have learned again from the classics what tyranny is, we shall be enabled and compelled to diagnose as tyrannies a number of contemporary regimes which appear in the guise of dictatorships. This diagnosis can only be the first step toward an exact analysis of present-day tyranny, for present-day tyranny is fundamentally different from the tyranny analyzed by the classics.

But is this not tantamount to admitting that the classics were wholly unfamiliar with tyranny in its contemporary form? Must one not therefore conclude that the classical concept of tyranny is too narrow and hence that

Excerpted from Leo Strauss, "Restatement on Xenophon's *Hiero*." See note 49 to Letter 21.

the classical frame of reference must be radically modified, i.e., abandoned? In other words, is the attempt to restore classical social science not utopian, since it implies that the classical orientation has not been made obsolete by the triumph of the biblical orientation?

This seems to be the chief objection to which my study of Xenophon's *Hiero* is exposed. At any rate, this is the gist of the only criticisms of my study from which one could learn anything. Those criticisms were written in complete independence of each other, and their authors, Professor Eric Voegelin and M. Alexandre Kojève, have, so to speak, nothing in common. Before discussing their arguments, I must restate my contention.

The fact that there is a fundamental difference between classical tyranny and present-day tyranny, or that the classics did not even dream of present-day tyranny, is not a good or sufficient reason for abandoning the classical frame of reference. For that fact is perfectly compatible with the possibility that present-day tyranny finds its place within the classical framework, i.e., that it cannot be understood adequately except within the classical framework. The difference between present-day tyranny and classical tyranny has its root in the difference between the modern notion of philosophy or science and the classical notion of philosophy or science. Present-day tyranny, in contradistinction to classical tyranny, is based on the unlimited progress in the "conquest of nature" which is made possible by modern science, as well as on the popularization or diffusion of philosophic or scientific knowledge. Both possibilities—the possibility of a science that issues in the conquest of nature and the possibility of the popularization of philosophy or science—were known to the classics. (Compare Xenophon, *Memorabilia* I.I.15 with Empedocles, fr. III; Plato, *Theaetetus* 180 c 7–d 5.) But the classics rejected them as "unnatural," i.e., as destructive of humanity. They did not dream of present-day tyranny because they regarded its basic presuppositions as so preposterous that they turned their imagination in entirely different directions.

Voegelin, one of the leading contemporary historians of political thought, seems to contend (*The Review of Politics*, 1949, pp. 241–44) that the classical concept of tyranny is too narrow because it does not cover the phenomenon known as Caesarism: when calling a given regime tyrannical, we imply that "constitutional" government is a viable alternative to it; but Caesarism emerges only after "the final breakdown of the republican constitutional order"; hence, Caesarism or "post-constitutional" rule cannot be understood as a subdivision of tyranny in the classical sense of tyranny. There is no reason to quarrel with the view that genuine

Caesarism is not tyranny, but this does not justify the conclusion that Caesarism is incomprehensible on the basis of classical political philosophy: Caesarism is still a subdivision of absolute monarchy as the classics understood it. If in a given situation "the republican constitutional order" has completely broken down, and there is no reasonable prospect of its restoration within all the foreseeable future, the establishment of permanent absolute rule cannot, as such, be justly blamed; therefore, it is fundamentally different from the establishment of tyranny. Just blame could attach only to the manner in which that permanent absolute rule that is truly necessary is established and exercised; as Voegelin emphasizes, there are tyrannical as well as royal Caesars. One has only to read Coluccio Salutati's defense of Caesar against the charge that he was a tyrant—a defense which in all essential points is conceived in the spirit of the classics—in order to see that the distinction between Caesarism and tyranny fits perfectly into the classical framework.

But the phenomenon of Caesarism is one thing, the current concept of Caesarism is another. The current concept of Caesarism is certainly incompatible with classical principles. The question thus arises whether the current concept or the classical concept is more nearly adequate. More particularly, the question concerns the validity of the two implications of the current concept which Voegelin seems to regard as indispensable, and which originated in nineteenth-century historicism. In the first place, he seems to believe that the difference between "the constitutional situation" and "the post-constitutional situation" is more fundamental than the difference between the good king or the good Caesar on the one hand and the bad king or the bad Caesar on the other. But is not the difference between good and bad the most fundamental of all practical or political distinctions? Secondly, Voegelin seems to believe that "post-constitutional" rule is not per se inferior to "constitutional" rule. But is not "post-constitutional" rule justified by necessity or, as Voegelin says, by "historical necessity"? And is not the necessary essentially inferior to the noble or to what is choiceworthy for its own sake? Necessity excuses: what is justified by necessity is in need of excuse. The Caesar, as Voegelin conceives of him, is "the avenger of the misdeeds of a corrupt people." Caesarism is then essentially related to a corrupt people, to a low level of political life, to a decline of society. It presupposes the decline, if not the extinction, of civic virtue or of public spirit, and it necessarily perpetuates that condition. Caesarism belongs to a degraded society, and it thrives on its degradation. Caesarism is just, whereas tyranny is unjust. But Caesarism is just in the way in which deserved punishment is just. It is as little choiceworthy for its own sake as is deserved punishment. Cato refused to see what his time demanded because he saw too clearly the degraded character of what his time demanded. It is much more important to realize the low level of Caesarism (for, to repeat, Caesarism cannot be divorced from the society which deserves Caesarism) than to realize that under certain conditions Caesarism is necessary and hence legitimate.

While the classics were perfectly capable of doing justice to the merits of Caesarism, they were not particularly concerned with elaborating a doctrine of Caesarism. Since they were primarily concerned with the best regime, they paid less attention to "post-constitutional" rule, or to late kingship, than to "pre-constitutional" rule, or to early kingship: rustic simplicity is a better soil for the good life than is sophisticated rottenness. But there was another reason which induced the classics to be almost silent about "post-constitutional" rule. To stress the fact that it is just to replace constitutional rule by absolute rule, if the common good requires that change, means to cast a doubt on the absolute sanctity of the established constitutional order. It means encouraging dangerous men to confuse the issue by bringing about a state of affairs in which the common good requires the establishment of their absolute rule. The true doctrine of the legitimacy of Caesarism is a dangerous doctrine. The true distinction between Caesarism and tyranny is too subtle for ordinary political use. It is better for the people to remain ignorant of that distinction and to regard the potential Caesar as a potential tyrant. No harm can come from this theoretical error which becomes a practical truth if the people have the mettle to act upon it. No harm can come from the political identification of Caesarism and tyranny: Caesars can take care of themselves.

The classics could easily have elaborated a doctrine of Caesarism or of late kingship if they had wanted, but they did not want to do it. Voegelin however contends that they were forced by their historical situation to grope for a doctrine of Caesarism, and that they failed to discover it. He tries to substantiate his contention by referring to Xenophon and to Plato. As for Plato, Voegelin was forced by considerations of space to limit himself to a summary reference to the royal ruler in the *Statesman*. As for Xenophon, he rightly asserts that it is not sufficient to oppose "the *Cyropaedia* as a mirror of the perfect king to the *Hiero* as a mirror of the tyrant," since the perfect king Cyrus and the improved tyrant who is described by Simonides "look much more opposed to each other than they really are." He explains this fact by suggesting that "both works fundamentally face the same historical problem of the new [sc., post-constitutional] rulership," and that one cannot solve this problem except by obliterating at the first stage, the distinction between king and tyrant. To justify this explanation he contends that "the very motivation of the *Cyropaedia* is the search for a stable rule that will make an end to the dreary overturning of democracies and tyrannies in the Hellenic polis." This contention is not supported by what Xenophon says or indicates in regard to the intention of the *Cyropaedia.* Its explicit intention is to make intelligible Cyrus's astonishing success in solving the problem of ruling human beings. Xenophon conceives of this problem as one that is coeval with man. Like Plato in the *Statesman,* he does not make the slightest reference to the particular "historical" problem of stable rule in "the post-constitutional situation." In particular, he does not refer to "the dreary overturning of democracies and tyrannies in the Hellenic polis": he speaks of the frequent overturning of democracies, monarchies, and oligarchies and of the essential instability of all tyrannies. As for the implicit intention of the *Cyropaedia,* it is partly revealed by the remark, toward the end of the work, that "after Cyrus died, his sons immediately quarreled, cities and nations immediately revolted, and all things turned to the worse." If Xenophon was not a fool, he did not intend to present Cyrus's regime as a model. He knew too well that the good order of society requires stability and continuity. (Compare the opening of the *Cyropaedia* with the parallel in the *Agesilaus* I.4.) He rather used Cyrus's meteoric success and the way in which it was brought about as an example for making intelligible the nature of political things. The work which describes Cyrus's whole life is entitled *The Education of Cyrus*: the education of Cyrus is the clue to his whole life, to his astonishing success, and hence to Xenophon's intention. A very rough sketch must here suffice. Xenophon's Cyrus was the son of the king of Persia, and until he was about twelve years old he was educated according to the laws of the Persians. The laws and polity of Xenophon's Persians, however, are an improved version of the laws and polity of the Spartans. The Persia in which Cyrus was raised was an aristocracy superior to Sparta. The political activity of Cyrus—his extraordinary success—consisted in transforming a stable and healthy aristocracy into an unstable "Oriental despotism" whose rottenness showed itself at the latest immediately after his death. The first step in this transformation was a speech which Cyrus addressed to the Persian nobles and in which he convinced them that they ought to deviate from the habit of their ancestors by practicing virtue no longer for its own sake, but for the sake of its rewards. The destruction of aristocracy begins, as one would expect, with corruption of its principle. (*Cyropaedia* I.5.5–14; compare Aristotle, *Eudemian Ethics* 1248 b 38ff., where the view of virtue which Xenophon's Cyrus instills into the minds of the Persian gentlemen is described as the Spartan view.) The quick success of Cyrus's first action forces the reader to wonder whether the Persian aristocracy was a genuine aristocracy, or, more precisely, whether the gentleman in the political or social sense is a true gentleman. This question is identical with the question which Plato answers explicitly in the negative in his story of Er. Socrates says outright that a man who has lived in his former life in a well-ordered regime, participating in virtue by habit and without philosophy, will choose for his next life "the greatest tyranny," for "mostly people make their choice according to the habits of their former life" (*Republic* 619 b 6-620 a 3). There is no adequate solution to the problem of virtue or happiness on the political or social plane. Still, while aristocracy is always on the verge of declining into oligarchy or something worse, it is the best possible political solution of the human problem. It must here suffice to note that Cyrus's second step is the democratization of the army, and that the end of the process is a regime that might seem barely distinguishable from the least intolerable form of tyranny. But one must not overlook the essential difference between Cyrus's rule and tyranny, a distinction that is never obliterated. Cyrus is and remains a legitimate ruler. He is born as a legitimate heir to the reigning king, a scion of an old royal house. He becomes the king of other nations through inheritance or marriage and through just conquest, for he enlarges the boundaries of Persia in the Roman manner: by defending the allies of Persia. The difference between Cyrus and a Hiero educated by Simonides is comparable to the difference between William III and Oliver Cromwell. A cursory comparison of the history of England with the history of certain other European nations suffices to show that this difference is not unimportant to the well-being of peoples. Xenophon did not even attempt to obliterate the distinction between the best tyrant and the king, because he appreciated too well the charms, nay, the blessings, of legitimacy. He expressed this appreciation by subscribing to the maxim (which must be reasonably understood and applied) that the just is identical with the legal.

Voegelin might reply that what is decisive is not Xenophon's conscious intention, stated or implied, but the historical meaning of his work, the historical meaning of a work being determined by the historical situation as distinguished from the conscious intention of the author. Yet opposing the historical meaning of Xenophon's work to his conscious intention implies that we are better judges of the situation in which Xenophon thought than Xenophon himself was. But we cannot be better judges of that situation if we do not have a clearer grasp than he had of the principles in whose light historical situations reveal their meaning. After the experience of our generation, the burden of proof would seem to rest on those who assert rather than on those who deny that we have progressed beyond the classics. And even if it were true that we could understand the classics better than they understood themselves, we would become certain of our superiority only after understanding them exactly as they understood themselves. Otherwise we might mistake our superiority to our notion of the classics for superiority to the classics.

According to Voegelin, it was Machiavelli, as distinguished from the classics, who "achieved the theoretical creation of a concept of rulership in the post-constitutional situation," and this achievement was due to the influence on Machiavelli of the biblical tradition. He refers especially to Machiavelli's remark about the "armed prophets" (*Prince* VI). The difficulty to which Voegelin's contention is exposed is indicated by these two facts: he speaks on the one hand of "the apocalyptic [hence thoroughly nonclassical] aspects of the 'armed prophet' in the *Prince*," whereas on the other hand he says that Machiavelli claimed "for [the] paternity" of the "armed prophet" "besides Romulus, Moses, and Theseus, precisely the Xenophontic Cyrus." This amounts to an admission that certainly Machiavelli himself was not aware of any nonclassical implication of his notion of "armed prophets." There is nothing unclassical about Romulus, Theseus, and Xenophon's Cyrus. It is true that Machiavelli adds Moses; but, after having made his bow to the biblical interpretation of Moses, he speaks of Moses in exactly the same manner in which every classical political philosopher would have spoken of him; Moses was one of the greatest legislators or founders (*fondatori: Discorsi* I.9) who ever lived. When reading Voegelin's statement on this subject, one receives the impression that in speaking of armed prophets, Machiavelli put the emphasis on "prophets" as distinguished from nonprophetic rulers like Cyrus, for example. But Machiavelli puts the emphasis not on "prophets," but on "armed." He opposes the armed prophets, among whom he counts Cyrus, Romulus, and Theseus, as well as Moses, to unarmed prophets like Savonarola. He states the lesson which he intends to convey with remarkable candor: "all armed prophets succeed and the unarmed ones come to ruin." It is difficult to believe that in writing this sentence Machiavelli should have been completely oblivious of the most famous of all unarmed prophets. One certainly cannot understand Machiavelli's remark on the "unarmed prophets" without taking into consideration what he says about the "unarmed heaven" and "the effeminacy of the world" which, according to him, are due to Christianity (*Discorsi* II.2 and III.1). The tradition which Machiavelli continues, while radically modifying it, is not, as Voegelin suggests, that represented by Joachim of Floris, for example, but the one which we still call, with pardonable ignorance, the Averroistic tradition. Machiavelli declares that Savonarola, that unarmed prophet, was right in saying that the ruin of Italy was caused by "our sins," "but our sins were not what he believed they were," namely, religious sins, "but those which I have narrated," namely, political or military sins (*Prince* XII). In the same vein Maimonides declares that the ruin of the Jewish kingdom was caused by the "sins of our fathers," namely, by their idolatry; but idolatry worked its effect in a perfectly natural manner: it led to astrology and thus induced the Jewish people to devote themselves to astrology instead of to the practice of the arts of war and the conquest of countries. But apart from all this, Voegelin does not give any indication of what the armed prophets have to do with "the post-constitutional situation." Certainly Romulus, Theseus, and Moses were "pre-constitutional" rulers. Voegelin also refers to "Machiavelli's complete drawing of the savior prince in the *Vita di Castruccio Castracani*" which, he says, "is hardly thinkable without the standardized model of the *Life of Timur*." Apart from the fact that Voegelin has failed to show any connection between the *Castruccio* and the *Life of Timur* and between the *Life of Timur* and the biblical tradition, the *Castruccio* is perhaps the most impressive document of Machiavelli's longing for classical *virtù* as distinguished from, and opposed to, biblical righteousness. Castruccio, that idealized condottiere who preferred in so single-minded a manner the life of the soldier to the life of the priest, is compared by Machiavelli himself to Philip of Macedon and to Scipio of Rome.

Machiavelli's longing for classical *virtù* is only the reverse side of his rejection of classical political philosophy. He rejects classical political philosophy because of its orientation by the perfection of the nature of man. The abandonment of the contemplative ideal leads to a radical change in the character of wisdom: Machiavellian wisdom has no necessary connection with moderation. Machiavelli separates wisdom from moderation. The ultimate reason why the *Hiero* comes so close to the *Prince* is that in the *Hiero* Xenophon experiments with a type of wisdom which comes relatively close to a wisdom divorced from moderation: Simonides seems to have an inordinate desire for the pleasures of the table. It is impossible to say how far the epoch-making change that was effected by Machiavelli is due to the indirect influence of the biblical tradition, before that change has been fully understood in itself.

The peculiar character of the *Hiero* does not disclose itself to cursory reading. It will not disclose itself to the tenth reading, however painstaking, if the reading is not productive of a change of orientation. This change was much easier to achieve for the eighteenth-century reader than for the reader in our century who has been brought up on the brutal and sentimental literature of the last five generations. We are in need of a second education in order to accustom our eyes to the noble reserve and the quiet grandeur of the classics. Xenophon, as it were, limited himself to cultivating exclusively that character of classical writing which is wholly foreign to the modern reader. No wonder that he is today despised or ignored. An unknown ancient critic, who must have been a man of uncommon discernment, called him most bashful. Those modern readers who are so fortunate as to have a natural preference for Jane Austen rather than for Dostoievski, in particular, have an easier access to Xenophon than others might have; to understand Xenophon, they have only to combine the love of philosophy with their natural preference. In the words of Xenophon, "it is both noble and just, and pious and more pleasant to remember the good things rather than the bad ones." In the *Hiero*, Xenophon experimented with the pleasure that comes from remembering bad things, with a pleasure that admittedly is of doubtful morality and piety.

Letter 21

3202 Oxford Ave., New York 63
21.1.49

Dear Mr. Voegelin,

I received your very amiable letter and sympathetic review, just in the middle of decamping and departing. I want to extend my heartfelt thanks to you. At this point, it interests me merely if there is at least one person who knows these ideas from a reading of the publication and not only from statements by word of mouth and who brings, against these ideas, understanding and a certain sympathy. I was already quite prepared to be hushed up or to be decried as not being a "liberal." In response to your pertinent critique, I cannot say anything, without more careful consideration than is at the moment possible.

Your critique could be interpreted as a supplement to my publication: I do not deny, but rather assume, that there is a fundamental difference between Machiavelli and Xenophon. You sketch out the way this difference should be understood *in concreto*. But you are right: my unexplained thoughts on this issue move in another direction from yours. Maybe I will argue this out with you in print.[49]

Letter 22

March 12, 1949

Dear Mr. Strauss,

Many thanks for your article on "Political Philosophy and History."[50] It is a very fine, clean work; I have the impression that we are in very much greater agreement in the direction of our work than I first supposed. Your main thesis—based on Hegel—that historical reflection is a peculiar requirement of modern philosophy seems completely right to me; and I view this motive also as the *raison d'etre* of my own historical studies. As I have only engaged myself with these questions in English, allow me my English formulation of the problem: To restore the experiences that have led to the creation of certain concepts and symbols; or: Symbols have become opaque; they must be made luminous again by penetrating to the experiences they express.—Very fine too is your critique of the attitude that would understand the thinker better than he would himself; and your insistence that the purpose of historical analysis is the production of meaning, as it was intended by the author.

I assume that this article is a type of advance notice of work, in which

49. In 1954 a French version of *On Tyranny* was published, *De le Tyrannie* (Paris: Gallimard, 1954). It contained a long review by Alexandre Kojève, "Tyrannie et sagesse," first published as "L'Action politique des philosophes," *Critique* 41–42 (1950): 46–55, 138–55; Strauss added a "mise au point" that responded briefly to Voegelin and at greater length to Kojève. The French reply by Strauss was in turn republished in English as "Restatement on Xenophon's *Hiero*," in *What Is Political Philosophy? And Other Studies* (Glencoe, Ill.: The Free Press, 1959), 95–133. The entire Strauss-Kojève debate has recently been reedited by Victor Gourevitch and Michael S. Roth, *On Tyranny* (New York: The Free Press, 1991).

50. Strauss, "Political Philosophy and History," *Journal of the History of Ideas* 10 (1949): 30–50.

you set out the problem; and I am already very curious to see the further studies.

With warmest greetings,
Eric Voegelin

Letter 23

17.3.49

My dear Mr. Voegelin,

I wanted to thank you warmly for your friendly and encouraging lines. It is very fine that you maintain the customs descended from another world, the Old World. Even more pleasing to me is the agreement in our intentions expressed by you, that so long as we have to combat the presently reigning idiocy, [that shared objective] is of greater significance than the differences, which I also would not wish to deny. Insofar as so slow a writer as I could take up something like this, I plan to say something, after its appearance, about your three-volume work, about which I have heard much: in case this occurs, I will specify in detail my standpoint as opposed to yours.

Your surmise regarding my article "Political Philosophy and History" is right: the article is to be thought of as one of the introductory chapters of a publication on classic principles of politics. But heaven only knows if I will manage with this publication: on the decisive questions, there are no preliminary studies, so that one would have to first lay the groundwork through a series of specialized investigations. At the moment I am studying Lucretius.[51] I have the desire to write freely and frankly on the meaning of his poem, that is, without footnotes, assuming that there is some prospect of publishing an essay of this sort. As far as Lucretius is concerned, the classical philologists are again remarkably blind.

With best wishes,

Yours,
Leo Strauss

51. Strauss later published "A Note on Lucretius," in *Natur und Geschichte: Karl Löwith zum 70. Geburtstag* (Stuttgart: Kohlhammer, 1967), 322–32, and an expanded version, "Notes on Lucretius," in Strauss, *Liberalism Ancient and Modern* (New York: Basic Books, 1968), 76–139.

Letter 24

March 22, 1949

Dear Mr. Strauss,

The way you fling your productions out—a fact that contradicts the claim in your friendly lines that you are a slow writer. Many thanks for the Spinoza study.[52] It came just at the right time—as, it seems, does everything that comes from you—in that I frequently consider the esoteric in Spinoza and the question of what he could actually mean. And so often an incidental comment was very illuminating for me: from some of your citations emerges the insight that Spinoza saw Christianity very precisely as a Lutheran-Calvinist might. Quite evidently he understands the problem of justification in the sense of the *sola fide* principle; whereas the Thomist problem of *amicitia* in faith is evidently unknown to him. Now I also understand better how Spinoza comes to his own religious attitude of *acquiescentia*, an attitude to which one can come from Lutheranism but hardly from classical Catholicism. This appears to me to be not insignificant for an understanding of Spinoza.

What you write about the plan for Lucretius fills me with mixed feelings. If you are only planning to write on Lucretius, this would certainly be welcome; if, however, this plan might become a prestudy to a systematic text of politics, and precisely through this a reason for its delay, it would be a shame. Lucretius is fine, but I would prefer your systematic politics. My encounters with Lucretius are unfortunately only occasional. I never really studied him, but rather always sniffed around at his work, in particular with regard to Santayana and Valéry; this little, however, lets me regret not knowing more. With Santayana and Valéry I have the impression that their Lucretianism is caused by what I would call spiritual fatigue. The inclination to let oneself drop into a depersonalized nature arises from a pseudo-aesthetic weakness of spirit, in particular in Valéry's moving *Cimetière Marin*. I was never quite clear if Lucretius's materialism might have itself a similar cause in the author's personality. I am anxious to hear something from you about it.

With warmest greetings,

Eric Voegelin

52. Strauss, "How to Study Spinoza's *Theologico-Political Treatise*," *Proceedings of the American Academy for Jewish Research* 17 (1948): 69–131. Reprinted in Strauss, *Persecution and the Art of Writing* (Glencoe, Ill.: The Free Press, 1952).

Letter 25

April 15, 1949

My dear Mr. Voegelin,

Your letter of March 22 remained unanswered for so long because in the meantime my first quarter in Chicago began and I was rather preoccupied with it. Yesterday I received a copy of the *Review of Politics* with your review of my work.[53] It pleased me greatly to see that it was printed *in toto* after all. Your review, with a single exception, will be and remain the only one that contributes to the discussion. The exception is a review promised by Alexander Kojève (the author of *Introduction à l'étude de Hegel*, an exceptional work [Gallimard, 1947])[54] in the journal *Critique*.[55] Kojève depicts himself as a Stalinist, but would be immediately shot in the USSR. As soon as Kojève's review appears, I intend to write a critique of both of your critiques. Gurian, who visited me two days ago, will leave me space in the *Review of Politics*.[56] Because I would like to do this, I will save my ammunition. I am doing this also since I want to think over your objections.

Regarding Spinoza, I attempted in my German work on Spinoza (1930) to define more exactly the connection with Calvinism (with Luther, in my opinion, there is no connection at all).[57] I believe now, that then I fell too much into the trap of Spinoza's accommodations. His intertheological preferences are essentially of a tactical nature except for the general one, that he prefers theological rationalism *qua* rationalism over every fideism. For me personally, the most important thing in the essay that you have read is that I succeeded in interpreting "*ad captum vulgi*" authentically. "Sometime" I will point out the coherence of Spinoza's moral philosophy: it is perhaps the most interesting example of an ethics based on modern natural science (in the sense of a modernity "more advanced" than the Hobbesian one).

53. See Letter 20.

54. Kojève, *Introduction à la lecture de Hegel*, ed. R. Queneau (Paris: Gallimard, 1947); trans. James H. Nichols, ed. A. Bloom, *Introduction to the Reading of Hegel* (New York: Basic Books, 1969).

55. See Letter 21, note.

56. Strauss's reply was not published in the *Review of Politics*; see Letter 21, note.

57. Strauss, *Die Religionskritik Spinozas als Grundlage seiner Bibelwissenschaft: Untersuchungen zu Spinozas theologisch-Politischem Traktat* (Berlin: Akadamie Verlag, 1930); trans. E. M. Sinclair, *Spinoza's Critique of Religion* (New York: Schocken, 1965).

Unfortunately, because the semester began, I had to leave Lucretius to one side in order to turn to the Lucretian-grounded Rousseau, the *Discours sur l'origine d'Inégalité*. I hope that this time I will cope with this political writing of J. J. and can in the fall submit an essay about it (a continuation of the essay in *Social Research*).[58] This work contains in germ all that comes later (for example Kant, Marx . . .). I do not yet know if it will be possible for me to point out everything that is in it.

I want to say only this about Lucretius today: his poem is the purest and most glorious expression of the attitude that elicits consolation from the utterly hopeless truth, on the basis of its being only the truth—there is no idea of the use of the hopeless, godless truth for some social purpose, as is almost always the case with other fashions or trends; nor is there any aestheticism or sentimentality. I do not believe that people like Santayana or Valéry can understand Lucretius. The next approximation in our world is the scientifically slanted aspect of Nietzsche.—As for Lucretius's "personality"? I do not believe it matters. Nor does his Romanness: his poem tries precisely *to be free from* "Romanness" (among other things): *primum Graius homo*—this means *not* the Romans.

Hope to hear from you soon. With warm wishes,

Yours,
Leo Strauss

Letter 26

17.12.49

My Dear Mr. Voegelin,

Warmest thanks for your analysis of the *Gorgias*, which I read with great interest.[59] Your position has become significantly clearer to me, and thus also the point at which I do not quite understand you. We are quite in agreement that in the dialogues *nostra res agitur*, [and] that it is therefore possible in particular to say that Plato's critique of the sophists is a critique of "intellectuals." The question is only whether you first of all interpret in the obvious way *nostra res* and therefore [believe] the reason for the reprehensibleness of the

58. See Letter 16.

59. Voegelin, "The Philosophy of Existence: Plato's *Gorgias*," *The Review of Politics* 11 (1949): 477–98.

intellectuals is identical to the Platonic one. The employment of the expression "existential" reveals the difficulty. "Existential" is opposed to the "objective," "theoretical," and thus betrays its anti-Platonic origin. The man who has thought through most clearly the problem of "existence"—Heidegger—therefore made Plato especially responsible for the actual "neglect." Kierkegaard's resistance to Socrates—the appeal to Socrates against Hegel is after all only provisional—expresses the same thought. In his critique of Plato, Heidegger tries to find the way by rejecting philosophy and metaphysics *as such. If* one wants to use the Kierkegaardian expression, one has to say that for Socrates-Plato, "existential" and "theoretical" are the same: insofar as I am serious and there are questions, I look for *the* "objective" truth. The sophist is a man to whom the truth does not matter—but in this sense all men except for the *gnēsios philosophounte* are sophists, especially the *polis* as *polis* (and not only the decadent ones). The passion for *knowledge* that moves the Platonic dialogue, this highest *mania*, cannot be understood within Kierkegaard's concept of "existence," and [the attempt to do so] must be discarded as a radical illusion. This *mania*, from which Faust himself turns away, [is] in opposition to the creature in paradise, on the Isles of the Blessed, or to the painstaking searches of Goethe himself.

The question Plato *or* existentialism is today the ontological question—about "intellectuals" we (you and I) do not need to waste words, unless it were about how they finally have to be interpreted, namely, within Platonic or existentialist philosophy; for this reason, I permit myself these brief remarks.

With warmest greetings,

Yours,
Leo Strauss

Letter 27

January 2, 1950

Dear Mr. Strauss,

Many thanks for your letter of 17.XII. I believe I owe you a few lines of explanation.

You are, of course, completely right to become indignant over existentialist philosophy and to ask what got into me. Let me then assure you that the misleading title of the article does not stem from me. I had titled it simply "Plato's Gorgias." Gurian added on "Philosophy of Existence" without asking me; I was embarrassingly surprised when I saw the journal.

Fortunately there are only a few readers, such as you, who would notice the scandal; and so I let it go. I swear that I am not straying on existentialist paths; we are in agreement also on the question of ontology.

Why and in what sense I use the term "existential" in the text of the article should be explained. Terminologically, the case is easy: I know no better expression; if I find one, I would be gladly prepared to use it; and if you could give me ideas I would be very grateful. It has to do then with the problem itself. I use the term "existential" in a sense that is very similar to that of Maritain in his *Court traité de l'existence*, which I just bought in New York and read in part on the trip.[60] The truth of ontology (including in particular philosophical anthropology) is not a datum that can be recognized by anyone at any time. Ontological knowledge emerges in the process of history and biographically in the process of the individual person's life under certain conditions of education, social context, personal inclination, and spiritual conditioning. *Epistēmē* is not just a function of understanding, it is also in the Aristotelian sense, a dianoetic *aretē*. For this *non*cognitive aspect of *epistēmē* I use the term "existential."

In a history of ideas I must use this term quite often. A history of ideas should not be a doxographic report, or a history of dogmas in the classical sense, but rather a history of existential transformations in which the "truth" comes to sight, is obscured, is lost, and is again recovered. A history of political ideas, in particular, should investigate the process in which "truth" becomes socially effective or is hindered in such effectiveness. You see, it does not have to do with a negation or relativization of ontology, but rather with the correlation between perception in the cognitive and existential sense; this correlation is for me the theme of "history." Existential special themes would be: theogony, the history of myth and revelation; destruction of the knowledge of truth through the *pleonexia* of intellectuals; the effectiveness of authority through existential readiness to reproduce the known truth imaginatively; the destruction of authority through the enclosing passion of self-assertion, etc.

These suggestions are brief; but they show what is at stake. I find, as said, no better term than "existential"; but I am at all times ready for a reform in terminology, if I find a better one.

With all best wishes for New Year,

Eric Voegelin

60. Jacques Maritain, *Court traité de l'existence et de l'existant,* trans. L. Galantière and G. B. Phélan as *Existence and the Existent*, new ed. (New York: Pantheon, 1964).

Letter 28

14.3.50

My Dear Mr. Voegelin,

Please excuse my long silence, but since I received your letter of January 2 I have been in such a whirl.

We are arguing as to whether, if one rejects existentialist philosophy, one can employ the expression "existential" without creating confusion. You admit the difficulty, but see no alternative. What is the problem? There are truths, you say, that cannot be seen by everyone at all times, the recognition of which therefore is bound to certain extratheoretical presuppositions, and thus are "existentially" conditioned. Therein lies an ambivalence: even Aristotle would have admitted that his conception of the whole was not factually possible at all times—it required leisure, that is to say, free communities within which there was the possibility for the unfolding of a higher humanity, and especially it required the continuity of a series of thinkers dedicated to the search for the truth of the whole. But: here "history" is no more than *condition* for the recognition of truth—"history" is not the source of truth. You say: the history of ideas is the "history of the existential transformations in which the 'truth' comes to view, is obscured, is lost, and then again won." Why do you place "truth" in quotation marks? Is truth only so-called truth, the illusion of the respective period? Or if there is *the* truth, which indeed under unfavorable circumstances, or deliberately, is obscured and then also not again won, this truth is itself and principally not "existentially" conditioned.

The concept "existential" requires a radical critique of the *vita contemplativa*, such that at the base of this critique one can only reject, but not understand, Plato. To my mind it will not do to identify Plato's critique of sophistry as a topic with the existentialist critique of *theoria*: the sophists (= intellectuals) were quite clearly not theoretical characters. Indeed, the *vita contemplativa* requires a turning around of the whole soul, but that does not mean that one can understand the *vita contemplativa* adequately in respect of its effects on the (if you forgive the expression) nontheoretical part of the soul.

The closest classical equivalent of "existential" is "practical," insofar as one understands "practical" in contradistinction to "theoretical." Existentialist philosophy will perhaps appear at some time in the future as the paradoxical effort to lead the thought of the praxis of the practical to its, in my mind, absurd last consequences. Under these conditions praxis ceases indeed to be actually praxis and transforms itself into "existence." If I am not totally mistaken, the root of all modern darkness from the seventeenth century on is the obscuring of the difference between theory and praxis, an obscuring that first leads to a reduction of praxis to theory (this is the meaning of so-called rationalism) and then, in retaliation, to the rejection of theory in the name of a praxis that is no longer intelligible as praxis.

In short, I do not believe that one can succeed with the terminology today at one's disposal (as the classic terminology is for the present completely unintelligible). That this is no mere "semantic" problem, I hardly need to say to you.

I warmly reciprocate your wishes for the New Year—please accept them despite the terrible delay.

Cordially yours,
Leo Strauss

Letter 29

10.4.50

My dear Mr. Voegelin,

You have misunderstood me, as you could not decipher my disgraceful handwriting.[61] I spoke not of "extrahuman" but rather of "extratheoretical" *presupposition*. The question is whether there is a pure grasp of truth as an *essential human possibility*, quite regardless of what the conditions and *actualization* of this possibility are, or whether there is *not* such a grasp as an essential possibility. When you say "only at such and such a time did that order of the soul emerge," you leave open the question whether this order of the soul is the natural telos of Man or a "coincidence"; that it also *could not* have emerged, does that not deprive it of the status of a telos? However that may be, it seems to me, nonetheless, that we are in more fundamental agreement than I believed.

May I ask you to let me know sometime what you think of Mr. Popper.[62] He gave a lecture here, on the task of social philosophy, that was beneath

61. Letter missing (Voegelin to Strauss).

62. Karl Popper, author of *The Open Society and Its Enemies* (1945) and several other works of an analytical nature.

contempt: it was the most washed-out, lifeless positivism trying to whistle in the dark, linked to a complete inability to think "rationally," although it passed itself off as "rationalism"—it was very bad. I cannot imagine that such a man ever wrote something that was worthwhile reading, and yet it appears to be a professional duty to become familiar with his productions. Could you say something to me about that—if you wish, I will keep it to myself.

Warmest greetings,
Leo Strauss

Letter 30

April 18, 1950

Dear Mr. Strauss,

The opportunity to speak a few deeply felt words about Karl Popper to a kindred soul is too golden to endure a long delay. This Popper has been for years, not exactly a stone against which one stumbles, but a troublesome pebble that I must continually nudge from the path, in that he is constantly pushed upon me by people who insist that his work on the "open society and its enemies" is one of the social science masterpieces of our times. This insistence persuaded me to read the work even though I would otherwise not have touched it. You are quite right to say that it is a vocational duty to make ourselves familiar with the ideas of such a work when they lie in our field; I would hold out against this duty the other vocational duty, not to write and to publish such a work. In that Popper violated this elementary vocational duty and stole several hours of my lifetime, which I devoted in fulfilling my vocational duty, I feel completely justified in saying without reservation that this book is impudent, dilettantish crap. Every single sentence is a scandal, but it is still possible to lift out a few main annoyances.

1. The expressions "closed [society]" and "open society" are taken from Bergson's *Deux Sources*.[63] Without explaining the difficulties that induced

63. Henri Bergson, *Les Deux Sources de la morale et de la religion*, trans. Ashley Audra and Cloudesley Bereton as *The Two Sources of Morality and Religion* (Garden City, N.Y.: Doubleday, 1935).

Bergson to create these concepts, Popper takes the terms because they sound good to him; [he] comments in passing that in Bergson they had a "religious" meaning, but that he will use the concept of the open society closer to Graham Wallas's "great society" or to that of Walter Lippmann. Perhaps I am oversensitive about such things, but I do not believe that respectable philosophers such as Bergson develop their concepts for the sole purpose that the coffeehouse scum might have something to botch. There also arises the relevant problem: if Bergson's theory of open society is philosophically and historically tenable (which I in fact believe), then Popper's idea of the open society is ideological rubbish. For this reason alone, he should have discussed the problem with all possible care.

2. The impertinent disregard for the achievements in his particular problem area, which makes itself evident with respect to Bergson, runs through the whole work. When one reads the deliberations on Plato or Hegel, one has the impression that Popper is quite unfamiliar with the literature on the subject—even though he occasionally cites an author. In some cases, as for example Hegel, I would believe that he has never seen a work like Rosenzweig's *Hegel and the State*.[64] In other cases, where he cites works without appearing to have perceived their contents, another factor is added:

3. Popper is philosophically so uncultured, so fully a primitive ideological brawler, that he is not able even approximately to reproduce correctly the contents of one page of Plato. Reading is of no use to him; he is too lacking in knowledge to understand what the author says. Through this emerge terrible things, as when he translates Hegel's "Germanic world" as "German world" and draws conclusions from this mistranslation regarding Hegel's German nationalist propaganda.

4. Popper engages in no textual analysis from which can be seen the author's intention; instead he carries the modern ideological clichés directly to the text, assuming that the text will deliver results in the sense of the clichés. It will be a special pleasure for you to hear that, for example, Plato experienced an evolution—from an early "humanitarian" period still recognizable in the *Gorgias*, to something else (I can't recall any more if "reactionary" or "authoritarian") in the *Republic*.

Briefly and in sum: Popper's book is a scandal without extenuating

64. Rosenzweig, *Hegel und der Staat* (Berlin: Oldenburg, 1920).

circumstances; in its intellectual attitude it is the typical product of a failed intellectual; spiritually one would have to use expressions like rascally, impertinent, loutish; in terms of technical competence, as a piece in the history of thought, it is dilettantish, and as a result is worthless.

It would not be suitable to show this letter to the unqualified. Where it concerns its factual contents, I would see it as a violation of the vocational duty you identified, to support this scandal through silence.

Eric Voegelin

Letter 31

8.8.50

My dear Mr. Voegelin,

I have never thanked you for your interesting letter dated 18.4. In confidence I would like to tell you that I showed your letter to my friend Kurt Riezler,[65] who was thereby encouraged to throw his not inconsiderable influence into the balance against Popper's probable appointment here. You thereby helped to prevent a scandal.

Today I write to you for the following reason. At the beginning of 1951, at Gallimard's wish, a French translation of my *Hiero* book is to appear in the following form:[66] 1) French translation of the *Hiero*; 2) my text omitting nearly all notes; 3) a sixty-page long critique of my writing titled "La tyrannie et la sagesse," written by Alexander Kojève, author of *Introduction à la lecture de Hegel*,[67] which is in every detail an outstanding interpretation of the *Phenomenology of Spirit*; 4) a "Restatement" from me, which I am just now writing. It seems important to me to begin the discussion with a response to your review. Because the critique of your views forms an integral part of the whole "Restatement," I am not sticking strictly to what you expressly said: I must come to terms with your unstated premises, which in part I know from your other publications, and in part presume. It occurred to me that you might wish to riposte. Unfortunately

65. See Strauss, *What Is Political Philosophy? And Other Studies* (Glencoe, Ill.: The Free Press, 1959), ch. 10.

66. See above, Letters 21, 25.

67. See above, Letter 25.

this is not possible in the French publication. But perhaps one could persuade Gurian to print the English original of my afterword together with your riposte in the *Review of Politics*, after the French publication has appeared. Please let me know what you think of this idea.[68]

Warmest greetings,

Yours,
Leo Strauss

Letter 32

August 21, 1950

Dear Mr. Strauss,

Many thanks for your letter of August 8. I returned only yesterday from a lengthy trip—as explanation as to why I answer your queries only today.

Let me say above all how much it pleases me that your *Hiero* found attention in France—one of the few good things that has been written today has not become lost. If I have understood your letter properly (I still have occasionally a little difficulty deciphering your handwriting—but it becomes better with every letter I receive from you)—if I understand you properly, then, you will add a "Restatement" to the French edition, in which I might at last clearly find out what the unstated presuppositions of my work are. Do not take this sentence, please, as ironic—I am very concerned myself at the moment with further explications on precisely these presuppositions, and I really hope for some help from your response. Thus far I am then very satisfied with your proposal. With regard to the further possibility of publishing your "Restatement" in English, accompanied by some of my remarks in the *Review of Politics*, you will find me, with the greatest pleasure, willing—if Gurian is interested.

Since the French edition will appear at the beginning of 1951, and the English publication will only take place later, we will have the opportunity to discuss at length these and other things, when I come to Chicago at the

68. This proposal by Strauss was not acted upon by Gurian.

end of January (to the Walgreen Lectures).[69] I am already looking forward to the opportunity of seeing you at some length.

Enclosed, a study on Marx;[70] one or another point may interest you.

Yours,
Eric Voegelin

Letter 33

25.8.50

My dear Mr. Voegelin,

Warmest thanks for your Marx essay, which I read with the greatest interest and with hearty agreement. In particular I am in total agreement with what you say regarding "Interpreting the world or changing it": that is, in fact, the root of the evil.[71] You are also completely right when you note the necessity of the *positive* image of the man of the future—this travesty as *homo universalis*, every oaf a Ph.D. I have doubt only with reference to p. 386: "M. was perfectly aware of the connection between his own thought and Genevan Protestantism." He believed in this connection, as did Hegel himself. But is it not, as you yourself subsequently seem to hint, an illusion? Is *liberal* Protestantism not a pseudo-Protestantism, whose real basis is not Protestantism, but rather a rational secularization? A small matter—top of 282, referring to note 18—compare Rousseau, *Discours sur les sciences et les arts*, part 1, 5th paragraph.

My terrible handwriting must have brought about a terrible misunderstanding. How could you ever believe that I wrote that you will learn finally with clarity from my "Restatement" what the unstated premises of your work are? From this response you will merely see that I take the classical teaching on tyranny as in principle completely sufficient. The longer section, which comes to terms with Kojève's tract "La tyrannie et la sagesse," deals, admittedly, with general matters and will, I believe, make

69. Published by Voegelin as *The New Science of Politics* (Chicago: University of Chicago Press, 1952).

70. Voegelin, "The Formation of the Marxian Revolutionary Idea," *Review of Politics* 12 (1950): 275–302.

71. The reference is to Marx's "Theses on Feuerbach," number eleven.

my premises clearer to you. They are very simple: *philosophari necesse est*, and philosophy is radically independent of faith—the root of *our* disagreement lies presumably in the second thesis.

I am *very* pleased that there is an opportunity to see you here in January. Here there reigns such atomization that I learned only from your letter that you are giving the Walgreen Lectures in the winter term.

With regard to the publication of the English original of my epilogue, now a new problem has arisen, insofar as the epilogue promises to run to forty printed pages. Gurian will probably not go along with it, and I must try to persuade Alvin Johnson that he too sometimes may also print a ruthless, reactionary utterance. I will keep you up to date.

With warm wishes

Yours,
Leo Strauss

Letter 34

December 4, 1950

Dear Mr. Strauss,

I have not yet responded to your friendly letter of August 25; and now your offprint on "Natural Right" has arrived.[72]

Let me at first thank you for the offprint. It really is an excellent analysis of historicism, with which I fully agree; and I am only eager to read what follows. I see that it is part of your Walgreen Lectures from last year—why has the book not yet appeared?[73] Or did it only pass me by? You suggest that in a further development you will provide a foundation for natural-law theory on the basis of classical political philosophy. And I would also like to know what the public in Chicago said of this effort; are there discussions after the lectures? And now to a point in your study that at the moment preoccupies me greatly. You say, on p. 425: "In the present state of our knowledge, it is difficult to say at what point in the modern development

72. Strauss, "Natural Right and the Historical Approach," *Review of Politics* 12 (1950): 422–42.

73. Published by Strauss as *Natural Right and History* (Chicago, University of Chicago Press, 1953).

the decisive break occurred with the 'unhistorical' approach that prevailed in all earlier philosophy." I must grant you that our "present state of knowledge" is not the best, but I like to believe that one can say something about the origin of the movement of ideas that comes to a head in historicism. It seems to me, the origin lies in the gnosticism of the Middle Ages and the attempt to give a "meaning" to the immanent course of history, as for example in the works of Joachim of Flora. When the attempt is made, first merely in principle, to immanentize the transcendent *eschaton* (in the Christian sense of the term), then everything follows from the logic of the approach, right down to the historical fact as the answer to the meaning of self-interpreting existence. From the approach of the Middle Ages, the modern inclination seems to follow in seeing something else in history besides political, profane history. From this point of view, I would permit myself a correction to your formulation, that "*all* earlier philosophy" was unhistorical. Philosophy [deformed into] the system, from Descartes to Hegel, seems to me to form a unity, insofar as the idea of a philosophical, closed "system" dominates. However, the idea of "system," of the possible exhaustive penetration of the mystery of the cosmos and its existence by the intellect, is itself a Gnostic phenomenon, a drawing in of eternity into the time of the individual thinker. I would therefore restrict your comment on philosophy in the Platonic-Aristotelian sense (Aristotle, as far as I know, had no concept of system; the systematization of Aristotle comes from the commentators).—This brings me to a comment in your letter regarding the derivation of Marx from liberal Protestantism. You mean that liberal Protestantism already should no longer be spoken of as Protestantism, but instead be seen as a result of secularization. I would agree with that, insofar as secularization in the sense of a radical immanentization must be distinguished from the half-baked immanentization of the Middle Ages and the Reformation. If we follow the logic of the problem (that is, immanentization) to its beginning, then I would see in orthodox Protestantism already the start of immanentization. Calvin flirts with the problem in the *Institutes*, where his concern for the *certitudo salutis* through the unequivocal "call" is quite clearly a Gnostic attempt to gain certitude of salvation, which is a bit more certain than orthodox *cognitio fidei*. Luther vacillates, but his hatred of the *fides caritate formata*, his wild efforts to take love out of faith, and to make deliberate knowledge into its substance, seems to me to lead in the same direction. One would perhaps have to say that there was enough Catholic substance in "orthodox" Protestantism to arrest a further development, the inner logic of which forces itself through in liberal Protestantism.

With regard to the "second thesis" of your letter, that philosophy is radically independent of faith, we will discuss that in Chicago. At the moment, I do not see how you get around the historical fact of the beginning of philosophy in the attitude of faith of Xenophanes, Heraclitus, and Parmenides.

The reason for my rather long silence is my work on the Walgreen Lectures. Naturally, it became something else than I had first anticipated. The title will read "Truth and Representation"; and the problem of modern gnosticism will take up a large part of it.

Yours,
Eric Voegelin

Letter 35

10.12.50

My dear Mr. Voegelin,

Just back from a trip to the east, I find your letter of the fourth of this month. I have just a bit of time, but unfortunately no proper paper. Excuse me.

My Walgreen Lectures have not yet appeared, because they are not yet ready to print. I have a bad conscience, but I would have even a worse one if I had already published them. The work remains a risk in either case, even though I do nothing more than present the *problem* of natural right as an unsolved problem. As to the reaction of the public here in Chicago, it was, I believe, favorable, especially among the younger ones, who at first see only an alternative between positivism-relativism-pragmatism and Neo-Thomism, and who can scarcely imagine that one can draw the consequence from one's ignorance that one must strive after knowledge, and that they see this immediately when one demonstrates it to them. There are *no* discussions after the Walgreen Lectures.

To your objections to the passage on page 425 of my article, I would say that of course I know of the idea of tracing back the turn to history to Joachim of Flora and the like (alone in the last two years the books of

Taubes and Löwith appeared, who do just this)[74] but also that it does not persuade me. I will not raise the objection that one would have to return from Joachim to the Islamic Shi'ah,[75] which for its part has a connection with Plato's *Statesman*, and so the clear lines and the clarity of the context fade away. Even if the lines from Joachim to Hegel exist, they would not bring out the turn to the thoroughly "this-worldly" philosophy, that is, from the eternal to a this-worldly process: one has to bring out as well the turn within philosophy. In this one must above all, as I see it, assume that "*all* earlier philosophy" was "ahistorical." "Ahistorical" is not the same as "systematic." Classical philosophy was not "systematic," but at the same time it was "ahistorical." "System" means the derivation of the whole sum of realities out of the *prōton physei*—it presumes that we can begin with the *prōton physei*, that the thinker stands at the beginning. Classical philosophy understands itself as the uncompletable ascent from *proteron pros hēmas* to *proteron physei*. Expressed otherwise: the "system" requires that the *hylē* be resolved into intelligible relations or the like, which classical philosophy denies. Classical philosophy is "ahistorical" insofar as it is a search for the *aie ōn*, within which all history has taken or can take place, for the *aie ōn* in no way opens up through "history": history is for classical philosophy infinitely unimportant, insofar as the decisive questions, the fundamental questions, necessarily relate to the *aie ōn*. The fundamental questions—(1) the question of the *archē* or the *archai*, (2) the question of the right life or the *aristē politeia*. "History" in the strict sense belongs in the practical dimension, in the dimension that is subordinated to the theoretical. Historicizing means the forgetting of eternity. This forgetting must be understood in terms of the rejection of the classical concept of philosophy. "*En brûlant les étapes*,"[76] one could say that historicism is a reaction to a system-philosophy, a reaction that has not freed itself from the ultimate presuppositions of system-philosophy—the obscuring of the radical difference between theory and praxis that lies at the basis of both forms of modern thinking. I say that historicism is a reaction to system-philosophy: the

74. Jacob Taubes, *Abendländische Eschatologie* (Bern: Franke, 1947), and Karl Löwith, *Meaning in History* (Chicago: University of Chicago Press, 1949).

75. Shi'ah is the smaller of the two major branches of Islam, as distinct from Sunnah. It began as an essentially political movement in early Islam but subsequently became a religious movement. Shi'is and Sunnis disagree chiefly on readings of the Qur'an and on the character of the imamate, the Shi'i religious leadership.

76. *Brûler une étape* means to pass by a halting-place without stopping; thus, Strauss proceeded directly to the "bottom line" regarding historicism and system-philosophy.

proto-Hegelian system is at first not "historical," except in an embryonic manner, as I think I said provisionally in chapter 6 of my Hobbes book.[77]

As to my remark on Protestant liberalism, namely that it cannot be understood alone from the religious tradition, I think above all of the overwhelming influence that modern science (critique of the possibility, or rather recognizability, of the miracles; denial of the simple reality of heaven and hell and the like) has had on the *whole* of modern thinking. One should think also of the influence of the discoveries as early as the sixteenth century that belongs by its structure to the influence of modern science. (Do you know my works, *Spinoza's Critique of Religion* [1930] and *Philosophy and Law* [1935], in which I tried to set out this connection in a somewhat more open-minded manner than usual?) Everything that I would write in response to your question would only be a misleading abbreviation of these explanations. Unfortunately, I do not have any copies of this book any more.

As to your question, "Philosophy and Faith," I deny that the "historical fact of the beginning of philosophy consists in the attitude of faith of Xenophanes, Heraclitus, and Parmenides," which you assume. Whatever *noein* might mean, it is certainly not *pistis* in some sense. On this point Heidegger in his *Holzwege* (who otherwise says many *adunatotata*) is simply right.

I am greatly looking forward to our reunion in January. We will not be in "agreement"—but for me it is always a great benefit and a rare joy to speak to a man who chooses the hard way.

With warm wishes,

Yours,

Leo Strauss

PS. Renewed apologies for the paper on which I have written today.

77. Strauss, *The Political Philosophy of Hobbes: Its Basis and Genesis*, trans. Elsa M. Sinclair (Chicago: University of Chicago Press, [1936] 1952).

Letter 36

February 21, 1951

Dear Mr. Strauss,

We have just begun our semester, but now the first assault has somewhat died down; and I hurry to thank you and your dear wife very warmly for your hospitality.

In particular I wish to thank you for the opportunity to read your *Philosophy and Law*. After reading it, your present position is actually more difficult for me to understand than before. I have the impression that you have retreated from an understanding of the prophetic (religious) foundation of philosophizing (with which I would heartily agree) to a theory of *epistēmē*, and that you refuse to see the problem of *epistēmē* in connection with experience, out of which it emerges. Why you do this, I do not know. And how this position can work, when it comes to the treatment of a concrete problem (for example, to an interpretation of a Platonic myth), I cannot predict—for that I would first have to see from you a concrete implementation.

With all best wishes,

Very cordially yours,
Eric Voegelin

Letter 37

25.2.51

My dear Mr. Voegelin,

I now have some time, but no proper paper. I fear when I do have the right paper, I will have no free time. So I dare to write to you on improper paper.

Warmest thanks for your letter. Your own thanks are quite unnecessary: we are very sorry not to see you more often—but these horrid flus, to say nothing of the demands of teaching duties. I could not even attend all your lectures. Therefore I also hesitate to say more than that they were most interesting. There is, as you can imagine, one point where our paths separate. I do not even want to try to describe it more exactly before I have read your lectures more closely. I have the intention to discuss them in detail in print.

With regard to *Philosophy and Law*, I believe that I basically still stand on the same ground. I hope, of course, that I have deepened my learning in the last fifteen years and would therefore express many things differently.

When I insisted at that time that the law has primacy, that was—leaving aside objective reasons—conditioned by the fact that I spoke of the Middle Ages. But you too would not deny that there is an essential distinction between the thinking of the Middle Ages, based on revelation, and the thinking of classical antiquity, not based on revelation. There is a double reason not to obscure this essential difference in any way. First, it is in the interest of revelation, which is by no means merely natural knowledge. Secondly, for the sake of human knowledge, *epistēmē*. You yourself have said that science matters very much to you. For me, it matters a great deal to understand it as such. Its classics are the Greeks and not the Bible. The classics demonstrated that truly human life is a life dedicated to science, knowledge, and the search for it. Coming from the Bible the *hen anagkaion* is something completely different. No justifiable purpose is served by obscuring this contradiction, by the postulating of the *tertium* from there [i.e., from the classics and the Bible].[78] Every synthesis is actually an option either for Jerusalem or for Athens.

Well, you speak of the religious foundation of classical philosophy. I would not do so simply for the reason that there is no Greek word for "religion." One would have to speak of the gods or of God or of the divine, and one would have to elucidate what different things the philosophers understood by God. But it was probably not the same as what the people understood by it. One would have to elucidate further which *experiences* of the divine the philosophers recognized as genuine. Plato and Aristotle attained, after all, *proof* of the existence of gods not from experience and customs but rather from the analysis of motion.

I believe still today that the *theioi nomoi* is the common ground of the Bible and philosophy—humanly speaking. But I would specify that, in any event, it is the problem of the multitude of *theioi nomoi* that leads to the diametrically opposed solutions of the Bible on the one hand and of philosophy on the other.

You seem to be quite sure that the Platonic myths are intelligible only on the basis of postulating a "religious" experience underlying them. I am not so sure about that. I confess my ignorance. It seems to me impossible really to solve the problem of the Platonic myth before one has solved the

78. Strauss's writing is very difficult to read in this passage.

problem of the Platonic dialogue, that is to say, the cosmos of the dialogues, since this whole work is a myth. Apart from that, those pieces that are usually designated as *the* myths of Plato are always elements of a dialogue. But as far as I know, so far nobody has been able to say clearly what the meaning of the dialogue is. That does not surprise me. Because without a complete understanding of the whole Platonic corpus, there remains inevitably a last doubt. I know of no one who could claim such an understanding. This much, I believe, emerges throughout from Plato, that he was less anxious to induce the better readers to believe than to induce them to think. And for that there is in fact no better means than the enigmatic quality of his work in general and the myths particularly.

I do not believe that the problem of the dialogues is irresolvable. It only seems to me that we are still quite far from doing so. Since when has the problem actually been noticed? Hardly before Schleiermacher, whose solution is demonstrably false. Then P. Friedländer began again—fundamentally [his interpretation was] only aesthetic. I find here and there good observations, but nowhere a clear exposition that goes to the bottom of things. Nearly the whole research is based on the hypothetical "development" theory, which cuts off all the central problems of interpretation by referring them to various periods of origin.

I do not know if you now understand my position better. Please do not hesitate to call me to account.

With warmest greetings,

Yours,
Leo Strauss

Letter 38

April 22, 1951

Dear Mr. Strauss,

I must thank you for a whole number of things—for your letter of February 25, for the offprints on Hobbes and Max Weber,[79] and for the

79. Strauss, "On the Spirit of Hobbes' Political Philosophy," *Revue internationale de philosophie* 4 (1950): 405–31, and "The Social Science of Max Weber," *Measure* 2 (1951): 204–30.

mimeographed article on Husik.[80] Thank you for everything and in particular for the Max Weber. It came just as I was working on the "Introduction" to the Walgreen Lectures; there I have also a few pages on Weber's value-free science and I see that to a considerable extent we agree in our analysis.

By mentioning the lectures I have also given you the reason why I left your letter lying for two months. My preoccupation with the Introduction left me no tranquility to "solve" either the problem of revelation or that of the Platonic dialogue, which you quite rightly identified in your letter as the cardinal points at which our views probably differ. You invite me very kindly to call you to account on these points. Surely that is not meant seriously. One can in such questions do nothing more than recognize the limitations of one's own knowledge and understanding. Let me in this sense, confess [my limitations] regarding the question of the relation between [human] knowledge and revelation.

The problem of revelation, to be at all discussable, must first of all be delimited. As "revelation," as "the word of God," one can first identify the contents of certain literary documents, which are canonized as "scriptures." By doing so, a historical problem of revelation is immediately raised, insofar as the canon was established by men (not by God) in lengthy and often very heated debate. At this point one could break off and push "revelation" to the side as the opinion of certain historical persons on the nature of these canonized literary works. If one remains at this point, then one would have to interpret (at least I see no other way) the phenomenon of faith in revelation psychologically (maybe even psychopathologically). Such a psychologization seems possible to me only under the condition that not only is the content of revelation psychologized, but also its presumed source, namely God, is denied. And that leads to metaphysical complications, which I need not go into any further.

If one allowed oneself to go beyond this point and enter into a discussion, then a number of consequences would follow. The people who fight over the inclusion or exclusion of works of literature in the canon are obviously in the possession of criteria for what is and what is not revelation. The problem of revelation seems thus to be inseparable from the problem of recognizing revelation as such; furthermore it seems

80. Strauss, "On Husik's Work in Medieval Jewish Philosophy," in *I. Husik's Philosophical Essays: Ancient, Medieval, and Modern* (Oxford: Blackwell, 1952), i–xli.

inseparable as well from the problem of interpretation. Revealed truth exists only insofar as it is received by humans and is communicable.

The contrast between human knowledge and revealed knowledge can, therefore, not be set up without qualifications. All knowledge, including revealed knowledge, is human insofar as it is the knowledge of concrete men. But some knowledge is understood by the men to whom it befalls as stemming from a divine source. This formulation is not meant pseudopsychologically, because it does not dispute that the source is rightly diagnosed.

These formulations seem to be necessary so as to understand certain historical facts appropriately, as, for example, the problem of levels of clarity of the revelation, which is suggested by the Pauline series of nature, law, and spirit. Knowledge can be revealed knowledge even when it is not understood as such as, for example, "natural" law. Thereto belongs also Clement of Alexandria's conception that Greek philosophy is the "old testament" of the heathens, or the patristic theory of the *anima naturaliter Christiana*. And above all the factum of the *doctrina Christiana*, understood as a two-thousand-year development of revelation, belongs here. The "word" of God is not a word that can be pronounced, but is instead a meaning that can be articulated in a very "free" interpretation that legitimates itself from the presence of the spirit in the historical community.

Revelation, then, is humanly debatable because it, like all knowledge, is human knowledge. Revealed knowledge is, furthermore, not simply everything that anybody assumes was revealed to him; rather, its contents can be determined sociohistorically. It can be interpreted and rationally clarified by men following criteria (Clement's *Criteria of Interpretation*,[81] the Vincentine canon, Augustinian *sapientia*). It distinguishes itself from "mere" human knowledge in that the experience of the contents of revealed knowledge is of "being addressed" by God. And through this experience of "being addressed," the essential contents of revealed knowledge are given: (1) a man who understands himself in his "mere" humanness in contrast to a transcendental being; (2) a world-transcendent Being who is experienced as the highest reality in contrast to all worldly being; (3) a Being who "addresses," and therefore is a person, namely, God; (4) a man who can be addressed by this Being and who thereby stands in

81. Reference is probably to Clement of Alexandria, "The Criterion by Which Truth and Heresy Are Distinguished."

a relation of openness to Him. In this sense I would venture the formulation: the fact of revelation is its content.[82]

When revelation is understood in this sense, very interesting problems for the history of thought present themselves. Revelation in the Jewish and Christian sense seems possible only when man historically developed a consciousness of his humanness, which clearly separates him from transcendence. Such consciousness is, for example, not yet given in Homer's polytheism or with Hesiod. Divine and human are still interconnected. This fact is veiled, in my mind, through the unfortunate theory of "anthropomorphism" in polytheistic cultures. So far as the Greek gods are concerned there is no anthropomorphic representation of the divine, but rather a theomorphic symbolization of the contents of the human soul. The development of the soul (as Jaeger and Snell worked through very well in opposition to Rohde)[83] appears to me to be the process in which man dedivinized himself and realized the humanity of his spiritual life. Only with this spiritual concentration will it be possible to experience oneself as being addressed by a world-transcendent God. Revelation seems to me to have a peculiar historical "curve." In a polytheistic culture the gods "reveal" themselves frequently through appearances, signs, and addresses. With the differentiation and concentration of the soul this diffuse revelation disappears. In Plato, and even more clearly in Aristotle, the maximum closure of the soul seems to have been reached, in which the maximally concentrated soul comes to an understanding of transcendent Being, and orients itself "erotically" to such Being, but without finding a response. In Christianity the understanding of the soul reached by the Greeks appears to have been absorbed and enriched by the restoration of the reciprocal relationship with the divine Being, now known as revelation. (Decisively in contrast to the Aristotelian *philia*, which is excluded between God and man, is the Thomistic *amicitia* between God and man; interesting is again the exclusion of *amicitia* by Luther, and the reliance on *fides* as a one-sided act of truth in a historically past, and spiritually not present, revelation).

With respect to the relationship of science (and especially metaphysics)

82. See Voegelin, *The New Science of Politics: An Introduction* (Chicago: University of Chicago Press, 1952), 78 and reference.

83. Werner Jaeger, *The Theology of the Early Greek Philosophers* (Oxford: Oxford University Press, 1947); Bruno Snell, *The Discovery of the Mind: The Greek Origins of European Thought*, trans. T. G. Rosenmeyer (Cambridge, Mass.: Harvard University Press, [1948] 1953); Erwin Rohde, *Psyche* (Tübingen: Mohr, 1921).

and revelation, Augustine seems to me in principle to have shown the way. Revealed knowledge is, in the building of human knowledge, that knowledge of the pregivens of perception (*sapientia*, closely related to the Aristotelian *nous* as distinguished from *epistēmē*). To these pregivens belongs the experience of man of himself as *esse, nosse, velle,* the inseparable primal experience: I am as knowing and willing being; I know myself as being and willing; I will myself as a being and a knowing human. (For Augustine in the worldly sphere, the symbol of the trinity: the Father—Being; the Son—the recognizable order; the Spirit—the process of being in history). To these pregivens belongs further the being of God beyond time (in the just characterized dimensions of creation, order, and dynamic) and the human knowledge of this being through "revelation." Within this knowledge pregiven by *sapientia* stirs the philosophic *epistēmē*.

I must confess that these pregivens appear to me quite acceptable. The distinction between *scientia* and *sapientia* removes from philosophizing a set of problems that in my opinion are not genuine problems of perception. Take for example a modern philosophical effort such as that of Husserl, who wishes to build up the world from stream of consciousness and from the noetics of the stream. And think of the tormenting constructions to which this project led in the construction of the "Thou" in the *Cartesian Meditations*. Husserl could have saved himself much time and unnecessary work if he had acknowledged that the human being is not a consciousness, that neither the "I" nor the "Thou" can be "constituted" out of consciousness, that one cannot construct self-consciousness as the act of perception after the model of a sensuous perception, etc., that instead what is involved here is the pregivens of perception.

Or, to take a classical example, think of the complications to which one is led when one constructs the recognizable order "metaphysically" as the imposition of form on matter; one is then led, following a craftsman's model, to the mythical demiurge of the *Timaeus*. On the other hand, materialism and idealism disappear as philosophical problems when the order of being and its recognition belong to the pregivens. In this case, one deals with the order itself and with the methods and boundaries of its recognition.

Problems of the kind indicated appear to be philosophic misconstructions because the genuine problems of human knowledge are not separable from the area of the *sapientia*. Augustine classifies these as *fantastica fornicatio* perpetrated by the injection of human fantasies into the fields of knowledge, which are clarified by "revelation." (I would be prepared to distinguish classical from Christian metaphysics, to accept to a considerable degree the position of Gilson, his *Esprit de la philosophie médiévale*). The philosophical worth of revelation appears to lie in the elimination of pseudoproblems.

And now to the second small problem—the Platonic dialogue. You are quite right when you say that nothing decent is available on the question and that the state of knowledge is rather unsatisfactory. That occurred to me too in my work on Plato, and I was puzzled because it appeared to me that the difficulty of understanding lay more in an *embarras de richesse* of motives than in the impossibility of finding them. Let me enumerate some of them:

1. Plato stands firmly under the influence of Aeschylus, particularly with regard to the problem of the *peithō*, the persuasive imposition of right order on the *daimonia* of desire. I would not understand *Prometheus*, for example, as Promethean in the romantic sense (as human revolt against a tyrannical fate), but instead as a drama of the soul, in which all persons represent forces of the soul, which struggle over the order of *Dike* in the soul—with the "solution" of a deliverance through the representative sufferings of Herakles hinted at the end. This drama of the soul is also the substance of the historical process (*Oresteia*) and the constitutional procedure (*Suppliants*). Aeschylus's sense of tragedy as a political cult seems to me to be (both individually and socially) the liturgy of political *Dike*. This cult loses its parenthetical meaning when the public is corrupt; the decisive symptom of corruption occurs when the representative of *Dike*, Socrates, is killed. The resolved tension of the Aeschylean tragedy becomes the unresolved tension of Socrates and Athens. There is now only one plot to tragedy, the tragedy of Socrates. Insofar as the Platonic dialogue is carried by the tension Socrates-Athens, it seems to be a continuation of Aeschylean tragedy under new historical-political circumstances.

2. But why tragedy at all, and why is it connected to the Platonic dialogue? The answer seems to me to lie in the Aeschylean and Platonic understanding of society as the order of the soul and the soul as the reflection of society. Apart from the explicit and basic principle, of the polis as man writ large, *Republic* VIII–IX seems to me to be important because of the splendid analysis of the decomposition of the soul—for example, of the oligarchs by the vices of society, which are perceived as forces of the soul; and at the end the magnificent analysis of tryanny as the social form of the

radically unsocial dream-fantasy of the tyrannical individual (here perhaps, as well, are Heraclitean overtones: the private worlds of the sleepwalkers). Insofar as the order of the soul is a properly functioning social conversation, the Platonic dialogue seems to be the required form of expression for the problem of the soul.

3. But for which public are these dialogues intended, when the decisive public, Athens, will not listen? Plato gives *one* answer to this question in the digression of the *Theaetetus*. Even the hardened pragmatist, who publicly will not listen to the philosophers, will become restless in private conversation, *in camera caritatis*. One can never know: the conversation must not stop. And the dialogue is no longer a political cult like the Aeschylean tragedy, but instead becomes an exoteric work of literature intended for every private person who may wish to listen.

4. But the conversation can only proceed when it is really a conversation. Decisive here are the scenes in the *Protagoras* and the *Gorgias* where Socrates threatens to break off the conversation if the partner does not respond to the argument and instead gives "speeches." Under this perspective, the dialogue is the weapon for the restoration of public order, which had been privately disturbed by the pseudopublic instrument of rhetoric.

5. These weapons can, however, break down in the individual case. The opponent is hardened and does not allow himself to be moved by the dialogic *peithō*. Is the dialogue then, in the end, a meaningless undertaking? Plato's answer is the myth of the judgment of the dead in the *Gorgias* and in the *Republic*. The dialogue continues, and the other-worldly leader of the dialogue is a judge who has healing and punishing sanctions at his disposal. One cannot escape the conversation. (This is not an explanation of all Platonic myths of judgment, but *only* the myths of the *Gorgias* and of the *Republic*.)

6. The relation between myth and dialogue is furthermore reversible. Not only is the myth the continuation of the dialogue, but the dialogue itself is a mythical tribunal. That is the idea of the *Apology*. In the *Apology* the action is played out at two levels. On the political level Socrates is judged by Athens; on the mythic level the tribunal of the gods (represented by Socrates) judges Athens. And the Socrates of the *Apology* does not leave his judges in doubt regarding the questions that they did not want to accept: in the future they would be posed as he posed them, to the people

of Athens. In this sense the dialogue is the continuation of the Socratic trial. The dialogue is a judicial proceeding.

7. When the conversation is carried on with success—in the Socratic-Platonic circle—then a further motive comes to light: the formation of the community through eros. This is the point that the members of the Stefan George Circle saw clearly. To see the image of the beautiful-good man (the *kalos k'agathos*) [or gentleman] in the other, to awaken it and draw it out (complicated by the mystery that the image in the other is one's own image), is possible only through the eroticism of conversation. For that one looks primarily to the *Symposium* and the *Phaedrus*, again with their specific mythic extrapolations. In this context the famous problem of the living and the written word seems to belong. Plato could not say it more clearly (especially when you add the episode with Dionysius) than that what is involved in his philosophizing is not a "doctrine," but instead a dialogic awakening through the living word. (For the esoteric explanation of this awakening, it would be necessary to draw from the less-known *Theages*). When this process is extended over the community of the spoken word, then the literary form of the dialogue (particularly, the factually resultless dialogue) seems to be again appropriate.

8. A further problem seems to arise from the linkage of the dialogues, especially from the large trilogy *Republic-Timaeus-Critias*. In the *Republic* itself, the dialogue is used (a) as a tribunal over sophistic Athens and (mediated by the typical silencing of Thrasymachus) (b) as erotic conversation with the clear goal to lead to the *periagōgē* of the *Agathon*. This whole dialogue with the "young ones" is told by Socrates to the "old ones" (as it follows from the *Timaeus*). It is therefore a constituent of the conversation of the "old ones," which is continued by the *Timaeus* and *Critias*—and obviously intended to be that way by Plato from the time of the composition of the *Republic*. With that consideration emerges a new aspect of the myth. Added to the relation of the myth to judgment (*Republic, Gorgias*), the myth to the erotic community (*Symposium, Phaedrus,* and *Republic*), there is now the relation of the myth to primordial history. From the myth of Atlantis is derived the Socratic knowledge of order, from which is derived the authoritative worth of the conversation with the "young ones" in the *Republic*. The Socratic knowledge of order is, then, the ultimate implication of the mythical dialogue that extends through the spiritual history of the cosmos up to the gods.

9. The intimate relation between dialogue and myth reaches its high point, to my mind, in the *Laws*. Here the dialogue itself has become a myth. But that is a complicated story and can be shown only through detailed analysis. (If it interests you, my very extensive study on the *Laws* stands at your disposal.) Just to hint at the principle: the arrangement of the dialogue into episodes, just as the contents of the episodes, follows a cosmic analogy that, in the explanation of the institutions of the polis, becomes the contents of the dialogue.

10. To conclude: I would say that the problem of the Platonic myth and dialogue has a close connection to the question of revelation. Plato propounds no truth that had been revealed to him; he appears not to have had the experience of a prophetic address from God. Therefore no direct announcement. The myth of Plato seems to be an intermediate form—no longer the polytheistic myth that, because of the concentration of his soul, had become impossible; but it is not yet the free diagnosis of the divine source of the knowledge of order. God does not speak unmediated, but only as mediated through Socrates-Plato. Insofar as the place of God as the addresser is taken by Socrates-Plato, as the speaker in the dialogue, the fullest expression of "theomorphic" polytheism seems to be the final reason for the dialogue form; the divine and the human are not yet completely separated. (By the way, for this reason all the literary efforts of the Renaissance that attempt to imitate the form of the Platonic dialogue are condemned to failure.) Plato seems to have been aware of this problem of his divinity in the polytheistic sense. As evidence I would introduce the uncanny figures of gods in the *Laws* (puppet players and board-game players); and quite particularly the myth of the *Statesman*, where the post-Saturnic age, the cycle of Zeus, is understood as the cycle of the Platonic *basileus*.

This has become a long letter. But technically you provoked me with the complaint that the question why Plato wrote dialogues has not been clarified. It is certainly not that such a question cannot be clarified, if one really goes to it. I am curious what you say about this attempt.

Yours,

Eric Voegelin

Letter 39

June 4, 1951

My dear Mr. Voegelin,

Again I face the alternative to write on poor paper or not to write at all. I elect to do as usual. Excuse me!

Warmest thanks for your detailed and enlightening letter of April 22, which I can only now answer at the end of the semester. I congratulate you on the completion of the Walgreen Lectures, which I look forward with excitement to study. Only on the basis of these lectures will it be possible for me really to argue with you.

You mistake me when you believe that I did not seriously mean the request to take me to task. Without *logon dounai te kai dexasthai* [without giving or being given accounts] I, at least, cannot live.

You are completely right when you assume that a "psychologizing," that is to say, atheistic interpretation of revelation leads to confusion. It is sufficient to remember the example of Heidegger, whose interpretation of conscience ends in the "calling" being grasped as *Dasein* calling itself—here guilt, conscience, action, lose their meaning. One has to assume that something coming from God happens to man. But this happening is not *necessarily* to be understood as call or address; this is a *possible* interpretation; the acceptance of this interpretation, *therefore*, rests on faith and not knowledge. I go further: there is a fundamental difference between the call of God itself and the human formulation of this call; what we face historically is the latter (in case one does not accept verbal inspiration, which one can, but *need* not). *Either* the human formulation is radically problematic, and then one ends up in the desert of Kierkegaard's subjectivism, to which leads the thought that one may believe *only* God himself and no human intermediary—a subjectivism, out of which Kierkegaard can save himself only by making the *contents* of faith (the mystery of the Incarnation) *intelligible* in a way, as no one perhaps had attempted previously.

Or, the human formulation is *not* radically problematic—that is to say, there are *criteria* that permit a distinction *between* illegitimate (heretical) and legitimate formulations. If I understand you correctly, the latter is your view. On the basis of the same, you accept Christian dogma. I do not know, however, if you do this in the Catholic sense. In case you did this, we would easily come to an understanding. Because my distinction between revelation and human knowledge to which you object is in harmony with the Catholic teaching. But I do not believe that you accept the Catholic teaching. Here a considerable difficulty could result, from your getting rid of the principle of tradition (in distinction from the principle of scripture), and Catholicism is most consistent in this respect.

It is with some reluctance that I as a non-Christian venture on this intra-Christian problem. But I can do so precisely because I can make it plain to myself that the problem, and the whole problem area, is, exactly, a Christian one and, through an appropriate extension, also a Jewish one; but then precisely it is not a "universal-human" one. That means that it presupposes a *specific* faith, which philosophy as philosophy does not and cannot do. Here and here alone it seems to me lies the divergence between us—also in the mere historical.[84]

I have no objections to your assertion that that which you designate as presupposition is, as you say, "acceptable." The only question is whether it is necessary.

To demonstrate this necessity, it is in no way sufficient to show the insufficiency of, for example, Husserl—all your objections to Husserl do not in any way affect Plato and Aristotle: because they were not "ideologues," there is no "problem of knowledge" for them. As to the ancients, they were *philosophoi* and knew therefore that there were difficulties with all human *sophia*: their understanding by no means fails if one or another of their attempted answers fails. The problems with which you occupied yourself will not become pseudoproblems because on the basis of faith, as distinct from knowledge, they may lose their seriousness; for knowledge, they keep their seriousness. I recall only what role within Christianity the problem of the immortality of the soul has played and *de jure* still plays. Certainly the demotion of the Platonic-Aristotelian problem area through Augustine, for example, was not bought at the price of his teaching on the cosmos, which was still meant to be historical, and which, humanly speaking, is no less fantastic than the teaching of the *Timaeus* you mentioned. Now, is there no problem in your quietly replacing this teaching on the cosmos with a modern view of history (ascent from polytheism to monotheism and the like)?

I read your exposition through again. You admit, of course, the distinction between a human knowledge inspired by revelation and "merely human" knowledge. It does not seem to me to contribute to greater clarity if one did not, in this distinction, recur to the tradition-sanctioned distinction between faith and knowledge.

84. See Letter 35.

I found your explanations with respect to the Platonic dialogue interesting and relevant in the highest degree. I can only allude to my reservations.

You say that the order of the soul is a properly functioning conversational community. I must assume you mean the *proper* order of the soul is a properly functioning conversational community. But the proper order of the soul corresponds to the proper order of the *polis*. Can one call the proper order of this *polis* (in Plato's *Laws*) a *conversation*? Here exists domination by command and legend, but precisely no conversation, which as such is based on the fiction or the reality of *equality*. In the Platonic sense, there is no Socratic dialogue. You yourself say that the dialogue is a means of combat for the restoration of public order: once it is restored the means of combat loses its sense. So: does the dialogue belong to the improper "order" or to the "unhealthy" soul or society?

Expressed otherwise: you speak of tragedy and you are silent about comedy, even though the dialogue just spoken about is a "synthesis" of tragedy and comedy. On the basis of known statements of Plato one might say that tragedy and *polis* belong together—correspondingly comedy and doubt about the *polis* belong together. From the standpoint of the philosophers the decay of the *polis* is not simply the worst thing. The whole *polis,* which believes in its eternity, has the inclination to hide the truly eternal, the *ontōs ōn*.

The Platonic dialogue cannot simply be understood from within the *polis* but rather only by philosophy. From this would follow that one cannot speak of "*the* conversation": it all depends with *whom* Socrates is speaking. The philosopher is in fact essentially speaking and not "doing"—in *this* sense the conversation may never stop. But the conversation that is not ultimately oriented toward philosophy is no conversation.

You are quite right: [Stefan] George understood more of Plato than did Wilamowitz, Jaeger, and the whole gang. But was that not a consequence of the fact that he did not think in biblical or secularized-biblical concepts? He is even right in doubting that there is a Platonic teaching in the sense that there is a Leibnizian teaching. But one should not go so far as to see the substance of the dialogues in an awakening to philosophic "existence," to a philosopher virtually without an object. Socrates knew that he knew nothing—this, if you will, is the Platonic teaching. But one cannot know *that* one does not know, if one does not [also] know what one does not know—that is to say, if one does not know what the actual questions and their rank of priority are. And Socrates knew that the *hen anagkaion* is *dêloun* or *skopein*. That, surely, is much less than a system, but also considerably more than the "maintenance of existence" and "divine faith."

Said in one sentence—I believe that philosophy in the Platonic sense is possible and necessary—you believe that philosophy understood in this sense was made obsolete by revelation. God knows who is right. But: insofar as it concerns the interpretation of *Plato*, it appears one must, before criticizing Plato, understand Plato in the sense in which *he* wanted [to be understood]. And this was, from the first and to the last, philosophy. Only here can the key to the dialogue be found.

Naturally, I do not say that someone who thinks in biblical concepts cannot understand Plato. I only say that one cannot understand Plato, if, in the undertaking of Platonic studies, one thinks in biblical concepts. In this sense the biblical question is to be separated from the philosophic one.

It pleases me to see that you think better of the "Thrasymachus"[85] than *hoi polloi*. I see no reason to judge this masterwork to be spurious.

The silence of Thrasymachus, I believe, is meant more comically than you take it. Do not forget that he comes back later two more times.

I would gladly read your interpretation of the *Laws*. But unfortunately I must wade through my Walgreen Lectures. They are already more than overdue and no end in sight.

Hoping to hear from you soon. With cordial greetings,

Yours,
Leo Strauss

Letter 40

August 5, 1952

Dear Mr. Strauss,

Many thanks for what you sent. The first two chapters of your *Persecution* bring the problem out superbly,[86] the problem that I believe I have observed has preoccupied you for many years. The confrontation of a series of old and new judgments on various philosophers and periods in the history of ideas is very instructive. And in any case the book will fulfill the need of showing the "young" what they must watch for.

85. *Republic*, book 1.
86. Strauss, *Persecution and the Art of Writing* (Glencoe, Ill.: The Free Press, 1952).

Thanks too for the study on Collingwood.[87] It comes quite conveniently. I am just working on a study of the "Oxford Political Philosophers"[88]—a command performance for the St. Andrew's *Philosophical Quarterly*—a reference to your article will substitute for the planned critique that is similar to your own.

Attached, a German article—the first written since 1938.[89]

With warmest greetings,
Eric Voegelin

Letter 41

April 20, 1953

Dear Mr. Strauss,

Many thanks for your offprints of "Walker's Machiavelli" and "Locke's Doctrine of Natural Right."[90]

Walker's translation of the *Discourses* does not in fact appear to be an outstanding achievement: The citations you give from the introduction are quite naive; and your technique, to contrast them with your careful individual references, is very skillful.

The Locke piece interested me greatly. (When will the *Natural Right* book finally come?) With regard to the general thesis—that Locke does not return to Hooker, but develops Hobbes further—I can on the basis of my own analyses heartily agree. The famous conflicts in Locke in fact do not exist. The *Second Treatise* does not base the theory of the right constitutional order upon some natural law but on a psychology of desire; and the way from this political psychology through Vauvenargues and Condillac to Helvétius seems clear to me.

Because I agree in total and in particular, I have a slight uneasiness in light of your handling of Locke as a representative of natural law—an uneasiness that will perhaps be dispersed when the obviously abbreviated parts are

87. Strauss, "On Collingwood's Philosophy of History," *Review of Metaphysics* 5 (1952): 559–86.

88. Voegelin, "The Oxford Political Philosophers," *Philosophical Quarterly* 3 (1953): 97–114.

89. Voegelin, "Gnostische Politik," *Merkur* 4 (1952): 307–17.

90. Strauss, "Walker's Machiavelli," *Review of Metaphysics* 6 (1953): 437–46, and "On Locke's Doctrine of Natural Right," *Philosophical Review* 61 (1952): 475–502.

presented completely in print. The theory of natural right is, as you superbly demonstrate, camouflage for something quite different. But, I ask myself, can, in light of this situation, Locke still be treated as a philosopher of natural right? And even more: Is Locke still a philosopher at all?

I believe I have understood you properly to say that, in the case of Locke, you wish to enrich your observations about the concealment of the actually intended theory on the part of the philosopher behind harmless-looking formulas. But is this case not after all different from that in your excellent studies, for example, on Arabic philosophers? In the one case, which I would call the legitimate one, a philosopher tries to hide his philosophizing against disturbance by the unqualified; in the other, in the case of Locke, a nonphilosopher, a political ideologue, tries to hide his dirty tricks against the attentiveness of the qualified. Isn't that, which might appear as camouflage of a philosopher, the bad conscience of "modern" man, who doesn't quite dare to say outright what he intends to do, and thus therefore hides his nihilism, not only from others but also from himself, through the rich use of a conventional vocabulary.

That is obviously no argument against your excellent analysis. The question only arises whether historical understanding, the ordering in a historical context, still allows Locke's politics to be approached from the side of natural right, or whether the result of the analysis, the ideological buttressing of the political status quo, should be standing in the center as the essential point.

Yours,
Eric Voegelin

Letter 42

April 15, 1953

Dear Mr. Strauss,[91]

Many thanks for your offprint of "Walker's Machiavelli" and "Locke's Doctrine of Natural Right."

Walker's translation of the *Discourses* does not in fact appear to be an outstanding achievement. The citations that you give from the "Introduc-

91. It is doubtful whether this letter was sent; it is housed in the Voegelin archive at the Hoover Institution. Letter 41, which it in part resembles closely, is in the Strauss collection at the University of Chicago Library.

tion" are quite naive; and your technique, to contrast with them your careful individual references, is very skillful.

The Locke piece interested me greatly. (When will the *Natural Right* book finally come?) With regard to the general thesis—that Locke does not return to Hooker, but develops Hobbes further—I can on the basis of my own analyses heartily agree. The famous conflicts in Locke in fact do not exist. The *Second Treatise* bases constitutional order on a psychology of desire; and the way from this political psychology through Vauvenargues and Condillac to Helvétius seems without doubt. The appearance of conflict arises through the conventional vocabulary of nature, reason, right, and law. Precisely in light of this agreement, however, I have a few questions of detail. They arise from a philological point, which disquiets me. On p. 479 you write:

> According to the traditional view, those sanctions are supplied by the judgment of God. Locke rejects this view. According to him, the judgment of the conscience is so far from being the judgment of God that the conscience "is nothing else but our opinion or judgment of the moral rectitude or depravity of our own actions."

My thoughts probably arise from ignorance—anyhow, which "traditional view" is here in opposition to Locke's? I consulted the index of my Regensburger edition of the *Summa Theologica* and found nine references to *conscientia*. C. is defined as *actus synderesis, spiritus corrector, paedagogus animae, dictamen rationis*—everything but "judgment of God." Gilson, in *L'Esprit de la philosophie médiévale*, with ample footnotes, also has only the act of scrutinizing our actions in the light of *ratio*. Locke's formula in the place quoted above could be by Thomas himself.

The difference in meaning at which you aim is obviously there. The question is only how does it arise in spite of the closest relationship of the linguistic formulas? In my opinion it rests on the changed meaning of the *ratio*. The Lockean *ratio* is in fact opinion, no longer participation in the *ratio divina*. With that, the question arises, essentially for the whole Age of Reason, whether a *ratio* that, unlike the classical and Christian, does not derive its authority from its share in divine being is still in any sense a *ratio*? For Locke, it is clear on the strength of your excellent study that it is no longer that. In the concrete realization he must drop the swindle of *ratio*, and in the last instance refer to desire.

The deliberate destruction of spiritual substance occurs throughout Locke's political work. In three places it becomes decisively visible. You have dealt with two of them. The first act of destruction concerns *ratio.* The second, man as *imago Dei* (in your note, p. 380). From this second destruction, the specific Lockean idea of man as "proprietor of his own person" should follow, on which the theory of ownership through incorporation of work into natural matter is based. This definition of the essence of man as property of oneself always seemed to me to be one of the most terrible atrocities in the so-called history of philosophy—and one perhaps not yet sufficiently noticed. The third act of destruction comes in the *Letter on Toleration*, on the occasion of a *separation* from a church community. Locke asks himself if, on such an occasion, conflicts over property could ensue that would make necessary the intervention of the state. He answers in the negative for the following reasons: the sole question of property could emerge from contributions to provisions that are consumed during the sacrament of communion. The contributions are too trifling to lead to a suit under common law. This conception of communion as a consumption of staples that cost money always fascinated me as much as the conception of property of oneself. Beyond these three main points, I believe, the systematic destruction of symbols can be demonstrated as a continuous feature in Locke.

This destruction leads now inevitably to conflict between the language of symbol, which is still used, and the new meanings that are substituted. It is not a conflict in Locke's theory (there you are quite right; he is consistent) but instead in the verbal construction. In the *Second Treatise*, the conflict is expressed in the fact that Locke must try three times to establish finally a political order that he wishes to have as the right one. The three attempts are (1) the natural state of pioneer squatters with approximate economic equality ("in the beginning all the world was America"), (2) the same egalitarian state, protected by state organization, (3) the consent to inequality (through money) in the context of state organization. The ultimate stage will then be protected by the new definition of consent by the fact of residency and by the exclusion of a state-run social policy. This final protection could refer, in a concrete historical sense, to the attempts of the politics of the Stuarts (Stafford and Laud) to protect the farmers of N. England and the slaves in Bermuda against extreme exploitation by the landlords and merchants, the attempts that were the material motive for revolt of the upper classes against Charles I. It is a brutal ideological construction to support the position of the English upper class, to which Locke belonged through his social relations. The construction is consistent, insofar as the *concupiscentia* is maintained from the beginning as the driving motive; it is inconsistent, insofar as the introduction of the vocabulary of natural right forces a repeated redefinition of the concept of nature.

And this leads, now, to the problem on which you have for so many years worked: the camouflage of the philosopher who wishes to protect the uncomfortable theories against conventional protests. If I understand you correctly, you see also in Locke such an effort at camouflage—and I believe you are right. But only then, when you considerably extend the problem of philosophic camouflage.

I mean the following: you follow a completely legitimate problem when you state that philosophers (I think for example about your Arabic studies) take precautionary measures to protect their philosophizing against disturbance by the unqualified. *But*: Is an ideological constructor, who brutally destroys every philosophical problem area in order to justify the political status quo, a philosopher? Is this not precisely the opposite case of a nihilistic destroyer, who wishes to cover his work of destruction from the attentiveness of the qualified? What difference, I ask myself, actually exists between Locke and that series of types that Camus deals with in *L'Homme révolté*? Isn't that which may still appear as camouflage of a philosopher already the bad conscience of "modern" man, who doesn't quite dare to declare the knavery that he actually intends; and so he hides it not only from others but also from himself, by the ample use of a conventional vocabulary? That possibility recalls the words of Karl Kraus; such a person knows already what he wants, only subconsciously. What is this political philosophy of Locke other than the roguery of which Anatole France in the *Île des Pengouins* makes fun: the majesty of the law that forbids equally the poor and the rich to steal. Finally, when one considers the development from Locke to Marx, what is this Lockean ideal picture of political order but the picture of bourgeois society that Marx believed he had to produce with laborious research and had to unmask. If England had not in fact been better than Locke, and had not again elevated itself through the Wesleyan Reformation, this nasty caricature of human order would have brought about some interesting revolutions.

Excuse the length of this letter. But when it comes to Locke, my heart runs over. He is for me one of the most repugnant, dirty, morally corrupt appearances in the history of humanity. But back to our technical problem: it seems questionable to me, at least where it concerns Locke's political work, whether it still falls within the area of philosophizing; and following from that, it seems questionable whether the substance of Locke's political work becomes accessible by attending to the question of philosophical camouflage. Perhaps what is involved is a phenomenon of a completely different order; Locke was one of the first very great cases of spiritual pathology, whose adequate treatment would require a different conceptual apparatus.

Let me thank you again cordially,
Eric Voegelin

Letter 43

April 29, 1953

My dear Mr. Voegelin,

Many thanks for your friendly lines. I am pleased that you agree with the central point of my presentation of Locke, which presumably will not meet all Anglo-Saxon wishes. I know that here in the Department of Philosophy the fundamental agreement between Locke and Aristotle is taught.

I believe that I do not go wrong when I designate Locke, as well as Hobbes, as natural-right theorists. In the previous chapter on Hobbes (in the *Revue de Philosophie*)[92] I pointed out the radical difference between modern and premodern natural right. Locke's teaching is modern natural right, which can be distinguished from utilitarianism and the like *only* by the recognition of natural right. I too take the modern natural right as untenable and narrow, or crude. But one must allow the fact that it *is* about natural right; otherwise one cannot understand the connection with Rousseau, Kant, and Hegel. In other words: German idealism is a return to the premodern on an "English" and therefore insufficient basis. I cannot develop this further here. You will find a further, but by no means sufficient explanation, in my small book on natural right and history, which will appear in the fall and which will be sent to you immediately after its appearance. A further hint perhaps: the German idealistic concept of freedom is a synthesis of the premodern concept of virtue with the Hobbesian-Lockean concept of subjective right as the morally fundamental fact.

You did very well to recognize that I wanted to enrich my observations on the esoteric by my remarks concerning Locke. The reason for this is that there is a fundamental distinction between the technique of true philoso-

92. Strauss, "On the Spirit of Hobbes' Political Philosophy," *Revue internationale de philosophie* 4 (1950): 405–31.

phy and that of modern philosophy. As to the last point, I believe that I explained the most urgent things in the essay "Persecution and the Art of Writing" (reprinted in the book under the same title).

Do you know, incidentally, Lawrence Thompson's *Quarrel with God*? It would be worth your interest.

I begin *lentissime* to write a small book on Machiavelli.[93] I can't help loving him—in spite of his errors.

Cordially yours,
Leo Strauss

Letter 44

May 22, 1953

My dear Mr. Voegelin,

Warmest thanks for your essay on the Oxford philosophers.[94] I do not need to say to you that I am on the main point completely in accord with you: the critique of nonphilosophy of "conscience," of the use of "rules of thumb" (or prudential devices, as you say) instead of authentic principles. Above all, it pleases me to see that you break even more decisively with historicism. "Externally," our efforts are to a surprising degree extensively in accord. I have doubts actually on only two points. The distinction (103, paragraph 3)[95] between principles and prudential measures, as you under-

93. Strauss, *Thoughts on Machiavelli* (Glencoe, Ill.: The Free Press, 1958).

94. Voegelin, "The Oxford Political Philosophers," *Philosophical Quarterly* 3 (1953): 97–114.

95. On pages 103–4 Voegelin wrote:

> The anachronistic use of terms, while impairing the theoretical value of the judgment, has nevertheless an intelligible purpose. Mr. D'Entrèves assumes three types of political principles: the medieval totalitarian, the modern totalitarian, and in between the preferred modern type characterized by free pursuit of truth, religious freedom according to conscience, and civil liberties. If we make the suggested distinction between philosophical anthropology (as a science of principles) and prudential measures that will, under given historical circumstances, create the best possible environment for the attainment of the highest good, the question concerning the status of the aforementioned freedoms cannot be avoided. Are these freedoms really fundamental principles,

stand them, would make impossible the Platonic-Aristotelian concept of the *aristē politeia* as a model necessary for the best life.[96] Or do I misunderstand you? When you say on p. 109 that we have little use for Greek *poleis* at present,[97] the meaning of the *polis* as the perfect form of human community, as Plato and Aristotle declared, would also not seem to matter. With respect to p. 111, n. 15,[98] I am sure that Thomas More's

---

> or are they perhaps no more than prudential devices? If the latter should be the case, the halo that surrounds them certainly would pale; the rude question, which can never be addressed to a principle, would have to be asked: whether they work or whether they have failed, perhaps quite as miserably as the medieval device of persecution. If, however, the distinction is not made, embarrassment will be avoided and the freedoms can be as inalienable, eternal, and ultimate as anyone desires. The cult of political institutions as incarnations of principles depends on the suspension of theoretical animation.

96. Strauss's writing is particularly difficult to read here. See Voegelin's remark in the following letter.

97. On page 109 Voegelin wrote:

> Aristotle did not create 'ideal states' (the very word 'ideal' has no equivalent in Greek), but developed imaginative paradigms, models of the best polis. What is 'best' again has nothing to do with 'ideals', but will be decided by the pragmatic suitability of the model to provide an environment for the 'best' or 'happiest life'; and the criterion of the best or happiest life in its turn will be established by the science of philosophical anthropology. The best life, according to the various formulations, is the life which leads to the unfolding of the dianoetic excellences, to one's existence as philosopher, to the *bios theōrētikos*, or to the cultivation of the noetic self. The models, thus, are based on a theory of the nature of man, which claims to be a science. Nobody, of course, will today unreservedly agree with the results of the Platonic-Aristotelian analysis of human nature; for in order to agree he would have to ignore the advances of philosophical anthropology that we owe to the Fathers and Scholastics, as well as to such contemporary thinkers as Bergson, Gilson, Jaspers, Lubac, or Balthasar; and as far as the classical models are concerned, our pragmatic interest in them will be mild since we have little use for Greek *poleis* at present. Such restrictions, however, do not affect the principle established by the classic philosophers that a philosophy of politics must rest on a theory of the nature of man, and that philosophical anthropology is a science—not an occasion for idealistic tantrums.

98. On page 111, footnote 15, Voegelin wrote:

> I have included the passages on preventive warfare in the account because they indicate a strain in Collingwood that goes farther back than Hobbes. Preventive

concept of a civilizing war goes back to the classical tradition: here lies really no *innovatio*.

Cordially yours,
Leo Strauss

n. I pass over our perennial difference of opinion concerning gnosis.

Letter 45

June 10, 1953

Dear Mr. Strauss,

I must thank you for two letters—the one from March and that of May 22. Excuse the long delay. I was quite ill with several operations (an intestinal problem) and am only now recuperating. The pressure of work has been increased by the hospitalization.

What you write about Locke is very valuable—but I must wait for your study on natural right to see the problem in the context at which you hint (the German natural right).

A misfortune has occurred with regard to your letter of May 22: despite the most ardent paleographic efforts I could not decipher the decisive sentence in which you formulate your doubts about the distinction between principles and prudential devices in connection with Aristotle-Plato. (At best I can usually read your Greek.)—Fortunately, I could read your sentence about More. That is an interesting point. You are certainly right when you say that the classical tradition plays a role in More's idea of a war of cultures. But does it not have to do, after all, with an *innovatio*, insofar as the war of cultures in a pre-Christian culture has a completely different spiritual status than in a Christian (or maybe post-Christian)? Until 1900 China still had a foreign ministry with the title of an office to supervise the barbaric border peoples; but that is something different from the differentiation of civilizations of More or Vitoria, which signifies something like the secularization of the Crusades.

During the last weeks I greatly regretted that we have no opportunity to

---

warfare against civilizationally inferior peoples was demanded and justified, for the first time in English political thought, by Thomas More in the *Utopia*. In the setting of the *Utopia* the origin of the argument in humanistic *hubris* is even clearer than in Collingwood's work.

speak occasionally. I am working on the Israelite chapter of my *History*—from the perspective that Israel articulated history as a symbolic form of the same order as the Mesopotamian and Egyptian cosmological myths, and Hellenic philosophy. It is quite delicate work, especially with regard to my absolutely insufficient knowledge of Hebrew.

We are driving to California in two days, to a summer school; we will be back at the end of July.

With warmest greetings,

Yours,
Eric Voegelin

Letter 46

University of California
Dept. of Political Science
Berkeley 4, California
June 23, 1953

Professor Eric Voegelin
741 Canal Street
Baton Rouge 2, Louisiana

Dear Mr. Voegelin:

Many thanks for your letter. You are not the first to complain about my handwriting. This explains why I dictate the present letter.

I was sorry to hear that you have been ill. I wish you a speedy and complete recovery.

I do not remember at the moment what I said about the distinction between principles and prudential devices in connection with Plato and Aristotle. I believe my objection had something to do with the fact that the distinction as understood by you did not make sufficient allowance for the classical concept of the best political or social order. I have dealt with this subject at some length in the fourth chapter of my forthcoming book on natural right. Maybe we can take up the discussion after you have had an opportunity to read that chapter. The book ought to be out sometime in September.

As regards the problem of history in the Old Testament, I regard this as one of the most complex problems in intellectual history. I think perhaps the utopian plan would be to devote about ten years to the solution of this problem.

As you can see from the letterhead, I am giving the summer course at Berkeley. I plan to be back in Chicago early in September.

With kindest regards,

Yours very sincerely,
Leo Strauss
Professor of Political Philosophy

LS:pv

Letter 47

June 3, 1956

Dear Mr. Strauss,

A few days ago I heard from Walter Berns[99] that you had a small heart attack but that you are already home from the hospital. And at the same time came the review of Riezler, addressed by you personally.[100] I hope from that, that it was nothing too serious. And now I just receive a letter from Stokes[101] [saying] that you had to decline your lecture in Buck Hills Falls and that you need, after all, a few months of complete convalescence.

I do not need to assure you how much your illness affected me. And in that is mixed a selfish concern, that I will again not see you. I had so looked forward to this opportunity of a longer conversation, and above all finally to see you in action.

We both wish you and your family best, and hope that you will soon be recovered.

Very warmly,

Yours,
Eric Voegelin

99. Walter Berns studied with Strauss and was a colleague of Voegelin at Louisiana State University.

100. Strauss, "Kurt Riezler, 1882–1955," *Social Research* 23 (1956): 3–34. Reprinted in *What Is Political Philosophy?* ch. 10.

101. Harold W. Stokes was dean of the Graduate School of Arts and Sciences, New York University, which sponsored the Buck Hills Falls conferences each year.

Letter 48

January 24, 1958

Dear Mr. Strauss,

Your Farabi study at last reached me here.[102] I see that you continue your inquiry into concealment through numerous methods. Every single one of these inquiries brings new fascinating material—like that of Farabi. Many thanks.

Tomorrow, I am leaving here. Mid-February I hope to be installed in Munich.[103] I hope we will see each other on occasion there.

With warmest greetings,
Eric Voegelin

Letter 49

The Univ. of Chicago
Dept. of Political Science
1126 East 59th Street
Chicago 37, Illinois
11 February 1960

Professor Eric Voegelin
Munich 2
Theresienstr. 3–5/IV

Dear Mr. Voegelin:

This is only to thank you for sending me your statement on "Democracy in the New Europe."[104] I am very much impressed by the clarity, sobriety, and conscientiousness of the statement with which I entirely concur. I just wrote to Hallowell asking him to bring out your statement in an English

102. Strauss, "How Farabi Read Plato's *Laws*," in *Melanges Louis Massignon* (Damascus: Institut francais de Damas, 1957), 3:319–44.

103. In 1958, Voegelin removed to Munich to establish and direct the Geschwister-Scholl Institut der Universität München.

104. Voegelin, "Demokratie im neuen Europa," *Gesellschaft Staat-Erzeihung* 4 (1959): 293–300.

translation in his *Journal*.[105] I do not have to tell you why it would be very good if it were made accessible to the American political scientists.

I hope you are happy in Munich.

With kindest regards.

Sincerely yours,
Leo Strauss

Letter 50

February 15, 1960

Professor Leo Strauss
Dept. of Political Science
The University of Chicago
1126 East 59th Street
Chicago 37, Illinois

Dear Mr. Strauss:

Thanks for your note of February 11.

I am glad you liked my address to the academy.

Notre Dame University has invited me to be a visiting professor in the winter semester 1960/61, and I have accepted. That will give us some occasion to get together—a possibility to which I look forward very much.

With all good wishes, I am,

Sincerely yours,
Eric Voegelin

105. John Hallowell, professor of political science, Duke University, was editor of the *Journal of Politics* and edited Voegelin's *From Enlightenment to Revolution*.

Letter 51

The Univ. of Chicago
Dept. of Political Science
1126 East 59th Street
Chicago 37, Illinois
22 February 1960

Professor Eric Voegelin
Theresienstrasse 3–5/IV
Munich 2, West Germany

Dear Voegelin:

I congratulate you on your invitation to Notre Dame. I regret very much that I will not be in Chicago at that time but somewhere in California. I am genuinely sorry about the fact that we shall miss one another.

Cordially yours,
Leo Strauss

Letter 52

Sept. 7, 1964
455

Professor Leo Strauss
Dept. of Political Science
The University of Chicago
1126 East 59th St.
Chicago 37, Illinois
U.S.A.

Dear Strauss:

Toward the beginning of the last term I received from the publisher a copy of *City and Man.*[106]

Let me thank you very much for this gift. At least, I have come round to reading it with the greatest care and I must say that I admire your analysis greatly. You will not be surprised if I say that I was most impressed

106. Strauss, *The City and Man* (Chicago: Rand McNally, 1964).

by the chapter on Thucydides. The analysis of the literary form seems to be in this case most felicitous.

In the springtime, that is, beginning with Feb. 1, I shall again be at Notre Dame, and I hope very much that it will be possible to get together with you in Chicago in this period.

With all good wishes,

Sincerely yours,
Eric Voegelin

Part 2

Essays

Jerusalem and Athens: Some Preliminary Reflections

Leo Strauss

I. The Beginning of the Bible and Its Greek Counterparts

All the hopes that we entertain in the midst of the confusions and dangers of the present are founded positively or negatively, directly or indirectly on the experiences of the past. Of these experiences the broadest and deepest, as far as we Western men are concerned, are indicated by the names of the two cities Jerusalem and Athens. Western man became what he is and is what he is through the coming together of biblical faith and Greek thought. In order to understand ourselves and to illuminate our trackless way into the future, we must understand Jerusalem and Athens. As goes without saying, this is a task whose proper performance goes much beyond my power, to say nothing at all of the still narrower limits set to two public lectures. But we cannot define our tasks by our powers, for our powers become known to us through performing our tasks; it is better to fail nobly than to succeed basely. Besides, having been chosen to inaugurate the Frank Cohen Memorial Lectureship at the City College of the City University of New York, I must think of the whole series of lectures to be given by other men—let us hope by better and greater men—in the coming years or decades.

The objects to which we refer by speaking of Jerusalem and Athens are today understood by the science devoted to such objects as cultures; "culture" is meant to be a scientific concept. According to this concept there is an indefinitely large number of cultures: *n* cultures. The scientist who studies them beholds them as objects; as scientist he stands outside of all of them; he has no preference for any of them; in his eyes all of them are of equal rank; he is not only impartial but objective; he is anxious not to distort any of them; in speaking about them he avoids any "culture-bound" concepts, i.e., concepts bound to any particular culture or kind of culture. In many cases the objects studied by the scientist of culture do or did not know that they are or were cultures. This causes no difficulty for him: electrons also do not know that they are electrons; even dogs do not know that they are dogs. By the mere fact that he speaks of his objects as cultures, the scientific student takes it for granted that he understands the people whom he studies better than they understood or understand themselves.

This whole approach has been questioned for some time, but this questioning does not seem to have had any effect on the scientists. The man who started the questioning was Nietzsche. We have said that according to the prevailing view there were or are *n* cultures. Let us say there were or are 1,001 cultures, thus reminding ourselves of the Arabian Nights, the 1,001 Nights; the account of the cultures, if it is well done, will be a series of exciting stories, perhaps of tragedies. Accordingly Nietzsche speaks of our subject in a speech of his Zarathustra that is entitled "Of 1,000 Goals and One." The Hebrews and the Greeks appear in this speech as two among a number of nations, not superior to the two others that are mentioned or to the 996 that are not mentioned. The peculiarity of the Greeks is the full dedication of the individual to the contest for excellence, distinction, supremacy. The peculiarity of the Hebrews is the utmost honoring of father and mother. (Up to this day the Jews read on their highest holiday the section of the Torah that deals with the first presupposition of honoring father and mother: the unqualified prohibition against incest between children and parents.) Nietzsche has a deeper reverence than any other beholder for the sacred tables of the Hebrews as well as of the other nations in question. Yet since he is only a beholder of these tables, since what one table commends or commands is incompatible with what the others command, he is not subject to the commandments of any. This is true also and especially of the tables, or "values," of modern Western culture. But according to him, all scientific concepts, and hence in particular the concept of culture, are culture-bound; the concept of culture is an outgrowth of nineteenth-century Western culture; its application to "cultures" of other ages and climates is an act stemming from the spiritual imperialism of that particular culture. There is then a glaring contradiction between the claimed objectivity of the science of cultures and the radical subjectivity of that science. Differently stated, one cannot behold, i.e., truly understand, any culture unless one is firmly rooted in one's own culture or unless one belongs in one's capacity as a beholder to some culture. But if the universality of the beholding of all cultures is to be preserved, the culture to which the beholder of all cultures belongs must be the universal culture, the culture of mankind, the world culture; the universality of beholding presupposes, if only by anticipating it, the universal culture which is no longer one culture among many. The variety of cultures that have hitherto emerged contradicts the oneness of truth. Truth is not a woman so that each man can have his own truth as he can have his own wife. Nietzsche sought therefore for a culture that would no longer be particular and hence in the last analysis arbitrary. The single goal of mankind is conceived by him as in a sense superhuman: he speaks of the superman of the future. The superman is meant to unite in himself Jerusalem and Athens on the highest level.

However much the science of all cultures may protest its innocence of all preferences or evaluations, it fosters a specific moral posture. Since it requires openness to all cultures, it fosters universal tolerance and the exhilaration deriving from the beholding of diversity; it necessarily affects all cultures that it can still affect by contributing to their transformation in one and the same direction; it willy-nilly brings about a shift of emphasis from the particular to the universal: by asserting, if only implicitly, the rightness of pluralism, it asserts that pluralism is *the* right way; it asserts the monism of universal tolerance and respect for diversity; for by virtue of being an ism, pluralism is a monism.

One remains somewhat closer to the science of culture as commonly practiced if one limits oneself to saying that every attempt to understand the phenomena in question remains dependent on a conceptual framework that is alien to most of these phenomena and therefore necessarily distorts them. "Objectivity" can be expected only if one attempts to understand the various cultures or peoples exactly as they understand or understood themselves. Men of ages and climates other than our own did not understand themselves in terms of cultures because they were not concerned with culture in the present-day meaning of the term. What we now call culture is the accidental result of concerns that were not concerns with culture but with other things and above all with the Truth.

Yet our intention to speak of Jerusalem and Athens seems to compel us to go beyond the self-understanding of either. Or is there a notion, a word, that points to the highest that the Bible on the one hand and the greatest works of the Greeks claim to convey? There is such a word: wisdom. Not only the Greek philosophers but the Greek poets as well were considered to be wise men, and the Torah is said in the Torah to be "your wisdom in the eyes of the nations." We must then try to understand the difference between biblical wisdom and Greek wisdom. We see at once that each of the two claims to be the true wisdom, thus denying to the other its claim to be wisdom in the strict and highest sense. According to the Bible, the beginning of wisdom is fear of the Lord; according to the Greek philosophers, the beginning of wisdom is wonder. We are thus compelled from the very beginning to make a choice, to take a stand. Where then do we stand? We are confronted with the incompatible claims of Jerusalem and Athens to our allegiance. We are open to both and willing to listen to each. We ourselves are not wise but we wish to become wise. We are seekers for wisdom, *philo-sophoi.* By saying that we wish to hear first and then to act to decide, we have already decided in favor of Athens against Jerusalem.

This seems to be necessary for all of us who cannot be orthodox and therefore must accept the principle of the historical-critical study of the Bible. The Bible was traditionally understood as the true and authentic account of the deeds of God and men from the beginning till the restoration after the Babylonian exile. The deeds of God include His legislation as well as His inspirations of the prophets, and the deeds of men include their praises of God and their prayers to Him as well as their God-inspired admonitions. Biblical criticism starts from the observation that the biblical account is in important respects not authentic but derivative or consists not of "histories" but of "memories of ancient histories," to borrow a Machiavellian expression.[1] Biblical criticism reached its first climax in Spinoza's *Theological-Political Treatise*, which is frankly antitheological; Spinoza read the Bible as he read the Talmud and the Koran. The result of his criticism can be summarized as follows: the Bible consists to a considerable extent of self-contradictory assertions, of remnants of ancient prejudices or superstitions, and of the outpourings of an uncontrolled imagination; in addition it is poorly compiled and poorly preserved. He arrived at this result by presupposing the impossibility of miracles. The considerable differences between nineteenth- and twentieth-century biblical criticism and that of Spinoza can be traced to their

1. *Discorsi* I.16.

difference in regard to the evaluation of imagination: whereas for Spinoza imagination is simply subrational, it was assigned a much higher rank in later times; it was understood as the vehicle of religious or spiritual experience, which necessarily expresses itself in symbols and the like. The historical-critical study of the Bible is the attempt to understand the various layers of the Bible as they were understood by their immediate addressees, i.e., the contemporaries of the authors of the various layers. The Bible speaks of many things that for the biblical authors themselves belong to the remote past; it suffices to mention the creation of the world. But there is undoubtedly much of history in the Bible, i.e., accounts of events written by contemporaries or near-contemporaries. One is thus led to say that the Bible contains both "myth" and "history." Yet this distinction is alien to the Bible; it is a special form of the distinction between *mythos* and *logos*; *mythos* and *historie* are of Greek origin. From the point of view of the Bible the "myths" are as true as the "histories": what Israel "in fact" did or suffered cannot be understood exept in the light of the "facts" of Creation and Election. What is now called "historical" is those deeds and speeches that are equally accessible to the believer and to the unbeliever. But from the point of view of the Bible the unbeliever is the fool who has said in his heart "there is no God"; the Bible narrates everything as it is credible to the wise in the biblical sense of wisdom. Let us never forget that there is no biblical word for doubt. The biblical signs and wonders convince men who have little faith or who believe in other gods; they are not addressed to "the fools who say in their hearts 'there is no God.'"[2]

It is true that we cannot ascribe to the Bible the theological concept of miracles, for that concept presupposes that of nature and the concept of nature is foreign to the Bible. One is tempted to ascribe to the Bible what one may call the poetic concept of miracles as illustrated by Psalm 114: "When Israel went out of Egypt, the house of Jacob from a people of a strange tongue, Judah became his sanctuary and Israel his dominion. The sea saw and it fled; the Jordan turned back. The mountains skipped like rams, the hills like lambs. What ails thee sea, that thou fleest, thou Jordan that thou turnest back? Ye mountains that ye skip like rams, ye hills like lambs? From the presence of the Lord tremble thou earth, from the presence of the God of Jacob who turns the rock into a pond of water, the flint into a fountain of waters." The presence of God or His call elicits a conduct of His creatures that differs strikingly from their ordinary conduct;

2. Bacon, "Of Atheism," *Essays*.

it enlivens the lifeless; it makes fluid the fixed. It is not easy to say whether the author of the psalm did not mean his utterance to be simply or literally true. It is easy to say that the concept of poetry—as distinguished from that of song—is foreign to the Bible. It is perhaps more simple to say that owing to the victory of science over natural theology the impossibility of miracles can no longer be said to be simply true but has degenerated to the status of an indemonstrable hypothesis. One may trace to the hypothetical character of this fundamental premise the hypothetical character of many, not to say all, results of biblical criticism. Certain it is that biblical criticism in all its forms makes use of terms having no biblical equivalents and is to this extent unhistorical.

How then must we proceed? We shall not take issue with the findings and even the premises of biblical criticism. Let us grant that the Bible and in particular the Torah consists to a considerable extent of "memories of ancient histories," even of memories of memories; but memories of memories are not necessarily distorting or pale reflections of the original; they may be re-collections of re-collections, deepenings through meditation of the primary experiences. We shall therefore take the latest and uppermost layer as seriously as the earlier ones. We shall start from the uppermost layer—from what is first for us, even though it may not be the first simply. We shall start, that is, where both the traditional and the historical study of the Bible necessarily start. In thus proceeding we avoid the compulsion to make an advance decision in favor of Athens against Jerusalem. For the Bible does not require us to believe in the miraculous character of events that the Bible does not present as miraculous. God's speaking to men may be described as miraculous, but the Bible does not claim that the putting together of those speeches was done miraculously. We begin at the beginning, at the beginning of the beginning. The beginning of the beginning happens to deal with *the* beginning: the creation of heaven and earth. The Bible begins reasonably.

"In the beginning God created heaven and earth." Who says this? We are not told; hence we do not know. Does it make no difference who says it? This would be a philosopher's reason; is it also the biblical reason? We are not told; hence we do not know. We have no right to assume that God said it, for the Bible introduces God's sayings by expressions like "God said." We shall then assume that the words were spoken by a nameless man. Yet no man can have been an eyewitness of God's creating heaven and earth;[3] the only eyewitness was God. Since "there did not arise in Israel a prophet like Moses whom the Lord saw face to face," it is

3. Job 38:4.

understandable that tradition ascribed to Moses the sentence quoted and its whole sequel. But what is understandable or plausible is not as such certain. The narrator does not claim to have heard the account from God; perhaps he heard it from some man or men; perhaps he retells a tale. The Bible continues: "And the earth was unformed and void. . . ." It is not clear whether the earth thus described was created by God or antedated His creation. But it is quite clear that while speaking about how the earth looked at first, the Bible is silent about how heaven looked at first. The earth, i.e., that which is not heaven, seems to be more important than heaven. This impression is confirmed by the sequel.

God created everything in six days. On the first day He created light; on the second, heaven; on the third, the earth, the seas, and vegetation; on the fourth, sun, moon, and the stars; on the fifth, the water animals and the birds; and on the sixth, the land animals and man. The most striking difficulties are these: light and hence days (and nights) are presented as preceding the sun, and vegetation is presented as preceding the sun. The first difficulty is disposed of by the observation that creation-days are not sun-days. One must add however at once that there is a connection between the two kinds of days, for there is a connection, a correspondence between light and sun. The account of creation manifestly consists of two parts, the first part dealing with the first three creation-days and the second part dealing with the last three. The first part begins with the creation of light and the second with the creation of the heavenly light-givers. Correspondingly the first part ends with the creation of vegetation and the second with the creation of man. All creatures dealt with in the first part lack local motion; all creatures dealt with the second part possess local motion.[4] Vegetation precedes the sun because vegetation lacks local motion and the sun possesses it. Vegetation belongs to the earth;[5] it is rooted in the earth; it is the fixed covering of the fixed earth. Vegetation was brought forth by the earth at God's command; the Bible does not speak of God's "making" vegetation; but as regards the living beings in question, God commanded the earth to bring them forth and yet God "made" them. Vegetation was created at the end of the first half of the creation-days; at the end of the last half the living beings that spend their whole lives on the firm earth were created. The living beings—beings that possess life in

4. Cf. U. Cassuto, *A Commentary on the Book of Genesis*, part I (Jerusalem, 1961), 42.

5. Cf. the characterization of the plants as engeia ("in or of the earth") in Plato's *Republic* 491 d 1. Cf. Empedocles A 70.

addition to local motion—were created on the fifth and sixth days, on the days following the day on which the heavenly light-givers were created. The Bible presents the creatures in an ascending order. Heaven is lower than earth. The heavenly light-givers lack life; they are lower than the lowliest living beast; they serve the living creatures, which are to be found only beneath heaven; they have been created in order to rule over day and night: they have not been made in order to rule over the earth, let alone over man. The most striking characteristic of the biblical account of creation is its demoting or degrading of heaven and the heavenly lights. Sun, moon, and stars precede the living things because they are lifeless: they are not gods. What the heavenly lights lose, man gains; man is the peak of creation. The creatures of the first three days cannot change their places; the heavenly bodies change their places but not their courses; the living beings change their courses but not their "ways"; men alone can change their "ways." Man is the only being created in God's image. Only in the case of man's creation does the biblical account of creation reportedly speak of God's "creating" him; in the case of the creation of heaven and the heavenly bodies, that account speaks of God's "making" them. Only in the case of man's creation does the Bible intimate that there is a multiplicity of God: "Let us make man in our image, after our likeness. . . . So God created man in his image, in the image of God he created him; male and female he created them." Bisexuality is not a preserve of man; but only man's bisexuality could give rise to the view that there are gods and goddesses: there is no biblical word for "goddess." Hence creation is not begetting. The biblical account of creation teaches silently what the Bible teaches elsewhere explicitly but not therefore more emphatically: there is only one God, the God who name is written as the Tetragrammaton, the living God Who lives from ever to ever, Who alone has created heaven and earth and all their hosts; He has not created any gods and hence there are no gods beside Him. The many gods whom men worship are either nothings that owe such being as they possess by man's making them, or if they are something (like sun, moon, and stars), they surely are not gods.[6] All nonpolemical references to "other gods" occurring in the Bible are fossils whose preservation indeed poses a question but only a rather unimportant one. Not only did the biblical God not create any gods; on the basis of the biblical account of creation one

6. Cf. the distinction between the two kinds of "other gods" in Deut. 4:15–19, between the idols on the one hand and sun, moon, and stars on the other.

could doubt whether He created any beings one would be compelled to call "mythical": heaven and earth and all their hosts are always accessible to man as man. One would have to start from this fact in order to understand why the Bible contains so many sections that, on the basis of the distinction between mythical (or legendary) and historical, would have to be described as historical.

According to the Bible, creation was completed by the creation of man; creation culminated in the creation of man. Only after the creation of man did God "see all that he had made, and behold, it was very good." What then is the origin of the evil or the bad? The biblical answer seems to be that since everything of divine origin is good, evil is of human origin. Yet if God's creation as a whole is very good, it does not follow that all its parts are good or that creation as a whole contains no evil whatever: God did not find all parts of His creation to be good. Perhaps creation as a whole cannot be "very good" if it does not contain some evils. There cannot be light if there is not darkness, and the darkness is as much created as is light: God creates evil as well as He makes peace.[7] However this may be, the evils whose origin the Bible lays bare after it has spoken of creation are a particular kind of evils: the evils that beset man. Those evils are not due to creation or implicit in it, as the Bible shows by setting forth man's original condition. In order to set forth that condition, the Bible must retell man's creation by making man's creation as much as possible the sole theme. This second account answers the question, not of how heaven and earth and all their hosts have come into being but of how human life as we know it—beset with evils with which it was not beset originally—has come into being. This second account may only supplement the first account but it may also correct it and thus contradict it. After all, the Bible never teaches that one can speak about creation without contradicting oneself. In postbiblical parlance, the mysteries of the Torah (*sithre torah*) are the contradictions of the Torah; the mysteries of God are the contradictions regarding God.

The first account of creation ended with man; the second account begins with man. According to the first account, God created man and only man in His image; according to the second account, God formed man from the dust of the earth and He blew into his nostrils the breath of life; the second account makes clear that man consists of two profoundly different ingredients, a high one and a low one. According to the first account, it would

7. Isa. 45:7.

seem that man and woman were created simultaneously; according to the second account, man was created first. The life of man as we know it, the life of most men, is that of tillers of the soil; their life is needy and harsh; they need rain, which is not always forthcoming when they need it, and they must work hard. If human life had been needy and harsh from the very beginning, man would have been compelled or at least irresistibly tempted to be harsh, uncharitable, unjust; he would not have been fully responsible for his lack of charity or justice. But man is to be fully responsible. Hence the harshness of human life must be due to man's fault. His original condition must have been one of ease: he was not in need of rain or of hard work; he was put by God into a well-watered garden that was rich in trees good for food. While man was created for a life of ease, he was not created for a life of luxury: there was no gold or precious stones in the garden of Eden.[8] Man was created for a simple life. Accordingly, God permitted him to eat of every tree[9] of the garden except of the tree of knowledge of good and evil (bad), "for in the day that you eat of it, you shall surely die." Man was not denied knowledge; without knowledge he could not have known the tree of knowledge or the woman or the brutes; nor could he have understood the prohibition. Man was denied knowledge of good and evil, i.e., the knowledge sufficient for guiding himself, his life. While not being a child, he was to live in childlike simplicity and obedience to God. We are free to surmise that there is a connection between the demotion of heaven in the first account and the prohibition against eating of the tree of knowledge in the second. While man was forbidden to eat of the tree of knowledge, he was not forbidden to eat of the tree of life.

Man, lacking knowledge of good and evil, was content with his condition and in particular with his loneliness. But God, possessing knowledge of good and evil, found that "it is not good for man to be alone, so I will make him a helper as his counterpart." So God formed the brutes and brought them to man, but they proved not to be the desired helpers. Thereupon God formed the woman out of a rib of the man. The man welcomed her as bone of his bones and flesh of his flesh but, lacking knowledge of good and evil, he did not call her good. The narrator adds that "therefore [namely, because the woman is bone of man's bone and flesh of his flesh] a man leaves his father and his mother, and cleaves to his

8. Cassuto, *A Commentary on the Book of Genesis*, part I, 77–79.
9. One does not have to stoop in order to pluck the fruits of trees.

wife, and they become one flesh." Both were naked but, lacking knowledge of good and evil, they were not ashamed.

Thus the stage was set for the fall of our first parents. The first move came from the serpent, the most cunning of all the beasts of the field; it seduced the woman into disobedience and then the woman seduced the man. The seduction moves from the lowest to the highest. The Bible does not tell what induced the serpent to seduce the woman into disobeying the divine prohibition against eating of the tree of knowledge of good and evil. It is reasonable to assume that the serpent acted as it did because it was cunning, i.e., possessed a low kind of wisdom, a congenital malice; everything that God had created would not be very good if it did not include something congenitally bent on mischief. The serpent begins its seduction by suggesting that God might have forbidden man and woman to eat of any tree in the garden, i.e., that God's prohibition might be malicious or impossible to comply with. The woman corrects the serpent and in so doing makes the prohibition more stringent than it was: "we may eat of the fruit of the other trees of the garden; it is only about the tree in the middle of the garden that God said: you shall not eat of it or touch it, lest you die." God did not forbid the man to touch the fruit of the tree of knowledge of good and evil. Besides, the woman does not explicitly speak of the tree of knowledge; she may have had in mind the tree of life. Moreover, God had said to the man: "thou mayest eat . . . thou wilt die"; the woman claims that God had spoken to both her and the man. She surely knew the divine prohibition only through human tradition. The serpent assures her that they will not die, "for God knows that when you eat it, your eyes will be opened and you will be like God, knowing good and evil." The serpent tacitly questions God's veracity. At the same time it glosses over the fact that eating of the tree involves disobedience to God. In this it is followed by the woman. According to the serpent's assertion, knowledge of good and evil makes man immune to death, but we cannot know whether the serpent believes this. But could immunity to death be a great good for beings that did not know good and evil, to men who were like children? But the woman, having forgotten the divine prohibition, having therefore in a manner tasted of the tree of knowledge, is no longer wholly unaware of good and evil: she "saw that the tree was good for eating and a delight to the eyes and that the tree was to be desired to make one wise"; therefore she took of its fruit and ate. She thus made the fall of the man almost inevitable, for he was cleaving to her: she gave some of the fruit of the tree to the man, and he ate. The man drifts into disobedience by following the woman. After they had eaten of the tree, their eyes were opened and they knew that they were naked, and they sewed fig leaves together and made themselves aprons: through the fall they became ashamed of their nakedness; eating of the tree of knowledge of good and evil made them realize that nakedness is evil (bad).

The Bible says nothing to the effect that our first parents fell because they were prompted by the desire to be like God; they did not rebel high-handedly against God; they rather forgot to obey God; they drifted into disobedience. Nevertheless God punished them severely. He also punished the serpent. But the punishment did not do away with the fact that, as God Himself said, as a consequence of his disobedience "man has become like one of us, knowing good and evil." As a consequence there was now the danger that man might eat of the tree of life and live forever. Therefore God expelled him from the garden and made it impossible for him to return to it. One may wonder why man, while he was still in the garden of Eden, had not eaten of the tree of life of which he had not been forbidden to eat. Perhaps he did not think of it because, lacking knowledge of good and evil, he did not fear to die and, besides, the divine prohibition drew his attention away from the tree of life to the tree of knowledge.

The Bible intends to teach that man was meant to live in simplicity, without knowledge of good and evil. But the narrator seems to be aware of the fact that a being that can be forbidden to strive for knowledge of good and evil, i.e., that can understand to some degree that knowledge of good and evil is evil for it, necessarily possesses such knowledge. Human suffering from evil presupposes human knowledge of good and evil and vice versa. Man wishes to live without evil. The Bible tells us that he was given the opportunity to live without evil and that he cannot blame God for the evils from which he suffers. By giving man that opportunity God convinces him that his deepest wish cannot be fulfilled. The story of the fall is the first part of the story of God's education of man. This story partakes of the unfathomable character of God.

Man has to live with knowledge of good and evil and with the sufferings inflicted on him because of that knowledge or its acquisition. Human goodness or badness presupposes that knowledge and its concomitants. The Bible gives us the first inkling of human goodness and badness in the story of the first brothers. The oldest brother, Cain, was a tiller of the soil; the youngest brother, Abel, a keeper of sheep. God preferred the offering of the keeper of sheep, who brought the choicest of the firstlings of his flock, to that of the tiller of the soil. This preference has more than one reason, but one reason seems to be that the pastoral life is closer to original simplicity than the life of the tillers of the soil. Cain was vexed and, despite his having been warned by God against sinning in general, killed his brother. After a futile attempt to deny his guilt—an attempt that increased his guilt ("Am I my brother's keeper?")—he was cursed by God as the serpent and the soil had been after the Fall, in contradistinction to Adam and Eve who were not cursed; he was punished by God, but not with death: anyone slaying Cain would be punished much more severely than Cain himself. The relatively mild punishment of Cain cannot be explained by the fact that murder had not been expressly forbidden, for Cain possessed some knowledge of good and evil, and he knew that Abel was his brother, even assuming that he did not know that man was created in the image of God. It is better to explain Cain's punishment by assuming that punishments were milder in the beginning than later on. Cain—like his fellow fratricide Romulus—founded a city, and some of his descendants were the ancestors of men practicing various arts: the city and the arts, so alien to man's original simplicity, owe their origin to Cain and his race rather than to Seth, the substitute for Abel, and his race. It goes without saying that this is not the last word of the Bible on the city and the arts, but it is its first word, just as the prohibition against eating of the tree of knowledge is, as one may say, its first word simply, and the revelation of the Torah, i.e., the highest kind of knowledge of good and evil that is vouchsafed to men, is its last word. One is also tempted to think of the difference between the first word of the first book of Samuel on human kingship and its last word. The account of the race of Cain culminates in the song of Lamech, who boasted to his wives of his slaying of men, of his being superior to God as an avenger. The (antediluvian) race of Seth cannot boast of a single inventor; its only distinguished members were Enoch, who walked with God, and Noah, who was a righteous man and walked with God: civilization and piety are two very different things.

By the time of Noah the wickedness of man had become so great that God repented of His creation of man and all other earthly creatures, Noah alone excepted; so He brought on the Flood. Generally speaking, prior to the Flood man's life span was much longer than after it. Man's antediluvian longevity was a relic of his original condition. Man originally lived in the garden of Eden, where he could have eaten of the tree of life and thus have become immortal. The longevity of antediluvian man reflects this lost chance. To this extent the transition from antediluvian to postdiluvian man is a decline. This impression is confirmed by the fact that before the

Flood rather than after it the sons of God consorted with the daughters of man and thus generated the mighty men of old, the men of renown. On the other hand, the fall of our first parents made possible or necessary in due time God's revelation of his Torah, and this was decisively prepared, as we shall see, by the Flood. In this respect the transition from antediluvian to postdiluvian mankind is a progress. The ambiguity regarding the Fall—the fact that it was a sin and hence evitable and that it was inevitable—is reflected in the ambiguity regarding the status of antediluvian mankind.

The link between antediluvian mankind and the revelation of the Torah is supplied by the first Covenant between God and men, the Covenant following the Flood. The Flood was the proper punishment for the extreme and well-nigh universal wickedness of antediluvian men. Prior to the Flood mankind lived, so to speak, without restraint, without law. While our first parents were still in the garden of Eden, they were not forbidden anything except to eat of the tree of knowledge. The vegetarianism of antediluvian men was not due to an explicit prohibition (cf. 1:29); their abstention from meat belongs together with their abstention from wine (cf. 9:20); both were relics of man's original simplicity. After the expulsion from the garden of Eden, God did not punish men, apart from the relatively mild punishment which He inflicted on Cain. Nor did He establish human judges. God as it were experimented, for the instruction of mankind, with mankind living in freedom from law. This experiment, just as the experiment with men remaining like innocent children, ended in failure. Fallen or awake, man needs restraint, must live under law. But this law must not be simply imposed. It must form part of a Covenant in which God and man are equally, though not equal, partners. Such a partnership was established only after the Flood; it did not exist in antediluvian times either before or after the Fall. The inequality regarding the Covenant is shown especially by the fact that God's undertaking never again to destroy almost all life on earth as long as the earth lasts is not conditioned on all men or almost all men obeying the laws promulgated by God after the Flood: God's promise is made despite, or because of, His knowing that the devisings of man's heart are evil from his youth. Noah is the ancestor of all later men just as Adam was; the purgation of the earth through the Flood is to some extent a restoration of mankind to its original state; it is a kind of second creation. Within the limits indicated, the condition of postdiluvian men is superior to that of antediluvian men. One point requires special emphasis: in the legislation following the Flood, murder is expressly forbidden and made punishable with death on the ground that man was created in the image of God (9:6). The first Covenant brought an increase in hope and at the same time an increase in punishment. Man's rule over the beasts, ordained or established from the beginning, was only after the Flood to be accompanied by the beast's fear and dread of man (cf. 9:2 with 1:26–30 and 2:15).

The Covenant following the Flood prepares the Covenant with Abraham. The Bible singles out three events that took place between the Covenant after the Flood and God's calling Abraham: Noah's curse of Canaan, a son of Ham; the excellence of Nimrod, a grandson of Ham; and men's attempt to prevent their being scattered over the earth through building a city and a tower with its top in the heavens. Canaan, whose land came to be the promised land, was cursed because of Ham's seeing the nakedness of his father, Noah, because of Ham's transgressing a most sacred, if unpromulgated, law; the curse of Canaan was accompanied by the blessing of Shem and Japheth, who turned their eyes away from the nakedness of their father; here we have the first and the most fundamental division of mankind, at any rate, of postdiluvian mankind, the division into a cursed and a blessed part. Nimrod was the first to be a mighty man on earth—a mighty hunter before the Lord; his kingdom included Babel; big kingdoms are attempts to overcome by force the division of mankind; conquest and hunting are akin to one another. The city that men built in order to remain together and thus to make a name for themselves was Babel; God scattered them by confounding their speech, by bringing about the division of mankind into groups speaking different languages, groups that cannot understand one another: into nations, i.e., groups united not only by descent but by language as well. The division of mankind into nations may be described as a milder alternative to the Flood.

The three events that took place between God's Covenant with mankind after the Flood and His calling Abraham point to God's way of dealing with men knowing good and evil and devising evil from their youth; well-nigh universal wickedness will no longer be punished with well-nigh universal destruction; well-nigh universal wickedness will be prevented by the division of mankind into nations in the sense indicated; mankind will be divided, not into the cursed and the blessed (the curses and blessings were Noah's, not God's), but into a chosen nation and the nations that are not chosen. The emergence of nations made it possible that Noah's Ark floating alone on the waters covering the whole earth be replaced by a whole, numerous nation living in the midst of the nations covering the whole earth. The election of the holy nation begins with the election of Abraham. Noah was distinguished from his contemporaries by his righteousness; Abraham separates himself from his contemporaries and in particular from his country and kindred at God's command—a command accompanied by God's promise to make him a great nation. The Bible does not say that this primary election of Abraham was preceded by Abraham's righteousness. However this may be, Abraham shows his righteousness by at once obeying God's command, by trusting in God's promise the fulfillment of which he could not possibly live to see, given the short life spans of postdiluvian men: only after Abraham's offspring will have become a great nation, will the land of Canaan be given to them forever. The fulfillment of the promise required that Abraham not remain childless, and he was already quite old. Accordingly, God promised him that he would have issue. It was Abraham's trust in God's promise that, above everything else, made him righteous in the eyes of the Lord. It was God's intention that His promise be fulfilled through the offspring of Abraham and his wife Sarah. But this promise seemed to be laughable to Abraham, to say nothing of Sarah: Abraham was one hundred years old and Sarah ninety. Yet nothing is too wondrous for the Lord. The laughable announcement became a joyous announcement. The joyous announcement was followed immediately by God's announcement to Abraham of His concern with the wickedness of the people of Sodom and Gomorra. God did not yet know whether those people were as wicked as they were said to be. But they might be; they might deserve total destruction as much as the generation of the Flood. Noah had accepted the destruction of his generation without any questioning. Abraham, however, who had a deeper trust in God, in God's righteousness, and a deeper awareness of his being only dust and ashes, than Noah, presumed in fear and trembling to appeal to God's righteousness lest He, the judge of the whole earth, destroy the righteous along with the wicked. In response to Abraham's insistent pleading, God as it were promised to Abraham that He would not destroy Sodom if ten righteous men were found in the city: He would save the city for the sake of the ten righteous men within it. Abraham acted as the mortal partner in God's righteousness; he acted as if he had some share in the responsibility for God's acting righteously. No wonder that God's Covenant with Abraham was incomparably more incisive than His Covenant immediately following the Flood.

Abraham's trust in God thus appears to be the trust that God in His righteousness will not do anything incompatible with His righteousness and that while or because nothing is too wondrous for the Lord, there are firm boundaries set to Him by His righteousness, by Him. This awareness is deepened and therewith modified by the last and severest test of Abraham's trust: God's command to him to sacrifice Isaac, his only son from Sarah. Before speaking of Isaac's conception and birth, the Bible speaks of the attempt made by Abimelech, the king of Gerar, to lie with Sarah; given Sarah's old age Abimelech's action might have forestalled the last opportunity that Sarah bear a child to Abraham; therefore God intervened to prevent Abimelech from approaching Sarah. A similar danger had threatened Sarah many years earlier at the hands of the Pharaoh; at that time she was very beautiful. At the time of the Abimelech incident she was apparently no longer very beautiful, but despite her being almost ninety years old she must have been still quite attractive;[10] this could seem to detract from the wonder of Isaac's birth. On the other hand, God's special intervention against Abimelech enhances that wonder. Abraham's supreme test presupposes the wondrous character of Isaac's birth: the very son who was to be the sole link between Abraham and the chosen people and who was born against all reasonable expectations was to be sacrificed by his father. This command contradicted not only the divine promise but also the divine prohibition against the shedding of innocent blood. Yet Abraham did not argue with God as he had done in the case of Sodom's destruction. In the case of Sodom, Abraham was not confronted with a divine command to do something and in particular not with a command to surrender to God, to render to God what was dearest to him: Abraham did not argue with God for the preservation of Isaac because he loved God, and not himself or his most cherished hope, with all his heart, with all his soul, and with all his might. The same concern with God's righteousness that had induced him to plead with God for the preservation of Sodom if ten just men should be found in that city induced him not to plead for the preservation of Isaac, for God rightfully demands that He alone be loved unqualifiedly: God does not command that we love His chosen people with all our heart, with all our soul, and with all our might. The fact that the command to sacrifice Isaac contradicted the prohibition against the shedding of innocent blood must be understood in the light of the difference between human justice and divine justice: God alone is

10. The Bible records an apparently similar incident involving Abimelech and Rebekah (26:6–11). That incident took place after the birth of Jacob; this alone would explain why there was no divine intervention in this case.

unqualifiedly, if unfathomably, just. God promised to Abraham that He would spare Sodom if ten righteous men should be found in it, and Abraham was satisfied with this promise; He did not promise that He would spare it if nine righteous men were found in it; would those nine be destroyed together with the wicked? And even if all Sodomites were wicked and hence justly destroyed, did their infants who were destroyed with them deserve their destruction? The apparent contradiction between the command to sacrifice Isaac and the divine promise to the descendants of Isaac is disposed of by the consideration that nothing is too wondrous for the Lord. Abraham's supreme trust in God, his simple, single-minded, childlike faith was rewarded, although or because it presupposed his entire unconcern with any reward, for Abraham was willing to forgo, to destroy, to kill, the only reward with which he was concerned; God prevented the sacrifice of Isaac. Abraham's intended action needed a reward although he was not concerned with a reward, because his intended action cannot be said to have been intrinsically rewarding. The preservation of Isaac is as wondrous as his birth. These two wonders illustrate more clearly than anything else the origin of the holy nation.

The God Who created heaven and earth, Who is the only God, Whose only image is man, Who forbade man to eat of the tree of knowledge of good and evil, Who made a Covenant with mankind after the Flood and thereafter a Covenant with Abraham which became His Covenant with Abraham, Isaac, and Jacob—what kind of God is He? Or, to speak more reverently and more adequately, what is His name? This question was addressed to God Himself by Moses when he was sent by Him to the sons of Israel. God replied: "Ehyeh-Asher-Ehyeh." This is mostly translated: "I am That (Who) I am." One has called that reply "the metaphysics of Exodus" in order to indicate its fundamental character. It is indeed the fundamental biblical statement about the biblical God, but we hesitate to call it metaphysical, since the notion of *physis* is alien to the Bible. I believe that we ought to render this statement by "I shall be What I shall be," thus preserving the connection between God's name and the fact that He makes covenants with men, i.e., that He reveals Himself to men above all by His commandments and by His promises and His fulfillment of the promises. "I shall be What I shall be" is as it were explained in the verse (Exod. 33:19), "I shall be gracious to whom I shall be gracious and I shall show mercy to whom I shall show mercy." God's actions cannot be predicted, unless He Himself predicted them, i.e., promised them. But as is shown precisely by the account of Abraham's binding of Isaac, the way in which He fulfills His promises cannot be known in advance. The biblical God is a mysterious God: He comes in a thick cloud (Exod. 19:9); He cannot be seen; His presence can be sensed but not always and everywhere; what is known of Him is only what He chose to communicate by His word through His chosen servants. The rest of the chosen people knows His word—apart from the Ten Commandments (Deut. 4:12 and 5:4–5)—only mediately and does not wish to know it immediately (Exod. 20:19 and 21, 24:1–2; Deut. 18:15–18; Amos 3:7). For almost all purposes the word of God as revealed to His prophets and especially to Moses became *the* source of knowledge of good and evil, the true tree of knowledge which is at the same time the tree of life.

This much about the beginning of the Bible and what it entails. Let us now cast a glance at some Greek counterparts to the beginning of the Bible and in the first place at Hesiod's *Theogony* as well as the remains of Parmenides' and Empedocles' works. They all are the works of known authors. This does not mean that they are, or present themselves as, merely human. Hesiod sings what the Muses, the daughters of Zeus, who is the father of gods and men, taught him or commanded him to sing. One could say that the Muses vouch for the truth of Hesiod's song, were it not for the fact that they sometimes say lies resembling what is true. Parmenides transmits the teachings of a goddess, and so does Empedocles. Yet these men composed their books; their songs or speeches are books. The Bible on the other hand is not a book. The utmost one could say is that it is a collection of books. But are all parts of that collection books? Is in particular the Torah a book? Is it not rather the work of an unknown compiler or of unknown compilers who wove together writings and oral traditions of unknown origin? Is this not the reason why the Bible can contain fossils that are at variance even with its fundamental teaching regarding God? The author of a book in the strict sense excludes everything that is not necessary, that does not fulfill a function necessary for the purpose that his book is meant to fulfill. The compilers of the Bible as a whole and of the Torah in particular seem to have followed an entirely different rule. Confronted with a variety of preexisting holy speeches, which as such had to be treated with the utmost respect, they excluded only what could not by any stretch of the imagination be rendered compatible with the fundamental and authoritative teaching; their very piety, aroused and fostered by the preexisting holy speeches, led them to make such changes in those holy speeches as they did make. Their work may then abound in contradictions and repetitions that no one ever intended as such, whereas in a book in the strict sense there is nothing that is not intended by the author. Yet by excluding what could not by any stretch of the imagination be rendered compatible with the fundamental and authoritative teaching, they prepared the traditional way of reading the Bible, i.e., the reading of the Bible as if it were a book in the strict sense. The tendency to read the Bible and in particular the Torah as a book in the strict sense was infinitely strengthened by the belief that it is the only holy writing or the holy writing par excellence.

Hesiod's *Theogony* sings of the generation or begetting of the gods; the gods were not "made" by anybody. So far from being created by a god, earth and heaven are the ancestors of the immortal gods. More precisely, according to Hesiod everything that is has come to be. First there arose Chaos, Gaia (Earth), and Eros. Gaia gave birth first to Ouranos (Heaven) and then, mating with Ouranos, she brought forth Kronos and his brothers and sisters. Ouranos hated his children and did not wish them to come to light. At the wish and advice of Gaia, Kronos deprived his father of his generative power and thus unintentionally brought about the emergence of Aphrodite; Kronos became the king of the gods. Kronos's evil deed was avenged by his son Zeus, whom he had generated by mating with Rheia and whom he had planned to destroy; Zeus dethroned his father and thus became the king of the gods, the father of gods and men, the mightiest of all the gods. Given his ancestors it is not surprising that while being the father of men and belonging to the gods who are the givers of good things, he is far from being kind to men. Mating with Mnemosyne, the daughter of Gaia and Ouranos, Zeus generated the nine Muses. The Muses give sweet and gentle eloquence and understanding to the kings whom they wish to honor. Through the Muses there are singers on earth, just as through Zeus there are kings. While kingship and song may go together, there is a profound difference between the two—a difference that, guided by Hesiod, one may compare to that between the hawk and the nightingale. Surely Metis (Wisdom), while being Zeus's first spouse and having become inseparable from him, is not identical with him; the relation of Zeus and Metis may remind one of the relation of God and Wisdom in the Bible.[11] Hesiod speaks of the creation or making of men not in the *Theogony* but in his *Works and Days*, i.e., in the context of his teaching regarding how man should live, regarding man's right life, which includes the teaching regarding the right seasons (the "days"): the question of the

11. *Theogony* 53–97 and 886–900; cf. Proverbs 8.

right life does not arise regarding the gods. The right life for man is the just life, the life devoted to working, especially to tilling the soil. Work thus understood is a blessing ordained by Zeus who blesses the just and crushes the proud: often even a whole city is destroyed for the deeds of a single bad man. Yet Zeus takes cognizance of men's justice and injustice only if he so wills (35–36, 225–85). Accordingly, work appears to be not a blessing but a curse: men must work because the gods keep hidden from them the means of life and they do this in order to punish them for Prometheus's theft, inspired by philanthropy, of fire. But was not Prometheus's action itself prompted by the fact that men were not properly provided for by the gods and in particular by Zeus? Be this as it may, Zeus did not deprive men of the fire that Prometheus had stolen for them; he punished them by sending Pandora to them with her box that was filled with countless evils such as hard toils (42, 105). The evils with which human life is beset cannot be traced to human sin. Hesiod conveys the same message by his story of the five races of men, which came into being successively. The first race, the golden race, was made by the gods while Kronos was still ruling in heaven; these men lived without toil and grief; they had all good things in abundance because the earth by itself gave them abundant fruit. Yet the men made by father Zeus lack this bliss; Hesiod does not make clear whether this is due to Zeus's ill will or to his lack of power; he gives us no reason to think that it is due to man's sin. He creates the impression that human life becomes ever more miserable as one race of men succeeds the other: there is no divine promise, supported by the fulfillment of earlier divine promises, that permits one to trust and to hope.

The most striking difference between the poet Hesiod and the philosophers Parmenides and Empedocles is that according to the philosophers not everything has come into being: that which truly is has not come into being and does not perish. This does not necessarily mean that what is always is a god or gods. For if Empedocles, e.g., calls one of the eternal four elements Zeus, this Zeus has hardly anything in common with what Hesiod, or the people generally, understood by Zeus. At any rate, according to both philosophers the gods as ordinarily understood have come into being, just as heaven and earth, and therefore will perish again.

At the time when the opposition between Jerusalem and Athens reached the level of what one may call its classical struggle, in the twelfth and thirteenth centuries, philosophy was represented by Aristotle. The Aristotelian god like the biblical God is a thinking being, but in opposition to the biblical God he is only a thinking being, pure thought: pure thought that thinks itself and only itself. Only by thinking himself and nothing but himself does he rule the world. He surely does not rule by giving orders and laws. Hence he is not a creator-god: the world is as eternal as god. Man is not his image: man is much lower in rank than other parts of the world. For Aristotle it is almost a blasphemy to ascribe justice to his god; he is above justice as well as injustice.[12]

It has often been said that the philosopher who comes closest to the Bible is Plato. This was said not the least during the classical struggle between Jerusalem and Athens in the Middle Ages. Both Platonic philosophy and biblical piety are animated by the concern with purity and purification: the "pure reason" in Plato's sense is closer to the Bible than the "pure reason" in Kant's sense or for that matter in Anaxagoras's and Aristotle's sense. Plato teaches, just as the Bible, that heaven and earth were created or made by an invisible God whom he calls the Father, who is always, who is good, and hence whose creation is good. The coming-into-being and the preservation of the world that he has created depends on the will of its maker. What Plato himself calls the theology consists of two teachings: (1) God is good and hence is no way the cause of evil; (2) God is simple and hence unchangeable. On the divine concern with men's justice and injustice, the Platonic teaching is in fundamental agreement with the biblical teaching; it even culminates in a statement that agrees almost literally with biblical statements.[13] Yet the differences between the Platonic and the biblical teaching are no less striking than the agreements. The Platonic teaching on creation does not claim to be more than a likely tale. The Platonic God is a creator also of gods, of visible living beings, i.e., of the stars; the created gods rather than the creator God create the mortal living beings and in particular man; heaven is a blessed god. The Platonic God does not create the world by his word; he creates it after having looked to the eternal ideas which therefore are higher than he. In accordance with this, Plato's explicit theology is presented within the context of the first discussion of education in the *Republic*, within the context of what one may call the discussion of elementary education; in the second and final discussion of education—the discussion of the education of the philosophers—theology is replaced by the doctrine of ideas. As for the thematic discussion of providence in the *Laws*, it may suffice here to say that it occurs within the context of the discussion of penal law.

12. *Metaphysics* 1072 b 14–30, 1074 b 15–1075 a 11; *De Anima* 429 a 19–20; *Eth. Nic.* 1141 a 33–b 2, 1178 b 1–12; *Eth. Eud.* 1249 a 14–15.

13. Cf. *Laws* 905 a 4–b 2 with Amos 9:1–3 and Psalm 139:7–10.

In his likely tale of how God created the visible whole, Plato makes a distinction between two kinds of gods, the visible cosmic gods and the traditional gods—between the gods who revolve manifestly, i.e., who manifest themselves regularly, and the gods who manifest themselves so far as they will. The least one would have to say is that according to Plato the cosmic gods are of much higher rank than the traditional gods, the Greek gods. Inasmuch as the cosmic gods are accessible to man as man—to his observations and calculations—whereas the Greek gods are accessible only to the Greeks through Greek traditions, one may ascribe in comic exaggeration the worship of the cosmic gods to the barbarians. This ascription is made in an altogether noncomic manner and intent in the Bible: Israel is forbidden to worship the sun and the moon and the stars, which the Lord has allotted to the other peoples everywhere under heaven.[14] This implies that the other peoples', the barbarians', worship of the cosmic gods is not due to a natural or rational cause, to the fact that those gods are accessible to man as man, but to an act of God's will. It goes without saying that according to the Bible the God Who manifests Himself as far as He wills, Who is not universally worshipped as such, is the only true god. The Platonic statement taken in conjunction with the biblical statement brings out the fundamental opposition of Athens at its peak to Jerusalem: the opposition of the God or gods of the philosophers to the God of Abraham, Isaac, and Jacob, the opposition of Reason and Revelation.

II. On Socrates and the Prophets

Fifty years ago, in the middle of World War I, Hermann Cohen, the greatest representative of German Jewry and spokesman for it, the most powerful figure among the German professors of philosophy of his time, stated his view on Jerusalem and Athens in a lecture entitled "The Social Ideal in Plato and the Prophets."[15] He repeated that lecture shortly before his death. We may then regard it as stating his final view on Jerusalem and Athens and therewith on *the* truth. For, as Cohen says right at the

14. *Timaeus* 40 d 6–41 a 5; Aristophanes *Peace* 404–13; Deut. 4:19.

15. *Hermann Cohens Jüdische Schriften* (Berlin, 1924), 1:306–30; cf. the editor's note, on p. 341.

beginning, "Plato and the prophets are the two most important sources of modern culture." Being concerned with "the social ideal," he does not say a single word on Christianity in the whole lecture. Crudely but not misleadingly one may restate Cohen's view as follows. *The* truth is the synthesis of the teaching of Plato and that of the prophets. What we owe to Plato is the insight that the truth is in the first place the truth of science but that science must be supplemented, overarched by the idea of the good, which to Cohen means, not God, but rational, scientific ethics. The ethical truth must not only be compatible with the scientific truth, the ethical truth even needs the scientific truth. The prophets are very much concerned with knowledge, with the knowledge of God, but this knowledge as the prophets understood it has no connection whatever with scientific knowledge; it is knowledge only in a metaphorical sense. It is perhaps with a view of this fact that Cohen speaks once of the divine Plato but never of the divine prophets. Why then can he not leave matters at Platonic philosophy? What is the fundamental defect of Platonic philosophy that is remedied by the prophets and only by the prophets? According to Plato, the cessation of evils requires the rule of the philosophers, of the men who possess the highest kind of human knowledge, i.e., of science in the broadest sense of the term. But this kind of knowledge, as to some extent all scientific knowledge, is according to Plato the preserve of a small minority: of the men who possess certain gifts that most men lack—of the few men who possess a certain nature. Plato presupposes that there is an unchangeable human nature. As a consequence, he presupposes that there is such a fundamental structure of the good human society as is unchangeable. This leads him to assert or to assume that there will be wars as long as there will be human beings, that there ought to be a class of warriors and that that class ought to be higher in rank and honor than the class of producers and exchangers. These defects are remedied by the prophets precisely because they lack the idea of science and hence the idea of nature, and hence they can believe that men's conduct toward one another can undergo a change much more radical than any change ever dreamed of by Plato.

Cohen has brought out very well the antagonism between Plato and the prophets. Nevertheless we cannot leave matters at his view of that antagonism. Cohen's thought belongs to the world preceding World War I. Accordingly he had a greater faith in the power of modern Western culture to mold the fate of mankind than seems to be warranted now. The worst things that he experienced were the Dreyfus scandal and the pogroms instigated by czarist Russia: he did not experience Communist Russia and Hitler Germany. More disillusioned regarding modern culture than Cohen was, we wonder whether the two ingredients of modern culture, of the modern synthesis, are not more solid than that synthesis. Catastrophes and horrors of a magnitude hitherto unknown, which we have seen and through which we have lived, were better provided for, or made intelligible, by both Plato and the prophets than by the modern belief in progress. Since we are less certain than Cohen was that the modern synthesis is superior to its premodern ingredients, and since the two ingredients are in fundamental opposition to each other, we are ultimately confronted by a problem rather than by a solution.

More particularly, Cohen understood Plato in the light of the opposition between Plato and Aristotle—an opposition that he understood in the light of the opposition between Kant and Hegel. We, however, are more impressed than Cohen was by the kinship between Plato and Aristotle on the one hand and the kinship between Kant and Hegel on the other. In other words, the quarrel between the ancients and the moderns seems to us to be more fundamental than either the quarrel between Plato and Aristotle or that between Kant and Hegel.

We prefer to speak of Socrates and the prophets rather than Plato and the prophets, for the following reasons. We are no longer as sure as Cohen was that we can draw a clear line between Socrates and Plato. There is traditional support for drawing such a clear line, above all in Aristotle; but Aristotle's statements on this kind of subject no longer possess for us the authority that they formerly possessed, and this is due partly to Cohen himself. The clear distinction between Socrates and Plato is based not only on tradition but on the results of modern historical criticism; yet these results are in the decisive respect hypothetical. The decisive fact for us is that Plato as it were points away from himself to Socrates. If we wish to understand Plato, we must take him seriously; we must take seriously in particular his deference to Socrates. Plato points not only to Socrates' speeches but to his whole life, to his fate as well. Hence Plato's life and fate do not have the symbolic character of Socrates' life and fate. Socrates, as presented by Plato, had a mission; Plato did not claim to have a mission. It is in the first place this fact—the fact that Socrates had a mission—that induces us to consider, not Plato and the prophets, but Socrates and the prophets.

I cannot speak in my own words of the mission of the prophets. Surely here and now I cannot do more than remind you of three prophetic utterances of singular force and grandeur. Isaiah 6: "In the year that King Uzziah died I saw also the Lord sitting upon a throne, high and lifted up, and his train filled the temple. Above it stood the seraphim: each one had six wings; with twain he covered his face, and with twain he covered his feet, and with twain he did fly. And one cried unto another, and said, Holy, holy, holy is the Lord of hosts: the whole world is full of his glory. And the posts of the door moved at the voice of him that cried, and the house was filled with smoke. Then I said, Woe is me! for I am undone; because I am a man of unclean lips, and I dwell in the midst of a people of unclean lips: for mine eyes have seen the King, the Lord of hosts. Then flew one of the seraphim unto me, having a live coal in his hand, which he had taken with the tongs from off the altar: And he laid it upon my mouth, and said, Lo, this hath touched thy lips; and thine iniquity is taken away, and thy sin purged. Also I heard the voice of the Lord, saying, Whom shall I send, and who will go for us? Then said I, Here am I; send me." Isaiah, it seems, volunteered for his mission. Could he not have remained silent? Could he refuse to volunteer? When the word of the Lord came unto Jonah, "Arise, go to Nineveh, that great city, and cry against it; for their wickedness is come up before me," "Jonah rose up to flee unto Tarshish from the presence of the Lord"; Jonah ran away from his mission; but God did not allow him to run away; He compelled him to fulfill it. Of this compulsion we hear in different ways from Amos and Jeremiah. Amos 3:7–8: "Surely the Lord God will do nothing but he revealeth his secret unto his servants the prophets. The lion hath roared, who will not fear? the Lord God hath spoken; who will not prophesy?" The prophets overpowered by the majesty of the Lord, by His wrath and His mercy, bring the message of His wrath and His mercy. Jeremiah 1:4–10: "Then the word of the Lord came unto me, saying, Before I formed thee in the belly I knew thee and before thou camest out of the womb I sanctified thee, and I ordained thee a prophet unto the nations. Then said I, Ah, Lord God! behold, I cannot speak; for I am a child. But the Lord said unto me, Say not, I am a child; for thou shalt go to all that I shall send thee, and whatsoever I command thee thou shalt speak. Be not afraid of their faces; for I am with thee to deliver thee, saith the Lord. Then the Lord put forth his hand, and touched my mouth. And the Lord said unto me, Behold, I have put my words in thy mouth. See, I have this day set thee over the nations and over the kingdoms, to root out, and to put down, and to destroy, and to throw down, to build, and to plant."

The claim to have been sent by God was raised also by men who were not truly prophets but prophets of falsehood, false prophets. Many or most hearers were therefore uncertain as to which kinds of claimants to prophecy were to be trusted or believed. According to the Bible, the false prophets simply lied in saying that they were sent by God: "they speak a vision of their own heart, and not out of the mouth of the Lord. They say . . . the Lord hath said, Ye shall have peace" (Jer. 23:16–17). The false prophets tell the people what the people like to hear; hence they are much more popular than the true prophets. The false prophets are "prophets of the deceit of their own heart" (ibid., 26); they tell the people what they themselves imagined (consciously or unconsciously) because they wished it or their hearers wished it. But: "Is not my word like as a fire? saith the Lord, and like a hammer that breaketh the rock in pieces?" (ibid., 29). Or, as Jeremiah put it when opposing the false prophet Hananiah: "The prophets that have been before me and before thee of old prophesied both against many countries, and against great kingdoms, of war, and of evil, and of pestilence" (28:8). This does not mean that a prophet is true only if he is a prophet of doom; the true prophets are also prophets of ultimate salvation. We understand the difference between the true and the false prophets if we listen to and meditate on these words of Jeremiah: "Thus saith the Lord; Cursed is the man, that trusteth in man, and makes flesh his arm, and whose heart departeth from the Lord. . . . Blessed is the man that trusteth in the Lord, and whose hope the Lord is." The false prophets trust in flesh, even if that flesh is the temple in Jerusalem, the promised land, nay, the chosen people itself, nay, God's promise to the chosen people if that promise is taken to be an unconditional promise and not as a part of a Covenant. The true prophets, regardless of whether they predict doom or salvation, predict the unexpected, the humanly unforeseeable—what would not occur to men, left to themselves, to fear or to hope. The true prophets speak and act by the spirit and in the spirit of *Ehyeh-Asher-Ehyeh.* For the false prophets on the other hand there cannot be the wholly unexpected, whether bad or good.

Of Socrates' mission we know only through Plato's *Apology of Socrates*, which presents itself as the speech delivered by Socrates when he defended himself against the charge that he did not believe in the existence of the gods worshipped by the city of Athens and that he corrupted the young. In that speech he denies possessing any more than human wisdom. This denial was understood by Yehudah Ha-levi among others as follows: "Socrates said to the people: 'I do not deny your divine wisdom, but I say that I do not understand it; I am wise only to human wisdom.'"[16] While this interpretation points in the right direction, it goes somewhat too far. At least Socrates refers, immediately after having denied possessing any more than human wisdom, to the speech that originated his mission, and of this speech he says that it is not his, but he seems to ascribe to it divine origin. He does trace what he says to a speaker who is worthy of credence to the Athenians. But it is probable that he means by that speaker his companion Chairephon, who is worthy of credence to the Athenians, more worthy of credence to the Athenians than Socrates, because he was attached to the democratic regime. This Chairephon, having once come to Delphi, asked Apollo's oracle whether there was anyone wiser than Socrates. The Pythia replied that no one was wiser. This reply originated Socrates' mission. We see at once that Socrates' mission originated in human initiative, in the initiative of one of Socrates' companions. Socrates takes it for granted that the reply given by the Pythia was given by the god Apollo himself. Yet this does not induce him to take it for granted that the god's reply is true. He does take it for granted that it is not meet for the god to lie. Yet this does not make the god's reply convincing to him. In fact he tries to refute that reply by discovering men who are wiser than he. Engaging in this quest he finds out that the god said the truth: Socrates is wiser than other men because he knows that he knows nothing, i.e., nothing about the important things, whereas the others believe that they know the truth about the most important things. Thus his attempt to refute the oracle turns into a vindication of the oracle. Without intending it, he comes to the assistance of the god; he serves the god; he obeys the god's command. Although no god had ever spoken to him, he is satisfied that the god had commanded him to examine himself and the others, i.e., to philosophize, or to exhort everyone he meets to the practice of virtue: he has been given by the god to the city of Athens as a gadfly.

While Socrates does not claim to have heard the speech of a god, he claims that a voice—something divine and demonic—occurs to him from time to time, his daimonion. This *daimonion*, however, has no connection with Socrates' mission, for it never urges him forward but only keeps him back. While the Delphic oracle urged him forward toward philosophizing, toward examining his fellow men, and thus made him generally hated and thus brought him into mortal danger, his *daimonion* kept him back from political activity and thus saved him from mortal danger.

16. *Kuzari* IV.13 and V.14. Cf. Strauss, *Persecution and the Art of Writing*, 105–6.

The fact that both Socrates and the prophets have a divine mission means, or at any rate implies, that both Socrates and the prophets are concerned with justice or righteousness, with the perfectly just society which as such would be free from all evils. To this extent Socrates' figuring out of the best social order and the prophets' vision of the Messianic age are in agreement. Yet whereas the prophets predict the coming of the Messianic age, Socrates merely holds that the perfect society is possible: whether it will ever be actual depends on an unlikely, although not impossible, coincidence, the coincidence of philosophy and political power. For, according to Socrates, the coming-into-being of the best political order is not due to divine intervention; human nature will remain as it always has been; the decisive difference between the best political order and all other societies is that in the former the philosophers will be kings or that the natural potentiality of the philosophers will reach its utmost perfection. In the most perfect social order as Socrates sees it, knowledge of the most important things will remain, as it always was, the preserve of the philosophers, i.e., of a very small part of the population. According to the prophets, however, in the Messianic age "the earth shall be full of knowledge of the Lord, as the waters cover the earth" (Isa. 11:9), and this will be brought about by God Himself. As a consequence, the Messianic age will be the age of universal peace: all nations shall come to the mountain of the Lord, to the house of the God of Jacob, "and they shall beat their swords into plowshares, and their spears into pruning hooks: nation shall not lift up sword against nation, neither shall they learn war any more" (Isa. 2:2–4). The best regime, however, as Socrates envisages it, will animate a single city which as a matter of course will become embroiled in wars with other cities. The cessation of evils that Socrates expects from the establishment of the best regime will not include the cessation of war.

The perfectly just man, the man who is as just as is humanly possible, is according to Socrates the philosopher and according to the prophets the faithful servant of the Lord. The philosopher is the man who dedicates his life to the quest for knowledge of the good, of the idea of the good; what we would call moral virtue is only the condition or by-product of that quest. According to the prophets, however, there is no need for the quest for knowledge of the good; God "hath shewed thee, o man, what is good; and what doth the Lord require of thee, but to do justly, and to love mercy, and to walk humbly with thy God" (Micah 6:8). In accordance with this the prophets as a rule address the people and sometimes even all the peoples, whereas Socrates as a rule addresses only one man. In the language of Socrates the prophets are orators, while Socrates engages in conversations with one man, which means he is addressing questions to him.

There is one striking example of a prophet talking in private to a single man, in a way addressing a question to him. 2 Sam. 12:1–7: "And the Lord sent Nathan unto David. And he came unto him, and said unto him, There were two men in one city; the one rich, and the other poor. The rich man had exceeding many flocks and herds: But the poor man had nothing, save one little ewe lamb, which he had brought and nourished up: and it grew up together with him, and with his children; it did eat of his own meat, and drank of his own cup, and lay in his bosom, and was unto him as a daughter. And there came a traveler unto the rich man and he spared to take of his own flock and of his own herd, to dress for the wayfaring man that was come unto him; but took the poor man's lamb, and dressed it for the man that was come unto him. And David's anger was greatly kindled against the man; and he said to Nathan, As the Lord liveth, the man that hath done this thing shall surely die; And he shall restore the lamb fourfold, because he did this thing, and because he had no pity. And Nathan said to David, Thou are the man." The nearest parallel to this event that occurs in the Socratic writings is Socrates' reproof of his former companion, the tyrant Critias. "When the thirty were putting to death many citizens and by no means the worst ones, and were encouraging many in crime, Socrates said *somewhere*, that it seemed strange that a herdsman who lets his cattle decrease and go to the bad should not admit that he is a poor cowherd; but stranger still that a statesman when he causes the citizens to decrease and go to the bad should feel no shame nor think himself a poor statesman. This remark was *reported* to Critias. . . ." (Xenophon, *Memorabilia* I.2.32–33.)

The Gospel and Culture

Eric Voegelin

The steering committee has honored me with the invitation to give a lecture on "the gospel and culture." If I have understood the intention of the committee correctly, they wanted to hear what a philosopher has to say about the Word's difficulty to make itself heard in our time and, if heard at all, to make itself intelligible to those who are willing to listen. Why could the gospel be victorious in the Hellenistic-Roman environment of its origin? Why did it attract an intellectual elite who restated the meaning of the gospel in terms of philosophy and, by this procedure, created a Christian doctrine? Why could this doctrine become the state religion of the Roman Empire? How could the church, having gone through this process of acculturation, survive the Roman Empire and become the chrysalis, as Toynbee has called it, of Western civilization?—And what has blighted this triumphant cultural force, so that today the churches are on the defensive against the dominant intellectual movements of the time, and shaken by rising unrest from within?

Quite an order, I must say. Still, I have accepted it—for what use is philosophy if it has nothing to say about the great questions which the men of the time rightly may ask of it? But if you consider the magnitude of the challenge, you will understand that I can promise no more than a humble attempt to justify the committee's confidence and to save the honor of philosophy.

I

I have pointed the initial questions toward the issue of gospel and philosophy, and I shall begin by presenting an early and a recent instance in which the issue has become thematic.

By absorbing the life of reason in the form of Hellenistic philosophy, the gospel of the early *ekklēsia tou theou* has become the Christianity of the church. If the community of the gospel had not entered the culture of the time by entering its life of reason, it would have remained an obscure sect and probably disappeared from history; we know the fate of Judaeo-Christianity. The culture of reason, in its turn, had arrived at a state that was sensed by eager young men as an impasse in which the gospel appeared to offer the answer to the philosopher's search for truth; the introduction to Justin's *Dialogue* documents the situation. In the conception of Justin the Martyr (d. ca. 165), gospel and philosophy do not face the thinker with a choice of alternatives, nor are they complementary aspects of truth which the thinker would have to weld into the complete truth; in his conception, the Logos of the gospel is rather the same Word of the same God as the *logos spermatikos* of philosophy, but at a later state of its manifestation in history. The Logos has been operative in the world from its creation; all men who have lived according to reason, whether Greeks (Heraclitus, Socrates, Plato) or barbarians (Abraham, Elias), have in a sense been Christians (*Apology* I.46). Hence, Christianity is not an alternative to philosophy, it is philosophy itself in its state of perfection; the history of the Logos comes to its fulfillment through the incarnation of the Word in Christ. To Justin, the difference between gospel and philosophy is a matter of successive stages in the history of reason.

With this early statement of the issue in mind, we shall now examine a recent pronouncement on it. I take it from *De Nieuwe Katechismus* of 1966, commissioned by the hierarchy of the Netherlands and conventionally called the *Dutch Catechism.* Its opening chapter bears the title "Man the Questioner"; and on the first page we find the following passage:

> This book . . . begins by asking what is the meaning of the fact that we exist. This does not mean that we begin by taking up a non-Christian attitude. It simply means that we, too, as Christians, are men with enquiring minds. We must always be ready and able to explain how our faith is the answer to the question of our existence.

The passage, though wanting in polish, is philosophy very much to the point. Its well-intentioned clumsiness sheds a flood of light on the difficulties in which the churches find themselves today. Note above all the difficulty the church has with its own believers who want to be Christians at the price of their humanity. Justin started as an inquiring mind and let his search, after it had tried the philosophical schools of the time, come to rest in the truth of the gospel. Today the situation is reversed. The believers are at rest in an uninquiring state of faith; their intellectual metabolism must be stirred by the reminder that man is supposed to be a questioner, that a believer who is unable to explain how his faith is an answer to the enigma of existence may be a "good Christian" but is a questionable man. And we may supplement the reminder by gently recalling that neither Jesus nor his fellowmen to whom he spoke his word did yet know that they were Christians—the gospel held out its promise, not to Christians, but to the poor in the spirit, that is, to minds inquiring, even though on a culturally less sophisticated level than Justin's. Behind the passage there lurks the conflict, not between gospel and philosophy, but rather between the gospel and its uninquiring possession as doctrine. The authors of the *Catechism* do not take this conflict lightly; they anticipate resistance to their attempt at finding the common humanity of men in their being the questioners about the meaning of existence; and they protect themselves against all too ready misunderstandings by assuring the reader they do not mean "to take up a non-Christian attitude." Assuming them to have carefully weighed every sentence they wrote, this defensive clause reveals an environment where it is not customary to ask questions, where the character of the gospel as an answer has been so badly obscured by its hardening into self-contained doctrine that the raising of the question to which it is meant as an answer can be suspect as "a non-Christian attitude." If that, however, is the situation, the authors have good reason to be worried indeed. For the gospel as a doctrine which you can take and be saved, or leave and be condemned, is a dead letter; it will encounter indifference, if not contempt, among inquiring minds outside the church, as well as the restlessness of the believer inside who is un-Christian enough to be man the questioner.

The *Catechism*'s intent to restore the inquiring mind to the position that is his due is a sensible first step toward regaining for the gospel the reality it has lost through doctrinal hardening. Moreover, however hesitant and tentative it may prove in the execution, the attempt is a first step toward regaining the life of reason represented by philosophy. Both Plato's eroticism of the search (*zētēsis*) and Aristotle's intellectually more aggressive *aporein* recognize in "man the questioner" the man moved by God to ask the questions that will lead him toward the cause (*archē*) of being. The search itself is the evidence of existential unrest; in the act of questioning, man's experience of his tension (*tasis*) toward the divine ground breaks forth in the word of inquiry as a prayer for the Word of the answer. Question and answer are intimately related one toward the other; the search moves in the *metaxy,* as Plato has called it, in the In-Between of poverty and wealth, of human and divine; the question is knowing, but its knowledge is yet the trembling of a question that may reach the true answer or miss it. This luminous search in which the finding of the true answer depends on asking the true question, and the asking of the true question on the spiritual apprehension of the true answer, is the life of reason. The philosopher can only be delighted by the *Catechism*'s admonition to make "faith" accountable in terms of an answer to questions about the meaning of existence.

Question and answer are held together, and related to one another, by the event of the search. Man, however, though he is truly the questioner, can also deform his humanity by refusing to ask the questions, or by loading them with premises devised to make the search impossible. The gospel, to be heard, requires ears that can hear; philosophy is not the life of reason if the questioner's reason is depraved (Rom. 1:28). The answer will not help the man who has lost the question; and the predicament of the present age is characterized by the loss of the question rather than of the answer, as the authors of the *Catechism* have seen rightly. It will be necessary, therefore, to recover the question to which, in Hellenistic-Roman culture, the philosopher could understand the gospel as the answer.

Since the question concerns the humanity of man, it is the same today as it ever has been in the past, but today it is so badly distorted through the Western deculturation process that it must, first, be disentangled from the intellectually disordered language in which we indiscriminately speak of the meaning of life, or the meaning of existence, or the fact of existence which has no meaning, or the meaning which must be given to the fact of existence, and so forth, as if life were a given and meaning a property it has or does not have.

Well, existence is not a fact. If anything, existence is the nonfact of a disturbing movement in the In-Between of ignorance and knowledge, of time and timelessness, of imperfection and perfection, of hope and fulfillment, and ultimately of life and death. From the experience of this movement, from the anxiety of losing the right direction in this In-Between of darkness and light, arises the inquiry concerning the meaning of life. But it does arise only because life is experienced as man's participation in a movement with a direction to be found or missed; if man's existence were not a movement but a fact, it not only would have no meaning but the question of meaning could not even arise. The connection between movement and inquiry can best be seen in the case of its deformation by certain existentialist thinkers. An intellectual like Sartre, for instance, finds himself involved in the conflict without issue between his assumption of a meaningless facticity of existence and his desperate craving for endowing it with a meaning from the resources of his *moi.* He can cut himself off from the philosopher's inquiry by assuming existence to be a fact, but he cannot escape from his existential unrest. If the search is prohibited from moving in the In-Between, if as a consequence it cannot be directed toward the divine ground of being, it must be directed toward a meaning imagined by Sartre. The search, thus, imposes its form even when its substance is lost; the imagined fact of existence cannot remain as meaningless as it is but must become the launching pad for the intellectual's ego.

This imaginative destruction of reason and reality is not Sartre's idiosyncrasy; it has representative character in history, because it is recognizably a phase in a process of thought whose mode has been set by Descartes. The *Meditations,* it is true, belongs still to the culture of the search, but Descartes has deformed the movement by reifying its partners into objects for an Archimedean observer outside the search. In the conception of the new, doctrinaire metaphysics, the man who experiences himself as the questioner is turned into a *res cogitans* whose *esse* must be inferred from its *cogitare;* and the God for whose answer we are hoping and waiting is turned into the object for an ontological proof of his existence. The movement of the search, furthermore, the eroticism of existence in the In-Between of divine and human, has become a *cogitare* demonstrating its objects; the luminosity of the life of reason has changed into the clarity of the *raisonnement.* From the reality of the search, thus, as it disintegrates in the *Meditations,* there are set free the three specters which haunt the Western scene to this day. There is, first, the God who has been thrown out of the search and is no longer permitted to answer questions: living in retirement from the life of reason he has shriveled into an object of unreasoned faith; and at appropriate intervals he is declared to be dead. There is, second, the *cogitare* of the Archimedean observer outside the movement: it has swollen into the monster of Hegel's Consciousness which has brought forth a God, man, and history of its own; this monster is still engaged in the desperate fight to have its dialectical movement accepted as real in place of the real movement of the search in the In-Between. And, finally, there is the man of the Cartesian *cogito ergo sum:* he has sadly come down in the world, being reduced as he is to the fact and figure of the Sartrean *sum ergo cogito*; the man who once could demonstrate not only himself but even the existence of God has become the man who is condemned to be free and urgently wants to be arrested for editing a Maoist journal.

The reflections on the search and its deformation in our time have been carried sufficiently far to allow for a few conclusions concerning the question and its recovery. First of all, the blight of deculturation has affected philosophy at least as badly as it has the gospel. An acculturation through the introduction of contemporary philosophy into the life of the church, the feat of the *patres* in the Hellenistic-Roman environment, would today be impossible, for neither have the churches any use for deformed reason nor do the representatives of deformation ask the questions to which the gospel offers the answer. Second, however, the situation is not quite so helpless as it may appear, for the question is present in the time even when reason is deformed. The search imposes its form even when its substance is rejected; the dominant *philosophoumena* of the time are intelligibly the debris of the search. Deculturation does not constitute a new society, or a new age in history; it is a process within our society, very much present to the public consciousness and arousing resistance. As a matter of fact, in these very lines I am analyzing the phenomenon of deformed reason, and recognizing it as such, by the criteria of undeformed reason; and I can do it because the Western culture of reason is quite alive enough, appearances notwithstanding, to furnish the criteria for characterizing its own deformation. This last observation will, in the third place, dispose of the ideological propagation of deculturation processes as a "new age." We do not live in a "post-Christian," or "postphilosophical," or "neopagan," age, or in the age of a "new myth," or of "utopianism," but plainly in a period of massive deculturation through the deformation of reason. Deformation, however, is not an alternative to, or an advance beyond, formation. One can speak of a differentiating advance in the luminosity of the search from myth to philosophy, or from myth to revelation, but one cannot speak of a pattern of differentiating progress from reason to unreason. Nevertheless, and fourth, the deculturation of the West is a historical phenomenon extending over centuries; the grotesque rubble into which the image of God is broken today is not somebody's wrong opinion about the nature of man but the result of a secular process of destruction. This character of the situation must be realized if one does not want to be derailed into varieties of action which, though suggestive, would hardly prove remedial. The question of the search cannot be recovered by stirring around in the rubble; its recovery is not a matter of small repairs, of putting a patch on here or there, of criticizing this or that author whose work is a symptom of deculturation rather than its cause, and so forth. Nor will the conflict be resolved by the famous dialogues where the partners do not step on each other's toes, less because of excessive gentility than because they don't know which toes need being stepped on. And least of all can anything be achieved by pitting right doctrine against wrong doctrine, for doctrinization precisely is the damage that has been inflicted on the movement of the search. There would be no doctrines of deformed existence today unless the search of both philosophy and the gospel had been overlaid by the late-medieval, radical doctrinization of both metaphysics and theology.

II

Only the millennial life of reason can dissolve its secular deformation. We do not have to stay in the ghetto of problems prescribed by the deformers as contemporary or modern. If the destruction can go back for centuries, we can go back for millennia to restore the question so badly damaged in our time.

The searching question for the meaning of life finds its classic expression, in fifth-century Greece, when Euripides develops the symbolism of the double meaning of life and death:

> Who knows if to live is to be dead,
> and to be dead to live.

Plato resumes the lines of Euripides in the *Gorgias* (492 e) and elaborates the symbolism in the myth of the judgment of the dead by which he concludes the dialogue. Jesus resumes the symbolism in the saying: "For whoever would save his life (*psychen*) will lose it; and whoever loses his life for my sake will find it. What, then will it profit a man, if he gains the whole world but has to suffer the destruction of his life?" (Matt. 16:25–26). Paul, finally, writes: "If you live according to the flesh, you are bound to die; but if by the spirit you put to death the deeds of the body, you will live" (Rom. 8:13). Variants could be multiplied. The earliest case known, though still couched in the language of the cosmological myth, is to be found in an Egyptian poem of the late third millennium B.C. But there must be remembered, because of its closeness to the gospel, the admonition of the Platonic Socrates, following the Myth of the Judgment of the Dead at the end of *Republic* (621 b–c): "The tale was saved . . . it will save us if we believe it . . . and keep our soul (*psychen*) undefiled. If we are persuaded by me, we shall believe the soul to be immortal . . . and so we shall hold ever to the upward way, pursuing righteousness with wisdom, so that we may be dear to ourselves and to the gods." Paul Shorey is right when, in his translation of the *Republic,* he adds a footnote to the phrase "keep our soul undefiled," referring to the parallels in James 1:27 and 2 Peter 3:14.

There is direction in existence; and as we follow it or not, life can be death, and death be life eternal. The philosophers were conscious of having gained this insight representatively for mankind. The question expressed by the double meaning of life and death is the question of everyman's, not only the philosopher's, existence. Hence, in the *Republic,* the tale that was saved and now is told by Socrates is attributed to Er the Pamphylian, the man of all tribes, or of the tribe of Everyman, who came back from death and told his fellowmen of the judgment he had witnessed in the underworld. Everyman can lose himself in the tangle of existence and, having returned from its death to life, can tell the tale of its meaning. Moreover, behind the tale there stands the authority of the representative death suffered by Socrates for its truth. The *Apology* concludes with the ironic parting word to the judges: "But now the time has come to go. I go to die, and you to live. But who goes to the better lot is unknown to anyone but the God."

The new insight became socially effective through the monument Plato erected to it in his work. By the time of Christ, four centuries later, it had become the self-understanding of man in the culture of the Hellenistic-Roman *oikumenē;* and again the universal truth of existence had to be linked with a representative death: the dramatic episode of John 12 is the Christian equivalent to the philosopher's *Apology.* The evangelist reports the triumphant entrance of Jesus in Jerusalem. The story of Lazarus has spread, and the crowd presses to see and hail the man who can raise the dead to life. The Jewish authorities want to take measures against him, because he draws the people away from them, but for the moment they must be cautious: "You see you can do nothing; look, the world (*kosmos*) is running after him!" This world of the Jewish authorities, however, is not the ecumenic world Jesus wants to draw to himself. Only when a group of Greeks approaches Philip and Andrew, and these apostles with the Greek names tell Jesus about the desire of the Greeks to see him, can he reply: "Now the hour has come for the Son of Man to be glorified" (12:23). The Greeks are coming—mankind is ready to be represented by the divine sacrifice. The Johannine Jesus can, therefore, continue:

> Most solemnly I tell you,
> unless a wheat grain falls into the earth and dies, it remains
> only a single grain,
> but if it dies, it bears much fruit.
> Who loves his life (*psychen*) loses it,
> but who hates his life in this world (*kosmos*), keeps it for
> life eternal.
> If anyone serves me, he must follow me,
> and wherever I am, my servant will be too.
> If anyone serves me, my Father will honor him.

In the Synoptic Gospels, as in the *Gorgias* and *Republic,* the question of life and death appears only in the forms of insight, persuasion, and admonition (Matt. 10:39, 16:25; Luke 14:26, 17:33); in John 12, as in the *Apology,* it is lived through by the representative sufferer, so that the insight becomes the truth of existence in reality by the authority of death. Even the daimonion that sustained Socrates in his course by not raising its warning voice has its equivalent in the reflection of Jesus:

> Now my soul is troubled. What shall I say?
> Father, save me from this hour?
> No, for this purpose I have come to this hour.
> Father, glorify your name.

To the prayer of submission by the troubled soul heaven answered with a roll of thunder—historians still are not sure whether the thunderer was Zeus or Yahweh—and to those who had ears to hear, the thunder came as a voice: "I have glorified it, and I will glorify it again." Assured by the thundering voice, Jesus can conclude:

> Now Judgment (*krisis*) has come to this world (*kosmos*),
> now the ruler of this world will be cast out.
> And I, when I am lifted up from this earth,
> will draw all men to myself.

The appearance of the Greeks is peculiar to John; we do not find them in the Synoptic Gospels. The interpretation I have given relies on John's literary form of letting a narrative of events or signs be followed by the exposition of their meaning through the response of Jesus, but the reader should be aware that most commentators tend to play down the Greeks, in order to assimilate the intent of John 12 to the Synoptic tradition. Still, I see no reason why the author should be denied the courtesy of having his literary work be taken seriously at the letter of the text just because his work is a gospel. The episode of John 12 expresses a Hellenistic-ecumenic conception of the drama of existence, culminating in the sacrificial death of Christ. It receives its peculiar atmosphere from the pregnostic play with the meanings of the word *kosmos*. In the usage of the Jewish authorities, the *kosmos* who runs after Jesus (12:19) probably means no more than *tout le monde*. With the appearance of the Greeks (12:20–22), the meaning grows toward the mankind of the *oikumenē*. With the hatred of one's life (*psychē*) in this world (12:25), the *kosmos* becomes a habitat from which this life must be saved for eternity. And in the concluding words (12:31), the *kosmos* is the domain of the prince of this world from whose rule Jesus, when he is "lifted up," will draw all men to himself, leaving the satanic *archōn* a ruler without a people. Jesus has become the rival of the *archōn* in a cosmic struggle for the rule of men. But is that not gnosticism? It would be rash to indulge in the assumption, for John moves the episode as a whole, including both the narrative and its exegesis by Jesus' response, into the literary position of a narrative on which a further exegetic response of Jesus is superimposed. In this superimposed response, Jesus emphatically declares (*ekrazen*):

> I, the light, have come into the world (*kosmos*),
> that whoever believes in me need not remain in darkness.
> If anyone hears my words and does not heed them, I do not judge him,
> for I have not come to judge the world (*kosmos*), but to save the world (*kosmos*).
> Who rejects me, and does not accept my words, has what judges him:

> The word I have spoken will be the word that judges him
> on the Last Day.
>
> (12:44)

The meaning of the *kosmos* reverts from the habitat to the inhabitants who are not to be evacuated but to be saved. From the cosmic struggle of *archōn* and Redeemer we return to the drama of existence—the light of the word has come into the darkness, saving those who believe it, and carrying judgment for those who close their eyes to it. At the present stage of the analysis, it would be difficult to find a major difference of function between Plato's Pamphylian tale of the last judgment and John's Last Day.

The search in the In-Between moves from the question of life and death to the answer in the Saving Tale. The question, however, does not arise from a vacuum, but from a field of reality, and points toward answers of a certain type; and the Saving Tale, be it Plato's Pamphylian myth or John's Gospel, is not an answer given at random, but must recognizably fit the reality of existence which in the question is presupposed as truly experienced. Question and answer are intimately related to one another in the movement as an intelligible whole. This relationship, which constitutes the truth of the tale, requires further analysis.

The double meaning of life and death is the symbolism engendered by man's experience of his being pulled in various directions among which he has to choose the right one. Plato has identified the plurality of pulls, the necessity of choosing among them, and the possibility of knowing the right one, as the complex of experiences from which arises the question of life and death. Corresponding to the variety of pulls, there can be distinguished a variety of existential modes and habits as we follow the one or the other. "When opinion leads through reason (*logos*) toward the best (*ariston*) and is more powerful, its power is called self-restraint (*sophrosyne*), but when desire (*epithymia*) drags us (*helkein*) toward pleasures and rules within us, its rule is called excess (*hubris*)" (*Phaedrus* 238 a). The pulls are in conflict, dragging us up or down. A young man may be "drawn (*helkein*) toward philosophy" (*Republic* 494 e), but social pressure may divert him toward a life of pleasure or success in politics. If he follows the second pull, however, the question of meaning is not settled for him, for the first pull continues to be experienced as part of his existence. By following the second pull he does not transform his existence into a question-free fact, but into a recognizably questionable course of life. He will sense the life he leads as "not his own and true life" (495 c)—he will live in a state of alienation. The play of the pulls, thus, is luminous with truth. By following the wrong course one does not make it the right one, but slides into existence in untruth. This luminosity of existence with the truth of reason precedes all opinions and decisions about the pull to be followed. Moreover, it remains alive as the judgment of truth in existence whatever opinions about it we may actually form.

The terms *seeking* (*zētein*) and *drawing* (*helkein*) do not denote two different movements but symbolize the dynamics in the tension of existence between its human and divine poles. In the one movement there is experienced a seeking from the human, a being drawn from the divine pole. I am deliberately avoiding the language of man and God at this point, because today these symbols are loaded with various doctrinal contents which derive from the insights which, in their turn, are the results of the existential movement that we call classic philosophy. Only from the travail of this movement there emerges man as the questioner, Aristotle's *aporon* and *thaumazon* (*Metaphysics* 982 b 18), and God as the mover who attracts or draws man to himself, as in Plato's *Laws* X or Aristotle's *Metaphysics*. These new insights into man's humanity and God's divinity which mark the end of the classic search must not be projected back into its beginning as doctrinal premises, or the reality of the process from which the answering symbols derive their truth would be eclipsed, if not destroyed. There is a long way from the compact experiences which engender the Homeric mortals and immortals to the differentiated movement of existence in the In-Between which Aristotle characterizes as an *athanatizein*, as an act of immortalizing (*Nicomachean Ethics* X.7, 8)—in historical time about as long as the way from classic philosophy to the gospel. The two components of the movement, now, need not always hold each other in the balance in which Plato keeps them in the construction of the dialogues where he demonstrates, for the pedagogical purpose of persuasion, the process and methods of seeking which lead to the right answer. Behind the dialogues, there stands the author who has found the answer before he engages in the work of literary composition; and his, as well as Socrates', way of finding it was not necessarily the way of dialogical persuasion. What happens in the life of the man who emerges from the movement of existence as the *paidagōgos* for his fellowmen can be apprehended rather in such episodes as the Parable of the Cave. There Plato lets the man who is fettered with his face to the wall be dragged up (*helkein*) by force to the light (*Republic* 515 e). The accent lies on the violence suffered by the man in the Cave, on his passivity and even resistance to being turned around (*periagōgē*), so that the ascent to light is less an action of seeking than a fate inflicted. If we accept this suffering of being dragged up as a realistic description of the movement, the parable evokes the passion of the Socrates who tells it: his being dragged up to the light by the God; his suffering the death for the light when he returns to let his fellowmen have their share in it; and his rising from the dead to live as the teller of the saving tale. Moreover, this passion of the parable evokes, if I may anticipate, the passion of conversion inflicted on the resisting Paul by Christ through the vision on the road to Damascus.

In Plato's experience, the suffering overshadows the action in the search so strongly that it becomes difficult to translate the *pathos* in his *tauta ta pathē en hemin* (*Laws* 644 e), "all these *pathē* in us." Does this *pathos* express only the experience of the pull (*helkein*) that gives direction to the search, or does it want to acknowledge the movement as so strongly tinged by suffering that the terms *experience* and *passion* approach synonymity? The context in which the passage appears, the Myth of the Puppet Player, leaves no doubt that the uncertainty is caused by Plato's exploration of the field of existential tension beyond the movement of the search that finds its fulfillment in the saving tale. For the surer we are of knowing the true answer to the question of life and death, the more puzzling it becomes that there should be a question at all. Why is the prisoner fettered in the Cave in the first place? Why must the force that binds him be overcome by a counterforce that turns him around? Why must the man who ascended to the light return to the Cave to suffer death at the hands of those who did not leave it? Why does not everybody leave, so that the Cave as an establishment of existence would be abandoned? Beyond the search that receives direction from the pull (*helkein*) of reason there extends the larger existential field of "counterpulling," of *anthelkein* (*Laws* 644–45). Behind the question to which the saving tale is the answer there looms the darker question why it remains the question of existence even when the answer is found. To these questions arising from the structure of "counterpulling" in existence Plato has given his answer in the symbolism of man as a puppet made by gods, "possibly as a plaything, possibly with a more serious purpose, but that we cannot know," and now being pulled by various cords toward opposite actions. On man it is incumbent always to follow the golden and sacred cord of judgment (*logismos*) and not the other cords of lesser metals. The component of human action, thus, has not disappeared from the movement, but it has now been fitted into the larger play of pull and counterpull. For the pull of the golden cord is gentle, without violence; in order to prevail in existence it needs the support of man who must counterpull (*anthelkein*) to the counterpull of the lesser cords. Man's self (*autos*) is introduced as the force which must decide the struggle of the pulls through cooperation with the sacred pull of reason (*logos*) and judgment (*logismos*). In brief: Rebellious questioners who want to complain about the structure of existence, in which the Cave persists to exert its pull even when the saving tale is found, are given the same brush-off they were given by an earlier great realist, by Jeremiah:

> Behold! What I have built, I will pull down;
> and what I have planned, I will tear up—
> and you seek great things for yourself?
> Seek them not!
> For behold! I will bring evil upon all flesh—
> says Yahweh—
> But your life will I give you, as a prize of war,
> in every place where you go.
>
> (45:4–5)

Life is given as a prize of war. Who wants to save his life in it will lose it. The Saving Tale is not a recipe for the abolition of the *anthelkein* in existence but the confirmation of life through death in this war. The death of Socrates which, just as the death of Jesus, could have been physically avoided, is representative because it authenticates the truth of reality.

These reflections have clarified the problem of truth so far that no more is needed than an explicit statement of the insights implied.

Neither is there a question vainly looking for an answer, nor is there a truth of the Saving Tale, imposing itself from nowhere on a fact of existence. The movement in the In-Between is indeed an intelligible whole of question and answer, with the experience of the movement engendering the language symbols for its expression. As far as the experiences are concerned, the movement has no "contents" other than its questioning, the *pathē* of pull and counterpull, the directional indices of the pulls, and the consciousness of itself that we have called its luminosity; as far as the symbols are concerned, they have nothing to express but the experiences enumerated, the placement of the reality experienced in the wider context of the reality in which the differentiated movement occurs, and the self-conscious movement as an event in man's existence in society and history in which hitherto it has not occurred. Such difficulties of understanding as these insights frequently encounter in the contemporary climate of deculturation are caused by the habits of hypostatizing and dogmatizing. The symbols developed in the movement, I want to stress therefore, do not refer to objects in external reality, but to the phases of the movement as it becomes articulate in its self-illuminating process. There is no In-Between other than the *metaxy* experienced in a man's existential tension toward the divine ground of being; there is no question of life and death other than the question aroused by pull and counterpull; there is no Saving Tale other than the tale of the divine pull to be followed by man; and there is no cognitive articulation of existence other than the noetic consciousness in which the movement becomes luminous to itself.

A further difficulty of understanding is encountered by the insight that the symbols belong as much to the In-Between as do the experiences symbolized. There is not, first, a movement in the In-Between and, second, a human observer, perhaps the philosopher, who records his observations of the movement. The reality of existence, as experienced in the movement, is a mutual participation (*methexis, metalēpsis*) of human and divine; and the language symbols expressing the movement are not invented by an observer who does not participate in the movement but are engendered in the event of participation itself. The ontological status of the symbols is both human and divine. Plato stresses that his Myth of the Puppet Player is an *alēthēs logos,* a true story, whether the *logos* be "received from a God, or from a man who knows" (*Laws* 645 b); and the same double status of the "word" is acknowledged by the prophets when they promulgate their sayings as the "word" of Yahweh, as in the Jeremiah passage previously quoted. This double status of the symbols which express the movement in the *metaxy* has been badly obscured in Western history by Christian theologians who have split the two components of symbolic truth, monopolizing, under the title of "revelation," for Christian symbols the divine component, while assigning, under the title of "natural reason," to philosophical symbols the human component. This theological doctrine is empirically untenable—Plato was just as conscious of the revelatory component in the truth of his *logos* as the prophets of Israel or the authors of the New Testament writings. The differences between prophecy, classic philosophy, and the gospel must be sought in the degrees of differentiation of existential truth.

There are, finally, in the climate of deculturation, the difficulties of understanding encountered by the problems of mythical imagination. Myth is not a primitive symbolic form, peculiar to early societies and progressively to be overcome by positive science, but the language in which the experiences of human-divine participation in the In-Between become articulate. The symbolization of participating existence, it is true, evolves historically from the more compact form of the cosmological myth to the more differentiated forms of philosophy, prophecy, and the gospel, but the differentiating insight, far from abolishing the *metaxy* of existence, brings it to fully articulate knowledge. When existence becomes noetically luminous as the field of pull and counterpull, of the question of life and death, and of the tension between human and divine reality, it also becomes luminous for divine reality as the Beyond of the *metaxy* which reaches into the *metaxy* in the participatory event of the movement. There is no In-Between of existence as a self-contained object but only existence experienced as part of a reality which extends beyond the In-Between. This experience of the Beyond (*epekeina*) of existence experienced, this consciousness of the Beyond of consciousness which constitutes consciousness by reaching into it, is the area of reality which articulates itself through the symbols of mythical imagination. The imaginative play of the *alēthēs logos* is the "word" through which the divine Beyond of existence becomes present in existence as its truth. The Saving Tale can be differentiated beyond classic philosophy, as it has historically happened through Christ and the gospel, but there is no alternative to the symbolization of the In-Between of existence and its divine Beyond by mythical imagination. The speculative systems of the Comtian, Hegelian, and Marxian type, favored today as alternatives, are not "science" but deformations of the life of reason through the magic practice of self-divination and self-salvation.

III

The God who plays with man as a puppet is not the God who becomes man to gain his life by suffering his death. The movement that engendered the Saving Tale of divine incarnation, death, and resurrection as the answer to the question of life and death is considerably more complex than classic philosophy; it is richer by the missionary fervor of its spiritual universalism, poorer by its neglect of noetic control; broader by its appeal to the inarticulate humanity of the common man; more restricted by its bias against the articulate wisdom of the wise; more imposing through its imperial tone of divine authority; more imbalanced through its apocalyptic ferocity, which leads to conflicts with the conditions of man's existence in society; more compact through its generous absorption of earlier strata of mythical imagination, especially through the reception of Israelite historiogenesis and the exuberance of miracle working; more differentiated through the intensely articulate experience of loving-divine action in the illumination of existence with truth. The understanding of these complexities by which the gospel movement differs from the movement of classic philosophy, though, cannot be advanced by using such topical dichotomies as philosophy and religion, metaphysics and theology, reason and revelation, natural reason and supernaturalism, rationalism and irrationalism, and so forth. I shall rather proceed by, first, establishing the noetic core the two movements have in common and by, second, exploring some of the problems which arise from the differentiation of divine action in the gospel movement, as well as from the reception of more compact strata of experience and symbolization.

The analysis will have to start at the point where the gospel agrees with classic philosophy in symbolizing existence as a field of pulls and counterpulls. I have previously quoted John 12:32 where the author lets Christ say that he will, when he is lifted up from the earth, draw (*helkein*) all men to himself. In John 6:44, then, this drawing power of Christ is identified with the pull exerted by God: "No one can come to me unless the Father who sent me draws (*helkein*) him." More austere on this point than the Synoptic evangelists, John makes it, furthermore, clear that there is no "message" of Christ but the event of the divine Logos becoming present in the world through the representative life and death of a man. The closing words of the great prayer before the Passion express the substance of this event:

> Father, Righteous One,
> the world has not known you, but I have known you,
> and they know that you have sent me.
> To them I have made known your name, and shall make it known,
> that the love by which you loved me will be in them, and I in them.
>
> (17:25–26)

To follow Christ means to continue the event of divine presence in society and history: "As you have sent me into the world, so I have sent them into the world" (17:18). And finally, since there is no doctrine to be taught but only the story to be told of God's pull becoming effective in the world through Christ, the Saving Tale that answers the question of life and death can be reduced to the brief statement:

> And this is life eternal:
> To know you, the only true God,
> and Jesus Christ whom you have sent.
> (17:3)

With an admirable economy of means, John symbolizes the pull of the golden cord, its occurrence as a historical event in the representative man, the illumination of existence through the movement from the question of life and death initiated by the pull to the saving answer, the creation of a social field through the transmission of the insight to the followers, and ultimately the duties incumbent on John to promulgate the event to mankind at large through writing the gospel as a literary document: "Now Jesus did many other signs in the presence of the disciples which are not recorded in this book. Those recorded, however, were written down so that you may believe that Jesus is the Christ, the Son of God, and that believing this you may have life in his name" (20:30–31). One can imagine how a young student of philosophy, who wanted to work himself out of the various doctrinal impasses into which the school philosophers of the time had maneuvered themselves, could be fascinated by the brilliance of these succinct statements that must have appeared to him as the perfection of the Socratic-Platonic movement in the In-Between of existence.

The symbol *helkein* is peculiar to John; it does not occur elsewhere in the New Testament. In the letters of Paul, the component of knowledge in the movement, the luminosity of its consciousness, dominates so strongly that the *pathos* of the pull is symbolized as a divine act of knowing which forcibly grips a man and illuminates his existence. In 2 Corinthians 4:6, Paul writes: "The God who said 'let light shine out of darkness' is the God who shone in our hearts to make them luminous (or: resplendent, *phōtismos*) with the knowledge (*gnōsis*) of God's glory, the glory on the face of Christ." The glory radiating on the face of Christ is the *phōtismos* on the face of the man who has seen God. Moses had still to hide it with a veil until it had faded; this veil that covered the Old Covenant of written letters has been drawn away from the New Covenant written by the spirit (*pneuma*) in the heart; "and we, with our unveiled faces, reflecting the brightness of the Lord, all grow brighter and brighter as we are turned into the image that we reflect" (2 Cor. 3:18).

That the resplendence of knowledge in the heart has its origin in divine action is explicitly stated in such passages as 1 Corinthians 8:1–3:

> We know that "all of us possess knowledge (*gnōsis*)."
> Knowledge (*gnōsis*) puffs up, love (*agapē*) builds up.
> If any one imagines he knows something, he does not yet
>   know as he ought to know.
> But if one loves God, one is known by him.

The words are addressed to members of the Corinthian community who "possess knowledge" as doctrine and unwisely apply it as a rule of conduct; such possessors of truth are reminded that the knowledge which forms existence without deforming it is God's knowledge of man. In a similar admonition to the Galatians Paul writes:

> Formerly, when you did not know God, you were enslaved to beings who are not really gods at all; but now that you have come to know God—or rather to be known by God—how can you want to return to the weak and beggarly elemental spirits and be their slaves?
> (Gal. 4:8–9)

The occasions which motivate Paul to clarify the dynamics of *gnōsis* in existence differ widely from the situation in which the classic philosophers do their differentiating work. In 2 Corinthians he wants to set off the radiance of the pneumatic covenant written in the heart against the more compact, "veiled" truth of the Law of Moses, using for this purpose a symbolism he takes from the prophets; in 1 Corinthians he has to warn off "idolothytes," men who are willing to partake of food sacrificed to idols, because they feel secure in their knowledge that the idols are no gods anyway; and in Galatians he has to issue a call to order to believers who relapse into their former worship of elemental spirits. This all too obvious difference of cultural context, however, must not obscure the fact that Paul strives to articulate a dynamics of existential knowledge which Aristotle compressed in the formula that human thought (*nous*) in search of the divine ground of being is moved (*kinetai*) by the divine Nous who is the object of thought (*noeton*) of the human Nous (*Metaphysics* 1072 a 30f.).

The noetic core, thus, is the same in both classic philosophy and the gospel movement. There is the same field of pull and counterpull, the same sense of gaining life through following the pull of the golden cord, the same consciousness of existence in an In-Between of human-divine participation, and the same experience of divine reality as the center of action in the movement from question to answer. Moreover, there is the same consciousness of newly differentiated insights into the meaning of existence; and in both cases this consciousness constitutes a new field of human types in history which Plato describes as, first, the spiritual man (*daimonios anēr*) in whom the movement occurs; second, the man of the earlier, more compact type of existence, the mortal (*thnētos*) in the Homeric sense; and third, the man who reacts negatively to the appeal of the movement, the dullard or foolish man (*amathēs*).

Though the noetic core is the same in the gospel, its spiritual dynamics has radically changed through the experience of an extraordinary divine irruption in the existence of Jesus. This irruption, through which Jesus becomes the Christ, is expressed by the author of Colossians in the words: "For in him the whole fullness of divine reality (*theotēs*) dwells bodily" (2:9). In its whole fullness (*pan to plērōma*), divine reality is present only in Christ, who, by virtue of this fullness, "is the image (*eikōn*) of the unseen God, the firstborn of all creation" (1:15). All other men have no more than their ordinary share of this fullness (*pepleromenoi*) through accepting the truth of its full presence in the Christ, who, by his iconic existence, is "the head of all rule (*archē*) and authority (*exousia*)" (2:10). Something about Jesus must have impressed his contemporaries as an existence in the *metaxy* of such intensity that his bodily presence, the *sōmatikos* of the passage, appeared to be fully permeated by divine presence.

The passage is precious, because the author has succeeded in conveying his impression without recourse to older, more compact symbols, such as the Son of God, which would not have done justice to the newly differentiated experience. This must have required a conscious effort on his part, for the term *theotēs* is a neologism coined by him for this occasion. To the various translations as *godhead, divinity,* or *deity,* which carry the implication of a personal God, I have preferred *divine reality* because it renders best the author's intention to denote a nonpersonal reality which allows for degrees of participation in its fullness while remaining the God beyond the In-Between of existence. If the author belonged to the Pauline "school," one can understand his symbol *theotēs* as an attempt to overcome certain imperfections in Paul's symbol *theiotēs.* In Romans 1:18ff., Paul speaks of the men who suppress the truth of God by their impiety and injustice: "For what can be known about God (*to gnōston tou theou*) is manifest in them, because God has made it manifest to them. For ever since the cosmos was made, God's invisible reality could be perceived by the mind (*nooumana*) in the things that were made, that is his everlasting power (*dynamis*) and divinity (*theiotēs*)." Paul is a quite impatient man. He wants the divine reality of the primary experience of the cosmos right away differentiated as the world-transcendent divinity that has become incarnate in Christ; he considers it inexcusable that mankind should have passed through a phase in history when the immortal God was represented by images "of mortal men, of birds, quadrupeds, and reptiles"; and he can explain such horror only by a deliberate suppression of the well-known truth. Moreover, in his Jewish disgust with pagan idols he makes the historical phenomenon of the cosmological myth responsible for cases of dissolute life he can observe in his environment and considers further adherence to them, with consequent moral dissolution, God's punishment for having indulged in idolatry in the first place (Rom. 1:26–32). Such zealous confusion of problems certainly needed to be disentangled; and the author of Colossians indeed extracted from the Pauline passage the distinction between the divine "invisibles" and the "visibles" of participatory experiences; he distinguished the invisible God, experienced as real beyond the *metaxy* of existence, from the *theotēs,* the divine reality which enters the *metaxy* in the movement of existence.

The distinction, it is true, was already made in *Theaetetus* 176 b, where Plato describes the purpose of man's flight from the evils of the world as the acquisition of the *homoiōsis theo kata to dynaton,* a becoming like God as far as that is possible. Nevertheless, though Plato's *homoiōsis theo* is the exact equivalent to the filling with *theotēs* by the author of Colossians, Plato's spiritual man, the *daimonios anēr,* is not the Christ of Colossians, the *eikōn tou theou.* Plato reserves iconic existence to the Cosmos itself: The cosmos is the image (*eikōn*) of the Eternal; it is the visible god (*theos aisthētos*) in the image of the Intelligible (*eikōn tou noētou*); it is the one and only begotten (*monogenēs*) heaven whose divine father is so recondite that it would be impossible to declare him to all men (*Timaeus* 28–29, 92 c). In the contraposition of the *monogenēs theos* in Plato's *Timaeus* and John 1:18 the barrier becomes visible which the movement of classic philosophy cannot break through to reach the insights peculiar to the gospel.

The obstacle to further differentiation is not some disability peculiar to the classic movement, such as the limitation of natural reason unaided by revelation, a topic still favored by theologians who ought to know better, but the cosmological mode of experience and symbolization dominant in the culture in which the movement occurs. For the experience of the movement tends to dissociate the cosmic-divine reality of the primary experience into the contingent being of things and the necessary being of the world-transcendent God; and a culture in which the sacrality of order, both personal and social, is symbolized by intracosmic gods will not easily give way to the *theotēs* of the movement whose victory entails the desacralization of traditional order. Moreover, the rearticulation and resymbolization of reality at large in accordance with the truth of the movement is a formidable task requiring centuries of sustained effort. One can discern a strong existential movement, driving toward an understanding of the hidden divinity, the *agnōstos theos,* behind the intracosmic gods, for instance, in the Egyptian Amon Hymns of the thirteenth century B.C., at about the same time when Moses broke with the Pharaonic mediation of divine order to society through his effort of constituting a people in immediacy under God, and yet it took thirteen centuries of history, and the shattering events of successive imperial conquests, to make people receptive for the truth of the gospel. Even then the movement might have proved socially and historically abortive, unless the classic movement, as well as its continuation by the Hellenistic thinkers, had provided the noetic instrument for the resymbolization of reality beyond the restricted area of reality of the movement itself in accordance with the truth of the gospel; and even when the gospel, favored by this cultural constellation, had become socially effective, it took another twelve hundred years for the problem of contingent and necessary being to be articulated by the Scholastic thinkers. If "revelation" is taken seriously, if the symbol is meant to express the dynamics of divine presence in the movement, the mystery of its process in history will assume more formidable proportions than it had to Paul when he struggled, in Romans 9–11, with the mystery of Israel's resistance to the gospel.

The dynamics of the process are still imperfectly understood, because the spectacular breakthroughs in history leave in their wake a sediment of Before-and-After symbols which severely distort reality when they are used in the interpretation of cultural history; before philosophy there was myth; before Christianity there were pagan idols and the Jewish law; before monotheism there was polytheism; and before modern science, of course, there were such primitive superstitions as philosophy and the gospel, metaphysics and theology, which no self-respecting person should touch nowadays. Not everybody is as tolerant and intelligent as the Jesus who could say: "Think not I have come to dissolve the law and the prophets; I have come not to dissolve (*katalysai*) but to fulfill (*plērōsai*)" (Matt. 5:17).

This sediment of phenotypes ignores that, as a matter of historical record, the truth of reality is always fully present in man's experience and that what changes are the degrees of differentiation. Cosmological cultures are not a domain of primitive "idolatry," "polytheism," or "paganism," but highly sophisticated fields of mythical imagination, quite capable of finding the proper symbols for the concrete or typical cases of divine presence in a cosmos in which divine reality is omnipresent. Moreover, the cases symbolized are not experienced as unrelated oddities, each case forming a species of reality by itself, but definitely as "the gods," i.e., manifestations of the one divine reality that constitutes and pervades the cosmos. This consciousness of divine oneness behind the multitude of gods can express itself in the mythospeculative constructions of theogonies and cosmogonies which compactly symbolize both the oneness of divinity and the oneness of the world it has created. The gods of cosmological culture, one may say, have a foreground of specific and a background of universal divine presence; they are specific divinities who partake of universal divine reality.

I shall now place the gospel movement in the context of the revelatory process in which the Unknown God separates from the cosmological divinities.

In the previously mentioned Amon Hymns of Dynasty XIX, Amon "came into being at the beginning, so that his mysterious nature is unknown." Not even the other gods know his form who is "the marvelous god of many forms." "All other gods boast of him, to magnify themselves through his beauty, according as he is divine. Re himself is united with his body." "He is too mysterious that his majesty might be disclosed, he is too great that man should ask about him, too powerful that he might be known" (ANET, ed. Pritchard, 1950, p. 368). Behind the known gods, thus, there emerges the unknown god from whom they derive their divine reality. This unknown Amon, however, though he is in the process of being differentiated from the specific Amon of Thebes, is not one more god in the cosmological pantheon, but the *theotēs* of the movement which, in the further process of revelation, can be differentiated to its climactic revelation in Christ. Moreover, since the unknown god is not a new god but the divine reality experienced as present also in the known gods, the revelatory process is bound to become a source of cultural conflicts as the differentiation of its truth progresses. "War and battle," the opening words of the *Gorgias*, are caused by the appearance of Socrates; and Jesus says: "I have come to cast fire on the earth. . . . Do you think I have come to bring peace on earth? No, I tell you, but rather division" (Luke 12:49, 51). For the men engaged in the movement tend to raise the divine reality they experience to the rank of a god in the image of the known gods and to oppose this true god to the specific gods who are demoted to the rank of false gods, while the cosmological believers, who are sure of the true divinity of their gods, will accuse the carriers of the movement of atheism, or at least of subverting the sacral order of society through the introduction of new gods. This conflict is still fundamentally the issue between Celsus in his attack on Christianity and Origen in his *Contra Celsum.*

The Amon Hymns are the representative document of the movement at the stage where the splendor of the cosmological gods has become derivative, though the gods themselves have not yet become false. Seven hundred years later, in the Deutero-Isaianic equivalent to the Amon Hymns (Isa. 40:12–25), the gods have become man-made idols who no longer partake of divine reality, while the Unknown God has acquired the monopoly of divinity. The author visibly struggles with the dynamics of the new situation. On the one hand, his god is alone with himself and his *ruach* from the beginning (40:12–14), thus being properly unknown like Amon; on the other hand, he is a known god and even berates men for not knowing him as well as they should, very much in the manner of Paul berating the pagans for not knowing God though he has revealed himself in his creation:

> Have you not known? Have you not heard?
> Has it not been told you from the beginning?
> Have you not understood from the foundation of the earth?
> (40:21)

Both the authors of the Amon Hymns and Deutero-Isaiah recognize the in-the-beginning as the true criterion of divine reality—in this point there is indeed no difference between the documents under discussion and Aristotle's *prōtē archē* in the speculation on the etiological chain in *Metaphysics*—but in the Amon Hymns the accent falls on the *causa sui* in the divine Beginning, while in Deutero-Isaiah it falls on the *causa rerum,* though in neither case is the other component of the Beginning neglected. The *causa sui* is what makes the differentiated divine reality of the movement the *agnōstos theos;* the *causa rerum* is what makes it the god who is known through creation. When universal divine reality has been differentiated from its compactly experienced presence in the cosmological gods, it returns to the cultural scene as the God of creation who invalidates the intracosmic gods. The god who returns from the beginning into which he has disappeared, however, is no more the same than the man who emerges from the movement. In the Deutero-Isaianic prophecy, the Yahweh of Israel returns as the God of all mankind,

> who created the heavens and stretched them out,
> who spread forth the earth and what comes from it,
> who gives breath to the people (*am*) upon it
> and spirit to those who walk in it.
> (42:5)

And the prophet, indistinguishable from Israel herself, has become the Suffering Servant, given by God

> as a covenant to the people (*am*), a light to the nations,
> to open the eyes that are blind,
> to bring out the prisoners from the dungeon,
> from the prison those who sit in darkness.
> (42:6–7)

The treasurer of the queen of Ethiopia had traveled to Jerusalem to worship. In the episode of Acts 8:26–40 we find him on the way back, on the road to Gaza, sitting on his cart, pondering the passage in Deutero-Isaiah: "Like a sheep he was led away to the slaughter." An angel of the Lord sends the apostle Philip to meet him: "Do you understand what you are reading?" "How can I," the Ethiopian replied, "without someone to guide me? . . . About whom, pray, does the prophet say this, about himself or about someone else?" Then Philip began, reports the historian of the apostles, and starting from this passage explained to him the good news (*evangelisato*) of Jesus. The revelation of the Unknown God through Christ, in conscious continuity with the millennial process of revelation I have adumbrated, is so much the center of the gospel movement that it may be called the gospel itself. The god of John 1:1ff., who in the beginning is alone with his Logos, is the God of Deutero-Isaiah (40:13), who in the beginning is alone with his *ruach*; the Word that shines as a light in the darkness (John 1:5, 9:5) is the Suffering Servant who is given as a light to the nations, to bring out from the prison those who sit in darkness (Isa. 42:6–7); and in 1 John 1, the light that was the Father, by manifesting itself through Christ his Son, constitutes the community of those who walk in the light. The Unknown God himself, then, becomes thematic in Acts 17:16–34, in the Areopagus speech attributed by Luke to Paul. Praising the Athenians for having devoted an altar to the *Agnōstos Theos,* the Paul of the speech assures them that the god whom they worship without knowing who he is, is the very god he has come to proclaim (*katangello*) to them. In Deutero-Isaianic terms he describes him as the god who made the world and all that is in it and, therefore, is not like the gods of the "handmade" shrines (Isa. 40:12, 18–20), and furthermore, as the god of the mankind to whom he has given life and spirit (Isa. 42:5). He is near enough to us to be found, for "in him we live, and move, and have our being." He will overlook our ignorance of representing him by man-made idols in the past, but now he commands (*apangellei*) everybody to repent (*metanoein*), everybody is now called to know him as the true god who will sit in judgment through the man whom he has resurrected from the dead. More could be added, as the *Nunc dimittis* of Luke 2:29–32, but the passage quoted will be sufficient to establish the Unknown God as the god who is revealed through Christ.

IV

In the historical drama of revelation, the Unknown God ultimately becomes the God known through his presence in Christ. This drama, though it has been alive in the consciousness of the New Testament writers, is far from alive in the Christianity of the churches today, for the history of Christianity is characterized by what is commonly called the separation of school theology from mystical or experiential theology which formed an apparently inseparable unit still in the work of Origen. The Unknown God whose *theotēs* was present in the existence of Jesus has been eclipsed by the revealed God of Christian doctrine. Even today, however, when this unfortunate separation is recognized as one of the great causes of the modern spiritual crisis; when energetic attempts are made to cope with the problem through a variety of crisis and existential theologies; and when there is no lack of historical information about either the revelatory process leading up to the epiphany of Christ, or about the loss of experiential reality through doctrinization; the philosophical analysis of the various issues lags far behind our preanalytical awareness. It will be necessary, therefore, to reflect on the danger that has given the Unknown God a bad name in Christianity and induced certain doctrinal developments as a protective measure, i.e., on the danger of the gospel movement derailing into gnosticism.

In his *Agnostos Theos* (1913; repr. 1956, pp. 73ff.) Eduard Norden has placed the problem in its historical context and refers back, on this occasion, to its first presentation by Irenaeus in *Adversus Haereses* (ca. 180). Irenaeus lets the doctrinal conflict between gnosticism and orthodox Christianity turn on the interpretation of Matthew 11:25–27:

> At that time Jesus declared:
> "I humbly acknowledge, Father, lord of heaven and earth,
> that you have hidden these things from the wise and
> understanding and revealed them to the simple;
> be it so, Father, for so it seemed good to your sight.
> All these things are delivered to me by my Father,
> and no one knows the Son except the Father,
> and no one knows the Father except the Son
> and any one to whom the Son chooses to reveal him."

In orthodox doctrine, the God revealed by Jesus is the same god as the creator god revealed by the prophets of Israel; in Gnostic doctrine, the Unknown God of Jesus and the Israelite demiurge are two different gods. Against the Gnostics, Irenaeus proposes to prove by his work that the god they distinguish as the Bythos, the Depth, is indeed "the invisible greatness unknown to all" and, at the same time, the world creator of the prophets (I.19.12). They make nonsense of the logion, when they interpret the words "no one knows the Father but the Son" as referring to an absolutely Unknown God (*incognitus deus*), for "how can he be unknown if they themselves know about him?" Should the logion really give the absurd counsel: "Don't seek God; he is unknown and you will not find him"? Christ did not come to let mankind know that Father and Son are unknowable, or his coming would have been superfluous (IV.6).

Neither Irenaeus's presentation of the issue nor his argument for the orthodox side is a masterpiece of analysis. If the Father and the Son in the critical logion be conceptualized as two persons who know one another to the exclusion of everybody else, then the statement would indeed be no more than a bit of information that one can believe or not. Nothing would follow from it for either orthodoxy or gnosticism. Moreover, if Jesus could advance this conceptualized statement about himself, anybody could; we might expect the sons of the Father to become numerous. In fact, something of this sort seems to have happened, for Irenaeus enumerates as Gnostics, "Marcion, Valentinus, Basilides, Carpocrates, Simon, and the others," implying that they claimed this status by adding: "But none of them has been the Son of God, but only Jesus Christ, our Lord" (IV.6.4). The situation must have resembled the modern outburst of new Christs in the persons of Fichte, Hegel, Fourier, and Comte. At least one important cause of the confusion, thus, is the conceptual and propositional deformation of symbols which make sense only in the light of the experience which has engendered them. Hence, I shall first place the logion in the experiential context of Matthew, recalling for this purpose only the most important passages, and then analyze the structure of the problem that may lead to the various doctrinal derailments.

At a time when the reality of the gospel threatens to fall apart into the constructions of a historical Jesus and a doctrinal Christ, one cannot stress strongly enough the status of a gospel as a symbolism engendered in the *metaxy* of existence by a disciple's response to the drama of the Son of God. The drama of the Unknown God who reveals his kingdom through his presence in a man, and of the man who reveals what has been delivered to him by delivering it to his fellowmen, is continued by the existentially responsive disciple in the gospel drama by which he carries on the work of delivering these things from God to man. The gospel itself is an event in the drama of revelation. The historical drama in the *metaxy,* then, is a unit through the common presence of the Unknown God in the men who respond to his "drawing" and to one another. Through God and men as the dramatis personae, it is true, the presence of the drama partakes of both human time and divine timelessness, but tearing the drama of participation asunder into the biography of a Jesus in the spatiotemporal world and eternal verities showered from beyond would make nonsense of the existential reality that was experienced and symbolized as the drama of the Son of God.

The episode on the way to Caesarea Philippi (Matt. 16:13–20) may be considered a key to the understanding of the existential context into which the logion 11:27 must be placed. There Jesus asks the disciples who the people say the Son of man is, and receives the answer that he is variously understood as an apocalyptic of the type of John the Baptist, the prophesied Elijah, a Jeremiah, or one of the other prophets. His questioning then moves on to who the disciples think he is, and he receives the reply from Simon Peter: "You are the Christ, the Son of the living God" (16:16). Jesus answers: "Blessed are you, Simon Bar-Jona; for flesh and blood has not revealed this to you, but my Father who is in heaven." The Matthean Jesus, thus, agrees with the Johannine (John 6:44) that nobody can recognize the movement of the divine presence in the Son unless he is prepared for such recognition by the presence of the divine Father in himself. The divine Sonship is not revealed through an information tendered by Jesus, but through a man's response to the full presence in Jesus of the same Unknown God by whose presence he is inchoatively moved in his own existence. The Unknown God enters the drama of Peter's recognition as the third person. In order to draw the distinction between revelation and information, as well as to avoid the derailment from one to the other, the episode closes with the charge of Jesus to the disciples "to tell no one that he was the Christ" (Matt. 16:20).

The motif of the silence that will guard the truth of revelation against abasement to a piece of knowledge available to the general public is carried by Matthew with particular care through the story of the Passion. In the trial before the Sanhedrin, Jesus does not answer the peripheral charges at all (26:13); the central charge of having proclaimed himself the Son of God he brushes aside with his "You said so," not committing himself one way or another; but then, speaking as a Jew to Jews, he reminds them of the apocalyptic Son of man who will come on the clouds of heaven. In the trial before Pilate, the apocalyptic threat would be senseless; when the representatives of the Sanhedrin repeat their charges, Jesus remains completely silent, "so that the governor wondered greatly" (27:11–14). In the mockery scene before the crucified, then, the vicious resistance is victorious: "If you are the Son of God, come down from the cross" (27:40). But ultimately, when Jesus sinks into the silence of death, with the cosmos breaking out in prodigies, the response comes from the Roman guards. "This really was the Son of God" (27:54).

By the time of the Passion, it appears, the great secret of Caesarea Philippi, the so-called *Messiasgeheimnis,* has become a matter of public knowledge after all. In order to explain this oddity, however, one must not accuse the disciples of loquacious disregard for the charge of silence, for between this episode and the Passion Matthew lets Jesus be quite generous with barely veiled allusions to his status as both the Messiah and the Son of God. Hence, the charge of the Sanhedrin that Jesus had proclaimed himself the Son of God was well founded. Moreover, even before the emphatic recognition by Peter, on the occasion of Jesus' walking on the water, the evangelist lets the disciples as a group acknowledge: "You really are the Son of God" (14:33). Farther back in the gospel, the symbol appears in the logion 11:25–27 as a self-declaration of Jesus, followed by the invitation:

> Come to me, all who labor and are heavy laden, and I will give you rest.
> Take my yoke upon you, and learn from me, for I am gentle and lowly in heart, and you will find rest for your soul.
> For my yoke is easy, and my burden is light.
> (11:28–30)

This complete logion 11:25–30 apparently is addressed, not to the disciples, but to the "crowds" mentioned in 11:7. And even earlier (8:29), the demoniacs of Gadara recognize Jesus, in the hearing of the bystanders, as the Son of God. The secret, thus, was known to everybody, including those who resisted—a point not to be forgotten if one wants to understand the conversion of Paul. And yet, Matthew is no more guilty of confusion in the construction of his gospel than the disciples are of loquacity. For a gospel is neither a poet's work of dramatic art nor a historian's biography of Jesus, but the symbolization of a divine movement that went through the person of Jesus into society and history. The revelatory movement, thus, runs its course on more than one plane. There is, first, the personal drama of Jesus from the constitution of his consciousness as the Son of God in the encounters with God (3:16–17) and the devil (4:1–11), to the full realization of what it means to be the Son of God (16:21–23), to the submission to the Passion and the last word: "My God, my God, why hast thou forsaken me?" (27:46). There is, second, the social drama of his fellowmen who recognize the divine authority, the *exousia,* in him by his words and miracles, with its bifurcation into the positive response of the plain people and the resistance of the wise and public authorities. And finally, the social blends into the historical drama; for neither the recognition of the divine Sonship in Jesus' lifetime nor the posthumous understanding that the Unknown God has suffered death in a man to carry him to his life would have been possible unless the *praeparatio evangelica* of the millennial movement had created the readiness of both experiential response and mythical imagination for the Son of God. The mystery of divine presence in existence had grown in the consciousness of the movement long before the drama of the gospel started; and the symbols which the evangelist uses for its expression—the Son of God, the Messiah, the Son of man, the kingdom of God—were historically at hand through the Egyptian Pharaonic, the Davidic royal, the prophetic and apocalyptic symbolisms, through Iranian traditions and the Hellenistic mysteries. Hence, the "secret" of the gospel is neither the mystery of divine presence in existence nor its articulation through new symbols, but the event of its full comprehension and enactment through the life and death of Jesus. The apparent contradictions dissolve into the use of the same symbols at various levels of comprehension, as well as at the different stages of enactment, until the Christ is revealed, not in a fullness of doctrine, but in the fullness of Passion and Resurrection.

What is meant by fullness, as against minor degrees, of comprehension can be gathered from the process of advancing differentiation in such chapters as 11 and 16.

In chapter 11, John the Baptist sends his disciples to inquire of Jesus whether he is the *malak,* the messenger of God, prophesied in Malachi 3:1, who will precede the coming of Yahweh to his temple. Evading a direct answer, Jesus asks the disciples to report to their master the miracles and healings of Jesus, knowing quite well that such deeds are not what is expected of Malachi's *malak;* he leaves them free to draw their own conclusions, but dismisses them with the warning to John and his followers that blessed is only who does not take offense at Jesus (11:2–6). Then he turns to the "crowds" and explains to them who John is: he is a prophet, but at the same time more than a prophet; in fact, John rather than Jesus is the true Malachian *malak.* In the quotation from Malachi, however, the Matthean Jesus changes the text from a messenger whom "I [the Lord] send . . . to prepare the way before me" to a messenger whom the Lord sends to prepare the way for "thee." By this change of the pronoun from "me" to "thee," the Baptist is converted from the forerunner of Israel's Yahweh to the forerunner of the Unknown God who is present in his Son Jesus (11:7–10). The prophetism of both the law and the prophets has, as a type of existence in the In-Between, come to its end with John (11:13); what is in the process of coming, and is even present in Jesus and the plain people who follow him, is the kingdom of the Unknown Father of the Sermon on the Mount and of the Lord's Prayer. The chapter, therefore, consistently closes with the self-declaration of the logion, 11:25–30.

In chapter 16, then, the Matthean Jesus resumes the differentiation of his own status from that of his predecessors. In the previously quoted 16:13–14, the people's classifications as a John the Baptist, an Elijah, a

Jeremiah, are dismissed for good by Peter's reply: "You are the Christ, the Son of the living God." The significance of the answer must be seen in the combination of the symbols Messiah-Christ and Son of God. Up to this passage, the symbol Christ had been used only by Matthew in his role of the narrator, but not by any of the persons in the drama; now the prophetic and apocalyptic savior-king of Israel is identified with the Son of God in the process of revelation itself. As the Malachian *malak* had to change his complexion to become the forerunner of Jesus, so now the Messiah has to acquire the characteristics of the Son of God which formerly he did not have. Or at least, that was the intention of the Matthean Jesus when he accepted Peter's recognition. Historically, however, the two symbols have influenced each other, for the absorption of the "Messiah" has brought into the history of Christianity, as well as of a Christianized Western civilization, the apocalyptic strand of violent fantasy that can degenerate into violent action in the world. Even in the New Testament itself, in Revelation 19:11–16, we see the Messiah coming:

> And now I saw heaven open, and a white horse appear:
> Its rider is called Faithful and True; and with righteousness he judges and makes war.
> His eyes are flames of fire; on his head are many diadems; and he has a name inscribed which no one knows but himself.
> He wears a robe soaked in blood; and he is known by the name: The Word of God (*ho logos tou theou*).
> Behind him, dressed in linen of dazzling white, ride the armies of heaven on white horses.
> From his mouth comes a sharp sword to strike the nations with; he will rule them with an iron rod; and he treads out the wine of fierceness and wrath of God the Pantocrator.
> On his robe and on his thigh the name is written: King of kings, and Lord of lords.

This blood-dripping Word of God is a far cry from the Matthean Jesus who calls to him the poor in spirit, the gentle, the pure in heart, the peacemakers, those who hunger and thirst after righteousness and are persecuted for righteousness' sake. In Matthew 16, Jesus certainly does not intend to transform the Son of God into the field marshal of the Pantocrator, but rather wants to transform the Messiah into the Son of God. Whatever meanings the symbolism of an Anointed of Israel may have carried hitherto, they are now relegated to the past by the presence of the Unknown God in the Son. The consciousness of the Sonship must now be unfolded. Hence, "from that time Jesus began to show his disciples that he must go to Jerusalem and suffer many things from the elders and chief priests and scribes, and be killed, and on the third day be raised." The pathos of the representative death to be suffered has entered the consciousness of Jesus. When Peter wants to dissuade him from this course, Jesus angrily rebukes him: "Get behind me, Satan! You are an obstacle (*skandalon*) to me; for the way you think is not the way of God but of men" (16:21–23). It is no accident that Jesus rebukes Peter with the same *hypage satana* he uses in the rejection of the tempter in 4:10; the formula is indeed meant to characterize the way "man" thinks as the way of the devil. This "man" who can be symbolized as the devil is the man who has contracted his existence into a world-immanent self and refuses to live in the openness of the *metaxy.* The Matthean Jesus lets the rebuke to Peter, administered in the older language of God and Satan, be followed by the translation of its meaning into the noetic symbolization of existence, previously discussed, through the double meaning of life and death:

> If a man wants to walk after me, let him radically deny
> himself, and take up his cross and follow me.
> For whoever would save his life will lose it, and whoever
> loses his life for my sake will save it.
> For what will it profit a man, if he gains the whole world
> and forfeits his life.
>
> (16:24–26)

The saying concludes with the poignant question: What has a "man," i.e., his life as an immanently contracted self, to offer in return for his "life" (*psychē*) in the second sense? The meaning of the rebuke, as well as the relation between the two strata of symbols, is further illuminated by the use of the verb *aparneistai* (*to deny, disown, repudiate*) in the denial of the self of 16:24. The same verb is used to denote man's denial of Jesus in the saying: "But whoever denies me before men, I also will deny before my Father who is in heaven" (10:33). Moreover, it is specifically used of Peter's denial in 26:33–34, 69–75, thus creating the great counterpoint of Peter's three denials of Jesus to Jesus' three rejections of the Devil. In the In-Between of existence, man is faced with the choice of denying his self and the devil or denying Jesus and the Unknown God.

The analysis of the experiential context into which the logion 11:27

must be placed, though far from being exhaustive, has been carried far enough to make the noetic problems of reality visible that lend themselves to misconstruction through doctrinal hypostases, through overemphasis on one area of reality as against others, or through plain lack of interest to engage in further noetic penetration. In the present context, I must confine myself to a brief enumeration of no more than the principal questions:

1. The various problems transmitted to us through two thousand years have their center in the movement in which man's consciousness of existence emerges from the primary experience of the cosmos. Consciousness becomes luminous to itself as the site of the revelatory process, of the seeking and being drawn. The experience of a cosmos full of gods has to yield to the experience of eminent divine presence in the movement of the soul in the *metaxy.* Hence, all symbolization of truth about reality, about God, man, society, and the world, must from now on be filtered through, and be made compatible with, the eminent truth of existential consciousness. Moreover, since the place of truth is historically preempted by the more compact symbolizations of the primary experience, existential consciousness is historical consciousness in the sense that, on the occasion of its differentiation, the truth of reality is discovered as an event in the process of a reality whose truth advances to higher stages of realization. If history is to be compatible with the truth of existence, it must be symbolized as a revelatory process: the cosmological past of experience and symbolization must be intelligibly related to the differentiated consciousness to which it has given birth; and the vision of the future must bear some intelligible relation to the insight into the double meaning of life and death. The responses to this problem have a wide range. Its amplitude can be gauged if one confronts the Augustinian conception of history, with its patient waiting for the eschatological events, with the Hegelian speculation, which enacts the eschatological event through the construction of the system; or if one confronts the position of a contemporary existentialist theologian who rejects the Old Testament as irrelevant to Christian theology, with the position of Clement of Alexandria who insists on adding Greek philosophy as the second Old Testament for Christians. Regarding visions of the future, one may confront the millennium introduced by an angel of the Lord in Revelation 20 with the millennia introduced by Cromwell and the Puritan army or by Lenin and the Communist party.

2. The cosmos does not cease to be real when the consciousness of

existence in the In-Between differentiates; but the emotional resistance to, and technical difficulty of, resymbolizing the order of the cosmos, which on its compact level had been quite adequately symbolized by the intracosmic gods, in the light of the new insight is enormous; especially because the new historical consciousness requires the older gods to be resymbolized as symbols of earlier stages in the process of revelation. In the movement of classic philosophy, as I have shown, the noetic analysis of the *metaxy* has gone as far as in the gospel movement, and in some points is superior to anything we find in the gospel, but the decisive step of making the experience of man's tension toward the Unknown God the truth to which all truth of reality must conform was never taken. To Plato, the *monogenēs* of the Unknown God is, not a man, but the cosmos. In the myth of the *Phaedrus,* then, he explicitly deals with the relation between the Unknown God and the intracosmic gods: on festival occasions, the Olympians rise steeply toward the top of their heaven; "there the utmost (*eschaton*) toil and struggle await the soul" when it wants to pass beyond and reach the outer surface of the vault; but when they take this stand, they can contemplate the things outside of heaven. The human followers of the gods are variously, but never completely, successful in achieving this state of contemplation, so that no poet in this world has ever worthily praised the *hyperouranion,* the region beyond the heaven, or ever will (247). Plato's mythical imagination, thus, endows the intracosmic gods with a tension of their psyche toward the Unknown God and lets them transmit their true knowledge to man. In the language of the cosmological myth, these Olympian god-seekers and mediators are the equivalent to the Son of God who alone knows the divine Father in the *plērōma* of presence, and mediates his knowledge to his followers according to their human receptiveness. This Platonic resolution to the problem had a durable success in philosophy: six hundred years later, when the Unknown God had been further differentiated as the Monad *epekeina nou* (*Enneads* v.3.11), Plotinus still went back to the myth of the *Phaedrus,* in order to symbolize the relation between the intracosmic gods and the Unknown God (*Enneads* v.8.10). Moreover, he used the argument of the gods who look up to the "king of the realm beyond" in his polemic against the Gnostic "sons of god" who want to elevate themselves above the gods of the cosmos and speak of this world as "the alien earth" (II.9.9).

3. The area of existential consciousness, though eminent of rank, is only one area of reality. If it is overemphasized, the cosmos and its gods will

become the "alien earth" of the Gnostics and life in the despised world will hardly be worth living. The tendency toward this imbalance is certainly present in the gospel movement. When Jesus prefers the plain people to the wise and the public authorities, he does not want to start a revolution that will bring the plain people to power but judges the kingdom of God more easily accessible to the "poor" than to men who have vested interests and positions of responsibility in the affairs of this world. His appeal is entirely different from [that of] Plato, who addressed himself to the sons of the ruling class, in order to make them existentially fit to be rulers in the paradigmatic polis that was meant to supersede the corrupt polis of the day, for the kingdom of God will have no social organization or ruling class in this world. In Matthew 16, Jesus concludes his analysis of existence with the assurance: "Truly, I say to you, there are some standing here who will not taste death before they see the Son of man coming in his kingdom" (16:28)—a vision that probably appeals to members of an establishment no more than to revolutionaries who want to establish themselves in their place. Moreover, not only may the future of history be lost, if one takes "no thought for the morrow" (Matt. 7:34), but there is also the danger of losing its past. The Matthean Jesus, it is true, has not come to destroy the law or the prophets but to fulfill them (5:17), but the fulfillment is difficult to distinguish from apocalyptic destruction. We have noted the subtle conversions of the *malak* of Yahweh into the forerunner of Jesus, as well as of the Messiah into the Son of God; and the Unknown Father of 11:27, whom nobody knows but the Son, is hardly the well-known God who thundered from Sinai and spoke through Moses and the prophets. Would not the Yahweh of Israel also have to become a god-seeker and mediator like the Olympians of the Platonic myth?

4. Because the issues of this type were insufficiently clarified in the gospel movement, the derailment into gnosticism became possible. The strength of the gospel is its concentration on the one point that is all-important: that the truth of reality has its center not in the cosmos at large, not in nature or society or imperial rulership, but in the presence of the Unknown God in a man's existence to his death and life. This very strength, however, can cause a breakdown if the emphasis on the center of truth becomes so intense that its relations to the reality of which it is the center are neglected or interrupted. Unless the Unknown God is the undifferentiated divine presence in the background of the specific intracosmic gods, he is indeed a god unknown to the primary experience of the

cosmos. In that case, however, there is no process of revelation in history, nor a millennial movement culminating in the epiphany of the Son of God, but only the irruption of an extracosmic god into a cosmos to whose mankind he hitherto had been hidden. Moreover, since the revelation of this extracosmic god is the only truth that existentially matters, the cosmos, its gods, and its history become a reality with the index of existential untruth. In particular, the Yahweh of Israel is imagined as an evil demon who has created the cosmos in order to indulge his lust of power and to keep man, whose destiny is extracosmic, prisoner in the world of his creation. This god of the Gnostics is certainly not the God of the gospel who suffers death in man to raise man to life, but he is a god who can emerge from the movement, when the consciousness of existence isolates itself, through an act of imagination, from the reality of the cosmos in which it has differentiated. I say advisedly that the Gnostic god can emerge from the movement at large, for he is not necessarily bound to the gospel movement as one of its possible derailments. The historians of religion who find the "origins" of gnosticism in Hellas or Persia, in Babylon or Egypt, in Hellenistic mystery religions or Jewish sectarian movements, and who diagnose the Gnostic elements in the New Testament itself, are not quite wrong, for the structural possibility of the derailment is present wherever the existential movement of differentiating the Unknown God from the intracosmic gods has begun. One should be clear, however, that the presence of the structural possibility is not itself gnosticism; it would be better to apply the term only to the cases where the imaginative isolation of existential consciousness becomes the motivating center for the construction of major symbolisms, as in the great Gnostic systems of the second century A.D. These systems, though they are products of mythical imagination, are neither myths of the intracosmic type, nor are they philosophers' myths like the Platonic or Plotinic, nor do they belong to the genus of New Testament Gospels. They are a symbolism *sui generis* which expresses a state of alienation from reality, more precisely to be characterized as an extracosmic isolation of existential consciousness.

Though the possibility of the Gnostic derailment is inherent to the movement from its beginning, only the full differentiation of the truth of existence under the Unknown God through his Son has created the cultural field in which the extracosmic contraction of existence is an equally radical possibility. With the gospel as the truth of reality, Western civilization has inherited extracosmic contraction as the possibility of its disruption. I have already intimated the cultural pattern of the new Christs in the late eighteenth and the early nineteenth centuries which repeats the pattern of the "sons of god" who aroused the wrath of Irenaeus and Plotinus. But on this occasion I cannot go beyond such intimations. We do not know what horrors the present period of cultural disruption has yet in store, but I hope to have shown that philosophy is not quite helpless in the noetic penetration of its problems. Perhaps its persuasion can help to restore the rule of reason.

Immortality: Experience and Symbol

Eric Voegelin

I

Immortality is one of the language symbols engendered by a class of experiences to which we refer as the varieties of religious experience. This term is perhaps no longer the technically best one, but it has the advantage of a great precedent, especially here at Harvard. Hence, its use will be convenient to secure, I hope, a common and immediate understanding about the subject matter of inquiry.

The symbols in question intend to convey a truth experienced. Regarding this intent, however, they suffer from a peculiar disability. For, in the first place, the symbols are not concepts referring to objects existing in time and space but carriers of a truth about nonexistent reality. Moreover, the mode of nonexistence pertains also to the experience itself, inasmuch as it is nothing but a consciousness of participation in nonexistent reality. As Hebrews 11:1 has it: "Faith is the substance of things hoped for, and the evidence of things unseen." And finally, the same mode also pertains to the meaning of the symbols, as they convey no other truth than that of the engendering consciousness. We have spoken, therefore, of a truth experienced rather than of a truth attaching to the symbols. As a consequence, when the experience engendering the symbols ceases to be a presence located in the man who has it, the reality from which the symbols derive their meaning has disappeared. The symbols in the sense of a spoken or written word, it is true, are left as traces in the world of sense perception, but their meaning can be understood only if they evoke, and through evocation reconstitute, the engendering reality in the listener or reader. The symbols exist in the world, but their truth belongs to the nonexistent experience which by their means articulates itself.

The intangibility of the experience just adumbrated exposes the symbols and their truth to strange vicissitudes of history. Because of the vanishing substratum, even the most adequate exegesis and articulation of an experience can achieve no more than symbols which remain as the exterior residue of an original full truth comprising both the experience and its articulation. As soon, however, as the symbols have separated from this fullness and acquired the status of a literary account, the intimate tension between a reality engendering and symbols engendered, holding in balance the identity and difference of the two poles, is liable to dissociate into a piece of information and its subject matter. There is no guarantee whatsoever that the reader of the account will be moved to a meditative reconstitution of the engendering reality; one may even say the chances are slim, as meditation requires more energy and discipline than most people are able to invest. The truth conveyed by the symbols, however, is the source of right order in human existence, we cannot dispense with it; and as a consequence, the pressure is great to restate the exegetic account discursively for the purpose of communication. It may be translated, for instance, into simple propositions, rendering what the translator considers its essential meaning, for use on the secondary level of instruction and initiation. If submitted to such proceedings, for quite respectable purposes, the truth of the account will assume the form of doctrine or dogma, of a truth at second remove, as for instance the propositions "Man is immortal" or "The soul is immortal." Moreover, dogmatic propositions of this kind are liable to condition corresponding types of experience, such as fideistic acceptance or even more deficient modes of understanding. There is the seminarian, as a Catholic friend once bitterly remarked, who rather believes in Denzinger's *Enchiridion* than in God; or, to avoid any suspicion of confessional partisanship, there is the Protestant fundamentalist; or, to avoid any suspicion of professional partisanship, there is the professor of philosophy who informs you about Plato's "doctrine" of the soul, or of the idea, or of truth, though to conceive of Plato as a promoter of doctrine is preposterous. Even the transformation into doctrine, however, is not the last loss that truth can suffer. When doctrinal truth becomes socially dominant, even the knowledge of the processes by which doctrine derives from the original account, and the original account from the engendering experience, may get lost. The symbols may altogether cease to be translucent for reality. They will, then, be misunderstood as propositions referring to things in the manner of propositions concerning objects of sense perception; and since the case does not fit the model, they will provoke the reaction of skepticism on the gamut from a Pyrrhonian suspense of judgment, to vulgarian agnosticism, and further on to the smart idiot questions of "How do you know?" and "How can you prove it?" that every college teacher knows from his classroom. We have reached T. S. Eliot's *Waste Land* with its broken images:

> What are the roots that clutch, what branches grow
> Out of this stony rubbish? Son of man,
> You cannot say, or guess, for you know only
> A heap of broken images, where the sun beats,
> And the dead tree gives no shelter, the cricket no relief,
> And the dry stone no sound of water.

II

I have tried to suggest the phenomena of original account, dogmatic exposition, and skeptical argument as a sequence that can attach itself to every experience of nonexistent reality when it becomes articulate and, through its symbols, enters society as an ordering force. In some instances, when the sequence attaches itself to the great ordering experiences of philosophy and Christian faith, it is discernible as a structure in historical processes of infinite complexity. A recall, even if it can be no more than the barest hint, of these wide-arched courses will be of help in determining not only our own position in them but the very sense we can make of an inquiry concerning immortality today.

In our civilization, the sequence has run its course twice: once in antiquity, and once in medieval and modern times. In antiquity, there emerges from the culture of the myth the noetic experience of the Hellenic thinkers. They have left, as the exegesis of their experience, the literary corpus of classic philosophy. The exegetic philosophy of Plato and Aristotle, then, is followed by the dogmatic philosophy of the schools. And the dogmatism of the schools, finally, is accompanied, ever since the first generation after Aristotle, by the skeptical reaction. At the turn from the second to the third century A.D., the vast, accumulated body of skeptical argument was collected and organized by Sextus Empiricus. The second cycle is more complicated than the first one, inasmuch as the sequence attaches itself to the truth of both philosophy and revelation. The crack in the precarious balance of a Christian order becomes unmistakable in the High Middle Ages, with the ominous bifurcation of faith and fideism in the parallel movements of mysticism and nominalism. In the sixteenth century, a Christianity that has become doctrinaire explodes in the wars of religion; and their devastations, both physical and moral, arouse wave after wave of disgust with dogmatism, be it theological or metaphysical. Still within the sixteenth century, the revulsion crystallizes in the so-called *crise pyrrhonienne* with its reintroduction of Sextus Empiricus into the arsenal of antidogmatic argument. And with the seventeenth century begins the incredible spectaculum of modernity—both fascinating and nauseating, grandiose and vulgar, exhilarating and depressing, tragic and grotesque—with its apocalyptic enthusiasm for building new worlds that will be old tomorrow, at the expense of old worlds that were new yesterday; with its destructive wars and revolutions spaced by temporary stabilizations on ever lower levels of spiritual and intellectual order through natural law, enlightened self-interest, a balance of powers, a balance of profits, the survival of the fittest, and the fear of atomic annihilation in a fit of fitness; with its ideological dogmas piled on top of the ecclesiastic and sectarian ones and its resistant skepticism that throws them all equally on the garbage heaps of opinion; with its great systems built on untenable premises and its shrewd suspicions that the premises are indeed untenable and therefore must never be rationally discussed; with the result, in our time, of having unified mankind into a global madhouse bursting with stupendous vitality.

Madness in the sense of the word here used—it is the Aeschylean sense of *nosos*—is a pneumopathological state, a loss of personal and social order through loss of contact with nonexistent reality. Where in this madhouse is there room for a rational discussion of immortality which presupposes the very contact with reality that has been lost—if there is any room at all?

Well, there is such room—and even more of it than we are sometimes inclined to suppose. For a man does not cease to be man, even when he runs amok in worlds of his own making, and a madness of the spirit is never quite undisturbed by a knowledge of its madness, however skillfully suppressed. The violent phase of the madness we call modernity is accompanied throughout by thinkers who, correctly diagnosing its cause, set about to remedy the evil by various attempts at recapturing reality. In the seventeenth century, a Descartes tries, in his *Meditations*, to find the safe ground of philosophizing beyond dogmatism and skepticism in an immediate experience. Early in the nineteenth century, Hegel states in so many words that we can escape from senseless dogmatism only through penetrating again to experience and he undertakes the dialectical speculation of his *Phänomenologie* for this purpose. In our own century, the work of William James and Henri Bergson has set great landmarks of such endeavor. This task of reestablishing contact with nonexistent reality, however, is not easy; and the task of making the attempts socially effective is even less so. It would be difficult to detect any lasting imprints the work of individual thinkers has left on the vast expanse of intellectual mud that covers the public scene; the madness seems to go as strong as ever, and only a Hobbesian fear of death puts on the brakes. And yet, discouraging as the results may be, progress of a sort seems to me undeniable.

In order to establish the criteria by which progress in this matter is to be gauged, I shall advert to a classic document of openness toward experiences of nonexistent reality, to William James's *Varieties of Religious Experience* (1902). If you examine the index of the book, you will find no reference to the most important literary texts that articulate such experiences and elaborate with care on the question of immortality. In vain you will look for the names of Plato and Aristotle; Christ is not mentioned; and the two references to St. Paul refer to passages in which he is quoted by other authors. These observations are not meant to criticize James; they rather want to characterize the situation of science at the beginning of the century, when the fundamental texts were so far below the threshold of general debate that even the catholicity of a James could not become aware of their relevance to his purpose. On immortality in particular, he has no more than a brief page, urbane in form but grumpy in mood—an understandable mood, as immortality presented itself to him in popular imaginings of the kind that were spoofed about the same time by E. M. Forster in his satirical short stories. The turn of the century, one must remember, was a difficult time for men of a philosophical bent, so bad a time indeed that a Wilhelm Dilthey refrained for a decade from publishing because he deemed the effort useless.

Since the beginning of the century, the situation has changed substantially. On the one hand, the spiritual disease has manifested itself massively in bouts of global war and revolution; on the other hand, the experiences of transcendence are being recaptured in a peculiarly backhanded manner. For the experiences which had been reduced to shadows by dogmatic incrustations, and seemed to be removed from the realm of the living by the successive attacks of antitheologism and antimetaphysicism, have returned from limbo by the back door of historical knowledge. To a field that apparently had been cleared of them so they would not disturb the futuristic dreams of *paradis artificiels*, they are being reintroduced as "facts of history"—through the exploration of myth, of the Old and New Testament, of apocalyptic and Gnostic movements, through comparative religion, Assyriology, Egyptology, classical philosophy, and so forth. This renewed knowledge about experiences on which depends the order in personal and social existence makes itself felt even now in an increasingly accurate diagnosis of the contemporary disorder and its causes; and it would be surprising if it did not become a living force, sooner or later, in the actual restoration of order.

Since the opening years of the century, thus, the intellectual scene has changed indeed. Today, a philosopher can responsibly engage in an inquiry concerning immortality, supported as he is by the comparative materials the historical sciences put at his disposition as well as by fairly advanced sciences of experiences and their symbolization. I shall now turn to the analysis of a representative case.

III

As the purpose of this inquiry is not a description of symbols but an analysis of the experiences engendering them, our choice of a case is narrowly determined by requirements of method. For on the one hand, the case selected should be a historically early one, in order to avoid questions which otherwise might arise with regard to the traditional character of the symbols and a correspondingly suspect authenticity of the experience. But on the other hand, it has to be culturally late enough for an exegesis of the experience to be so articulate that the connection between the truth experienced and the symbols expressing it will be intelligible beyond a doubt. The case that will satisfy both requirements is an anonymous text from the Egypt of the First Intermediate Period, ca. 2000 B.C., an early reflection on the experiences of life, death, and immortality, distinguished by excellence of analysis. The text is known as the "Dispute of a Man, Who Contemplates Suicide, with His Soul."

The first part of the *Dispute,* only imperfectly preserved, presents an argument between the Man and his Soul. The Man is driven to despair by the troubles of a disordered age and wants to cast off a life that has become senseless; the Soul is introduced as the speaker who militates against the decision. As far as the imperfect state of preservation permits us to understand the rationale of speech and counterspeech, the argument moves through three phases. The first bout of the struggle between Man and his Soul is concerned with the idea of life as a gift of the gods. Since life is not a man's property to be thrown away when it becomes burdensome but an endowment to be treated as a trust under all conditions, the Soul can point to the command of the gods and the wisdom of the sages which both prohibit the shortening of the allotted span. But Man knows how to plead: the disintegration of order, both personal and public, in the surrounding society deprives life of any conceivable meaning, so that exceptional circumstances will justify a violation of the rule before the gods. In the second bout, there arises the question of immortality in the conventional sense. Man tries to make the decision palatable to his Soul by promising proper provision for burial and sacrifice, so that its sojourn in the beyond will be pleasant. Unfortunately, however, the Soul belongs to the sophisticated variety and proves impervious to conventional promises. It seems to be familiar with skeptical thought about the probabilities of afterlife; it knows that nobody has ever come back from over there to tell the living about the state of the soul in the beyond. But Man proves no less resistant than his Soul. A third and last bout becomes necessary because he is not to be swayed by skepticism. That makes for a difficult situation. For what can you do with a man who will not find his peace of mind either with conventional belief or with conventional skepticism! Hence, the Soul now has to proceed to a radical attack on the core of Man's misery: Man is in deadly anguish, because he takes life seriously and cannot bear existence without meaning. But why be so serious? Why not simply not despair? Man should enjoy the pleasures of the moment as they come: "Pursue the happy day and forget care." This ultimate argument was in common use at the time, as we know from other sources, such as the "Song of the Harper." In the present context, however, it gains a new meaning, because it is not accepted as a counsel of worldly wisdom but sensed as the ultimate indignity inflicted on Man in the agony of his existence. The counsel sets off the spiritual crisis that had been in the making. Man is incensed by the baseness of the advice and expresses his distaste:

> Behold, my name will reek through thee
> More than the stench of bird droppings
> On summer days, when the sky is hot.

Before this outburst the Soul falls silent; its resources are exhausted. Man is now alone with himself to face the decision.

A brief reaction on this first part will clarify its function in the *Dispute* as well as its import with regard to some questions raised earlier in this inquiry.

The arguments of the Soul try to open ways out of an impasse that characteristically may induce a solution through suicide. These arguments, however, suffer from a curious tinge of unreality; we can bring it out by wording them colloquially: This life is god-given and not yours to throw away at will; besides, you can't be sure of a life beyond, so better hold on to what you've got; and finally, don't be so pompous about the meaning of life, don't assume that holier-than-thou attitude, be one of the boys and have a good time like everybody else. If in this manner we transpose the essence of the argument into American colloquialism, its seriousness will become suspect. The first part would, then, appear as an ironic exhibition of popular arguments used at the time in debates about the meaning of life; and the irony would imply an understanding of the arguments as expressions of existence in a deficient mode. It looks as if the surrounding society were to be characterized as suffering from a severe loss of ordering reality, manifesting itself in the vulgarian character of the argument; as if the troubles of the age were to be understood, not simply as a breakdown of government on the pragmatic level, perhaps caused by the disfavor of the gods, but as events somehow connected with a disintegration of existential order. A characterization of this type is possible, of course, only if the alternative to the deficient mode is a living force in the author, so that he can use the presence of reality experienced as a standard by which to judge society. The situation of the Man in the *Dispute,* then, would not differ very much from that of a man in our own time: to live in a society that lives by vulgar clichés of piousness, skepticism, and hedonism is trying enough to make a man look for an oasis of reality—even if, in order to reach it, he will not necessarily resort to the radical means of suicide.

This interpretation, though it sounds anachronistic, is not a piece of venturesome surmise. It is confirmed by the construction of the *Dispute* as a drama of existence. The argument is carefully phased so as to lead up to the spiritual outburst—which could not occur unless there was a spirit to burst out. Hence, the argument must be read in retrospect from the outburst it has provoked. In the light radiating from the climax the difference between a traditional lamentation about the iniquities of the age and the existential revolt against the indignity of participating in corruption, even if the participation should assume the respectable form of ineffectual lament, becomes clear. The author of the *Dispute* rises above lamentation to dramatic judgment and action. His Man is pitted against the disorder of society and can emerge as victor from the struggle because he carries in himself the full reality of order. Such reality can grow to its full presence, however, only through a growth of consciousness; and the consciousness of reality is made to grow precisely by Man's dramatic resistance to the Soul's counsel. Only through his ultimate rejection of society, its persuasion and pressure, does he find the freedom and clarity to articulate both the reality living in him and the negative state of society from which he disengages himself. Having disposed of the temptation to become a conformist and make his name a stench, he can be at one with himself and find the language adequate to his experience.

The second part of the *Dispute* articulates the experience of reality; the account is organized in four sequences of tristichs. The first sequence expresses Man's revulsion at becoming a stench to himself by continuing life on the level of corrupt existence. After this outburst of a reality that has become sure of itself as distinct from unreality, the second sequence characterizes life in the mode of unreality; the third one deals with death as the liberator from the sickness of life; the fourth one, with faith in the fullness of life to be achieved through death. This pattern of articulation—revulsion at the dead life, description of the living death, liberation through death from death in life, and fullness of life through death—renders the structure of the experience with an exactitude hardly to be surpassed. It is true, the accounts rendered by Plato or St. Paul move on the more differentiated level of noetic and revelatory experiences, they have at their disposition a more diversified arsenal of symbols, their expression has become more supple as it is no longer hampered by the blocklike compactness of myth, but fundamentally they are—as all accounts invariably must be if they are true—variations of the motifs that were articulated by the unknown Egyptian thinker.

From the first sequence, expressing Man's revulsion, I have quoted an example. The other tristichs of this series do no more than amplify the theme by listing further unappetizing odors. I shall now present one or two samples from each of the following sequences to give an idea of the degree to which the experience has become articulate in detail.

Each of the tristichs of the second sequence opens with the line "To whom can I speak today?" The destruction of community among men through destruction of the spirit is their great theme. Specifically, the author complains:

> To whom can I speak today?
> One's fellows are evil;
> The friends of today do not love.

Transposing the thought into the language of classic philosophy, one might say: The *philia politike* in the Aristotelian sense, deriving from the love of the divine Nous that is experienced as constituting the very self of man, has become impossible, because the divine presence has withdrawn from the self. As a consequence, the complaint goes on:

> To whom can I speak today?
> Faces have disappeared:
> Every man has a downcast face toward his fellows.

When reality has receded from the self, the face becomes faceless—with various consequences. The present tristich seems to point to the consciousness of the loss and its torment; the lines sound like a description of the phenomena of which today we speak as the "lonely crowd" and the "quiet despair." To the Man of the *Dispute* the phenomenon becomes conscious as his own loneliness.

> To whom can I speak today?
> There is no one contented of heart;
> The man with whom one went, no longer exists.

But the loss of self can also assume the form of wickedness and consent to it. Further tristichs dwell on the wicked man who stirs no more than laughter, on the social dominance of criminality, and on the dreary prospect of evil without end.

In such utter loneliness, Man turns toward death as the salvation from senseless existence:

Death faces me today
 Like the recovery of a sick man,
 Like going out into the open after a confinement.

Or:

Death faces me today
 Like the longing of a man to see his home again,
 After many years that he was held in captivity.

The tristichs of this third sequence vary the themes of life as a sickness, as a land of darkness under clouds, as an exile and a prison; and the themes of death as the recovery, as the light that leads from darkness to the hitherto unknown, as the longing for return to one's home, and as a release from prison. The symbols of this group arouse our attention because we are familiar with them from Platonic and Gnostic texts. Hence, it seems, they are not specific to any of the varieties, but rather characteristic of a genus of experience. We shall return to this problem presently.

The tristichs of the fourth sequence express the speaker's faith in entering the fullness of life through death.

Why surely, he who is yonder
 Will be a living god,
 Punishing the sin of him who commits it.

Why surely, he who is yonder
 Will stand in the bark of the sun,
 Causing the choicest therein to be given to the temples.

Why surely, he who is yonder
 Will be a man of wisdom,
 Not hindered from appealing to Re when he speaks.

From this sequence one should especially note the symbolism of Man's transformation into a living god, riding in the bark of the sun. For transformed into a divine companion of the sun-god, Man will function as his adviser and as a judge concerning affairs of man and society on earth. The theme of judgment, it appears, is no more specific to Hellenic or Christian experiences than the symbols of alienation, sickness, imprisonment, and so forth; it rather is, like the others, a constant in the whole class of experiences from which the symbolism of Immortality emerges.

The precise degree of differentiation which the author of the *Dispute* has achieved will become clear only if we confront the assurances of the last sequence with the Egyptian experience of cosmos and empire.

In the primary experience of the cosmos all the things it comprehends—the gods, heaven and earth, man and society—are consubstantial. Since the realm of Egypt is a partner in the cosmos, its order is supposed to manifest the *ma'at*, the divine-cosmic order, while the Pharaoh is supposed to be the mediator of this order to society. At the time of the author's writing, however, Egypt was in disorder because of the Pharaoh's malfunctioning; and according to the traditional conception of empire, this unfortunate situation could be repaired only by the epiphany of a new Pharaoh who again would effectively channel the flow of *ma'at* from the gods to society. Set against this traditional conception, the *Dispute* must be considered an extraordinary, if not a revolutionary, event in the history of empire, inasmuch as it offers a substitute for the mediating function of the Pharaoh. For the author of the *Dispute* is neither interested in life at all cost nor in the immortality in the sense of conventional imaginings—such topics belong to the mode of unreality from which he is disengaging himself—but in a quite different kind of immortality that is meant to become instrumental in restoring order to Egypt. The living god Man will shoulder the burden of the living god Pharaoh who has failed. There can be no doubt, we are witnessing a spiritual outbreak, bursting the primary experience of the cosmos and moving in the direction of a personal experience of transcendence. The author is on the verge of the insight that Man's order, both personal and social, will have to depend on Man's existence in immediacy under God. In view of the very articulate symbolization, it would even be tempting to press the interpretation one step further and to consider the insight into Man's nature as *imago Dei*, without benefit of Pharaonic mediation, as achieved. But that would be going too far. For the unknown author does not radically break with that primary experience but, the phenomena of social disorder notwithstanding, preserves his faith in the cosmos. His Man is not everyman, and therefore, he cannot translate his personal breakthrough into a revolution against sacred kingship. The acceptance of status as counselor to the sun-god remains the only method conceivable to make the newly discovered reality of Man effective in the economy of cosmos and society—and in order to achieve that status, Man must commit suicide. The time has not yet come for the transfer of authority from the cosmological ruler to the prophet, sage, or philosopher as the nucleus of a new communal order.

IV

The Western philosopher in the twentieth century A.D. finds himself in substantially the same position as the Egyptian thinker in the twentieth century B.C.: both the philosopher and the author of the *Dispute* are disturbed by the disorder of the age, they both are in search of a reality no longer alive in the surrounding images, and they both want to recover the meaning of symbols from their misuse in everyday debate. The contemporary quarrel between doctrinaire beliefs and equally doctrinaire objections is the counterpart of the first, argumentative part of the *Dispute*; and today's philosopher has to wind his way in search of truth through the very type of imagery and argument that has been recognized as expressing a deficient mode of existence by his predecessor of four thousand years ago.

On the strength of this parallel, we can lay down two rules for the philosopher. On the one hand, he is not permitted to side with the believers and, in particular, he must not let himself be betrayed into arguing the doctrinal question whether man, or his soul, is immortal or not. For in doctrinal argument, symbols are erected into entities: and when he participates in it, he involves himself in the error that Whitehead has named the fallacy of misplaced concreteness. On the other hand, he is not permitted to side with the objectors, as they deny validity to propositions concerning God, the soul, and immortality, on the ground that they cannot be verified or falsified like propositions concerning objects of sense perception. This argument, however, is pointless, as nobody maintains that doctrinal propositions refer to the external world; the appearance of an objection accrues to it from the false premise that doctrinal truth is not derivative but original. Nevertheless, while treading the narrow path between the contestants, the philosopher must remain aware of their respective merits both intellectual and existential. He must grant the intellectual advantage to the objector, because he escapes the believer's fallacy of operating with hypostatized symbols. He must grant the existential advantage to the believer, because the objector pays for his intellectual cleanliness the price of denying truth altogether, while the believer preserves truth experienced at least in its doctrinal derivation. But then again, the sympathetic weighing must not degenerate into the sentimentalisms of either condemnation or indecision. The philosopher must not condemn—for the tension between faith and reason, their conspiracy and conflict in time, is a mystery. Whether the traditionalist believer who professes truth in doctrinal form is not perhaps farther removed from truth than the intellectual objector who denies it because of its doctrinal form, he does not know. God alone knows who is nearer to the end that is the beginning. Nor must the philosopher remain undecided because he cannot penetrate the mystery—for as far as he can see within the limitations of his human understanding, the objector who cannot sense an unbroken reality behind the broken images moves on the same level of deficient existence as the traditionalist who, perhaps desperately, believes his broken image to be whole. Indecision would cast the philosopher in the role of the Soul in the *Dispute,* while it is his burden to act the part of Man.

The philosopher moves in the field of tensions just adumbrated. We have to note its properties with regard to extension and structure. With regard to its extension Plato has formulated the principle that society is man writ large—a principle that must be amplified today so as to include history. Both society and history are man writ large. The field, that is to say, is not confined to man as a single person, but embraces the manifold of human beings in society and history: for the tensions Man experiences in his personal existence are the same he recognizes as structuring the other sectors of the field. With regard to the structure of the field, then, we can distinguish two principal dimensions. There is, first, the tension between existence in truth and the deficient modes of existence. This is the very tension in which the philosopher lives and moves himself. His concern is, therefore, not with truth as a bit of information that has escaped his contemporaries, but as a pole in the tension of order and disorder, of reality and loss of reality, he experiences as his own. His existence comprehends the disorder by which he feels repelled as much as the order toward which his desire moves him. There are, second, the tensions on the level of deficient existence. When the reality of truth has declined to traditionalist belief in symbols, the scene is set for the appearance of unbelief and reasoned objection to belief. For belief, when losing contact with truth experienced, not only provokes objection but even gives aid to the enemy by creating the doctrinaire environment in which objection can become socially effective. This class of tensions, i.e., the dynamics of belief and unbelief, I shall call the subfield of doctrinaire existence. The philosopher's concern, now, is not with this or that part of the field, but with the whole of it—to its full extension and in all of its structural dimensions—for his search would lose direction if he were to disregard the points of orientation. In particular, he must resist the professional temptation of taking his stance at the pole of the tension toward which his desire moves him; if he were to start sermonizing on existence in truth as if it were an absolute object in his possession, he would derail into doctrinaire existence.

Though the author of the *Dispute* and the modern philosopher move in the same type of field, their respective fields differ concretely, inasmuch as the issue of history is present in the Egyptian field only compactly, while in the modern Western field it has become an explicit theme for the philosopher as well as for the believer and the objector. I shall deal, first, with the issue of history as it appears in the subfield of doctrinaire existence.

In the modern variant of the subfield we find a class of symbols that has no counterpart on the Egyptian scene, i.e., the so-called ideological objections to doctrinal belief. Their prodigious success in our society can be explained only if we have recourse to the rule that doctrinaire belief prefigures the pattern of ideological argument, and, thus, makes society receptive to it. As a representative case, I shall select for analysis the modern objector's *pièce de résistance:* "The experience is an illusion."

First, the intellectual structure of the objection: the proposition is a piece of loose thinking, quite common in everyday speech. Speaking carefully, one would have to say that an experience is never an illusion but always a reality; the predicate *illusion* should be used with reference, not to the experience, but to its content, in case it has illusionary character. Taken by itself, the incorrect wording is worth not more attention than is necessary to avoid a misunderstanding. In the context of ideological polemic, however, the transfer of the predicate is subtly used for the very purpose of creating a misunderstanding, viz., that the incorrectly worded proposition in the foreground carries, in its own right, the possible sense of the background proposition. The transfer diverts attention from the inarticulate premise. The result is a nonsense proposition designed to forestall the question whether the possible sense in the background really makes sense in the concrete case. Let us, therefore, break the taboo and ask the question we are supposed not to ask: What does it mean when the content of an experience is to be characterized as an illusion? It can mean one of two things: either, radically, that the object experienced by a subject does not exist at all; or, gradationally, that the object exists but on closer inspection reveals characteristics different from those apparent in the object as experienced. In either case, the judgment of illusion rests on control experiences of the potentially or actually existent object outside the experience. With this observation, however, the reason—or at least one of the reasons—why the possible sense in the background must be kept in the dark becomes visible. For a judgment of illusion can pertain only to experiences of existent objects, not to experiences of participation in nonexistent reality. Thus, the veiled sense in the background, if made articulate, proves to be just as much nonsense as the proposition in the foreground.

The intellectual error, though it takes a paragraph to trace it out, is too obvious for the proposition to survive, in a critical environment, for any length of time; in order to explain its social effectiveness in polemics, we must introduce the factor of existential assent. To one part this assent is determined by the general readiness, in our society, to think (if *think* is the right word) in doctrinal form. Since the objector's argument accepts the believer's doctrine at its face value, the intellectual error which should discredit the argument becomes the source of its credibility in a predominantly doctrinaire society. This general readiness, however, is characteristic also of other civilizations and periods in the history of mankind. For the specific cause of assent, we must look to the specifically Western and modern ambience of language and opinion as it has grown through two centuries of ideologies.

The modern Western ambience to which I refer is an intellectual and emotional jungle of such denseness that it would be unreasonable to single out a particular ideology as the great culprit. Nevertheless, the most important strands in the matted growth can be discerned and enumerated. First rank among them must be accorded to the psychology developed by Feuerbach in his *Essence of Christianity*. Feuerbach was disturbed—as Kant in the *Critique of Pure Reason* had been before him—by the fact that dogmatic propositions, be they theological or metaphysical, survive socially, even when their fallacious character has been thoroughly analyzed and exhibited to public view. There must be some reality engendering them and sustaining their life, after all; and since to a doctrinaire believer, if he is well shaken by rationalism, this reality can neither be a transcendent entity nor a truth experienced, the symbols must have some world-immanent cause. In the *Critique of Pure Reason*, Kant had already used the term *illusion*, but had not been overly clear about the reality responsible for the illusions and their pertinacity. In the nineteenth century, when the attempt to solve the riddle of the missing reality through Gnostic speculation had run its course and failed, the question had become desperate: after the great "idealistic" systems, the time had come for unequivocal, of somewhat exacerbated, answers through recourse to human nature as the cause of the illusions. Thus Feuerbach interpreted the symbols as projections of the world-immanent consciousness of man. His psychology of projection has remained one of the pillars of the ideologist's creed ever since, and one may even say it is a stronger force today than it was in Feuerbach's time, as in our century it has been fortified by the psychoanalysis of Freud and Jung. Another important component of the ideological ambience is Marx's critique of religion. Marx relied on Feuerbach's psychology, but elaborated it further by the introduction of "Being," in the sense of *Produktionsverhältnisse*, as the cause of the various states of consciousness which induce or prevent the illusionary projections. There must be mentioned, furthermore, Comte's *philosophie positive* which interpreted the symbols of truth experienced as peculiar to a doctrinaire "theological phase" in history, followed by an equally doctrinaire "metaphysical phase," both of them now to be superseded by the dogmatism of "positive science." And finally, we must not forget Freud's *Future of an Illusion*, as the title of the work has become a popular phrase endowing the ideologist's language of illusion with the authority of so undoubted a science as psychology. The list could be continued, but it is sufficiently long to establish the issue: the conventionally so-called ideologies are constructions of history which interpret the doctrinal mode of truth as a phase of human consciousness, now to be superseded by a new phase that will be the highest as well as the last one in history.

The proposition "The experience is an illusion," thus, operates with two intellectual tricks. First, it obscures the fallacy of misplaced concreteness which its background premise has taken over from doctrinal truth; and second, it hides the implied ideology which carves history into a series of blocklike segments, each governed by a state of consciousness. That the second trick is, just like the first one, prefigured by the doctrine it criticizes, is too obvious a point to be labored; I shall recall only the most blatant figuration of the prefigured, i.e., the replacement of the era of Christ by the era of Comte, the Fondateur de la Religion de l'Humanité. As the doctrinaire believer gives his existential assent to the tricky device, he is caught both ways: by the first trick, he becomes the victim of his own fallacy; by the second one, he is shoved aside as the relic of a past that has become obsolete. The proposition is an excellent polemical device, indeed.

The question how the issue of history presents itself to the philosopher has been answered, to a large part, by the preceding analysis. It is true, we have described the issue as it appears on the level of doctrinaire existence, but we have not described it as it appears to the doctrinaire. To the people who live in it, the subfield is a closed world; there is nothing beyond it, or at least nothing they care to know about, should they uneasily sense that something is there after all. Our analysis, on the contrary, while describing this world of theirs, did not move inside it but described it as the subfield in the philosopher's larger horizon of reality. As a consequence, the point has come into view on which hinges a philosophical understanding of history: that truth experienced is excluded from the subfield, while the larger field is characterized by its inclusion. The implications of this difference in structure for a comprehensive view of history must now be unfolded.

Doctrinaire existence affects the operations of the mind. Since the deficient mode of existence belongs to the comprehensive field of history, the pathological deformations which characterize the subfield are historical forces. We must take note of the two principal deformations that have become visible in our analysis:

1. Truth experienced can be excluded from the horizon of reality but not from reality itself. When it is excluded from the universe of intellectual discourse, its presence in reality makes itself felt in the disturbance of mental operations. In order to save the appearances of reason, the doctrinaire must resort, as we have seen, to such irrational means as leaving premises inarticulate, as the refusal to discuss them, or the invention of devices to obscure them, and the use of fallacies. He does no longer move in the realm of reason but has descended to the underworld of opinion, in Plato's technical sense of *doxa*. Mental operations in the subfield, thus, are characterized by the doxic as distinguished from the rational mode of thought.

2. A critical study of history, based on empirical knowledge of phenomena, is impossible, when a whole class of phenomena is denied cognizance. Since the appearances of empirical knowledge, as well as of critical science, must be saved just as much as the appearances of reason, a considerable apparatus of devices has been developed for the purpose of covering the defect. Such devices I shall call doxic methodology; the resulting type of doctrinaire science, doxic empiricism. The problem is set by the constructions of history to which our analysis had to advert: they draw their strength from their opposition, not to faith and philosophy, but to late doctrinal forms of theology and metaphysics; and they remain themselves on the very level of doctrine whose specific phenomena they oppose. The persuasive trick of carving history into ascending phases or states of consciousness, for the

purpose of placing the carver's consciousness at the top of the ladder, can be performed only under the assumption that man's consciousness is world-immanent and nothing but that; the fact that man is capable of apprehending

> The point of intersection of the timeless
> With time

as well as the symbolisms expressing such apprehension must be ignored. The field of historical reality, furthermore, has to be identified and defined as a field of doctrine; and since the great events of participation do not disappear from reality, they must be flattened and crushed until nothing but a rubble of doctrine is left. Especially Plato had to go through the oddest deformations to make him fit the doctrinaire fashions of the moment. During the last one hundred years, selections from his *disjecta membra* were used to let him appear as a Socialist, a Utopian, a Fascist, and an authoritarian thinker. For its legitimation, the butchery performed by ideologists on history requires the covering devices which go under the name of methods—be they of the psychological or materialistic, the scientistic or historicist, the positivist or behaviorist, the value-free or rigorous-method varieties. In the latter half of the nineteenth century, when doxic constructions of history had become so numerous that their mutual incompatibility attracted attention, the fact of doctrinaire construction was even transformed into a methodological principle: "history" was to be a constructive selection of materials, in agreement with somebody's private view or standpoint; such standpoints were called "values," while the assembly of materials under them was named "value-free science"; the standpoints or values themselves were to be exempt from critical examination; and the postulate of exemption was buttressed by the strict refusal to admit the existence of criteria. Not the least grotesque feature of a grotesque age is the speed at which standpoints roll off the production line of consciousness. In fact, the public scene has become so crowded with them that, in the twentieth century, the Open Society—Popper's, not Bergson's—had to be invented, in order to prevent public collisions between private opinions. Regrettably, however, the device for securing peace among opinions, if not of mind, is not foolproof. For every now and then, there happens a standpointer who takes himself seriously and faces everybody else with the alternative of either joining him in his intellectual prison or being put in a concentration camp.

Iron laws of segmented history are constructed, in order to frighten the contemporaries into a state of consciousness that seems desirable to the respective doxic thinker. The conception of the iron law is a terrorist's dream. History has no phases governed by states of consciousness, because there is no such thing as a world-immanent consciousness that would politely exude this or that type of projection in obedience to a doctrinaire's prescription. For History is Man—not: the Doctrinaire—writ large; and as man's consciousness is the reality of tension toward the divine ground of his existence, history is the struggle between existence in truth and the deficient modes of existence. A representative sector of this struggle has been illuminated by the analysis of the "Dispute." There is the wasteland of argument; this wasteland presupposes a truth experienced that has engendered the symbols now broken; and a spiritual outburst occurs in revolt against the untruth of existence. The sector is representative in the sense that we have no empirical knowledge of a different pattern in history: neither is there a wasteland of literalist doctrine and skepticism not recognizably deriving from a truth experienced; nor are there spiritual outbursts in a field empty of previous truth and its decline. There is no beyond in time to the struggle in time; or if we want to express the same thought in an older language, the *civitas Dei* and the *civitas terrena* are intermingled in history throughout its course from the beginning of mankind to its end. The history of mankind, thus, is an open society—Bergson's, not Popper's—comprehending both truth and untruth in tension. It is true, the balance of the tension can shift—personally, socially, and historically—toward one or the other of the poles; and certainly, the shifts in balance can be used to characterize periods of history. Our present age, for instance, must be characterized as an age in which deficient existence, as well as its symbolic expression, is socially predominant. But social predominance of one pole does not abolish the other one and together with it the tension. To speak of periods characterized by one of the poles to the exclusion of the other would be equivalent to saying that there are periods in the history of mankind characterized by the nonexistence of Man—though sometimes one is tempted to indulge in this fancy.

The doctrinaire segmentation of history has found its climactic expression in the formula: "We are living in a post-Christian age." Every style, even the doctrinaire, has its beauties of perfection—and the philosopher cannot suppress his admiration for the neat trick of turning the "post-Christ" of the Christians into the "post-Christian" of the ideologues. Thanks to existential assent, the formula has become widely accepted in our society. Thinkers who otherwise rank above the level of ordinary intellectuals propound it with a serious, if sorrowful, face; and even theologians, who ought to know better, are softening under constant pressure and display a willingness to demythologize their dogma, to abandon the most charming miracles, to renounce the virgin birth, and glumly to admit that God is dead. The attitude is regrettable; for a truth whose symbols have become opaque and suspect cannot be saved by the doctrinal concessions to the *Zeitgeist,* but only by a return to the reality of experience which originally has engendered the symbols. The return will engender its own exegesis—as it does in the present lecture—and the exegetic language will make the older symbols translucent again.

The social effectiveness of the formula indicates a widespread confusion and helplessness; I shall clarify, therefore, the several levels of its meaning. The symbolism belongs to the self-interpretation of a revolutionary movement in the deficient mode of existence. To one part its meaning reaches, like the top of an iceberg, into the reality of the historical process; this realistic stratum of meaning I shall isolate first. To the larger part, the meaning is submerged in the dreamworld of doctrinaire existence that has cut loose from the reality of existential tension; with this large block of submerged meaning I shall deal second. As the "post-Christian" derives from the "post-Christ," I shall deal, third, with the implications of the symbolism for the Christian "post-."

As far as the formula of the "post-Christian age" expresses a revolutionary consciousness of epoch, we can make sense of it. The eighteenth-century revolt, enacted in the name of science and reason against the incubus of doctrinaire theology and metaphysics, was certainly an "epoch," and the unfolding of its momentum up to the present definitely marks an "age" in history. Moreover, the consummation of the revolt through social predominance of its doctrine may well infuse latter-day conformists with a warm glow that theirs is the epoch which in fact was that of the eighteenth century. Inasmuch as the revolt against doctrinaire Christianity has been remarkably successful in our society, there are solid reasons to speak of the age as "post-Christian." As soon, however, as the realistic meaning of the formula is brought out, the limits to its sense as well as to the age it denotes become visible. Regarding the sense, we must not forget that the revolt occurred in the subfield of deficient existence; its wrath was directed against a Christian doctrine that had become opaque, not against Christian faith. Hence, to distinguish the age of ideological revolt as a "post-Christian age" would attribute to the revolt a depth which it does not have—it would be too much of an honor. Regarding the limits to the age, they are set by this very lack of depth. For the revolt against theology and metaphysics did not recover the tension of existence that had seeped from the older symbols but abandoned truth experienced altogether, with the inevitable result of flattening out into a new doctrine of world-immanent consciousness. The loss of reality was not repaired but only further aggravated by the development of ideological doctrines which now in their turn have become opaque and lost their credibility. Still the revolt had to be lived through, it seems, in order to bring the issue of truth v. doctrine to acute consciousness: in the twentieth century, at least the beginnings of a truly radical revolt against all varieties of doctrine, including the ideological ones, can be discerned—as I have pointed out in an earlier part of this lecture. What the ideologues style the "post-Christian age" appears to be receding into the past, and those among us who prefer to live in the present will characterize their age rather as postdoctrinal.

In the realistic sense of the "post-Christian age" is an antidoctrinal revolt which, having failed to recapture the reality of existential tension, has derailed into a new dogmatism. The adherent of an ideological sect, however, would not accept our interpretation as the meaning which he attaches to his symbol. He would be aroused to indignation by the idea that his particular "post-" should ever become a past, with a new "post-" moving into the present; for he, on his part, intends the symbol "post-" to denote the establishment of a final state of society on earth. Moreover, he would ridicule our charge that he failed to recapture truth experienced; he would rightly plead he had never tried such nonsense, as "the experience is an illusion." And finally, he would insist that he objects to theology and metaphysics, not because doctrine is a secondary mode of truth, but because they are wrong conceptions of the world and have long enough obscured the reality in which alone he is interested. This energetic protest cannot be brushed aside. The ideologue's position seems to have a basis in reality; we must ascertain what this reality is, and how it is transformed into the dream constructions of history.

The ideologue appeals to the reality, not of truth experienced, but of the world, and for good reason. For the ideological revolt against the older type of doctrine derives indeed the better part of its strength from the contemporaneous experience of power to be gained over nature through the use of science and reason. Ideology is a commensal of modern science, drawing for both its pathos and aggressiveness on the conflicts of scientists with church and state. In the sixteenth century, and in some regions of

Western civilization well into the twentieth, the Christian *contemptus mundi* still cast its shadow over nature; and the exploration of nature was specifically handicapped by the literalists' belief in Christian doctrine as the infallible source of information about the structure of the world. Inevitably, the explorers of the reality hitherto neglected had to suffer from the persecutions of literalist doctrinaires. There is nothing dreamlike about these facts: science, technology, industry, and the memories of the struggle are the solid ground on which the ideologue can take his stand. Nevertheless, the terrorism of ideological groups and regimes is also real; and the claim of the ideologies to be "sciences," as well as the development of the doxic methodologies, leaves no doubt that somehow the nightmare is connected with science in the rational sense. There must be a factor whose addition will change the reality of power over nature, with its rational uses in the economy of human existence, into a terrorist's dream of power over man, society, and history; and there can hardly be a doubt what this factor is: it is the *libido dominandi* that has been set free by the draining of reality from the symbols of truth experienced. At the time when the reality of science and power was gained, the reality of existential tension was lost, so that from the combination of gain and loss, with the *libido dominandi* as the catalyst, the new dream could arise. The technique by which the symbols of the dream are produced is well known. The shell of doctrine, empty of its engendering reality, is transformed by the *libido dominandi* into its ideological equivalent. The *contemptus mundi* is metamorphosed into the *exaltatio mundi*; the City of God into the City of Man; the apocalyptic into the ideological millennium; the eschatological metastasis through divine action into the world-immanent metastasis through human action; and so forth. The center from which the particular symbols receive their meaning is the transformation of human power over nature into a human power of salvation. Nietzsche has developed the symbol of self-salvation in order to express the alchemic *opus* of man creating himself in his own image. In this dream of self-salvation, man assumes the role of God and redeems himself by his own grace.

Self-salvation, however, is self-immortalization. Since the dream of participation in a "post-Christian age" secures to the ideological believer the immortality which in terms of the broken image has become incredible, he can accept neither the realistic meaning of his own phrase nor rational argument in general. His problem will become clear, as soon as we state the alternatives to persistence in his dream. In order to accept reason, he would have to accept truth experienced—but the reality of existential tension is difficult to revive, once it has atrophied. If the prison of his dream, however, were broken in any other manner than by a return to reality, the only vista opening to him would be the bleakness of existence in a world-immanent time where everything is post-everything-that-has-gone-before *ad infinitum*. The second alternative would release a flood of anxiety, and the dread of this flood keeps the doors of the prison closed. We should be aware of this horror, when sometimes we wonder about an ideologue's resistance to rational argument. The alternative to life in the paradise of his dream is death in the hell of his banality. His self-made immortality is at stake; and in order to protect it, he must cling to his conception of time. For the time in which the ideologue places his construction is not the time of existence in tension toward eternity, but a symbol by which he tries to pull the timeless into identity with the time of his existence. Though the reality of tension between the timeless and time is lost, thus, the form of the tension is preserved by the dream act of forcing the two poles into oneness. We can characterize the ideologue's "post-Christian age," therefore, as a symbol engendered by his libidinous dream of self-salvation.

The philosopher, too, has his troubles with the "post-." For participation in the nonexistent reality of the ground is participation in the timeless; the consciousness of the ground is the area of reality where the timeless reaches into time. Where, then, does the existential tension belong? To time with its "post-," or to the timeless where presumably there is no "post-"? The experience of a reality intermediate between the two poles is excellently symbolized by two passages from T. S. Eliot's *Four Quartets*: "History is a pattern of timeless moments"; and "the point of intersection of the timeless with time." To express the same experience of reality, Plato has developed the symbol of the *metaxy*, of the In-Between, in the sense of a reality that partakes of both time and eternity and, therefore, does not wholly belong to the one or the other. There appears to be a flow of existence that is not existence in time. Since modern philosophy has not developed a vocabulary for describing the *metaxy*, I shall use the term *presence* to denote the point of intersection in man's existence; and the term *flow of presence* to denote the dimension of existence that is, and is not, time. The question then will arise what sense the symbol "post-" does make if history is a flow of presence; and inversely, what sense the symbol "presence" does make if the presence of intersection is a timelike flow.

The question has agitated the Christian thinkers. For the truth of salvation and immortality through faith in Christ, if converted into doctrine, is apt to condemn to hell all mankind that happened to live before Christ. Setting aside the brutality of the procedure, a philosopher will not be too happy about such doctrine, because he knows the tension of faith toward God to be not a Christian privilege but a trait of human nature. A St. Augustine, for instance, was well aware that the structure of history is the same as the structure of personal existence; and he did not hesitate to use, inversely, historical symbols to express the reality of personal tension. In the *Enarrationes in Psalmos* 64.2 he lets the historical symbols of the Exodus and of Babylon express the movement of the soul when it is drawn by love toward God:

> Incipit exire qui incipit amare.
> Exeunt enim multi latenter,
> et exeuntium pedes sunt cordis affectus:
> exeunt autem de Babylonia.
>
> He begins to leave who begins to love.
> Many the leaving who know it not,
> for the feet of those leaving are affections of the heart:
> and yet, they are leaving Babylon.

His conception of history as a tale of two cities, intermingling from the beginning of mankind to its end, conceives it as a tale of man's personal exodus writ large. But how does the "historical Christ," with a fixed date in history, fit into this philosophical conception? St. Thomas has asked the question and sharpened it to its critical point: he asks "whether Christ be the head of all men" (*ST* III 8.2), and answers unequivocally that he is the head of all men, indeed, and that consequently the mystical body of the church consists of all men who have, and will have, existed from the beginning of the world to its end. Philosophically, the proposition implies that Christ is both the "historical Christ," with a "pre-" and "post-" in time, and the divine timelessness, omnipresent in the flow of history, with neither a "pre-" nor a "post-." In the light of these implications, then, the symbolism of incarnation would express the experience, with a date in history, of God reaching into man and revealing him as the Presence that is the flow of presence from the beginning of the world to its end. History is Christ writ large. This last formulation is not in conflict with the Platonic "man writ large." To be sure, the two symbolisms differ, because the first one is engendered by a pneumatic experience in the context of Judaic-Christian revelation, while the second one is engendered by a noetic experience in the context of Hellenic philosophy; but they do not differ with regard to the structure of the reality symbolized. In order to confirm the sameness of structure expressed in different symbolisms, I shall quote the essential passage from the Definition of Chalcedon (A.D. 451), concerning the union of the two natures in the one person of Christ: "Our Lord Jesus Christ . . . truly God and truly man . . . recognized in two natures . . . the distinction of natures being in no way annulled by the union, but rather the characteristics of each nature being preserved and coming together to form one person and subsistence." This valiant attempt of the *patres* to express the two-in-one reality of God's participation in man, without either compromising the separateness of the two or splitting the one, concerns the same structure of intermediate reality, of the *metaxy,* the philosopher encounters when he analyzes man's consciousness of participation in the divine ground of his existence. The reality of the Mediator and the intermediate reality of consciousness have the same structure.

In the intellectual climate of the age, our analysis of equivalent symbols may lead to misunderstanding. Let me caution therefore: the philosopher can help to make revelation intelligible, but no more than that; a philosophy of consciousness is not a substitute for revelation. For the philosopher is a man in search of truth; he is not God revealing truth. The warning is necessary, because Hegel has tried to combine philosophy and revelation in the act of producing a system of dialectical speculation. He imagined an inchoative revelation of God through Christ to have come to its fulfillment through consciousness becoming self-conscious in his system; and correspondingly he imagined the God who had died in Christ now to be dead. I do not have to go into details—we are familiar with the Hegelian aftermath of existentialist theology and the God-is-dead movement. This Hegelian dream of making God a consciousness, so that consciousness can be revelation, belongs to the "post-Christian age." Our inquiry is neither a "post-Christian" construction of history nor a revelation of truth; it rather is an anamnestic venture to recover presence from "the general mess of imprecision of feeling." T. S. Eliot has caught the essence of such a venture in the following lines:

> And what there is to conquer
> By strength and submission, has already been discovered
> Once or twice, or several times, by men whom one
> cannot hope

To emulate—but there is no competition—
There is only the fight to recover what has been lost
And found and lost again and again; and now, under
conditions
That seem unpropitious

Perhaps the conditions are less unpropitious than they seemed to the poet when he wrote these lines, almost a generation ago. Anyway, we must immerse ourselves now in the flow of presence, in order to recover the meaning of immortality that has flared up in the Egyptian *Dispute.*

V

Man, while existing in time, experiences himself as participating in the timeless. The experience engenders the type of symbolism of which the Egyptian *Dispute* is a variant. This rather large complex of symbols must be considered a unit, because its various parts—of which "immortality" is one—are the expressive ramifications of the one originating experience. We must describe the nature of the complex and its variants before we can use the *Dispute* in the analysis of certain issues surrounding the problem of immortality.

The complex is not an accidental assemblage of symbols but reveals a structure in which the member symbols have a definite place. The *Dispute* suggests at least the following groups as typical: (1) there is a nuclear group consisting of the symbols "life," "death," "mortality," and "immortality"; (2) another group is formed by the symbols which refer to the entities involved in the fate of life and death, such as man, his soul, or part of his soul, and the gods, or God; (3) a further group concerns the order of the cosmos and society, justice and judgment; (4) we have drawn attention, then, to a group that also appears in Hellenic philosophy, in Christianity, and gnosis, i.e., the group of life as a prison, as a sickness, a darkness, and an exile, and of death as a release from a prison, a recovery from sickness, a light shining in the darkness, and a return to one's home; (5) and finally, there is a group of imagery concerning the topography of the upper and nether worlds and the destinies of their inhabitants.

The historical variants of the complex do not actualize the several groups all in the same manner or with the same relative weight. The accents may fall on the consequences of immortality for the ordering of existence in earthly life, as in classical ethics. The tension of existence may snap, so that the injustice of social order will appear irreparable in the present *aiōn* and just order is to be expected only from a metastasis of the world through divine intervention, as in apocalyptic; or it may be deformed by the libidinous attempt at pulling the timeless into identity with time, as in ideological speculations on politics and history. The cosmos may be considered a demonic prison, so that the purpose of human action will be reduced to finding the means of escape from it, as in gnosis. The expectation of immortality may rise to Egyptian comforts, or shrink to the Hellenic shadow existence in Hades, or expand ecstatically to Christian glorification. The drama of fall and redemption may assume the form of a cosmological myth, as in Gnostic systems; or of a historical myth, as in Marxian speculation. The imagery of afterlife may be richly elaborated, as in the apocalyptic and Gnostic symbolisms; and then again, the mythical imagery may disappear under pressure of enlightenment and demythization, to be replaced by the hedonistic imagery of perfect realms to be achieved through progress and revolutionary action, as in our own time. Nevertheless, wherever the accents fall and however the groups of symbols are balanced or imbalanced, the pattern of the complex remains recognizable.

The relations between the complex and its variants, as well as the relations between the variants, are problems in the logics of experience and symbolization, too intricate to be suitable for treatment on this occasion. It must be sufficient to state that the variants of the complex are not individuals of a species but historical variants in a technical sense: they have a recognizable pattern in common because they all express the tension of existence between time and the timeless; and they are variants of the pattern because they express modalities of the tension. The flow of presence with its changing modalities of experience is the common source of both the single variants and their sequence. The variants are, therefore, subunits of meaning in the unit of the sequence which derives its meaning from the one engendering flow of presence. The fact that the sequence of variants is a unit of meaning makes it possible for our inquiry to move backward and forward in the sequence, in order to let the variants elucidate one another. For the variants, however remote in time, will never sink into a dead past without meaning, once they have arisen from the flow of truth that has "presence"; they will remain phases in the historical process of living truth of which neither the beginning nor the end is known; and by virtue of this character the truth of each variant is supplementary to the truth of the others. A later variant may have differentiated an aspect of truth experienced that has been insufficiently articulated in an earlier one; while the compact earlier variant may have expressed aspects of truth which, under pressure of a newly differentiated and therefore more heavily accented problem, do not receive their proper weight in, or have disappeared completely from, the later one. Moreover, the movement of inquiry from one variant to the other is apt to let the meaning of the sequence as a whole emerge—though *meaning of the whole*, I should warn, is not the proper term for a perspective of truth that must be gained from a position inside the process of emergent truth.

In my concluding remarks I shall use the *Dispute* to clarify a few problems of immortality that must remain obscure as long as we concentrate too firmly on later variants. I shall deal, first, with the issue of alienation as it provides the setting for the problem of immortality; and second, with the experiential motivations of the symbol "immortality."

I shall use the term *alienation* to denote a certain mood of existence. Whenever the mood is aroused to intense consciousness, it engenders a characteristic group of symbols. We have encountered this group, in the *Dispute,* in the symbols referring to life as a prison, and so forth; the same group appears in pre-Socratic and Platonic philosophy; and in the Gnostic ambience it flowers so richly that the authorities in the field are inclined to accept it as the specific difference of gnosticism. The term *alienation* (*allotriosis, Entfremdung*) itself, however, does not appear in philosophical discourse, as far as I know, before Plotinus. In its Neoplatonic context it refers to a remoteness of God so great that God is "alien" to the world and man; and this meaning is quite close to the language of the "alien" or "hidden God," or of the "alien Life," that we find in the Mandaean and other Gnostic writings. In modern usage, especially since Hegel and Marx, the term has come to refer to the state of existence which is apt to engender this group of symbols—a change of meaning which indicates the new critical attitude of existential analysis. I shall continue the modern usage, but give it more philosophical precision by letting the term refer to a mood of existence that is rooted in the very structure of existence itself. By this procedure it will be possible to connect the plurality of meanings which the alienation group of symbols has acquired in the course of history with similar pluralities of meaning developed by other groups. Of primary interest to our purpose is the connection between the developments of plural meanings in the alienation group and in the life-death group of symbols.

We know life ending in death to be only part of the life we experience. Under the pressure of circumstances, this suspense between a temporal life that is not all of life, and a nontemporal life that makes no sense on the conditions of time and death, can be sharpened to a conflict in which the meaning of life changes to death and of death to life. In the *Gorgias* 492–93, Socrates addresses Callicles:

> Well, but on your own view, life is strange. For I tell you I should not
> wonder if Euripides' words were true, when he says:
> Who knows if to live is to be dead,
> and to be dead to live?
> and we really, it may be, are dead; in fact, I once heard one of our sages
> say that now we are dead, and the body is our tomb.

The Platonic double meaning of life and death, current in Hellenic culture probably as early as Pythagoras, is substantially the same as in the *Dispute*; and in the *Dispute* and the *Gorgias* it prepares the vision of just order restored through judgment in afterlife. We can speak of a state of alienation, therefore, when the existential mood that engenders the double meanings of life and death has reached a stage of acute suffering—as it has for the Man in the *Dispute.* The symbol "alienation" is meant to express a feeling of estrangement from existence in time because it estranges us from the timeless: we are alienated from the world in which we live when we sense it to be the cause of our alienation from the world to which we truly belong; we become strangers in the world when it compels conformity to a deficient mode of existence that would estrange us from existence in truth. In further elaboration of the symbolism, existence in time can become an "alien world," or a "foreign country," or a "desert" in which the wanderer from another world has lost his way; or the man thrown into this alien environment may find his direction and engage in a "pilgrim's progress," or an "ascent from the cave," or a prolonged "wandering in the desert" that will ultimately lead him to the "promised land"; or he may adapt himself to the ways of the strangers and find his home among them, so that the alien world becomes the true world and the true world would be an alien world—a problem that has occupied the Hellenic poets and philosophers from Hesiod to Plato.

I have followed the symbolism of alienation from its experiential core into some of its ramifications, in order to make it clear beyond a doubt that there is no other way to make sense of the variety of symbols but the way back to their point of origin in the structure of existence. Alienation, it appears from the symbols, is a mood of existence just as fundamental as anxiety. For the symbols of alienation are recognizable as hypostases of the poles of existential tension. The "world" we discern in the perspective of our existence to partake of both time and the timeless is dissociated, under the pressure of the mood, into "this world" of existence in time and the "other world" of the timeless; and as we "exist" in neither the one nor the other of these worlds but in the tension between time and the timeless, the dissociation of the "world" transforms us into "strangers" to either one of the hypostatized worlds. The symbolism of the two worlds can then be further elaborated in the manner that we know from the *Dispute,* or the Platonic and Gnostic myths, or modern ideological speculations. With regard to the historical situations that will arouse a feeling of alienation strong enough to engender the great symbolic expressions, a survey of the variants suggests the breakdown of traditional order and the subsequent periods of disorder, both personal and social, as their typical setting. In the case of the *Dispute,* the situational pressure is supplied by the breakdown of imperial order, the prolonged disorder of the First Intermediate Period, and skepticism with regard to traditional symbols of order; in the case of the pre-Socratics and Plato, by the waning power of the *poleis*, of continuous warfare among them, the threat to their very existence posed by the rise of power organizations on the imperial scale, and the disintegration of the *patrios doxa* through skepticism and sophistic; that Apocalypse, Gnosis, and Christianity were conditioned by the expansion of empire and the destruction of traditional community order is generally acknowledged; and in the case of modern alienation, the pressure is supplied by the decline of Christianity into dogmatic belief, the wave of enlightenment, the dissolution of traditional economic and social forms through the rise of industrial society, and the global wars.

Symbolisms of alienation are conventionally associated with gnosis. It will be appropriate, therefore, to formulate the bearing which our analysis has on this question.

In the present state of science we are still torn between the older historicist methods and the critical methods of existential analysis. Historicism is a doxic method, connected with the general decline of truth experienced to belief in doctrine; symbols, when conceived as doctrine, are cut off from their engendering experience and become historical phenomena in their own right. Once a symbolism has attracted his attention for one reason or another, the historicist scholar will describe it conscientiously on the basis of the sources and then proceed to explore its historical filiation as far back as the knowledge of materials will allow. The method has been applied to gnosis. Gnostic systems certainly are spectacular phenomena in the "history of ideas" and deserve attention; symbolisms of alienation and the famous "dualism" are so strongly developed that one is justified in considering them the specific difference of Gnostic thought; and both Hellenic and Iranian symbolisms are similar enough to permit the construction of a long prehistory of Gnostic thought. The Egyptian *Dispute* has hitherto escaped attention—but I would not be surprised if sooner or later it were used to extrapolate the history of gnosis beyond Iran to its true beginning in Egypt. Nevertheless, even at the time of historicist exuberance Eugène de Faye had insisted, in his *Gnostiques et gnosticisme* (1913), that Gnostic symbolisms could not be understood without recourse to the experience engendering them. Today, with our wealth of comparative materials, we must be even more insistent on the point. If alienation is indeed a fundamental mood of existence, its symbolization is to be expected whenever a situation of disorder has built up sufficient pressure; since, however, the alienation symbols are no more than one group in the comprehensive complex, nothing follows from their appearance for the meaning of the variant as a whole. The mood of alienation can affect the tension of existence in more than one way, and the resulting modes of experience and variants of symbolization are not necessarily Gnostic. Neither the argument of the *Dispute* nor the philosophizing of Plato has anything to do with gnosis; and we hardly shall consider St. Paul a Gnostic thinker because he counsels us to live in this world as if we were not of it. If we want to overcome the confusion caused by historicism, we had better remember the treatment accorded to the issue by Clement of Alexandria. For the purpose of his polemic against Marcion and other Gnostics he presents (*Stromateis* III.3.12–21) a formidable collection of alienation symbols gleaned from Hellenic poets and philosophers; and then he goes on to explain that the collection is as acceptable to him as it is to Marcion as a true interpretation of the human condition, but that he will not for that reason agree with Marcion on the conclusions to be drawn from them. Clement presents us with the model case of a single body of alienation symbols that can serve in three experiential contexts differing as widely as Pagan Philosophy, Gnosis, and Christianity. I conclude, therefore, that the appearance of alienation symbols does not mark any of the historical variants as Gnostic, even though in the Gnostic context they are remarkably elaborate. The problems of Gnosis lie elsewhere.

The problems posed by the symbol "immortality," or rather by the pair "mortality"-"immortality," will be brought into focus by the following statements:

1. The symbolism of immortality is not peculiar to Christianity and revelation. It is well articulated as early as the *Dispute,* i.e., in a strictly cosmological variant of the complex.
2. Immortality is a predicate presupposing a subject. In Homeric language man is mortal, the gods are immortal; in classic philosophy the soul, or at least its noetic part, is immortal; in early Christianity immortality means the bodily resurrection of man assured by the resurrection of Christ; in the *Dispute* the subject of immortality is the soul, or rather one of the souls, of Man.
3. Whatever the subject of which immortality be predicated, the symbol pertains to the lasting or duration of an entity.
4. The symbol "immortality" presupposes the experience of life and death. The symbols "life"-"death" are not synonyms for man's spatiotemporal existence, its coming-into-being and its passing away, seen from the outside, but express man's consciousness of existing in tension toward the divine ground of his existence. We have noted the double meanings of life and death engendered by the consciousness of participating, while existing in time, in the timeless. The pair "mortality"-"immortality" is related to the pair "life"-"death" and its double meanings.

The problems arise from the changing modes of experience and the corresponding plurality of variant symbols. The four statements suggest at least two historical modes of experience: on the first level, that of the primary experience of the cosmos, there appear the entities of whom mortality or immortality is predicated; on the second level, that of differentiated consciousness, the symbols express the poles of existential tension. The movement from the earlier to the later mode of experience, however, is not accompanied by the development of a new set of symbols; the older symbols are retained and change their meanings. Moreover, it seems the earlier meanings cannot be dispensed with when the later modality is reached, so that in the later context the symbols appear with two meanings; the symbolizations of truth experienced do not exclude but supplement one another. The result is a not inconsiderable confusion of meanings. I shall try to unravel this problem at least on principle.

A famous passage from Aristotle's *Nicomachean Ethics* X,VII,.8 will show the symbolism of immortality at the point of transition from the earlier to the later mode of experience:

> The life of the intellect (*nous*) is higher than the human level; not in virtue of his humanity will a man achieve it, but in virtue of something within him that is divine; and by as much as this something is superior to his composite nature, by so much is its activity superior to the exercise of other sorts of virtue. If then the intellect is something divine in comparison with man, so is the life of the intellect divine in comparison with human life. Nor ought we to obey those who enjoin that a man should have man's thoughts and a mortal the thoughts of mortality, but we ought to immortalize (*athanatizein*) as much as possible and do everything toward a life in accordance with the highest thing in man.

The two modes of experience and symbolization are clearly recognizable and the confusion of meanings is impressive. On the older level we find the entities, i.e., the immortal gods and mortal men; on the new level, represented by Plato and Aristotle, we find the tension of existence with its poles of mortality and immortality. The passage alludes to a sharp conflict between the guardians of tradition and the philosophers. For the traditionalists believe in gods and men as distinct entities and insist that men should have only thought proper to their status of mortals; while the philosophers have discovered that man is not quite mortal but partakes of divine immortality and insist, therefore, that his thought should be principally concerned with the divine. It is a clash between two theologies: the philosophers abolish the gods of the polytheistic tradition and identify their own God as the *Nous* who reveals himself, through noetic search, as the Ground of existence. In the passage, however, the conflict is not expressed with full clarity, because tradition is strong enough to overlay the newly discovered tension of existence with the older symbolization of gods and men. Even to Aristotle man is still the mortal who can think only mortal thought; if he can think about the divine nevertheless, he is enabled to do so by some part in him, the intellect, that is a divine entity. Is the Aristotelian man, then, a temporary union of a human-mortal with a divine-immortal entity to be dissolved through death? The answer must be no; for at this point the tension of existence, in its turn, makes its influence felt and engenders the magnificent symbol of *athanatizein*. I have translated the *athanatizein* by an intransitive *to immortalize*; for the symbol is meant to characterize noetic life as a habit of action by which man can, and ought to, increase his potential immortality to its full stature. The practice of "immortalizing" is to Aristotle a virtue superior to all other. Since in *Nicomachean Ethics* Aristotle has distinguished only between ethical and dianoetic virtues, not giving a name to the highest class—to which also belong *phronēsis* and *philia*—I propose the term *existential virtues*.

The state of confusion in which Aristotle has left the problem has become a historical force causing confusion even in modern thought. For if *Nous* is both the god beyond man and the divine entity within man, then the two are liable to collapse into one as soon as they are not firmly held apart by the tension of existence. This is what has happened in Hegel's *Begriffsspekulation*: the two *Nous* entities of Aristotle blend into the one *Geist* of Hegel; the separate entities become moments in the dialectical process; and the tension between them reappears as the dialectical movement internal to the *Geist*. When the consciousness of existential tension has atrophied—as it has in doctrinal theology and metaphysics of the eighteenth century—we are not thrown back to a pre-Aristotelian belief in mortals and immortals. From the state of confusion, there rather emerges the new type of system which transforms experienced participation in the divine into a speculative possession of the divine. The system has had prodigious success, and still has, because it furnishes the intellectual apparatus for the various ideological and theological attempts at bringing God and the world, society and history, under the control of man.

In order to dissolve the fateful confusion, I shall first give more precision to its crucial points.

1. The confusion arises at the point of transition from the primary experience of the cosmos to the consciousness of man's participation in the divine ground. The language of the cosmological myth will not adequately express the newly discovered reality of interaction and mutual participation between God and man.

2. The pre-Socratic and classic philosophers have developed a host of new symbols that will express the experience of an area of reality intermediate between God and man. There are, first of all, the Platonic symbols of the In-Between (*metaxy*) and of the spiritual man (*daimonios anēr*) who exists in the tension of the In-Between. Curiously enough, there was developed a wealth of symbols expressing the nuances of existential

tension, such as "love" (*philia, erōs*), "faith" (*pistis*), "hope" (*elpis*), while the symbol "tension" (*tasis*) itself appears only in Stoic philosophy as expressing the structure of reality in general. The nature of the In-Between as a mutual participation of human and divine is symbolized by the Platonic *methexis* and the Aristotelian *metalēpsis*, the active life in the tension by the existential virtues previously mentioned. Symbols for consciousness are inchoatively developed by pressing *aisthēsis* and *nous* into service; as a symbol for the site of the experience, the *psychē* must do. The experience itself, however, is carefully described as a search (*zētēsis*) from the side of man and attraction (*kinēsis*) from the side of God.

3. In spite of the highly developed symbolism expressing the In-Between of participation, certain difficulties arise from the side of the participants. For the divine and human partners to the tension are not the immortals and mortals of tradition, but a new type of God and man. We have seen Plato developing the *daimonios anēr*, in order to distinguish the new man from the mortal (*thnētos*) of old; when the distinction is not made, we encounter the difficulties of the Aristotelian passage. In a modern language of consciousness the problem of the new man can be formulated in the following manner: when man discovers his existence in tension, he becomes conscious of his consciousness as both the site and the sensorium of participation in the divine ground. As far as consciousness is the site of participation, its reality partakes of both the divine and the human without being wholly the one or the other; as far as it is the sensorium of participation, it is definitely man's own, located in his body in spatiotemporal existence. Consciousness, thus, is both the time pole of the tension (sensorium) and the whole tension including its pole of the timeless (site). Our participation in the divine remains bound to the perspective of man. If the distinction between the two meanings of consciousness be neglected, there arises the danger of derailing into the divinization of man or the humanization of God.

4. In the primary experience of the cosmos, mortality is man's way of lasting; immortality the gods' way. On the level of differentiated consciousness, the meaning of the symbolism subtly changes in a manner that will become apparent when we link the pair "mortality"-"immortality" with the double meanings of life-death in the *Gorgias* passage. We would then have to say: Mortality means that man's life having lasted for a while will succumb to death; immortality means that man's life will outlast death. The meaning carried by the two sentences will be more clearly conveyed when they are combined into one statement: Man's life is structured by

death. The symbol "life" in this last formulation will express with exactitude the experience of the In-Between that has also engendered the Platonic *daimonios anēr*. For the life structured by death is neither the life of the mortals nor the lasting of the gods, but the life experienced in the tension of existence. It is the life lived in the flow of presence.

5. Even though the symbolization may be exact, we have the uneasy feeling that something has escaped us. Is that really all we know about immortality? Some of the more robust will say they don't care about this sort of anemic immortality. What has become of the mythopoetic imagery of afterlife, as for instance of the position of a counselor in the bark of the sun-god, as in the *Dispute*; or that of a follower in the suite of the God, as in the *Phaedrus*; to say nothing of Dante's Hell, Purgatory, and Paradise? Well, as far as the tension of existence is concerned, I am afraid that is all—though it is a good deal, for we have traced the symbolism of immortality to its origin in the experience that life is more than the life of mortals. Nevertheless, the rebellious questioning motivated by a desire for fulfillment beyond tension, for a purpose to the exodus from Sheol, for a destination to the wandering in the desert, and so forth, is quite healthy, for the experience of existential tension is indeed not all of man's experience. We have to account for the fact that the symbol "immortality" unequivocally means lasting in the manner of the gods, though man's existence in tension toward the divine ground will give him no information about the mode of divine existence. How, then, do we know that gods are "everlasting" (*aiōnios*), and what does the lasting of the gods mean, if they so distinctly do not last in time that the most appropriate symbolism for man's existence is the tension between time and the timeless?

The answer to the question to which our series of precisions has led will come through recourse to the *Dispute*.

The Egyptian variant of the symbolism reveals an acute suffering from alienation and the desire to preserve existence in truth against the pressure to conform to a deficient mode of existence. Since, however, the consciousness of existential tension has not yet differentiated, its problems must be expressed in the compact language of the cosmological myth. It is the language, not of tension, but of the entities involved in the fate of life and death; and the understanding of the entities is hardly affected by the theological conflict characteristic of the transition from the experience of the cosmos to that of existential participation. The entities are man, his soul, the realm of Egypt, and the sun-god; the order (*ma'at*) pervading the entities has its source in the sun-god and flows from him, through the

Pharaoh, into the administration of the realm, and ultimately to the people living in the realm. When something goes wrong with the order of the Pharaoh, the realm, and man, the solution envisaged is the restoration of order through Man's cooperation at its source in the bark of the sun-god. The entities, thus, form a community of consubstantial partners in divine order. This divinely ordered community—to which we apply the later Greek term *kosmos*—is experienced by Man as the lasting reality of which he is part. The lasting of the cosmos is the lasting of the gods who create and maintain its order; and the Man of the *Dispute* can participate in its lasting by attuning his existence to the order of the gods. The primary experience of cosmic reality, thus, provides the spaces and times for the life of the gods and the afterlife of man. The imagery of immortality is engendered by the primary experience of man's conduration with the cosmos.

The confusion will dissolve if we acknowledge the historical stratification in man's experience of reality. There is, first, the compact experience of the cosmos and, second, the differentiated experience of existential tension. For their adequate expression, the two types of experience engender two different sets of symbols. To the first set there belong among others:

(*a*) the time of the cosmos; and conduration with the cosmos
(*b*) the intracosmic gods
(*c*) the language of the mythical tale and its personnel

To the second set there belong among others:

(1) the polarization of cosmic time into the time and the timeless of the tension; and the flow of presence
(2) the world-transcendent God
(3) the language of noetic and spiritual life

With regard to the symbol "immortality" we can say therefore: The imagery of afterlife originates in the compact experience of cosmic reality; the symbolism of life structured by death originates in man's experience of his existence in tension toward the divine ground.

We can dissolve confusion and misconstruction once they have arisen—but we cannot prevent the disturbances of existential order that will historically arise from changes in the modes of experience and cause ever new confusion and misconstruction. Let me advert, in conclusion, briefly to this problem, as we are living in an age of major disturbances from this source.

The two experiences do not pertain to different realities but to the same reality in different modes. The experience of cosmic reality includes in its compactness the existential tension; and the differentiated consciousness of existence has no reality without the cosmos in which it occurs. On the level of cosmic experience we find, as a consequence, a rich variety of hymns and prayers expressing the personal tension of existence, and even such documents as the *Dispute*; while on the level of existential experience man has to cope with the problems of cosmic reality which require resymbolization as far as the older symbolism has become incompatible with the new insights of existential tension. Plato, for instance, was acutely aware of the philosopher's quandary: he developed a new type of symbolism, the philosophic myth, in order to express on the noetic level the cosmic reality that formerly had been the domain of traditional myth. Moreover, in the *Epinomis* he earnestly warned against discrediting traditional myth, because people whose faith in the myth is destroyed will not necessarily become philosophers, but rather will become spiritually disoriented and derail into some deficient mode of existence. Christianity, then, has inherited, through both the Old and New Testaments, a solid body of cosmic myth and lived with it by letting it stand and digesting theologically only so much of it as the philosophical instrumentarium of the moment seemed to allow. Compact symbolisms, in sum, may become obsolete in the light of new insights, but the reality they express does not cease to be real for that reason. If we let any part of reality drop out of sight by refusing it public status in the world of symbols, it will lead a sort of underground life and make its reality felt in intense moods of alienation, or even in outright mental disturbances. C. G. Jung had a few things to say on this problem. Even though we should have to reject all traditional symbolizations of cosmic reality as incompatible with our present mode of experience, we still are living in the reality of the cosmos and not in the universe of physics, the brainwashing propaganda of our scientistic ideologues notwithstanding. The ideological constructions of history which ignore the historical stratification of experience and relegate compact strata, under the title of obsolete "states of consciousness," to a dead past should be understood, with regard to one of their motivations, as acts of despair caused by an acute state of alienation; for they try to annihilate by magic-murder a disturbing reality that has not yet found satisfactory resymbolization. These remarks, though they can be no more than the barest hints, will perhaps suggest a new understanding of some problems that move the age.

The Mutual Influence of Theology and Philosophy

Leo Strauss

I

When we attempt to return to the roots of Western civilization, we observe soon that Western civilization has two roots which are in conflict with each other, the biblical and the Greek philosophic, and this is to begin with a very disconcerting observation. Yet this realization has also something reassuring and comforting. The very life of Western civilization is the life between two codes, a fundamental tension. There is therefore no reason inherent in the Western civilization itself, in its fundamental constitution, why it should give up life. But this comforting thought is justified only if we live that life, if we live that conflict, that is. No one can be both a philosopher and a theologian or, for that matter, a third which is beyond the conflict between philosophy and theology, or a synthesis of both. But every one of us can be and ought to be either the one or the other, the philosopher open to the challenge of theology or the theologian open to the challenge of philosophy.

There is a fundamental conflict or disagreement between the Bible and Greek philosophy. This fundamental conflict is blurred to a certain extent by the close similarity in points. There are, for example, certain philosophies which come seemingly close to the biblical teaching—think of philosophic teachings which are monotheistic, which speak of the love of God and of man, which even admit prayer, etc. And so the difference becomes sometimes almost invisible. But we recognize the difference immediately if we make this observation. For a philosopher or philosophy there can never be an absolute sacredness of a particular or contingent event. This particular or contingent is called, since the eighteenth century, the historical. Therefore people have come to say that revealed religion means historical religion, as distinguished from natural religion, and that philosophers could have a natural religion, and furthermore, that there is an essential superiority of the historical to the natural. As a consequence of this interpretation of the particular and contingent as historical, it came to be held, and that is very frequently held today, that the Bible is in an emphatic sense historical, that the Bible, as it were, discovered history (or the biblical authors), whereas philosophy as philosophy is essentially nonhistorical. This view is underlying much of present-day interpretation of biblical thought. What is called existentialism is really only a more elaborate form of this interpretation. I do not believe that this approach is very helpful for the understanding of the Bible, at least as far as its basic parts are concerned; and as an explanation, I will suggest here only one consideration: that these present-day concepts, such as History with a capital *H*, are very late concepts, very derivative, and by this very fact not as capable of unlocking to us early thought, thought which is in no way derivative, but at the beginning of a tradition.

One can begin to describe the fundamental disagreement between the Bible and Greek philosophy, and doing that from a purely historical point of view, from the fact that we observe first a broad agreement between the Bible and Greek philosophy regarding both morality and the insufficiency of morality; the disagreement concerns that "x" which completes morality. According to Greek philosophy, that "x" is *theoria*, contemplation, and the biblical completion we may call, I think without creating any misleading understanding, piety, the need for divine mercy or redemption, obedient love. To be more precise (the term "morality" itself is one of these derivative terms which are not quite adequate for the understanding of earlier thought), we may replace the term "morality" by the term "justice," a term common to both sources; and justice means primarily obedience to law, and law in the full and comprehensive sense, divine law. Going even back behind that, we suggest as a starting point of the whole moral development of mankind, if we may say so, a primeval identification of the good with the ancestral. Out of this primeval equation which we still understand, of which we still make use in actual life, the notion of a divine law necessarily arose. And then in a further step, the problem of divine law: the original notion of a divine law or divine code implies that there is a large variety of them. The very variety and, more specifically, the contradiction between the various divine codes makes the idea of a divine law in the simple and primary sense of the term radically problematic.

There are two diametrically opposed solutions to this problem possible, the one is the philosophic and the other is the biblical solution. The philosophic solution we may describe in the following terms: The philosophers transcend the dimension of divine codes altogether, the whole dimension of piety and of pious obedience to a pregiven code. Instead they embark on a free quest for the beginnings, for the first things, for the principles. And they assume that on the basis of the knowledge of first principles, of the first principles, of the beginnings, it will be possible to determine what is by nature good, as distinguished from what is good merely by convention. This quest for the beginnings proceeds through sense perception, reasoning, and what they called *noēsis*, which is literally translated by "understanding" or "intellect," and which we can perhaps translate a little bit more cautiously by "awareness," an awareness with the mind's eye as distinguished from sensible awareness. But while this awareness has certainly its biblical equivalent and even its mystical equivalent, this equivalent in the philosophic context is never divorced from sense perception and reasoning based on sense perception. In other words, philosophy never becomes oblivious of its kinship with the arts and crafts, with the knowledge used by the artisan and with this humble but solid kind of knowledge.

Now turning to the biblical alternative, here the basic premise is that one particular divine code is accepted as truly divine; that one particular code of one particular tribe is the divine code. But the divine character of all other allegedly divine codes is simply denied, and this implies a radical rejection of mythology. This rejection of mythology is also characteristic of the primary impulse of philosophy, but the biblical rejection of mythology proceeds in the opposite direction as philosophy does. To give some meaning to the term mythology which I am here forced to use, I would say that mythology is characterized by the conflict between gods and impersonal powers behind the gods. What is in Greek sometimes called *moira*, for example. Now philosophy replaces this impersonal fate, as we might say, by nature and intelligible necessity. The Bible, on the other hand, conceives of God as the cause of everything else, impersonal necessities included. The biblical solution then stands or falls by the belief in God's omnipotence. The notion of omnipotence requires, of course, monotheism, because if you have more than one God clearly none of them can be omnipotent. Only the biblical authors, we may say, understand what omnipotence really means, because only if God is omnipotent can one particular code be the absolute code. But an omnipotent God who is in principle perfectly knowable to man is in a way subject to man, insofar as knowledge is in a way power. Therefore a truly omnipotent God must be a mysterious God, and that is, as you know, the teaching of the Bible. Man cannot see the face of God, and especially the divine name, "I shall be that I shall be," means it is never possible in any present to know that, what God shall be. But if man has no hold whatever over the biblical God, how can there be any link between man and God? The biblical answer is the Covenant, a free and mysterious action of love on the part of God, and the corresponding attitude on the part of man is trust, or faith, which is radically different from theoretical certainty. The biblical God is known in a humanly relevant sense only by his actions, by his revelations. The book, the Bible, is the account of what God has done and what he has promised. It is not speculation about God. In the Bible, as we would say, men tell about God's actions and promises on the basis of their experience of God. This experience, and not reasoning based on sense perception, is the root of biblical wisdom.

This radical difference between the Bible and Greek philosophy shows itself also in the literary character of the Bible, on the one hand, and of Greek philosophic books, on the other. The works of the Greek philosophers are really books, works, works of one man, who begins at what he regards as the necessary beginning, either the beginning simply or the best beginning for leading up people to what he regards as the truth. And this one man—one book, was characteristic of Greek thought from the very beginning: Homer. But the Bible is fundamentally, as is today generally held, a compilation of sources, which means the Bible continues a tradition with a minimum of changes, and therefore the famous difficulties with which the biblical scholars are concerned. The decisive point, I think, is this: here is no beginning made by an individual, no beginning made by man, ultimately. There is a kinship between this art of writing and the favored form of writing, favored in the Jewish tradition, namely, the commentary, always referring back to something earlier. Man does not begin.

In my analysis I presupposed that the equation of the good with the ancestral is the primeval equation. That may be so in chronological terms, but one cannot leave it at that, of course, because the question arises, why should this be so, what evidence does this equation have? That is a very long question, and I do not propose to answer it now. I would only refer to a Greek myth according to which Mnemosyne, memory, is the mother of the muses, meaning the mother of wisdom. In other words, primarily the good, the true, however you might call it, can be known only as the old because prior to the emergence of wisdom memory occupied the place of wisdom. Ultimately, I think, one would have to go back to a fundamental dualism in man in order to understand this conflict between the Bible and Greek philosophy, to the dualism of deed and speech, of action and thought—a dualism which necessarily poses the question as to the primacy of either—and one can say that Greek philosophy asserts the primacy of thought, of speech, whereas the Bible asserts the primacy of deed. That is, I know very well, open to misunderstandings, but permit me to leave it at this for the moment.

II

Now we are at any rate confronted with the fact that there is a radical opposition between Bible and philosophy, and this opposition has given rise to a secular conflict from the very beginning. This conflict is characteristic of the West, the West in the wider sense of the term including even the whole Mediterranean basin, of course. It seems to me that this conflict is the secret of the vitality of the West. I would venture to say that as long as there will be a Western civilization there will be theologians who will suspect the philosophers and philosophers who will be annoyed or feel annoyed by the theologians. But, as the saying goes, we have to accept our fate, and it is not the worst fate which men could imagine. We have this radical opposition: the Bible refuses to be integrated into a philosophical framework, just as philosophy refuses to be integrated into a biblical framework. As for this biblical refusal, there is the often-made remark, that the god of Aristotle is not the God of Abraham, Isaac, and Jacob, and therefore any attempt to integrate the biblical understanding into philosophic understanding means to abandon that which is meant by the God of Abraham, Isaac, and Jacob. As for philosophy, that is perhaps a little bit obscured by a number of facts and therefore we must dwell upon it for a moment. The obscuration, I believe, is ultimately due to the fact that in the discussions regarding the relation of theology and philosophy, philosophy is identified with the completed philosophic system, in the Middle Ages, of course, primarily with Aristotle—by which I do not mean to say that Aristotle has a system, although it is sometimes believed that he had—but certainly with Hegel in modern times. That is, of course, one very special form of philosophy: it is not the primary and necessary form of philosophy. I have to explain that.

In a medieval work, the *Kuzari*, by Yehuda Halevi, we find this statement: "Socrates says to the people, 'I do not reject your divine wisdom, I simply do not understand it. My wisdom is merely human wisdom.'" Now in the mouth of Socrates, as in this apothegm, human wisdom means imperfect wisdom or quest for wisdom, that is to say, philosophy. Since he realizes the imperfection of human wisdom, it is hard to understand why he does not go from there to divine wisdom. The reason implied in this text is this: as a philosopher, he refuses assent to anything which is not evident to him, and revelation is for him not more than an unevident, unproven possibility. Confronted with an unproven possibility, he does not reject, he merely suspends judgment. But here a great difficulty arises which one can state as follows: it is impossible to suspend judgment regarding matters of utmost urgency, regarding matters of life and death. Now the question of revelation is evidently of utmost urgency. If there is revelation, unbelief in revelation or disobedience to revelation is fatal. Suspense of judgment regarding revelation would then seem to be impossible. The philosopher who refuses to assent to revelation because it is not evident therewith rejects revelation. But this rejection is unwarranted if revelation is not disproved. Which means to say that the philosopher, when confronted with revelation, seems to be compelled to contradict the very idea of philosophy by rejecting without sufficient grounds. How can we understand that? The philosophic reply can be stated as follows: the question of utmost urgency, the question which does not permit suspense, is the question of how one should live. Now this question is settled for Socrates by the fact that he is a philosopher. As a philosopher, he knows that we are ignorant of the most important things. The ignorance, the evident fact of this ignorance, evidently proves that quest for knowledge of the most important things is the most important thing for us. Philosophy is then evidently the right way of life. This is in addition, according to him, confirmed by the fact that he finds his happiness in acquiring the highest possible degree of clarity which he can acquire. He sees no necessity whatever to assent to something which is not evident to him. And if he is told that his disobedience to revelation might be fatal, he raises the question, what does fatal mean? In the extreme case, it would be eternal damnation. Now the philosophers of the past were absolutely certain that an all-wise God would not punish with eternal damnation or with anything else such human beings as are seeking the truth or clarity. We must consider later on whether this reply is quite sufficient. At any rate, philosophy is meant, and that is the decisive point, not as a set of propositions, a teaching, or even a system, but as a way of life, a life animated by a peculiar passion, the philosophic desire or eros, not as an instrument or a department of human self-realization. Philosophy understood as an instrument or as a department is, of course, compatible with every thought of life, and therefore also with the biblical way of life. But this is no longer philosophy in the original sense of the term. This has been greatly obscured, I believe, by the Western development, because philosophy was certainly in the Christian Middle Ages deprived of its character as a way of life and became just a very important compartment.

I must therefore try to restate why, according to the original notion of philosophy, philosophy is necessarily a way of life and not a mere discipline, if even the highest discipline. I must explain, in other words, why philosophy cannot possibly lead up to the insight that another way of life apart from the philosophic one is the right one. Philosophy is quest for knowledge regarding the whole. Being essentially quest and being not able ever to become wisdom, as distinguished from philosophy, the problems are always more evident than the solutions. All solutions are questionable. Now the right way of life cannot be fully established except by an understanding of the nature of man, and the nature of man cannot be fully clarified except by an understanding of the nature of the whole. Therefore, the right way of life cannot be established metaphysically except by a completed metaphysics, and therefore the right way of life remains questionable. But the very uncertainty of all solutions, the very ignorance regarding the most important things, makes quest for knowledge the most important thing, and therefore a life devoted to it, the right way of life. So philosophy in its original and full sense is then certainly incompatible with the biblical way of life. Philosophy and Bible are the alternatives or the antagonists in the drama of the human soul. Each of the two antagonists claims to know or to hold the truth, the decisive truth, the truth regarding the right way of life. But there can be only one truth: hence, conflict between these claims and necessarily conflict among thinking beings; and that means inevitably argument. Each of the two opponents has tried since millennia to refute the other. This effort is continuing in our day, and in fact it is taking on a new intensity after some decades of indifference.

III

Now I have to say a few words about the present-day argument. The present-day argument in favor of philosophy, we can say, is practically nonexistent because of the disintegration of philosophy. I have spoken on a former occasion of the distinction between philosophy and science as understood today, a distinction which necessarily leads to a discrediting of philosophy. The contrast between the lack of results in philosophy and the enormous success of the sciences brings this about. Science is the only intellectual pursuit which today successfully can claim to be the perfection of the human understanding. Science is neutral in regard to revelation. Philosophy has become uncertain of itself. Just one quotation, a statement of one of the most famous present-day philosophers: "Belief in revelation is true, but not true for the philosopher. Rejection of revelation is true for the philosopher, but not true for the believer." Let us turn to the more promising present-day argument in favor of revelation. I shall not waste words on the most popular argument which is taken from the needs of present-day civilization, the present-day crisis, which would simply amount to this: that we need today, in order to compete with Communism, revelation as a myth. Now this argument is either stupid or blasphemous. Needless to say, we find similar arguments also with Zionism, and I think this whole argument has been disposed of in advance a long time ago by Dostoievsky in *The Possessed.*

Now the serious argument in favor of revelation can be stated as follows: there is no objective evidence whatever in favor of revelation, which means there is no shred of evidence in favor of revelation except, first, the experience, the personal experience, of man's encounter with God, and secondly, the negative proof of the inadequacy of any nonbelieving position. Now as to the first point—there is no objective evidence in favor of revelation except the experience of one's encounter with God—a difficulty arises. Namely, what is the relation of this personal experience to the experience expressed in the Bible? It becomes necessary to distinguish between what the prophets experience, what we may call the call of God or the presence of God, and what they said, and this latter would have to be called, as it is today called by all nonorthodox theologians, a human interpretation of God's action. It is no longer God's action itself. The human interpretation cannot be authoritative. But the question arises, is not every specific meaning attached to God's call or to God's presence a human interpretation? For example, the encounter with God will be interpreted in radically different manners by the Jew on the one hand and by the Christian on the other, to say nothing of the Muslim and others. Yet only one interpretation can be the true one. There is therefore a need for argument between the various believers in revelation, an argument which cannot help but to allude somehow to objectivity. As for the second point—the negative proof of the inadequacy of any nonbelieving position—that is usually very strong insofar as it shows the inadequacy of modern progressivism, optimism, or cynicism, and to that extent I regard it as absolutely convincing.

But that is not the decisive difficulty. The decisive difficulty concerns classical philosophy, and here the discussions, as far as I know them, do not come to grips with the real difficulty. To mention only one point, it is said that classical philosophy is based on a kind of delusion which can be proved to be a delusion. Classical philosophy is said to be based on the unwarranted belief that the whole is intelligible. Now this is a very long question. Permit me here to limit myself to say that the prototype of the philosopher in the classical sense was Socrates, who knew that he knew nothing, who therewith admitted that the whole is not intelligible, who merely wondered whether by saying that the whole is not intelligible we do not admit to have some understanding of the whole. For of something of which we know absolutely nothing, we could of course not say anything, and that is the meaning, it seems to me, of what is so erroneously translated by the intelligible, that man as man necessarily has an awareness of the whole. Let me only conclude this point. As far as I know, the present-day arguments in favor of revelation against philosophy are based on an inadequate understanding of classical philosophy.

Now, to find our bearings, let us return to a more elementary stratum of the conflict. What is truly significant in the present-day argument will then become clearer, and we shall understand also the reasons for the withdrawal from objectivity in the argument in favor of revelation in present-day theology. The typical older view regarding revelation and reason is today accepted fully only by the Catholic Church and by Orthodox Jews and orthodox Protestants. I speak of course only of the Jewish version. The question is, how do we know that the Torah is from

Sinai or the word of the living God? The traditional Jewish answer is primarily that our fathers have told us, and they knew it from their fathers, an uninterrupted chain of a reliable tradition, going back to Mount Sinai. If the question is answered in this form, it becomes inevitable to wonder, is the tradition reliable? I will mention only one specimen from the earlier discussion. At the beginning of his legal code, Maimonides gives the chain of tradition from Moses down to Talmudic times, and there occurs the figure of Ahijah the Shilonite who is said to have received the Torah from King David and also is introduced as a contemporary of Moses who had received the Torah from Moses. Now, whatever Maimonides may have meant by the insertion of this Talmudic story, from our point of view it would be an indication of the fact that this chain of the tradition, especially in its earlier parts, contains what today is called "mythical," that is to say, unhistorical elements. I shall not dwell on the very well-known discrepancies in the Bible. The question of who wrote the Pentateuch was traditionally answered, as a matter of course, by Moses, so much so that when Spinoza questioned the Mosaic origin of the Torah it was assumed that he denied its divine origin. Who wrote the Pentateuch, Moses himself, or men who knew of the revelation only from hearsay or indirectly? The details are of no interest to us here; we have to consider the principle.

Is a historical proof of the fact of revelation possible? A historical proof of the fact of revelation would be comparable to the historical proof of the fact, say, of the assassination of Caesar by Brutus and Cassius. That is demonstrably impossible. In the case of historical facts proper, or historical facts in the ordinary sense of the term, there is always evidence by impartial observers or by witnesses belonging to both parties. For example, here, friends and enemies of Caesar. In the case of revelation, there are no impartial observers. All witnesses are adherents and all transmitters were believers. Furthermore, there are no pseudoassassinations or pseudowars, but there are pseudorevelations and pseudoprophets. The historical proof presupposes, therefore, criteria for distinguishing between genuine and spurious revelation. We know the biblical criterion, at least the decisive one in our context: a prophet cannot be a genuine prophet if he contradicts the preceding classic revelations, the Mosaic revelation. Therefore the question is, how to establish the classic revelation?

The usual traditional answer was, "miracles." But here the difficulty arises in this form: miracles as miracles are not demonstrable. In the first place, a miracle as a miracle is a fact of which we do not know the natural causes, but our ignorance of the cause of a given phenomenon does not entitle us to say it cannot have been produced by any natural cause but only supernaturally. Our ignorance of the power of nature—that is Spinoza's phrasing of the argument—our ignorance of the power of nature disqualifies us from ever having recourse to supernatural causation. Now this argument in this form is not quite adequate for the following reasons: because while our knowledge of the power of nature is certainly very limited, of certain things we know, or at least men like Spinoza believed to know, that they are impossible by nature. I mention only the resurrection of a dead man, to take the strongest example, which Spinoza would admit could never have taken place naturally. Therefore the argument taken from the ignorance of the power of nature is supplemented by the following argument: that it might be possible theoretically to establish in given cases that a certain phenomenon is miraculous, but it so happens that all these events regarding which this claim is made are known only as reported, and many things are reported which have never happened. More precisely, all miracles which are important, certainly to the Jew and even to the Protestant (the case of Catholicism is different), took place in a prescientific age. No miracle was performed in the presence of first-rate physicists, etc. Therefore, for these reasons, many people today say, and that was also said by certain famous theologians of the past, that miracles presuppose faith; they are not meant to establish faith. But whether this is sufficient, whether this is in accordance with the biblical view of miracles, is a question. To begin with, one could make this objection: that if you take the story of the prophet Elijah on Carmel, you see that the issue between God and Baal is decided by an objective occurrence, equally acceptable to the sense of perception of believers as well as unbelievers.

The second ordinary traditional argument in favor of revelation is the fulfillment of prophecies. But I need not tell you that this again is open to very great difficulties. In the first place, we have the ambiguity of prophecies, and even in cases like unambiguous prophecies—for example, the prophecy of Cyrus in the fortieth chapter of Isaiah, that is today generally taken to be a prophecy after the event, the reasoning being that such a prophecy would be a miracle if established; but it is known only as reported, and therefore the question of historical criticism of the sources comes in.

Much more impressive is the other line of the argument which proves revelation by the intrinsic quality of revelation. The revealed law is the best of all laws. Now this, however, means that the revealed law agrees with the rational standard of the best law; but if this is the case, is then the allegedly revealed law not in fact the product of reason, of human reason, the work of Moses and not of God? Yet the revealed law, while it never contradicts reason, has an excess over reason; it is suprarational, and therefore it cannot be the product of reason. That is a very famous argument, but again we have to wonder what does suprarational mean? The supra has to be proved and it cannot be proved. What unassisted reason sees is only a nonrational element, an element which, while not contradicting reason, is not in itself supported by reason. From the point of view of reason, it is an indifferent possibility: possibly true, possibly false, or possibly good, possibly bad. It would cease to be indifferent if it were proved to be true or good, which means if it were true or good according to natural reason. But again, if this were the case, it would appear to be the product of reason, of human reason. Let me try to state this in more general terms. The revealed law is either fully rational—in that case it is a product of reason—or it is not fully rational—in that case it may as well be the product of human unreason as of divine superreason. Still more generally, revelation is either a brute fact, to which nothing in purely human experience corresponds—in that case it is an oddity of no human importance—or it is a meaningful fact, a fact required by human experience to solve the fundamental problems of man—in that case it may very well be the product of reason, of the human attempt to solve the problem of human life. It would then appear that it is impossible for reason, for philosophy, to assent to revelation as revelation. Moreover, the intrinsic qualities of the revealed law are not regarded as decisive by the revealed law itself. Revealed law puts the emphasis not on the universal, but on the contingent, and this leads to the difficulties which I have indicated before.

Let us turn now to the other side of the picture; these things are, of course, implied in all present-day secularism. Now all these and similar arguments prove no more than that unassisted human reason is invincibly ignorant of divine revelation. They do not prove the impossibility of revelation. Let us assume that revelation is a fact, if a fact not accessible to unassisted reason, and that it is meant to be inaccessible to unassisted reason. For if there were certain knowledge, there would be no need for faith, for trust, for true obedience, for free surrender to God. In that case, the whole refutation of the alleged rejection of the alleged objective historical proofs of revelation would be utterly irrelevant. Let me take this simple example of Elijah on Carmel: were the believers in Baal, whom Elijah or God convinced, impartial scientific observers? In a famous essay,

Francis Bacon made a distinction between idolators and atheists and said that the miracles are meant only for the conviction, not of atheists, but of idolators, meaning of people who in principle admit the possibility of divine action. These men were fearing and trembling, not beyond hope or fear like philosophers. Not theology, but philosophy, begs the question. Philosophy demands that revelation should establish its claim before the tribunal of human reason, but revelation as such refuses to acknowledge that tribunal. In other words, philosophy recognizes only such experiences as can be had by all men at all times in broad daylight. But God has said or decided that he wants to dwell in mist. Philosophy is victorious as long as it limits itself to repelling the attack which theologians make on philosophy with the weapons of philosophy. But philosophy in its turn suffers a defeat as soon as it starts an offensive of its own, as soon as it tries to refute, not the necessarily inadequate proofs of revelation, but revelation itself.

IV

Now there is today, I believe, still a very common view, common to nineteenth- and twentieth-century freethinkers, that modern science and historical criticism have refuted revelation. Now I would say that they have not even refuted the most fundamentalistic orthodoxy. Let us look at that. There is the famous example which played such a role still in the nineteenth century and, for those of us who come from conservative or orthodox backgrounds, in our own lives. The age of the earth is much greater than the biblical reports assume, but it is obviously a very defective argument. The refutation presupposes that everything happens naturally; but this is denied by the Bible. The Bible speaks of creation; creation is a miracle, the miracle. All the evidence supplied by geology, paleontology, etc., is valid against the Bible only on the premise that no miracle intervened. The freethinking argument is really based on poor thinking. It begs the question. Similarly, textual criticism—the inconsistencies, repetitions, and other apparent deficiencies of the biblical text: if the text is divinely inspired, all those things mean something entirely different from what they would mean if we were entitled to assume that the Bible is a merely human book. Then they are just deficiencies, but otherwise they are secrets.

Historical criticism presupposes unbelief in verbal inspiration. The attack, the famous and very effective attack by science and historical criticism on revelation, is based on the dogmatic exclusion of the possibility of miracles and of verbal inspiration. I shall limit myself to miracles, because verbal inspiration itself is one miracle. Now this attack, which underlies all the scientific and historical arguments, would be defensible if we knew that miracles are impossible. Then we would indeed be able to draw all these conclusions. But what does that mean? We would have to be in possession either of a proof of the nonexistence of an omnipotent God, who alone could do miracles, or of a proof that miracles are incompatible with the nature of God. I see no alternative to that. Now the first alternative—a proof of the nonexistence of an omnipotent God—would presuppose that we have perfect knowledge of the whole, so as it were we know all the corners, there is no place for an omnipotent God. In other words, the presupposition is a completed system. We have the solution to all riddles. And then I think we may dismiss this possibility as absurd. The second alternative—namely, that miracles are incompatible with the nature of God—would presuppose human knowledge of the nature of God: in traditional language, natural theology. Indeed the basis, the forgotten basis, of modern free thought, is natural theology. When the decisive battles were waged, not in the nineteenth century, but in the eighteenth and seventeenth, the attempted refutation of miracles, etc., was based on an alleged knowledge of the nature of God—natural theology is the technical name for that.

Let us sketch the general character of this argument. God is the most perfect being. This is what all men mean by God, regardless of whether He exists or not. Now the philosophers claim that they can prove the incompatibility of revelation and of any other miracle with divine perfection. That is a long story, not only in the seventeenth and eighteenth centuries but of course also in the Middle Ages. I will try to sketch this argument by going back to its human roots. Fundamentally, the philosophic argument in natural theology is based on an analogy from human perfection. God is the most perfect being. But we know empirically perfection only in the form of human perfection, and human perfection is taken to be represented by the wise man or by the highest human approximation to the wise man. For example, just as the wise man does not inflict infinite punishment on erring human beings, God, still more perfect, would do it even less. A wise man does not do silly or purposeless things, but to use the miracle of verbal inspiration, for example, in order to tell a prophet the name of a pagan king who is going to rule centuries later, would be silly. I mean, that is the argument underlying these things or something of this kind. To this I would answer as follows: God's perfection implies that he is incomprehensible. God's ways may seem to be foolish to man; this does not mean that they are foolish. Natural theology would have to get rid, in other words, of God's incomprehensibility in order to refute revelation, and that it never did.

There was one man who tried to force the issue by denying the incomprehensibility of God's essence, and that man was Spinoza. (May I say this in passing that I have leaned very heavily in my analysis of these things on Spinoza.) One can learn much from Spinoza, who is the most extreme, certainly of the modern critics of revelation, not necessarily in his thought but certainly in the expression of his thought. I like to quote the remark of Hobbes, you know, a notoriously bold man, who said that he had not dared to write as boldly as Spinoza. Now Spinoza says, "We have adequate knowledge of the essence of God," and if we have that, God is clearly fully comprehensible. What Spinoza called the adequate knowledge of the essence of God led to the consequence that miracles of any kind are impossible. But what about Spinoza's adequate knowledge of the essence of God? Let us consider that for one moment, because it is really not a singular and accidental case. (Many of you will have seen Spinoza's *Ethics*, his exposition of that knowledge.) Spinoza's *Ethics* begins, as you know, with certain definitions. Now these definitions are in themselves absolutely arbitrary, especially the famous definition of substance: substance is what is by itself and is conceived by itself. Once you admit that, everything else follows from that; there are no miracles possible then. But since the definitions are arbitrary, the conclusions are arbitrary. The basic definitions are, however, not arbitrary if we view them with regard to their function. Spinoza defines by these definitions the conditions which must be fulfilled if the whole is to be fully intelligible. But they do not prove that these conditions are in fact fulfilled—that depends on the success of Spinoza's venture. The proof lies in the success. If Spinoza is capable of giving a clear and distinct account of everything, then we are confronted with this situation. We have a clear and distinct account of the whole, and, on the other hand, we have obscure accounts of the whole, one of whom would be the biblical account. And then every sane person would prefer the clear and distinct account to the obscure account. That is, I think, the real proof which Spinoza wants to give. But is Spinoza's account of the whole clear and distinct? Those of you who have ever tried their hands, for example, at his analysis of the emotions, would not be so certain of that. But more than that, even if it is clear and distinct, is it necessarily true? Is its clarity and distinctness not due to the fact that Spinoza abstracts from those elements of the whole which are not clear and distinct and which can never be rendered clear and distinct? Now fundamentally, Spinoza's procedure is that of modern science according to its original conception—to make the universe a completely clear and distinct, a completely mathematizable unit.

Let me sum this up: the historical refutation of revelation (and I say here that this is not changed if you take revelation in the most fundamentalist meaning of the term) presupposes natural theology because the historical refutation always presupposes the impossibility of miracles, and the impossibility of miracles is ultimately guaranteed only by knowledge of God. Now a natural theology which fills this bill presupposes in its turn a proof that God's nature is comprehensible, and this in its turn requires completion of the true system of the true or adequate account of the whole. Since such a true or adequate, as distinguished from a merely clear and distinct, account of the whole, is certainly not available; philosophy has never refuted revelation. Nor, to come back to what I said before, has revelation, or rather theology, ever refuted philosophy. For from the point of view of philosophy, revelation is only a possibility; and secondly, man, in spite of what the theologians say, can live as a philosopher, that is to say, untragically. It seems to me that all these attempts, made, for example, by Pascal and by others, to prove that the life of philosophy is fundamentally miserable, presuppose faith; it is not acceptable and possible as a refutation of philosophy. Generally stated, I would say that all alleged refutations of revelation presuppose unbelief in revelation, and all alleged refutations of philosophy presuppose already faith in revelation. There seems to be no ground common to both, and therefore superior to both.

If one can say colloquially, the philosophers have never refuted revelation and the theologians have never refuted philosophy, that would sound plausible, considering the enormous difficulty of the problem from any point of view. And to that extent we may be said to have said something very trivial; but to show that it is not quite trivial, I submit to you this consideration in conclusion. And here when I use the term *philosophy*, I use it in the common and vague sense of the term where it includes any rational orientation in the world, including science and what have you, common sense. If this is so, philosophy must admit the possibility of revelation. Now that means that philosophy itself is possibly not the right way of life. It is not necessarily the right way of life, not evidently the right way of life, because this possibility of revelation exists. But what then does the choice of philosophy mean under these conditions? In this case, the choice of philosophy is based on faith. In other words, the quest for evident knowledge rests itself on an unevident premise. And it seems to me that this difficulty underlies all present-day philosophizing and that it is this difficulty which is at the bottom of what in the social sciences is called the value problem: that philosophy or science, however you might call it, is incapable of giving an evident account of its own necessity. I do not think I have to prove that showing the practical usefulness of science, natural and social science, does not of course prove its necessity at all. I mean I shall not speak of the great successes of the social sciences, because they are not so impressive; but as for the great successes of the natural sciences, we in the age of the hydrogen bomb have the question completely open again whether this effort is really reasonable with a view to its practical usefulness. That is of course not the most important reason theoretically, but one which has practically played a great role.

Part 3

Commentaries

Reason and Revelation as Search and Response: A Comparison of Eric Voegelin and Leo Strauss

James L. Wiser

I

In two articles, published on two separate occasions, Leo Strauss summarized his understanding of the relationship between Greek philosophy and the biblical tradition. Although these two traditions have functioned as the historical sources for Western civilization and although they both refer to a highest good that may be described in general terms as wisdom, the biblical and philosophical traditions exist, according to Strauss, in fundamental tension. The codes expressed by the two traditions are in conflict with one another, and it is a conflict that permits neither a compromise nor an alternative: "No one can be both a philosopher and a theologian or, for that matter, a third which is beyond the conflict between philosophy and theology, or a synthesis of both."[1]

According to Strauss, a synthesis is not possible due to the fact that the core teachings of each tradition necessarily deny the ultimate legitimacy of the other. "We must then try to understand the difference between biblical wisdom and Greek wisdom. We see at once that each of the two claims to

1. Strauss, "The Mutual Influence of Theology and Philosophy," *Independent Journal of Philosophy* 3 (1979): 111. [See page 217 in this volume.]

be the true wisdom, thus denying to the other its claim to be wisdom in the strict and highest sense."[2]

In the articles in which the above quotations are found, Strauss presents his analysis of the specific teachings of the biblical and philosophic codes, which he believes justifies the conclusion he has drawn. Among these justifications/arguments are included the following:

1. For the Greeks philosophy is more than a discipline; it is a way of life. As described by Plato, it is a never-ending quest for knowledge of the good. Thus, its wisdom begins in and is continually nourished by wonder. For biblical prophets, on the other hand, there is no need to seek for knowledge of the good because such knowledge has been revealed by God. As a consequence the wise person is one who preserves this revelation, and that person's wisdom begins in piety and fear of the Lord.

2. Whereas the Greeks understood contemplation as the completion of morality, the Bible places morality's completion in piety or obedient love.

3. Whereas Greek philosophy asserts the primacy of thought and speech—and thus, for example, Aristotle's God is pure thought thinking itself—the Bible asserts the primacy of deed, and its God, in turn, is a creator-God who not only thinks but also acts and rules.

4. Whereas the Greek belief that nature is intelligible found its final expression in Aristotle's doctrine of the eternity of the visible universe, the biblical doctrine of creation ultimately led some to the position that the world as created by God cannot be known by human reason alone.

5. For the Greeks philosophy is the free quest for the whole, for the first things or principles, and seeks that which has intelligible necessity and is, as a consequence, capable of producing theoretical certainty. The Bible, on the other hand, sees an omnipotent God as the cause of all things. Inasmuch as the biblical God is omnipotent, He is by necessity beyond the control of knowledge and, as a consequence, must remain essentially mysterious to all. According to the biblical

2. "Jerusalem and Athens: Some Preliminary Reflections," *Commentary* 43 (1967): 46. [See page 112 here.]

tradition, then, faith (*pistis*) replaces knowledge (*epistēmē*) as the proper link between man and God.

In a letter to Voegelin dated 4 June 1951, Strauss stated that he believed that his "distinction between revelation and human knowledge . . . is in harmony with the Catholic teaching." Although Voegelin's reply to this particular statement is not extant, it is highly likely that he would have accepted it as historically accurate. The problem for Voegelin was not with any individual's position, vis-à-vis the traditional Christian teaching on revelation and reason, but rather with the adequacy of that very tradition itself. From Voegelin's perspective the traditional dichotomy between reason and revelation was itself an example of a type of doctrinal deformation that could be traced down to ancient Stoicism:

> Moreover, the Stoic deformation had a decisive influence on Christian theology in fostering a dichotomy of reason-revelation. There is nothing "natural" in the noetic illuminations of consciousness of Plato and Aristotle. That the insights of the classic philosophers have something to do with "natural reason" as distinguished from "revelation" is a conceit developed by the *patres* when they accepted the Stoic symbols of nature and reason uncritically as "philosophy."[3]

For Voegelin the error that explains this deformation can be found in the general tendency to interpret symbols without giving appropriate attention to those experiences for whose articulation they were first created. This tendency, in turn, recurs as it does because of the multiply paradoxical quality of reality, consciousness, and language.

According to Voegelin, reality encompasses more than just those things that are intended as the objects of consciousness. It also exists as a comprehending whole that includes not only those things of the object world and that form of consciousness which intends them but also that all-encompassing horizon within which such objects and their corresponding forms of intending consciousness are revealed as existing together. This all-encompassing, nonobjective horizon, in turn, is made accessible to us by a form of consciousness that, because it is included within the horizon

3. Voegelin, *The Ecumenic Age* (Baton Rouge: Louisiana State University Press, 1974), 48.

of being, cannot stand apart from it. Thus, rather than intending this all-encompassing reality as an object, this second form of consciousness necessarily participates within it as its source of self-illumination. Whereas intentional consciousness creates concepts by which to express its comprehension of objective reality, luminal consciousness creates symbols by which to articulate its experience of participation within the all-encompassing horizon or movement of being itself.

In volume 5 of his *Order and History*, Voegelin devoted considerable effort to an examination of the structures of reality, consciousness, and language. These structures are both complicated and paradoxical inasmuch as each component is in itself a complex one. According to Voegelin, the term "reality" refers to both an objective order and the order of the all-encompassing (or, as in his terms, a "thing-reality" and an "It-reality"). Consciousness includes both an intentional form and a luminal form, and language may function either conceptually or symbolically.[4] Inasmuch as there are distinct modes of reality, each with its own appropriate form of apprehending consciousness and each with its own set of rules as to proper language usage, failure to respect these differences inevitably leads to the doctrinal deformations referred to earlier. In such cases language, which was originally created to function as a meditative symbol, comes to be understood as the conceptual description of specific metaphysical entities or "things." In short, the creation of dogma replaces noetic participation as the proper activity of the philosophical imagination. Once the focus of analysis is no longer on the experience of luminosity itself but rather on the coherence of various dogmatic systems, differences at the level of language eventually obscure the underlying equivalences common to all instances of participatory consciousness.

This, according to Voegelin, explains why the medieval distinction between natural reason and divine revelation is inappropriate. By focusing upon the explicit dogmas of the Greek and biblical traditions, this distinction obscures the underlying and controlling fact that both traditions are in effect dogmatized expressions of the same fundamental form of human existence-in-truth. In an effort to emphasize this commonality, Voegelin referred to that "noetic core" which is shared by both classical philosophy and the Gospels.

4. The contemporary philosopher whose ideas are most similar on this issue is Karl Jaspers. Voegelin's distinctions parallel somewhat Jaspers's efforts to differentiate between world and transcendence, consciousness-at-large and existential consciousness, and concepts and ciphers.

> The noetic core, thus, is the same in both classic philosophy and the gospel movement. There is the same field of pull and counter-pull, the same sense of gaining life through following the pull of the golden cord, the same consciousness of existence in an In-Between of human-divine participation, and the same experience of divine reality as the center of action in the movement from question to answer. Moreover, there is the same consciousness of newly differentiated insights into the meaning of existence; and in both cases this consciousness constitutes a new field of human types in history. . . .[5]

At this point in the analysis the differences between Leo Strauss's and Eric Voegelin's understanding of reason and revelation should be clear. Strauss sees the traditions of Athens and Jerusalem as antithetical to one another. Revelation is understood as a form of superhuman information that is transmitted to us by the authority of the prophets. As such, it is essentially hearsay and, thus, maintained by the faith of that particular community which trusts in the legitimacy of its ancestral codes. Philosophy, on the other hand, is the unaided quest for first things, guided by an awareness that "is never divorced from sense perception and reasoning based on sense perception."[6] As such, philosophy holds revelation to a test it cannot pass as long as it remains true to itself as revelation. According to Strauss, revelation is always a particular act directed toward a particular group; reason, on the other hand, seeks by its very nature the universal, not the particular; the necessary, not the contingent. Thus it demands that what is, in fact, particular deny its own particularity. The revealed must demonstrate its truth before all:

> When it was demanded that the distinction between hearsay and seeing with one's own eyes be applied to the most weighty matters, it was demanded that the superhuman origin of all alleged superhuman information must be proved by examination in the light . . . of such criteria as ultimately derived in an evident manner from the

5. Voegelin, "The Gospel and Culture," in D. Miller and D. G. Hadidian, eds., *Jesus and Man's Hope*, vol. 2 (Pittsburgh, Pa.: Pittsburgh Theological Seminary Press, 1971), 80. [See pages 158–59 here.]

6. Strauss, "Mutual Influence," 112. [See page 219 here.]

> rules which guide us in matters fully accessible to human knowledge.[7]

Given that revelation can never meet the test of reason as long as it preserves its own character as revelation, there can never be, according to Strauss, a synthesis between the two traditions.

Voegelin, on the other hand, sees biblical revelation and classical Greek philosophy as sharing a common noetic core. There are differences. For indeed revelation supplements the Greek experience of an individual's noetic quest with its own particular appreciation of God's inrush into history. Or to use Voegelin's terms, whereas revelation emphasizes the pneumatic movement of the divine toward man, Greek philosophy emphasizes the human experience of man's noetic quest for the divine.[8] At the same time, however, both movements are but singular aspects of that mutual participation of the human and the divine that constitutes the all-encompassing reality of existence.

II

A disagreement about the relationship between revelation and reason could occur because of differing understandings as to the nature of

7. Strauss, *Natural Right and History* (Chicago: University of Chicago Press, 1953), 88.

8. These differences are important and do have consequences:

> The movement that engendered the Saving Tale of divine incarnation, death, and resurrection as the answer to the question of life and death is considerably more complex than classic philosophy; it is richer by the missionary fervor of its spiritual universalism, poorer by its neglect of noetic control; broader by its appeal to the inarticulate humanity of the common man; more restricted by its bias against the articulate wisdom of the wise; more imposing through its imperial tone of divine authority; more imbalanced through its apocalyptic ferocity, which leads to conflicts with the conditions of man's existence in society; more compact through its generous absorption of earlier strata of mythical imagination, especially through the reception of Israelite historiogenesis and the exuberance of miracle working; more differentiated through the intensely articulate experience of loving-divine action in the illumination of existence with truth. (Voegelin, "Gospel and Culture," 77. [See pages 154–55 here.])

revelation itself. Indeed, there is evidence in these materials that suggests that this is the case in the dispute under consideration. In his letter of 22 April 1951, Voegelin refers approvingly to Augustine's understanding of biblical revelation as a "knowledge of the pregivens" (*sapientia*). This knowledge includes a primary apperception of the existence of a transcendent God, the order of being, and an appreciation of the human person as *esse, nosse,* and *velle*. From this perspective, biblical revelation is understood as contributing toward the "building of human knowledge" and is, as a consequence, a necessary component of philosophic speculation.[9] Strauss, on the other hand, argues that the Bible "is not speculation about God." It is rather "the account of what God has done and what he has promised."[10] In his article "Jerusalem and Athens" Strauss refers to that tradition of biblical criticism which sees in the Bible evidence of human intelligence functioning as a "vehicle of religious or spiritual experience, which necessarily expresses itself in symbols and the like."[11] One could easily imagine that Strauss would place Voegelin in this group. This approach, according to Strauss, necessarily leads to a distinction between "myth" and "history," and although it has been adopted by a number of commentators, this distinction is, in fact, "alien to the Bible" itself.[12]

Although the above suggests that Voegelin and Strauss disagree as to both their specific readings of the Bible and as to the very way in which the Bible should be read, I believe that the most important factor explaining their disagreement concerning the relationship of reason and revelation is to be found, not in their differing understandings of revelation, but rather in their disagreement as to the nature of reason itself.

As was shown earlier, Voegelin has argued consistently that the medieval distinction between natural reason and divine revelation was an error from its very inception. Typically, this error was due to a failure to appreciate the true structure of rational or noetic consciousness as first articulated in Greek philosophy.

> The consciousness of questioning unrest in a state of ignorance becomes luminous to itself as a movement in the psyche toward

9. Within this knowledge pregiven by *sapientia* stirs the philosophic *epistēmē*" (Voegelin to Strauss, 22 April 1951).

10. "Mutual Influence," 112. [See page 220 here.]

11. "Jerusalem and Athens," 46. [See page 113 here.]

12. Ibid. [See page 113 here.]

> the ground that is present in the psyche as it moves. The precognitive unrest becomes a cognitive consciousness, a *noēsis*, intending the ground as its *noēma*, or *noēton*; at the same time the desire (*oregesthai*) to know becomes the consciousness of the ground as the object of desire as the *orekton*. . . . The ground can be reached in this process of thought and can be recognized as the object desired by the meditative ascent through the *via negativa*. The ground is not to be found among the things of the eternal world . . . but lies beyond this world.[13]

This account, according to Voegelin, is theoretically correct because it properly emphasizes both the noetic movement of man toward the divine ground and the pneumatic experience of being moved by that which can only be intuitively apprehended as the goal of reason's quest. In other words, the divine is both the origin and the goal of rational thought. According to Voegelin, however, it is precisely this insight that is lost by the medieval dichotomy between reason and revelation:

> Christian theology has denatured the platonic *Nous* by degrading it imaginatively to a "natural reason," a source of truth subsidiary to the overriding source of revelation. . . . But history has taken its revenge. The non-revelatory reason imagined by the theologians as a servant has become a self-assertive master. In historical sequence the imagined non-revelatory reason has become the real anti-revelatory reason of the Enlightenment revolt against the church.[14]

For Voegelin, then, the Western understanding of reason has evolved from an original and essentially correct classical or noetic-pneumatic understanding to a modern nonrevelatory and ultimately antirevelatory one. The challenge, according to this perspective, therefore, is to save the truths of revelation by recapturing the spirit of the classical appreciation.

In a letter to Voegelin written 25 August 1950, Strauss specified the premises of his own work. "They are very simple: *philosophari necesse est*, and philosophy is radically independent of faith—the root of our disagreement lies presumably in the second thesis." Certainly Strauss is correct in

13. Voegelin, "Reason: The Classic Experience," *Southern Review* 10, no. 2 (1974): 244–45.

14. *In Search of Order* (Baton Rouge: Louisiana State University Press, 1987), 43.

pointing to the importance of the second thesis. However, I believe that the two theses are fundamentally related to one another and that this association, in turn, clarifies the root causes of the Strauss-Voegelin disagreement.

The necessity of philosophy can be taken in several ways. I believe that there are at least two ways operative in Strauss's own writings. First, Strauss believed that philosophizing is necessary for human well-being because it is the right way of life. In this he followed the classics who he believed had demonstrated that the truly human life is a life dedicated to knowledge and its unending pursuit. According to Strauss, the classical Greeks had shown that absent a knowledge of the whole and thus lacking an understanding of the whole of human nature, the right way of life must necessarily remain questionable. It is this very situation, however, that makes the quest for such an understanding the most important thing one can undertake, and thus, a life devoted to such a quest is the right way of living.

The necessity of philosophy, however, can have another meaning. Philosophical understanding can be regarded as necessary in the sense of its being compelling or evident to a properly formed human mind. This second sense is also operative in Strauss's writings and for several reasons. First, Strauss appears to have followed Aristotle in accepting the argument that a truly theoretical inquiry is concerned with those things that cannot be other than they are. They are as they are necessarily so:

> The philosophic quest for the first things presupposes not merely that there are first things but that the first things are always and that things which are always or are imperishable are more truly beings than the things which are not always. . . . In other words, the manifest changes would be impossible if there did not exist something permanent or external, or if the manifest contingent beings require the existence of something necessary and therefore eternal.[15]

According to Strauss, one of the real achievements of classical philosophy was its insistence upon recognizing this distinction between the realm of the theoretical and that of the practical. The theoretical was the realm of the eternal and the necessary, and all the decisive philosophical questions are related to this realm. To forget the eternal and turn toward

15. Strauss, *Natural Right*, 89.

the contingent (as does historicism), or to treat the practical as if it were capable of generating theoretical insight (as does Enlightenment rationalism), is to deny the possibility of true philosophy.

The second reason for Strauss's association of philosophical knowledge with necessity is found in his understanding of the structure of reasoning itself. Strauss admits, along with Aristotle, that there may be certain historical conditions necessary for the recognition of truth, e.g., the existence of leisure and the presence of teachers to inculcate the intellectual virtues, but maintains that the structure of reason itself is self-sufficient and, thus, does not depend upon such externalities as either an act of God or the events of history. Reason begins with sense perception and logical analysis and proceeds to a level of awareness that is "never divorced from sense perception and reasoning based on sense perception."[16] As such, according to Strauss, "philosophy recognizes only such experiences as can be had by all men at all times in broad daylight."[17] This insistence that philosophical experience be available in principle to all men at all times is equivalent to an expectation that all philosophical knowledge be made fully explicit. In short, we must be able to demonstrate what we know. "Judgment . . . is suspended until the facts upon which the claims are based have been manifested or demonstrated. They must be made manifest—manifest to all in broad daylight."[18] Knowledge that can be fully manifest and made available to all is necessary knowledge. It is knowledge that carries its own persuasive authority because its reasons are fully apparent. It is clear, cogent, self-evident, and compelling.[19] Any given individual may not recognize these qualities in a specific philosophical truth, but that is a failing of the individual and not a denial of the nature of philosophic truth itself. According to Strauss, then, it would appear that philosophical truth is necessary in that it both refers to necessary things and does so in a compelling and explicit manner. Obviously, revelation as understood by Strauss cannot meet these expectations. Revealed truth is not necessary; rather it is only that truth which God has chosen to

16. Strauss, "Mutual Influence," 112. [See page 219 here.]

17. Ibid., 116. [See page 229 here.]

18. Strauss, *Natural Right*, 87.

19. "Who can say that he understands what Plato means by the idea of the good if he has not discovered by himself, though guided by Plato's hints, the exact or scientific argument which establishes the necessity and the precise character of that 'idea' . . ." (Strauss, "On a New Interpretation of Plato's Political Philosophy," *Social Research* 13 [September 1946]: 351).

communicate and, inasmuch as it has been chosen, it is not truly required. At the same time, revealed truth is neither explicit nor compelling. It is not compelling because its promulgation requires the external authority of that particular community which accredits its legitimacy. And it is not explicit because according to Strauss, "God has said or decided that He wants to dwell in mists."[20]

Voegelin's willingness, on the other hand, to accept the epistemic claims of revelation is due in large part to this expanded appreciation of reason's experiential structure. According to Voegelin, reason draws from the full range of human experience (not just from sense perception) and seeks to elucidate and explore that which was originally only intimated. As such, the "results" of rational inquiry are more akin to affirmations than they are to demonstrations.[21] Whereas for Strauss reason seeks to uncover contradictions and, therefore, assumes that truth is specifiable in principle if not in fact, for Voegelin reason participates in the profoundly mysterious and, therefore, must accept truth's principled unspecifiability. For Strauss reason is characterized by clarity, precision, and logical rigor, whereas for Voegelin, its qualities are more properly described in terms of its fecundity, promise, and openness.

Voegelin's appreciation of reason's characteristics is based upon his understanding of its structure. Rational insight is essentially a participatory event. It begins with an often intuitive perception of a promised meaning. Inasmuch as this is only an intimation of meaning, the movement of reason must be guided by its original engendering experience rather than by any necessary logic or method of discovery. As a consequence, neither the principles of induction nor those of deduction can adequately explain noetic "logic." Reason does not move solely according to some specified rules of thought, and although such rules may help clarify certain aspects of thinking, they do not, according to Voegelin, explain the necessary and appropriate role of faith and imagination.

Just as the movement of reason cannot be reduced to a set of specific logical rules, so, too, is it impossible to find a necessary and precise philosophical vocabulary. According to Voegelin, the nature of philosophical language is symbolic rather than conceptual, and the test of the

20. "Mutual Influence," 116. [See page 229 here.]

21. "One cannot prove reality by a syllogism; one can only point to it and invite the doubter to look" (Voegelin, "Quod Deus Dicitur," *Journal of the American Academy of Religion* 53 [December 1985]: 579).

appropriateness of any specific set of symbols is not its rigor or precision but rather its ability to recall to our consciousness that engendering experience which first gave rise to its creation. Thus, it is the evocative power of language that makes it the appropriate instrument of philosophical inquiry. Finally, the purpose of philosophical argument, according to Voegelin, is not to demonstrate the necessity of any particular conclusion. Rather, true philosophical persuasion seeks to make available to others those fundamental human experiences that first excited the philosopher's quest. It is an attempt to turn one toward that which is most important. In other words, according to Voegelin, philosophy culminates in a personal conversion experience. Through it one is turned away from those things that cause us to forget that we are essentially participants in an all-encompassing reality grounded in the divine. For Voegelin, then, reason and revelation, or faith and intellect, are not opposed. They are, in fact, aspects of the same primary event that he has described as existence-in-truth: "The process of our *intellectus* in quest of our *fides*, a process that can also be formulated as our *fides* in quest of our *intellectus*, is a primary event."[22]

In the above I have attempted to show that the differences between Voegelin and Strauss on the issue of the relationship between reason and revelation proceed not only from their different understandings of the meaning of revelation but, more importantly, from their different conceptions of reason itself. For Strauss, revelation must fail to meet the test of reason because it lacks that quality of logical specificity which he appears to accept as a fundamental given in rational discourse. Voegelin, on the other hand, has an experiential rather than a logical conception of reason and, thus, is open to the epistemic claims of revelatory experience. Given such a fundamental disagreement as to what could even count as rational evidence, it is not altogether surprising that their correspondence became increasingly infrequent and formal after it became clear to both what the issue really was.

22. "Quod Deus Dicitur," 569.

Philosophizing in Opposition: Strauss and Voegelin on Communication and Science

Hans-Georg Gadamer

The correspondence between Leo Strauss and Eric Voegelin is a document of particular appeal. Here two German scholars encounter one another while in exile. The actual correspondence begins in 1942. It reflects a little of the unusual situation in which German scholars found themselves when they had been driven out of their homeland and yet remained attached to the German conviction regarding science. In this foreign land, both again found themselves in opposition, this time to the prevailing conditions that gave the American academic world its form. What is revealed in this opposition is no longer merely the primary political questions, but rather the form which science, and above all philosophy, retained in the respective national cultures. Thus, the bond between the two scholars consisted not least in their similar distance from their native origins, which had fallen victim to national socialism. Both, moreover, testified to an at times astonished, at times perplexed, encounter with a quite different cultivation of the sciences, as this was practiced in the United States. Especially Strauss often had harsh words for the governing "idiocy." For Voegelin too, however, the new academic surroundings were so alien that he could delineate his own working disposition largely only in opposition to it. Clearly, this situation does not exclude the fact that although there was considerable agreement between the two scholars and their scientific dispositions, the two men certainly never reached complete agreement.

By the time that the correspondence began in 1942, one must have observed the world situation with some clarity. Even if the collapse of France and preparations for the invasion of Great Britain may have left German émigrés as well as the Americans themselves holding their breath—with Hitler's invasion of Russia the signs were clear for the perspicacious both here and abroad. Naturally, there is in the letters scarcely even a hint concerning such matters. It is clear that two German scholars like Strauss and Voegelin, living in the United States after its entry into the war, did not engage in political correspondence and in general never mentioned political matters in their letters. The two scholars begin their exchange in a kind of "utopia," a nowhere. Apparently, they only rarely saw each other in person. Thus the expanse of the American continent led to an increasingly rare and precious form of communication, a correspondence of remarkable continuity.

Both correspondents were already distinguished in their scholarship, Leo Strauss first of all through his German publications, which he had been able to publish before and during the first years of the national socialist terror in Germany. Strauss had then shown himself with his book on Hobbes to be an important and independent thinker in the Anglo-Saxon world. His later works, which are reflected in this correspondence and which Strauss sent to his correspondent at the time, also show the inner consistency of Strauss's philosophical thought.

Strauss's primary theme, which already set the tone of his book on Spinoza, was the "querelle des anciens et des modernes," the literary dispute that accompanied the European Enlightenment and that reigned over the great French century. This quarrel also radiated in manifold ways into the German intellectual world. In his correspondence and in his later works, Strauss took the side of the ancients with increasing resolve. This meant above all a radical opposition to the historicism of the modern centuries. The result of this literary quarrel had been the acknowledgment of the role of the culture of antiquity as a model. This acknowledgment led to the development of a historical consciousness, which implied that the alternative between the ancients and moderns was relativized. If the writers of eighteenth-century France, insofar as they were counted among the ancients, found the model of antiquity far superior to all modern attempts, the conclusion of the quarrel was nonetheless sealed with the progress of history, the success of French classicism, and the permeation of the German classicism of the Goethe era with historical consciousness. In contrast, Strauss now undertook with polemical verve to extend the option of the ancients to the entire realm of historical, philological, and philosophical investigation.

That had its consequences. The greatest representatives of the German mode of scientific inquiry of the time—Max Weber, the great philologist Wilamowitz, and then later Werner Jaeger—actually became for Strauss the targets of his critique, and to the extent that Heidegger could already be recognized in the beginning as a radical critic of modernity, Strauss shared with him some things that he had come to understand from his student years in Germany. Strauss enjoyed telling the story of how in 1922 he attended Martin Heidegger's lecture on an interpretation of the beginning of Aristotle's *Metaphysics*, and how Werner Jaeger later interpreted the same text in Berlin. Strauss was so overwhelmed by the penetrating force of Heidegger's energetic questioning that he used to comment, "compared to this man, even the great Max Weber is merely an orphan child."[1] The superiority of the Heideggerian questioning and energy of thought, and likewise the weakness of the historical justification that ruled contemporary classical philology and that obtained its concept of objectivity from intellectual history, had clearly become apparent to him. In fact, Heidegger sought ultimately to gain a critical distance from the philosophical premises of the Greeks with his interpretations of Greek philosophy. It was the peculiar genius of Heidegger, however, that not this critique, but only the overpowering presence of his thought, came to light in the face of the force of his appropriation and recovery of Greek thought. Thus, Heidegger's mode of thought could appear in Strauss's eyes to be closely related to his own preference for the ancients. What one could, in the terminology of the time, call the phenomenological element in Heidegger was in fact the immediacy with which Heidegger pursued the matters themselves, whereby he in fact maintained a critical distance from any kind of intellectual history in the style of Dilthey and his followers.

Strauss saw his own choice of the ancients as a serious recovery and a taking up of the Socratic question, the question of the good. This was, in fact, contrary to the spirit of historicism. One might seek to recognize oneself in particular past phenomena and indeed, on the face of it, in all of them. Certainly, however, giving preeminence to the fundamental, normative question of Socrates was a challenge that opposed the basic

1. [Trans. note.] Strauss's own recounting of this story can be found in Strauss, *The Rebirth of Classical Political Rationalism: An Introduction to the Thought of Leo Strauss*, ed. Thomas Pangle (Chicago: University of Chicago Press, 1989), 28.

premises of historicism. In this, Strauss and Voegelin are in agreement. The correspondence allows important differences to become visible, to be true in the background, but it is also concerned with retaining the common character of their concerns. Both are agreed that the self-evidentness accorded to the concept of progress in the modern world and likewise in Anglo-Saxon philosophy and scientific inquiry, although belonging properly and without dispute to scientific research, is entirely out of place and suppresses actual philosophizing when it is directed toward the most important questions concerning man.

In the later letters between the two researchers, which are exchanged in the fifties, the argument about the major differences between them begins to open up. On Voegelin's part there are long letters that are nearly short essays. They betray the need to defend his own intentions against the extreme positions of Strauss, even if both share in the same challenge to the reigning mode of scientific inquiry. Strauss's choice of classical philosophy is sharpened into the antithesis that a later essay in 1967 expresses in its title, "Jerusalem and Athens."[2] Correspondence between the two later dried up, especially after Voegelin in 1958 took over the chair for political philosophy in Munich. Voegelin, however, did not neglect a reply to the extreme position of Strauss: "The Gospel and Culture."[3]

The two aforementioned later essays of the two writers are concerned with precisely the point of difference that is intimated in the letters between them. Thereby arises the task of using the early letters, which date back nearly two decades, as commentaries on the essays—or, obversely, of reading the later essays in light of the earlier letters.

Strauss insists on the decisive separation of faith and knowledge. This separation had been long prepared in Strauss's development. It was already announced in his dissertation, dedicated to Jacobi, which he submitted under Cassirer in Hamburg in 1922. Thus, he continually expressed doubt in the letters concerning Voegelin's perspective. Voegelin sees classical philosophy as a kind of preliminary stage to gnosticism. In this he follows the tendency of the Church Fathers, especially Justin Martyr and Clement. They attempted to mediate between the New Testament and

2. "Jerusalem and Athens: Some Preliminary Reflections," *Commentary* 43 (1967): 45–57. [Reprinted in this volume.]

3. "The Gospel and Culture," in D. Miller and D. G. Hadidian, eds., *Jesus and Man's Hope*, vol. 2 (Pittsburgh, Pa.: Pittsburgh Theological Seminary Press, 1971), 59–101. [Reprinted in this volume.]

philosophy and believed that they had found this mediation in the concept of the *logos*. In fact, it is not so much the classical philosophy of the *logos* of Plato and Aristotle which thereby comes into view, as rather the Platonic myths and the *logos spermatikos* of Stoic philosophy, treated as doctrines. Classical philosophy is thereby seen in truth as already on the way to the Christian doctrine of the Incarnation. It appears as a stage on the way to "reason." The Christian message is that the *Logos*, the Word, has come into the world and with that the apparent contradiction between revelation and human knowledge is dissolved. Voegelin writes, "the noetic analysis of the intermediate position of man is equal in rank with that found in the New Testament." The only thing missing is the tension "the Unknown God."[4] Thus, the alien character of the worldly is already laid out for the true philosopher in Plato. Certainly, this alienation is not yet, as in gnosticism, the fall of the soul into the alien world and the ascent from this fall through one's own path of realization. Voegelin attempts nevertheless to read into classical philosophy the same pull of the *Logos*, of the same seeking for God—both seeking and being drawn. The distinction between human knowledge and revelation upon which Strauss rigorously insists is therefore problematized by Voegelin in a long letter in 1952. He even interprets the Platonic relationship of *logos* and *mythos* in this way: "God does not speak immediately, but only mediately through Socrates and Plato."

Both thinkers naturally find themselves situated on the soil of the scientific enlightenment belonging to modernity. Even Strauss's choice of the "ancients" cannot be established without further ado or historical investigation. It is on this that Strauss bases his claim that one must understand every author "exactly" as he understood himself, and that in this way one could learn to avoid the errors of modernity.

To examine Strauss's studies in their particular details would exceed my competence. Certainly even I would not disagree that one must seek to understand a text in the sense the author intended. But this always includes above all understanding the matter about which the text speaks. A person who intends to engage in philosophy cannot dispute this claim. Let us attempt to test the matter. What happens when a narrow concept of authorship fails due to the conditions of transmission themselves, because we know nothing about the author? In his essay, "Jerusalem and Athens," Strauss deals in his description of Jerusalem with the book of Genesis, whose exegesis he then attempts. There he is quite rightly concerned with

4. Ibid., 97–98. [See page 173 here.]

the meaning of the creation story. Even if he rejects contemporary biblical criticism and its methodical separation of myth from the historicity of facts—and this rejection is convincing—he nevertheless behaves in a hermeneutical way. That is to say, he reads this text in the sense of a Holy Scripture, and seeks to question it as such on the basis of its rationally understood meaning. Here is a text that clearly cannot be attributed to one single author, but at best to one editor to whom the origin of the text may be retraced. But this would be a completely imaginary author, of whose understanding one can hardly raise a claim of unity of meaning. But in any case, it is a text that one is reading here, and that one is supposed to understand. One therefore arrives at the heretical idea that as a reader who seeks to understand this text as a unified discourse, one is rather better situated than the critical philologist of today. The reader as such knows the individual parts as such, and their origin not at all, and has solely the unity of the meaning of the whole in view. In the introduction to "Jerusalem and Athens," Strauss himself presents an impressive demonstration of how the so obviously incoherent text of Genesis can nevertheless be read reasonably and understandably.

Strauss acquired his perspective of calling for a return to classical philosophy from a study of the tensions to which modern science, as it arose, found itself exposed in its intercourse with the Christian and humanistic traditions. At that time, the Christian church exercised a determinative political power. In his book on Spinoza, Strauss uncovered contradictions in Spinoza's text that he interpreted as a conformity to censorship and therefore as an occlusion of the author's true meaning. It is a matter of examining individual cases to determine how widely this principle of Strauss's may be applied. I am not competent to apply such a test in the area of the Age of Enlightenment, and certainly not in Arabic-Jewish philosophy. I also gladly confess that his book on Hobbes generally persuaded me. As Strauss shows, the conventional interpretation, which has come to predominance in recent scholarship, namely that Hobbes's theory can be seen as simply an application of mathematical method, seems to me, to be superficial. Deeper-lying motivations of social criticism and of an understanding of human nature are the background determinants in Hobbes.

I really do not wish to go into the general standpoint from which Strauss gives political philosophy the weight that he does." But in truth such a return to classical philosophy and to the Socratic question leads to the roots from which the concept of political philosophy can be considered at all; and this is truly the concern of philosophy. The meaning and range of that which can be called rationality, and its relationship to revelation, is thereby brought into play to a full extent. Voegelin clearly interprets knowledge through revelation in a very broad sense. But what is the case in political philosophy? Since Aristotle (and at bottom since Socrates and Plato), political philosophy has signified a well-circumscribed field of questions. It is a part of practical philosophy. The relationship of practical philosophy and theoretical philosophy, however, which Aristotle introduces, is highly complex even in Aristotle's eyes. Practical reason, which governs human activity, is in a certain sense the precondition for a free contemplation of that which is. Voegelin would call this rather a "knowledge of order," and indeed Aristotle himself says that such a free contemplation, that is, theory, is the mode of existence of the gods, and as such the highest form of *praxis*.

But now the texts of classical philosophy are supposed to serve *praxis*, which is to say, offer an orientation to the good. Insofar as such theories and texts exist within the framework of the *polis*, they always have, in addition to their theoretical philosophical function, an undeniable relationship to political practice itself. Indeed there is no *praxis* that does not encompass everything that occurs in the *polis*. Not only the teacher and the political speaker but, in literary times, the author too stands in this space of the *polis*. Teachings and writings are, at the same time, activities. This is the reason why everywhere in his studies of classical philosophy, Strauss poses the question whether the true intention of the author is openly voiced or more or less expressed in disguise. *Persecution and the Art of Writing* is the title of one of Leo Strauss's most interesting publications. This title has a nearly Goethean ring and universal scope. It did not escape Goethe that the pressure of censorship always resulted in a refinement of thought and the art of writing. This perspective ultimately has an impact on the so-called freedom of expression and even on the freedom of science, and thus does not necessarily have meaning only for political philosophy.

Nevertheless it is not so self-evident that one is dealing with conscious camouflage in this case. This would mean that the discerning reader, who is supposed to be the actual addressee of the text, must pick up the signals in the text that point to a hidden or concealed meaning. To plant such signals is, in truth, an extremely difficult task, demanding great skills in writing, and moreover great skill in reading. Thus arises the most difficult question, namely, when one can be certain of the meaning of texts that are clearly expressed, or whether one must also second-guess and look behind such texts. But this question becomes almost unanswerable if one is sure that in public expressions of speech or writing, unconscious conformity to public opinion and to the prejudice of the addressee is ubiquitous. The true intention of the author can thereby be more or less distorted or disguised. This is a thesis with which the reader is well acquainted from the critiques of ideology in our century. In its ultimate generalization, it reproduces Nietzsche's principle, always to value "truth" only as a condition of the preservation and enhancement of the "will to power," and thereby to degrade ideas into ideologies. One must make this consequence clear to oneself, and in particular focus on that other universal expansion of the hermeneutic of suspicion which between human beings leads to the attempt to interpret all communication from the perspective of psychoanalytic enlightenment. If one would make such a search for unconscious motives a rule and would see in this the goal of all "deconstruction," it would bring the dissolution of all communication as such. In fact, only when the failure or disturbance of communication is experienced can such a search be legitimate.

Ultimately, this principle must hold true even for an author who consciously dissembles and makes his or her true motives unrecognizable. Here too, communication will only become possible if the intended addressee is invited or forced to second-guess an apparent intention, because the expectation of meaning, with which one reads, is not fulfilled.

The Platonic dialogue plays a special role in the correspondence between Strauss and Voegelin. Indeed, it is actually only in dialogue that we can grasp the Socratic question. But the entangled relationship of *logos* and *mythos*, of compelling argument and suggestive narration, plays a major part in the main Platonic dialogue. If one conceives of *mythos* in the wider sense of "narrative," then the Platonic dialogues are ultimately all myths. They report occasions of dialogue between others, and it is not Plato himself who speaks or teaches in them. The excursus in Plato's Seventh Letter should remind us not to forget this. There it is stated explicitly that there is no text from Plato himself presenting his own teachings. It is not for nothing that this circumstance has led to the controversy concerning an esoteric and exoteric Plato, somewhat in the manner in which both are attested to in the practice of the Pythagorean order. In any case, however, there can be no doubt that we are not supposed to guess a hidden intention of Plato from the dialogues and their role-playing, not even when the Platonic Socrates demurs from a final answer to the question of what the good is. Rather, we are supposed to keep ourselves free of any prior opinion or prior orientation concerning Plato's true teaching, and to raise questions ourselves, and to ask oneself about the good. Neither is Socrates Plato in disguise, even if in the end he develops beyond the role of an aporetic speaker and utopian or mythical thought-games are put into his mouth. The same is true when other interlocutors, and no longer Socrates, play out their roles.

If one insists with Strauss that one must understand authors exactly as they understood themselves, then one can certainly understand the intention of an author in this way; but doing so requires only that one carry on the conversation with oneself and not simply repeat the conversation that forms the text of the Platonic dialogue. In this I would even expressly agree with Strauss against Voegelin, that these dialogues are not to be read as political actuality, meant to restore the disturbed order. Rather, they are to be regarded as partners in the search for truth, as directed toward the consummation of a philosophical, theoretical goal. In this regard, one will also have to agree with Strauss that as philosophers "we have already decided in favor of Athens and against Jerusalem."[5]

Here the difference that always lurks in the background of the correspondence comes to the fore. To determine the intentions of authors as they understood themselves, including for example whether something is said in jest, or ironically, or is to be understood literally, is of irrefutable interest if one intends to examine the consequences of this activity. This cannot be denied. But what is the case when dealing with texts of great artistic craftsmanship, such as the comedies of Aristophanes or the Socratic dialogues of Plato? The standard of logical coherence, or of the intention of the author, loses its applicability in this case. The apparent contradictoriness that art can tolerate without repudiating itself or motivating the reader to second-guess it links it to the element of play that attends all art. "They kill only in fun." One need think only of the dramas of Shakespeare, which clearly present the actor with tasks of re-creation, but precisely such as the actor knows how to accomplish, and in such a way that the contradictoriness, unseemliness, and incoherence of the text is not perceived as a contradiction at all—everything is so tremendously real. The seductive daring of art consists in its trying out every conceivable form of play. The philological study of Shakespeare has ranged all the way from poetic vision to textbook montage. In this regard, his dramas are a particularly extreme example of what a work of art allows and demands.

5. "Jerusalem and Athens," 45. [See page 112 here.]

The presentation of a poetic work in the theater palpably reveals the degree of freedom that is in play in every experience of art.

But is this actually the case only in art? It seems to me, in fact, that when we are concerned with reading and understanding anywhere, there are hardly great differences to be made. The word of the one who speaks or who is encountered in a text is always exposed to a latitude in understanding. Thus, I remain doubtful when Strauss seeks to secure his deep-questioning method applied to a Platonic dialogue with the argument that when a contradiction becomes clear, this signifies a conscious conformity and veiling. Not much can be accomplished with this principle in regard to an author like Plato, because his entire work invites argument and thought. Such a master of irony cannot be adequately understood by the rigid category of noncontradiction. Instead, one must return to the situation of the respective conversations that Plato creates and presents in his work. One is meant to take part as a listener in precisely these conversations and in doing so to follow the conversation of one's own soul with itself; and this is thinking. In this there is neither total agreement nor total contradiction. This is, as I see it, for the bold questioning that takes place in philosophy not a bad principle, namely, to leave questions open. Only in this way can there be conversation. A Platonic dialogue does not put forward an itemized series of teachings, but rather initiates a movement of thought that surely, when confronted with an issue, continually asks itself if the matter is this way or otherwise. This is true of all thinking that we call philosophy, whether dialogue or tentative dialectic or dialectical method, whether of Plato, Aristotle, or Hegel. One can say it with a statement of Hegel's, "Speculative truths are not suited to the form of a proposition," or with a statement of Plato's, "Thinking is the conversation of the soul with itself." Conversation with Greek thought is indispensable for many reasons. Only in such conversations, in contrast to the encumbered concepts of modern times, can one learn to return to the original experiences out of which philosophy and the Socratic question developed in the Greek *polis*. In doing so, however, it is important to employ and engage one's own thinking, especially in one's choice of words and development of concepts. To presuppose that classical thought is simply the voice of truth which one may not question and go behind seems to me to be a mistake. Above all it seems to me to be wrong to want to restrict oneself to the concepts and vocabulary of the authors and texts of antiquity. Actually, this is an impossibility. Understanding demands that one enter into conversation with the classical texts and their thoughts in a living language. One must remain conscious that this is a conversation between today and then, even more than between Jerusalem and Athens; one comes thereby to recognize the dialectic of repetition as well as the dialectic of understanding. To interpret is always a speaking that stands between, and it has meaning only when it is helpful to the conversation.

I know from the published correspondence that Strauss carried on with me concerning *Truth and Method*, that the reflexive stance of philosophical hermeneutics appeared erroneous to him.[6] In my eyes, however, every thinking conversation remains a search for and a discovery of the common language in which we understand each other. The other is indeed an other. But who does not change and learn when participating in a conversation? I side with Plato's Socrates: "It is not my word, whatever I also may say!"

6. "Correspondence with Hans-Georg Gadamer concerning *Wahrheit und Methode*," *Independent Journal of Philosophy* 2 (1978): 5–12.

Politics or Transcendence? Responding to Historicism

Stanley Rosen

This exchange between two of the most influential political thinkers of the twentieth century is in my view especially striking for the shared perception that historicism, or the surrender of reason to perspectival interpretation, can only be overcome by the hermeneutical mastery of history. It is not enough to say that one finds in Strauss and Voegelin a genuine respect for the great thinkers of the past, and hence for reading the decisive texts of Western tradition. To leave it at that would be to trivialize what these men represented as a pedantic aestheticism. They would accordingly amount to nothing more than an old-fashioned counterpart to postmodern textual athleticism, with a consequent juxtaposition of the musty scent of libraries on the one hand and the sweat of deconstructive liberation on the other.

In fact, Strauss and Voegelin were both engaged in a deconstructive enterprise of their own, and one with positive political implications. With due allowance to the difference between them, one may suggest that in both cases the enterprise was intended as a preemptive strike against an anticipated postmodern crisis, predicted by Nietzsche, and which we are now experiencing. One would be tempted to judge their work a failure, if by success is meant the suppression of one's opponent. In my opinion, this temptation should be resisted for two reasons. First, success requires a more extended definition. Second, the clarifications and theses of Strauss and Voegelin are themselves a part of the crisis of late modernity; it could be argued, and it is in fact my view, that the only possibility of a salutary resolution is to allow the crisis, which is in fact a complex dispute, to carry itself to completion. A radical reinstitution of some past "golden age" is impossible, and if it were possible, it would be undesirable. Freedom is not acquired by suppression of the dialectic intrinsic to its own inner movement.

To make a slightly different approach to the same issue, one might say that Strauss and Voegelin wished to inoculate their students and readers with a vaccine against the more virulent form of late-modern decadence. It is too early to pronounce the vaccine a success or a failure. And it must be admitted that there are two vaccines here, not one. The most pressing question raised by their correspondence is then: can one effectively fight a common enemy by pressing simultaneously in two different directions? Is the degree to which Strauss and Voegelin were allies not offset by the decisive disagreement between them?

The virus of historicism destroys the self-confidence and clarity of reason. For both Strauss and Voegelin, an almost unstated assumption of these letters is the ability of reason to communicate with reason across the span of centuries. I say "almost unstated" because the principle is defended in the common attempt to grasp the roots of historicism, rather than to ground the principle in epistemological or ontological constructions (see the important exchange of 25 August and 4 December 1950). This agreement is qualified by a difference that may be stated as follows: whereas Voegelin appears to be more concerned, negatively as well as positively, with metaphysical reflection, and so too with epistemology and ontology, than is Strauss, there is a sense in which Strauss takes metaphysics more seriously than does Voegelin. I mean by this, not that Strauss is the more serious metaphysician of the two, but that he tacitly rejects metaphysics altogether. Strauss never stated the full reasons for this rejection, and certainly there is no basis in these letters for reconstructing his argument. Strauss gives the impression of a tactical intention to bypass excessive theoretical construction for a more direct approach to the political phenomena. He thus implies that the political phenomena do indeed present themselves to us with a sufficient directness, and so too that the phenomenon of historicism is equally accessible. For Voegelin, historicism arises precisely when the transcendent is "immanentized," or brought into history. But this entails the view that the transcendent must be kept free from immanentization, or in other words remain the bastion of pure reason. And this transcendence of reason is certainly connected for

Voegelin with religious faith. It is of course quite true that Voegelin grounds "pure" reason, at least in the case of politics, in existential perception. However, the perception is of political phenomena not in their own terms but as symbols of transcendence. Voegelin's position is thus in sharp contrast to that of Strauss: Voegelin does not question the fundamental role of metaphysics, whereas Strauss does not explain the tacit (or not so tacit) rejection of metaphysics as fundamental to political inquiry.

Strauss includes a declaration of first principles in his letter of 25 August 1950: *philosophari necesse est* and philosophy is radically independent of faith. The same point is implied in the following remark from a letter by Strauss dated 4 June 1951: "there is a fundamental difference between the call of God itself and the human formulation of this call." Voegelin describes the *raison d'etre* of his historical work as follows: "to restore the experiences which have led to the creation of certain concepts and symbols; or: Symbols have become opaque; they must be made luminous again by penetrating to the experiences which they express" (12 March 1949) and so also to the "existential" or "*non*cognitive aspect of *epistēmē*" (2 January 1950). He is clearly referring to the Christian theme of historical existence as the symbolic representation of divine transcendence. How the symbolic is to be kept free of the risk of "immanentization" is not explained in these letters. That Voegelin's orientation as a political thinker is Christian is evident from the beginning of the correspondence; I cite his letter of 9 December 1942 on "the superiority of the Christian anthropology over the Hellenic" because of its universalizing of man: "the Hellenocentric man has been replaced by the individual, the person in direct communication with God."

The importance of metaphysics for Voegelin emerges once more from his criticism of Husserl. In Voegelin's account (26 September 1943), epistemology is central for Husserl; for Voegelin, epistemology is not *the* question. Accordingly, it is metaphysics rather than (as for Husserl) egology that is decisive. Metaphysics as the interpretation of symbols of the transcendent has a Kantian flavor; it should not, despite Voegelin's emphasis upon the experiential or existential component of metaphysics, be confused with Kierkegaard's Christian existentialism. By contrast, in an earlier letter, Strauss defends Husserl against a similar criticism by Voegelin. For Strauss (9 May 1943), egology is "the less correct side" of Husserlian phenomenology. One may discern here the unspoken influence of Heidegger. The following passage must be cited at length:

> Husserl's phenomenological analysis ended in the radical analysis of the whole development of modern science . . . I know nothing in the literature of our century that would be comparable to this analysis in rigor, depth, and breadth. Husserl has seen with incomparable clarity that the restoration of philosophy or science—because he denies that that which today passes as science is genuine science—presupposes the restoration of the Platonic-Aristotelian level of questioning. His egology can be understood only as an answer to the Platonic-Aristotelian question regarding the *Nous* and only on the level of this question is that answer to be discussed adequately.

This in 1942: whatever modifications may have transpired in Strauss's later position, one thing, in my opinion, remains constant, and certainly in his discussions with Voegelin. Strauss is a spokesman for Platonic-Aristotelian *science*, and not for the metaphysics that descends from the Judeo-Christian tradition. It is this "paganism," and the correlative estimate of Husserl, that underlies and qualifies Strauss's agreement with Voegelin on a central point: "Above all, I completely agree that the radical doubt about the dogmas of the last three or four centuries is the beginning of every pursuit of wisdom" (13 February 1943). In other words, Strauss rejects "egology" together with epistemology and ontology as artificial constructions emanating from the mistaken or unphilosophical conception of science that Husserl, despite his "infection" by modernity, so effectively criticizes. His deeper acceptance of science is a rejection of metaphysics as that term is employed by Voegelin.

This is not to suggest that Strauss conceived of himself, whether in 1942 or later, as a scientific thinker at the level of Husserl, to say nothing of Plato and Aristotle. It could even be denied that Strauss conceived of his own task as a follower, in the narrow sense, of such a scientific philosophy. This point can best be expressed at the outset in terms of Strauss's account of Husserl. Strauss saw Husserl as a defective but nevertheless useful paradigm for the task of returning, by way of a "desedimentation" of modern (philosophically nongenuine) scientific thought, to the natural world of political experience. Husserl's own process of desedimentation is for Strauss defective precisely because it is in the service of a doctrine of egology, and so returns us, not to *doxa* in the Greek sense (despite Husserl's own statement on this point), but rather to a theoretical construction: the *Lebenswelt.* All the steps in Strauss's assessment of Husserl are not visible in the correspondence with Voegelin. Without the remark I have just added, it might seem that Strauss had failed to grasp the link in Husserl between egology and the critique of modern science. One may nevertheless ask whether Strauss's own "desedimentation" of the history of political thought is valid apart from an enterprise analogous to that of Husserl but free of Husserl's "modernism." In other words: can Strauss simply *combine* Husserl's analysis of the origins of modern science with his own analysis of the origins of historicism at the level of political experience?

This is not a question that can be explored in the present series of remarks. It must be left to the reader to consider the validity of Strauss's implication that his work stands either on the Husserlian or, still more problematically, on the Platonic-Aristotelian foundation. What can be said here is this: Strauss does not praise Husserl in defense of either metaphysics *or* epistemology. On the other hand, Strauss would certainly have agreed with Voegelin that self-consciousness is pregiven, that, as Voegelin says (contra Husserl: 22 April 1951), "one cannot construct self-consciousness as the act of perception after the model of a sensuous perception." One could summarize this agreement as follows: both Strauss and Voegelin rejected the contention of the English and French Enlightenment that mathematical and experimental science provides the paradigm of rationality, and specifically the paradigm for understanding human being. Whereas Voegelin turned (not exclusively, but decisively) for illumination to the Judeo-Christian tradition, Strauss, even in his role as commentator on the medieval Jewish and Arabic texts, was a *pagan.* It is an exaggeration, but one that I believe points us in the right direction, to say that Strauss's approach to Plato and Aristotle is illuminated by his understanding of Thucydides. It is not an exaggeration to say that Voegelin's approach to Plato and Aristotle is illuminated by his understanding of the Bible.

The previously cited letter of 5 December 1942 is perhaps the clearest example in this correspondence of Voegelin's orientation. For a powerful statement of Strauss's paganism I recommend the letter of 15 April 1949, and in particular the final paragraph's praise for Lucretius. To conclude these remarks, it is plain that neither Strauss nor Voegelin is likely to achieve a paramount position among postmodernists who, despite their frequent invocation of Nietzsche, are denounced prophetically in paragraphs 44 and 200–203 of *Beyond Good and Evil.* And yet I have the impression that Strauss's paganism is somewhat more appealing (whether as traced back to Aristotle or to Machiavelli), hence more politically effective in today's environment than is Voegelin's transcendental or metaphysical approach to politics. In slightly different terms, Strauss is closer than Voegelin to Nietzsche. Whereas both Strauss and Voegelin are critics of the Enlightenment, Strauss, like Nietzsche, shares the Enlightenment taste for "the attitude that elicits consolation from the utterly hopeless truth, on the basis of its being only the truth" (15 April 1949), a phrase used by Strauss in conjunction with Lucretius, but secondarily with Nietzsche ("the next approximation in our world is the scientifically slanted aspect in Nietzsche"). For a confirmation of Strauss's view, see *Beyond Good and Evil*, paragraph 210. This in turn raises the difficult question, with which I began, whether Strauss and Voegelin, despite their apparently common enemy, are fighting the same battle. Is adherence to the Judeo-Christian tradition closer to the heart of the contemporary crisis than is paganism? And if Strauss is closer to Nietzsche's scientific slant than is Voegelin, who is closer to historicism?

The Theological Conflict Between Strauss and Voegelin

Thomas J. J. Altizer

The deep conflict between Leo Strauss and Eric Voegelin was a conflict over the very identity of Western history and civilization; that identity is a consequence of the dual sources of Western history in Greek philosophy and the Bible; and while both Strauss and Voegelin were thinkers who were each ultimately committed to the Bible and Greek philosophy, Strauss accepted an irresoluble opposition between reason and revelation, whereas the center of Voegelin's work and mission was a reconciliation and union of Athens and Jerusalem. Voegelin is alone among twentieth-century thinkers in exercising this vocation; and while Strauss's position would appear to be common among religious thinkers, it was, in fact, deeply uncommon, and this because of Strauss's total commitment to Greek philosophy. For Strauss the opposition between Greece and the Bible is the source of the deepest vitality of the West; and not only is that opposition irreconcilable, but, as Strauss asserts, "philosophy and Bible are the alternatives or the antagonists in the drama of the human soul."[1] If Strauss believed that no one could be both a philosopher and a theologian,[2] Voegelin was certainly both, or, at least, he was a religious and a philosophical thinker simultaneously, and a thinker most deeply dedicated

1. "The Mutual Influence of Theology and Philosophy," *Independent Journal of Philosophy* 3 (1979): 114. [See page 223 in this volume.]
2. Ibid., 111. [See page 217 here.]

to a synthesis of the Bible and Greek philosophy, a synthesis that Strauss believed to be a literal impossibility. True, Strauss began as a Maimonides scholar, and he clearly shows the impact of Rosenzweig in his book on Spinoza, a book dedicated to Rosenzweig. But *Spinoza's Critique of Religion* was based on the premise that a return to premodern philosophy is impossible,[3] a premise whose reversal is the primary ground of Strauss's mature work; and one can only assume that it was upon the basis of his Greek philosophical orientation that Strauss could know such a deep contradiction between reason and revelation.

Nothing so determined Strauss's mature thinking as his opposition to historicism, a historicism he believed to be the spirit of our time, and a historicism he identified as the forgetting of eternity. Believing that Greek philosophy was ahistorical, Strauss strove to reverse modern historical thinking; and one sign of this reversal is his understanding of modern philosophy. Thus Strauss refuses to see that it was not until the twentieth century that modern philosophy fully liberated itself from the Bible, even if he does see that Nietzsche himself was both a biblical and an antibiblical thinker, and that the "new thinking" of Heidegger does not succeed in its intention of liberating philosophy from the last relics of Christian theology.[4] The truth is that modern philosophical thinking from Descartes through Heidegger has been both biblical and philosophical thinking, even if the biblical ground of that thinking has been extraordinarily various and obscure; and therein modern philosophical thinking is in a kind of continuity with scholastic philosophical thinking; and it is precisely modern historical thinking and scholarship which has again and again demonstrated that continuity, as shown by no less a work than Strauss's own book on Spinoza. Neither Plato nor Aristotle directed such labor to the problem of God as have the greatest thinkers of modern philosophy, and if this appears to be untrue of Kant, it was the creator of neo-Kantianism, Hermann Cohen, who centered his most mature thinking upon the problem of God. Nevertheless, Strauss can declare in a letter to Voegelin (25 February 1951) that every synthesis between reason and revelation is actually an option either for Athens or Jerusalem.

Presumably Maimonides chose Jerusalem, even as Spinoza chose Athens, but such a judgment historically could be only meaningless or absurd,

3. Preface to Strauss, *Spinoza's Critique of Religion* (New York: Schocken Books, 1982), 31.

4. Ibid., 12.

for clearly Maimonides was a profoundly philosophical thinker even as Spinoza was a profoundly religious thinker; and even as Maimonides was a Platonic and Aristotelian thinker, Spinoza was a Christian and Jewish thinker. When Strauss again and again declares that philosophy is wholly independent of faith, one wonders what actual or historical philosophy he could possibly have in mind, except perhaps the philosophy of the contemporary classroom, or those innumerable species of philosophical positivism that Strauss holds wholly in contempt. If nothing else, Voegelin clearly and decisively demonstrated the deep grounding in faith of Plato's philosophical thinking, and this does not go against historical scholarship but rather deepens it, a deepening here revolving about a resurrection of modern Neoplatonism. But despite his Neoplatonism, Voegelin is clearly a modern thinker, and most so in his historical thinking, a thinking in which "history is Christ writ large."[5] While Voegelin is surely unique in finding the noetic core in classical philosophy and in the gospel to be the same,[6] he not only offers serious arguments for this position, he has offered us a full philosophy of history culminating with this thesis. That is an achievement of the highest order, and even if Strauss was opposed to the very possibility of a philosophy of history, the fact remains that Voegelin gave us one which is classical and biblical at once. Apparently, Strauss never responded to *Order in History*, a work whose very title must have been anathema to him, but no other work of our time has been such a deep challenge to Strauss.

That challenge is the reconciliation of reason and revelation, a reconciliation that collapsed upon impact with modernity, a collapse that seemingly was only reversed by German Idealism, an idealism that in Hegel is Christian and atheistic at once. If Hegel is the first philosopher of the death of God, a death inaugurated by the French Revolution, he is nevertheless a Christian philosopher, and nowhere more so than in his philosophy of history. That philosophy is the only fully Christian philosophy of history, at least until Voegelin, and it is dedicated to understanding the whole of history as theodicy. That marks a decisive and ultimate break from Augustine's *City of God*—which with its descendents is the one

5. Voegelin, "Immortality: Experience and Symbol," *Harvard Theological Review* 60 (1967): 263. [See page 201 here.]

6. "The Gospel and Culture," in D. Miller and D. G. Hadidian, eds., *Jesus and Man's Hope*, vol. 2 (Pittsburgh, Pa.: Pittsburgh Theological Seminary Press, 1971), 80. [See page 157 here.]

orthodox Christian philosophy of history—with the notable result that it is only Christian atheism or Christian heresy that even intends to understand the totality of history as the providence of God. Hegel, however, was not only the creator of the philosophy of history, he was also the creator of historical thinking itself, or of historical philosophical thinking, a thinking that not only Strauss but virtually all major modern conservative thinkers have dedicated themselves to destroying. In Hegel, this thinking is atheistic and Christian at once, and while one could not accuse Hegel of forgetting eternity, one could accuse him of dedicating his thinking to the negation and reversal of a transcendent eternity, and thereby as being the father of historicism.

Hegel is our deepest modern ancestor, an ancestor whom even the French deconstructionists openly concede as such, and Voegelin has again and again opposed Hegel as his deepest enemy. Thereby, and not only thereby, Voegelin has profoundly opposed modernity itself; and not only Voegelin but Strauss as well. Nothing so unites Strauss and Voegelin as does their mutual opposition to modernity, and this opposition is centered on their assault upon modern historical and political thinking, and at this point historical and political thinking are inseparable. For it was the French Revolution that gave birth to modern conservatism, and the French Revolution was not only a product of the historical thinking given birth by the Enlightenment but was also a consequence of the modern historical realization of the death of God. This is a major motif of Hegel's *Phenomenology of Spirit*, a work which itself was only made possible by the French Revolution, and a work which in due term gave birth to Marxism. But the *Phenomenology of Spirit* is an openly and profoundly Christian philosophical work, for here the death of God is the consequence of the Incarnation itself, and is ultimately the historical embodiment and final actualization of absolute Spirit. So it is that in Hegelian terms the French Revolution is a realization of the Incarnation, and with this realization the ancient world is finally ended. This is an ending that the conservative thinker must oppose, and oppose not only by way of an opposition to political modernity but also by way of an opposition to the totality of modern historical thinking, a thinking that is itself finally inseparable from the French Revolution.

Voegelin believed that the primary task of genuine historical thinking is to penetrate the spiritual-historical form of the other to its experience of transcendence, and in such penetration to train and clarify one's own experience of transcendence. Such "spiritual-historical understanding is a catharsis, a *purificatio* in the mystical sense, with the personal goal of *illuminatio* and *unio mystica*"; and it can lead to working out the sequences of order in the historical revelation of Spirit and in this way can factually and finally produce a philosophy of history.[7] Thus the revelation of Spirit is both the "factual" and the final ground of the philosophy of history, and that revelation is a historical revelation, a revelation to be found in Athens and Jerusalem alike. But this revelation is manifest only as a consequence of the breakdown of an original mythical and cosmological consciousness, a breakdown giving birth to the individual consciousness, and now that consciousness actually experiences a world-transcendent Being who "addresses" that individual consciousness.[8] An openness to that address is possible only for one who is clearly separated from transcendence, and separated from it as the Homeric and Hesiodic consciousness was not, a consciousness which was not present in Greece until Socrates, whose life and death therein and thereby becomes the paradigmatic source of the Greek noetic consciousness. Accordingly, the historical revelation of spirit is inseparable from the actual and historical presence of individual consciousness, an individual consciousness that is a dedivinized consciousness, but a dedivinized consciousness that is now open to transcendence. This is a consciousness that was present in both Greece and Israel, but it is also a consciousness that was profoundly assaulted if not reversed by the triumphant advent of the modern consciousness.

That advent, for Voegelin, is a rebirth of ancient gnosticism, a rebirth revolving about a Gnostic murder of God, a murder intending a redivinization of consciousness by way of the actual and historical realization of total immanence. Thereby Voegelin, and Voegelin alone, understands Hegel as a Gnostic thinker, a thinker in quest of a divinization of consciousness, a divinization that can be realized only by way of the destruction of the noetic consciousness, and therefore and thereby the destruction of Athens and Jerusalem alike. If Hegel was a mystical thinker with the personal goal of *illuminatio* and *unio mystica*, that goal was not transcendence but rather absolute immanence; and if this goal did make possible the construction of the Hegelian philosophy of history, that is a philosophy of history transforming transcendence into immanence, so that the realization of total immanence is the ultimate goal of absolute Spirit,

7. Letter from Voegelin to Alfred Schütz on Edmund Husserl, reprinted in this volume, page 30.

8. Voegelin to Strauss, 22 April 1951.

and a goal that is realized here and now. Nothing could be more catastrophic than Hegelian thinking, a thinking issuing not only in Marxism but in that whole world or worlds of ideology that is the driving force of twentieth-century totalitarianism. Thus Hegel could father both Communism and Fascism, for it was Hegelian thinking in all its forms that unthought transcendence itself, an unthinking reversing the transcendence revealed in Greece and Israel, and that reversal is nothing less than the modern historical realization of the death of God. Nothing is or could be more real to us than this event, for it dominates the modern intellectual, imaginative, political, and social worlds. If our age is the most catastrophic age in history, it would certainly appear to be a new age and world, and an infernal world with no real precedent in history. Yes, ours is a post-Christian age, and an age driven by a terrorism of the *libido dominandi* that has been released by the draining of reality from the symbols of experienced truth.

> The shell of doctrine, empty of its engendering reality, is transformed by the *libido dominandi* into its ideological equivalent. The *contemptus mundi* is metamorphosed into the *exaltatio mundi*; the City of God into the City of Man; the apocalyptic into the ideological millennium; the eschatological metastasis through divine action into the world-immanent metastasis through human action; and so forth. The center from which the particular symbols receive their meaning is the transformation of human power over nature into a human power of salvation. Nietzsche has developed the symbol of self-salvation in order to express the alchemic *opus* of man creating himself in his own image. In this dream of self-salvation, man assumes the role of God and redeems himself by his own grace.[9]

Voegelin is a demonologist of the highest order, and he surpasses his historical predecessors by finding demons everywhere in our world, a world that was possible only as a consequence of the erosion and collapse of Christianity, a collapse that was realized in the French Revolution. While Voegelin believed that the truth of reality is always fully present in man's experience and that what changes are the degrees of differentiation,[10] it would appear that the full presence of that truth is very rare in our world, and so rare that it would be difficult to name another thinker who understood that presence.

9. Voegelin, "Immortality," 260. [See page 199 here.]
10. "Gospel and Culture," 84. [See page 161 here.]

Is Strauss such a thinker? Certainly Strauss shares with Voegelin a profound commitment both to Greek philosophy and the Torah, and he also shares with Voegelin a profound opposition to the spirit of modernity, a spirit that is the primary source of the illusions and the terrors of the modern world. While Strauss was Jewish and Voegelin Christian, neither was orthodox in his thinking, and Strauss could even understand philosophy as the alternative to and antagonist of revelation. Nevertheless, Strauss deeply affirmed revelation, and that affirmation paralleled his philosophical vocation, even as that vocation could be understood as a clearing of the path in our world for revelation. Certainly the illusions that he assaulted are obstacles to revelation, just as the thinking that he pursued is open to revelation, and perhaps even open to what the Christian knows as revelation. This places Strauss in a very small corner in our world, although not so small as Voegelin's, and if Strauss thus far has had a far greater impact than Voegelin, that may well be due to the fact that he was a realist as Voegelin could never be, and a realist who resolutely refused all speculative thinking. For Strauss was a Jew who was awaiting the Messiah, whereas Voegelin was a Christian who not only knew the Messiah to be present but knew him as that Christ who is history writ large. There is a violence in Voegelin's opposition to modernity that is absent in Strauss, and absent not only because of Strauss's realism but also perhaps because Strauss never made the absolute commitment to history that is so manifest in Voegelin, a commitment that can neither tolerate nor understand any kind of opacity to revelation.

That opacity, for Voegelin, interiorly arose and became ever more overwhelming in the historical drama of revelation itself, as the Unknown God ultimately becomes the God "known" through his presence in Christ.

> This drama, though it has been alive in the consciousness of the New Testament writers, is far from alive in the Christianity of the churches today, for the history of Christianity is characterized by what is commonly called the separation of school theology from mystical or experiential theology which formed an apparently inseparable unit still in the work of Origen. The Unknown God whose *theotēs* was present in the existence of Jesus has been eclipsed by the revealed God of Christian doctrine.[11]

11. Ibid., 88. [See page 164 here.]

It was the doctrinization of Christianity that was a decisive source of its fall and collapse, a doctrinization most fully realized in the late medieval world, and such a scholastic dogmatism is inevitably followed by a skeptical reaction. That skeptical reaction ushered in the modern world, but the fact remains that this advent arose out of the history of Christianity itself, and even out of the history of revelation. Nothing is more critical in Voegelin's philosophy and theology of history than an understanding of this transition; for even if it had a precedent in the birth of the Hellenistic philosophical schools, that birth played a decisive role in the end of the ancient world, even as its medieval counterpart is a primary source of the disintegration of Christianity. That disintegration certainly occurred, or did so for Voegelin, and nothing less than this could historically make possible the comprehensive triumph of a demonic "self-salvation" in the modern world.

Voegelin apparently saw dogmatic thinking and understanding as an inversion of an openness to and participation in revelation, yet he devoted very little analysis to an explication of its meaning, and almost wholly isolated it from the historical worlds in which it occurred. Yet, and all too significantly, this problem does seem to lie at the center of his final reflections, and most explicitly so in his attempt to unravel the modern deformation of the symbol "God," a deformation occurring throughout the whole of modern thinking, and a deformation that has become actual in the development of the "public unconscious" from the eighteenth to the twentieth century. In the tortuous language of the unfinished and unrevised *In Search of Order*, and in the context of attempting to understand how the seeds of this deformation are present in Saint Bonaventura's *Itinerarium mentis in Deum*, Voegelin can say:

> The radical distinction of Being and non-Being, replacing the Platonic symbolism of a formative Beyond and its Parousia in formed reality, stresses the formative eminence of the Beyond in the experienced tension of reality so strongly that it acquires an ontic monopoly that cannot be sustained in the course of the analysis; the "Non-Being" cannot avoid becoming synonymous with "restricted Being"; and "restricted Being," while not the *ipsum esse* of Being, is some sort of Being after all. The ambiguity, it appears, must be read as the consequence of an attempt to ward off a threatening disruption of the paradox of consciousness: a publicly noticeable

> inclination to identify the thing-reality with Being is compensated by according the monopoly of Being to the comprehending reality.[12]

Once again Voegelin is attempting to maintain a Platonic and Aristotelian continuity between Being and Becoming, a continuity that was broken philosophically by Plotinus and Middle Platonism, and theologically by Paul and the Fourth Gospel, and it was Augustine who brought these definitive endings together in his construction of the foundations of the Western theological tradition.

This is the tradition that is finally Voegelin's deepest opponent, and if only for this reason, Hegel is his deepest philosophical enemy, for the Hegelian system both negated and preserved the Western dogmatic tradition. All of the fundamental moments and categories of Western dogmatics are present in the Hegelian system, whereas they are absent in Voegelin's system, as witness his Herculean labors to reverse the dogmatic category of beginning in the opening of *In Search of Order*. Indeed, Voegelin is nowhere more fully a classical thinker than in his refusal to accept the ultimacy or finality of any particular event, and he could join Strauss in his assertion that for a philosopher or for philosophy there can never be an absolute sacredness for a particular or contingent event.[13] Thus Voegelin can respond in this spirit to the question of how the "historical Christ," with a fixed date in history, can fit into a philosophical conception.

> St. Thomas has asked the question and sharpened it to its critical point: he asks "whether Christ be the head of all men" (*ST* III.8.2.), and answers unequivocally that he is the head of all men, indeed, and that consequently the mystical body of the church consists of all men who have, and will have, existed from the beginning of the world to its end. Philosophically, the proposition implies that Christ is both the "historical Christ," with a "pre-" and "post-" in time, and the divine timelessness, omnipresent in the flow of history, with neither a "pre-" nor a "post-." In the light of these implications, then, the symbolism of incarnation would express the experience, with a date in history, of God reaching into man and

12. *In Search of Order* (Baton Rouge: Louisiana State University Press, 1987), 84.
13. Strauss, "Mutual Influence," 111. [See page 218 here.]

> revealing him as the Presence that is the flow of presence from the beginning of the world to its end. History is Christ writ large.[14]

The seemingly uniquely Christian affirmation that history is Christ writ large is in full continuity with Classical thinking and understanding, and this is precisely the point that Voegelin himself makes, even going so far as doing it by way of a quotation of the essential passage from the Definition of Chalcedon concerning the union of the divine and human natures in the one person of Christ.

> "Our Lord Jesus Christ . . . truly God and truly man . . . recognized in two natures . . . the distinction of natures being in no way annulled by the union, but rather the characteristics of each nature being preserved and coming together to form one person and subsistence." This valiant attempt of the *patres* to express the two-in-one reality of God's participation in man, without either compromising the separateness of the two or splitting the one, concerns the same structure of intermediate reality, of the *metaxy*, the philosopher encounters when he analyzes man's consciousness of participation in the divine ground of his existence. The reality of the Mediator and the intermediate reality of consciousness have the same structure.[15]

One might well wonder whether there is an ultimate difference between Strauss and Voegelin, unless perhaps it is theological, and that not deriving from their respective Jewish and Christian identities, but rather from the deepest of all theological centers, the name or symbol or identity of God. Finally, Voegelin must find the Western theological tradition as a whole to be a deformation of "God," a deformation annulling the *metaxy* or the *In-Between*, that very In-Between which is the sole arena of revelation and whose disappearance results in an apprehension of the world as world and God as Being itself, or *ipsum esse*. This formula is, of course, the formula of St. Thomas, and beyond Thomas, of the Western theological world as a whole, a world grounded in an ontological gulf between the creature and the Creator. True, that gulf has ever deepened in the history of Western Christianity, becoming an impenetrable chasm in modern Christianity, as

14. Voegelin, "Immortality," 263. [See page 201 here.]
15. Ibid.

witness Kierkegaard. This is that chasm which produced a Hegel, just as it produced the Deism of the eighteenth century, and as it has produced a Voegelin in the twentieth century. Clearly that chasm has ever deepened in our history, and deepened above all for the Christian thinker, a thinker who in believing in Christ believes in the historical coming together of the creature and the Creator. That historical coinherence is transformed by Voegelin into a universal history of revelation, a revelation occurring in the *metaxy* or the In-Between, an intermediate consciousness between divinity and humanity that has the same structure as the Mediator or Christ, and which is eternally present in history as a whole. That eternal presence is obscured by a cosmological and mythical consciousness, just as it is virtually lost in modern consciousness, and virtually forgotten today.

Or is it? Does the philosophy of Voegelin promise the possibility of a breakthrough, a breakthrough that would be a return to our beginning, to the beginning of the drama of the history of revelation? The philosophy of Strauss certainly seems to offer the possibility of a breakthrough, and of a breakthrough to the ancient world, indeed, a breakthrough dissolving all fundamental or ultimate distinctions between the ancient and the modern worlds. These distinctions themselves are the product of modernity and of modernity alone, so that with the reversal or erasure of these distinctions one might well expect not only a remembrance of eternity but a return to a transcendental consciousness, and therewith an end of all our ideological terrors and illusions. Voegelin can know a "God" who is the source of such a call to eternity, a "God" who is both the Unknown God and the All, and a "God" who is eternally present. Strauss did not and perhaps would not recognize such a "God" as God, as that one God who is the sole Creator, and who is the giver of that Torah which is irreconcilable with all philosophy. Perhaps it is not the Christian and the Jew who are in contention with each other in Voegelin and Strauss, but rather the Jew and the pagan, the Jew who knows God to be God and only God, and the pagan who knows God as the Unknown All. Now if it was Strauss who was the realist in their mutual conflict with modernity and Voegelin who was driven into a lonely isolation, can these be consequences of their respective choices of the name and identity of God? Or is it possible that the far lonelier path of Voegelin is a consequence of a deeper turn of mind? Only time will tell.

Philosophy, Faith, and the Question of Progress

Timothy Fuller

Leo Strauss and Eric Voegelin, in rethinking political philosophy in the modern situation, confront Hegel's thought as that which has not yet been overcome. In confronting Hegel's thought, each questions the principle of philosophical progress as Hegel formulated it. Questioning philosophical progress cannot be separated from critical examination of Hegel's claim to have reached a philosophical reconciliation of the age-old conflict between faith and philosophy, or reason and revelation. Hegel argues for their convergence through the agency of Christianity. Hence to criticize the Hegelian idea of philosophical progress with respect to the question of reason and revelation, Strauss and Voegelin also must eventually criticize certain features of Christianity itself.

Hegel argues that truth is one, and that variation and disagreement among philosophers is no proof that truth cannot be found or does not persist through history.[1] These affirmations are both congenial to and among the sources for the defenses of philosophy offered by Strauss and Voegelin themselves. This being so, why do Strauss and Voegelin reject Hegel? It is because of the progressive principle. Hegel repeatedly contends that we know more than our predecessors, that the enigmas of the human condition are progressively illuminated and resolved.

1. See G.W.F. Hegel, *Introduction to the Lectures on the History of Philosophy*, trans. T. M. Knox and A. V. Miller (Oxford: Clarendon Press, 1987), for example, 48–52, 58–59.

If the fundamental question is the relation between philosophy and faith, or reason and revelation, Hegel argues for the necessary convergence of the two through Christianity. The Christian outlook, evolving through the agency of the human faculties, constitutes the process by which faith and reason become known as modes of what is one.[2] Hegel is decisively a philosopher with a Christian frame of mind. Under his progressive principle, the Protestant era supersedes the medieval Catholic era, supplanting Scholastic philosophy with what eventuates in Hegel's own philosophy, the latter being the culmination of the events set in motion by the Reformation.[3] On Hegel's view, Western civilization culminates in the "modern time" presided over (explained) by his own philosophy. Christianity, in various institutional forms, may dissolve, but only to carry through to fulfillment the convergence of faith and reason. The modern era supersedes its predecessors, carrying forward those continuingly relevant elements that provide the basis for the convergence. Western civilization thus solves its fundamental problem in a fundamentally Christian way—whether official Christians acknowledge or accept the way this happens or not, whether they see it or not. Strauss and Voegelin, each in his own way, take issue with this formulation.

Strauss, for example, insists that the hallmark of Western civilization is the question of the irresolvable conflict between faith and reason.[4] To resolve or permanently overcome this conflict would involve a radical transformation in Western civilization, bringing it to an end and paving the way for something new.

Hegelian thought can and has encouraged a longing, increasingly dominant from the seventeenth century on, to bring the historically repetitive experience of death and rebirth to fruition or resolution; radical activism comes into being, the "longing for total revolution,"[5] implicated

2. Ibid., and also G.W.F. Hegel, *Lectures on the Philosophy of World History; Introduction: Reason in History*, trans. H. B. Nisbet with an introduction by Duncan Forbes (Cambridge: Cambridge University Press, 1980). Hereafter cited as *Reason in History*.

3. G.W.F. Hegel, "The Modern Time," in *Lectures on the Philosophy of History*, trans. J. Sibree (London: G. Bell and Sons, 1914), part 4, section 3.

4. Strauss to Voegelin, 24 November 1942; and "Jerusalem and Athens: Some Preliminary Reflections," *Commentary* 43 (1967): 45–57. [Both appear in this volume.]

5. See Bernard Yack, *The Longing for Total Revolution: Philosophic Sources of Social Discontent from Rousseau to Marx and Nietzsche* (Princeton, N.J.: Princeton University Press, 1986). See Voegelin's own discussion in *From Enlightenment to Revolution*

in Hegel's claim to go beyond "providence" to a "more serious" comprehension of history's meaning. Enlightenment turns into "secularization," the latter not to be understood as "irreligious," but rather as a process in which the radical transformation is dissociated from the ecclesiastical formalities of the Christian tradition.[6] Because Hegel also insists upon our growing self-consciousness as agents of this massive change—we alone must carry it through—progress, so to speak, baptizes human brutality to the degree it is unavoidable in seeking to overcome or supersede everything that cannot accommodate to the convergence or resolution of the opposition that is the paradigmatic opposition for the past as a whole, the opposition of faith and reason.

In opposing the coerciveness of the modern project's effort to bring convergence to its completion, by showing that Enlightenment actually demands suppression of some forms of knowing for the sake of others, and in pointing to the obvious signs that the twentieth century's utmost brutality has not effected the convergence, Strauss and Voegelin are compelled to deny neither Hegel's defense of the centrality of philosophy nor the oneness of truth, but to purge Hegel's formulations of the progressive principle.[7]

To oppose Hegel's progressive principle implies skepticism toward some characteristic Christian claims about the convergence of faith and reason; without them Hegel's position loses its immediate plausibility to those who must receive his teaching. Voegelin would urge that it is Christianity itself, when undistorted by Hegel's reformulation of its claims, that deprives Hegel's position of its plausibility. Strauss implicitly denied that there could be "Christian philosophy," in denying in principle the possibility of ever

---

(Durham, N.C.: Duke University Press, 1975). For Hegel's claim, see *Reason in History*, 35–36, 40, 42.

6. "We cannot, therefore, be content with this (if the word be permitted) trivial faith in providence, nor indeed with a merely abstract and indeterminate faith which conceives in general terms of a ruling providence but refuses to apply it to determinate reality; on the contrary, we must tackle the problem seriously" (Hegel, *Reason in History*, 36). For "secularization," see Owen Chadwick, *The Secularization of the European Mind in the Nineteenth Century* (Cambridge, Eng.: Cambridge University Press, 1975).

7. Thus they show us an alternative to the nihilistic response to the problem that is itself a continuation of the Enlightenment frame of mind in the name of a critique of the Enlightenment. This has been well analyzed by Stanley Rosen in *Hermeneutics as Politics* (New York: Oxford University Press, 1987).

reconciling reason and revelation.[8] Anyone who seeks such a synthesis must subordinate either faith or philosophy, creating the mere appearance of a synthesis. Voegelin would agree to this when it comes to a Hegelian synthesis that appears to work by subordinating the radical otherness of the transcendent to the power of human explanation; in other words, Hegel makes faith into the human acknowledgment of its own reason in a particular mode. For Voegelin the balance to be struck between the "noetic" understanding and the "pneumatic" is not a "synthesis," and neither mode of knowing is privileged against the other. The tense relationship between them forever breaks apart and renews itself; Voegelin entirely rejects the hope of tranquillity in "synthetic" (humanly constructed) unity.

Strauss's strikingly different method in "Jerusalem and Athens" is to persuade us that, as soon as we start to consider the issue posed by reason and revelation, we will already have chosen sides. In weighing the claims of Jerusalem and Athens, we have already opted for Athens.[9] There is no "opting" for Jerusalem; one is either with Jerusalem or against Jerusalem. For example, that Strauss or anyone else listens to, and takes seriously, modern biblical criticism means that he or she is no longer loyal to Jerusalem (no longer understands the biblical writers as they understood themselves). This makes sense as the statement of one who began in faith and later left it, although it is obvious there are those who think themselves loyal to Jerusalem while engaging in biblical criticism. Perhaps Strauss understands the audience of this essay to be those who began in faith and have become open to leaving it. Or perhaps Strauss thinks that all of us today look back to the Scriptures through the veil of the modern critical consciousness. But that could equally suggest an audience comprising many who have never begun in faith and thus have not yet had the chance to leave it behind. Surely, those who have not begun in faith, who are seeking that which they have not yet found, would weigh alternatives (including alternative ideas of what it means to be faithful) before committing themselves; they can certainly think that they have not yet heard the voice of the Lord, even though they may long to. Strauss adopts a peculiarly nonvoluntarist stance, leaving the status of human participation in relation to the sources of religious authority unresolved (is simple piety the only religious answer to modern scholarship?).

8. See "Jerusalem and Athens," 55. [See page 112 in this volume.]

9. Ibid., 55. [See page 112 here.]

Strauss defends this stance in his delineation of insuperable differences between scriptural belief and philosophical reason on the character of wisdom. This is his summary: According to the Bible, the prophets are summoned by the Lord; according to Plato's *Apology of Socrates*, Socrates is prompted by Chairephon's questioning of the oracle. The prophets predict the messianic age; Socrates "merely holds that the perfect society is possible."[10] The prophets see universal knowledge; Socrates is confident only of the philosophic minority. The messianic age is understood to be an era of universal peace; Socrates' best regime is a single regime in a world of regimes still at war. The "faithful servant" who knows the good is categorically different from the "philosopher" who can only quest for the good.

Strauss presents each side as a stark alternative to the other but, on his own initial premise, in doing this he must be giving aid and comfort to the side of Athens. To put it differently, a detached comparison of the claims of philosophic science with the claims of prophetic revelation may excite the reader to choose, but the author, in making the alternatives as dichotomous as possible, remains outside the choice. Strauss as philosopher is reminiscent of Max Weber urging us to choose our way of life by choosing our way of knowing, while remaining himself in the role of the detached observer who cannot participate in making the choice he has clarified. Nevertheless, in doing this, Strauss is also using the detachment of the modern social scientist against modern social science—a lesson he could take from careful observation of Weber's method.

On the other hand, here, surely, is an opportunity for Strauss to discuss the divine drama as marked out by Plato (and as elaborated, as Strauss well knew, by Voegelin). Strauss rightly sees Plato pointing away from himself to Socrates. But Strauss downplays, if he does not dismiss, alternative views of Socrates' "divine mission." For example, he asserts that Socrates took the Delphic pronouncement seriously only in trying to disprove it. Strauss does not comment on the result of the attempt. He also insists that it was only on Chairephon's initiative (i.e., only through human agency) that the matter arose. Strauss in no way whatever discusses here the motive of Chairephon's initiative—the divine mystery of Socrates' life itself. Moreover, he does not consider that Socrates, in saying that he knows nothing, may be comparing what he does know to the divine reality yet to be known (as suggested, for example, in the Parable of the Cave). None of

10. Ibid., 57. [See page 137 here.]

this is unknown to or forgotten by Strauss; it is pointedly not mentioned. He gives no qualifications or alternatives to his interpretation of Plato's Socrates.

Strauss is obviously rejecting, by failing to mention, Voegelin's effort through his categories "noetic consciousness" and "pneumatic consciousness," each of which is a mode of appreciating theophany (the manifestation to us of the divine), to evoke the proximity of faith and philosophy. Noetic consciousness emphasizes man reaching out to the divine; pneumatic consciousness, the divine irrupting into human consciousness; together, in Voegelin's formulation, they form the dimensions of a complex of experiences in which humanity must locate itself (the *metaxy*, the in-between condition that is the human condition). Likewise, Strauss must reject Voegelin's notion of the believer as questioner who resists religion's "hardening into self-contained doctrine."[11] In short, Voegelin's Christianity is philosophical from the outset, a continuation of philosophical-theological speculation in which he understands Socrates, Plato, Aristotle, the

11. "The Gospel and Culture," in D. Miller and D. G. Hadidian, eds., *Jesus and Man's Hope*. vol. 2 (Pittsburgh, Pa.: Pittsburgh Theological Seminary Press, 1971), 60–61. [See page 141 here.] Strauss and Voegelin agree that the central issue for the whole history of political philosophy is the issue of the correct understanding of Plato and Aristotle. They proceed to disagree on what that understanding is. The disagreement depends on whether the Christian experience is an essential supplement to, a further unfolding of, the insights of the Platonic-Aristotelian philosophy. Voegelin holds that Plato and Aristotle did not have a universal political science because they did not transcend their foundation in the Greek experience but only pointed toward such transcendence. It was, Voegelin argues, the emergence of Christianity and the historical consciousness that led to the universalization of the image of man, establishing the "superiority of the Christian anthropology." Voegelin suggests that the "belief in the universality of the Hellenic image of man seems to be a product of the Renaissance," that is, of a Christianized classicism (Voegelin to Strauss, 9 December 1942). Strauss "decisively denies" the limitation Voegelin imputes to Plato and Aristotle but, he continues, even if this were so, the attribution of universality to Greek philosophy was already to be found in the ninth century among Moslem and Christian thinkers. The only way for the disagreement to be settled, if it can be, is through "radical, relentless interpretation of every Platonic dialogue" (Strauss to Voegelin, 20 December 1942). Apart from other considerations, it is clear that Strauss intuited a "latent progressivism" (a Hegelian historicist taint?) in Voegelin's formulation of the problem at that time. This latency can be felt through *The New Science of Politics* and the early volumes of *Order and History*. Volumes 4 and 5 of the latter work seek to purge this residuum. They express an interpretation that tends to equalize the insights, if not to lean toward Plato, while otherwise conceding nothing to the Straussian interpretation of the dialogues.

Prophets, and Paul all to play indispensable roles. For Voegelin, raising questions is not only not against faith, it is of the essence of faith.

Strauss, in fact, pointedly does not take up Christianity at all, invoking the authority of Hermann Cohen in leaving Christianity out when discussing Plato, the Prophets, and the "social ideal."[12] Christianity, perhaps, not being tied to a polis or a nation, has no "social ideal," but rather an aspiration to transcend all social ideals. Voegelin's Christianity is a philosophical religion responding to a divine pressure to question, which opens the way to reformulating the relation of religion and philosophy. Modernity starts to emerge with Christianity. Modernity is ancient, not necessarily Hegelian.[13] The seeds of our modern intellectual and spiritual deformity lie waiting to be fertilized by what Voegelin calls "late-medieval, radical doctrinization of both Metaphysics and Theology,"[14] and by what Strauss discovers to be the project of the modern political philosophers.

Strauss describes Hegel as continuing the modern tradition of competitive struggle for glory "originated by Machiavelli and perfected by such men as Hobbes and Adam Smith."[15] But he also describes Hegel as attempting a synthesis of classical and biblical morality, effecting "the miracle of producing an amazingly lax morality out of two moralities both of which made very strict demands on self-restraint." Strauss's concern for the morality of self-restraint principally emphasizes, in this context, political self-restraint. If we ask what will liberate us from a sense of restraint on the human longing for fulfillment through political and military glory, it is the conviction that we have attained an absolute insight into history's end or goal. By imagining the confluence of divine wisdom

12. "Jerusalem and Athens," 56. [See pages 131–32 here.]

13. "Gospel and Culture," 62. [See page 142 here.]

14. Ibid., 66. [See page 147 here.] See also "Gnosticism—the Nature of Modernity," in *The New Science of Politics: An Introduction* (Chicago: University of Chicago Press, 1987).

15. Strauss, "Restatement on Xenophon's *Hiero*," in *On Tyranny, Revised and Enlarged* (Ithaca, N.Y.: Cornell University Press, 1968), 205. Hereafter cited as "Restatement." And, "the root of all modern darkness from the seventeenth century on is the obscuring of the difference between theory and praxis, an obscuring that first leads to a reduction of praxis to theory (this is the meaning of so-called rationalism) and then, in retaliation, to the rejection of theory in the name of a praxis that is no longer intelligible as praxis" (Strauss to Voegelin, 14 March 1950). That is, the movement runs from Machiavelli to Hegel, and thenceforth proceeds ever more rapidly into the abyss of "existential philosophy." This argument seems to have persuaded Voegelin not to rely too heavily on the word "existential" in future writings.

and human agency, Hegel could, as Strauss insists, conjure up a man who "lacks awareness of sacred restraints."[16]

Religion is prone to zeal and passion. To incorporate the prestige of philosophy into the revelatory claim of certain knowledge is to prompt a frame of mind ill-suited to protect itself against excess and fanaticism. It will at least be difficult to control those who appropriate religious symbolism to a fanaticism that is religiously inauthentic but easily confused with the genuine article by the unreflective to whom "final solutions" appeal. On this point, Voegelin and Strauss are quite agreed.

On the other hand, for Strauss, philosophy cannot subsume revelation without demythologizing it, and philosophy cannot simply assume, or conclusively prove, religion to be mistaken. Philosophy's self-questioning makes it unsuitable to lead, although it can question and undermine leadership. Philosophy must remain open, questioning, seeking, and nonsectarian: "As long as there is no wisdom but only quest for wisdom, the evidence of all solutions is necessarily smaller than the evidence of the problems. Therefore the philosopher ceases to be a philosopher at the moment at which the 'subjective certainty' of a solution becomes stronger than his awareness of the problematic character of that solution. At that moment the sectarian is born."[17]

Christianity, implicitly from the start, according to Voegelin, gave rise to the thought of a reconciliation of faith and philosophy culminating in the thought of Thomas Aquinas.[18] The Reformation, in teaching reliance on faith alone, may be said to have encouraged "subjective certainty." Hegel located this emergence in a process whose latent aim was to overcome the radical dichotomy of the flesh and the spirit, to identify the

16. "Restatement," 205.

17. Ibid., 209–10. Strauss continues: "The difference between the philosopher and the political man will then be a difference with respect to happiness. The philosopher's dominating passion is the desire for truth, i.e., for knowledge of the eternal order, or the eternal cause or causes of the whole. As he looks up in search for the eternal order, all human things and all human concerns reveal themselves to him in all clarity as paltry and ephemeral, and no one can find solid happiness in what he finds paltry and ephemeral. . . . The political man must reject this way altogether. . . . He could not devote himself to his work with all his heart or without reservation if he did not attach absolute importance to man and to human things" (211–12). Needless to say, such a man does not need the encouragement of believing that he is in possession of a divinely inspired insight, expressed in a "theory" that drives his "praxis."

18. Strauss recognizes this in discussing Thomas in *Natural Right and History* (Chicago: University of Chicago Press, [1953] 1968), 157–59.

divine with the human. If the Word was made flesh, so must the flesh be made Word, and the latter through the agency of the "I" who can do no other. Thus revelation could be turned into the claim of self-generated human insight into the path it must commit itself to travel, with Hegel its prophet. Here too Strauss and Voegelin could agree on what happened.

The implication in Strauss's analysis is that to oppose Hegel one cannot help but oppose certain features of the Christian frame of mind (even though this does not rule out the possibility of another kind of Christianity, which Strauss does not speculate on). This seems to imply that Hegel's "Christian philosophy" is the form of Christianity likely to be "practical" for our time. Strauss's admonition, always to keep the character of our own time clearly in mind as we analyze past thought,[19] has to mean keeping our time's peculiar form of Christianization-secularization in mind.

To go back to the ancients is to take seriously the antiprogressive view, to bring the "progressive" and the "antiprogressive" before us for contemplation. Then the decisive feature of the ancients already will have been appropriated to a modern context in which the antiprogressive view opposes "progress," losing its immediate appearance of naturalness, becoming a counterrevolutionary, politicized or political principle. In the context of modern partisanship, this view cannot function simply as the ground from which all reflection begins. The difficulty of showing that antiprogressive philosophy is not merely opinion but knowledge imposes itself upon us. Not only in Hegel but in writers such as J. S. Mill and throughout the last two centuries, the principle of "order" has been interpreted as ancillary to "progress," which, although usefully restrained from incautious self-development by the necessities of order, nevertheless must proceed relentlessly forward, liberating itself from the flatness of custom by continually redefining order as its insights accumulate. Perhaps Hegel did not live up to the requirements of philosophy insofar as he took progress for granted. For example, Hegel both insists that each philosopher must be studied in his or her own terms, not in terms invented later, and also asserts, repeatedly, that later philosophy is better than earlier.[20] Thus, for Hegel, to study each philosopher in his or her own terms is to identify that philosopher's limits (even though truth is expressed within those limits). Strauss calls us to consider that we have gone wrong and that, where we believe we have proven past thinkers are limited, it is possible they saw true

19. See "Jerusalem and Athens."
20. *Introduction to the Lectures on the History of Philosophy*, passim.

limits we are either too ignorant or loath to admit. In forcing ourselves to rethink, we will have already distanced ourselves from simple acceptance of the progressive principle.

Both Strauss and Voegelin, in identifying what they take to be the deformities of modern thought, are moved to study the ancients. For both, the modern problem cannot be isolated from the problem of Christianity. Voegelin responds by resituating Christianity in a larger complex of experiences where it loses its claim of privilege, contributing to but not becoming the arbiter of the understanding of the universal structure of reality; Strauss insists on the unmediable opposition between philosophy and religion.

Can the progressive principle be opposed without opposing Christianity? Voegelin certainly thinks so. But this leads him into visualizing the unity of faith and reason, not in a process of convergence through time, but in identifying primordial experiences common to both faith and philosophy, underlying both and directive to the expressions of either as their practitioners attempt to respond to and articulate the meaning of the experiences. According to Voegelin, the task of the philosopher is "to preserve the balance between the experienced lastingness and the theophanic events in such a manner that the paradox becomes intelligible as the very structure of existence itself . . . the postulate of balance." And "the life of reason, thus, is firmly rooted in a revelation" that is obscured when we report philosopher's ideas without looking at the "experiences that have motivated them."[21] There is one God. But "when God lets himself be seen, whether in a burning thornbush or in a Promethean fire, he is what he reveals himself to be in the event."[22]

21. *Order and History,* vol. 4, *The Ecumenic Age* (Baton Rouge: Louisiana State University Press, 1974), 228–29. Hereafter cited as *The Ecumenic Age*. See also the letter from Voegelin to Strauss, 12 March 1949. There Voegelin describes his aim "to restore the experiences that have led to the creation of certain concepts and symbols," for the "symbols have become opaque; they must be made luminous again." In saying this, Voegelin, in agreement with Strauss, is expressing his method, which does not attempt an understanding of past thinkers better than their understanding of themselves. Strauss responds that opposing the "presently reigning idiocy" is far more crucial than dwelling on their differences (Strauss to Voegelin, 17 March 1949). Strauss goes on to say that "Plato *or* existentialism is today the ontological question" (Strauss to Voegelin, 17 December 1949). It is clear in the context of the letters that "existentialism" to Strauss means "historicism."

22. *The Ecumenic Age*, 229. Also, Voegelin says, Plato knew that the "divine

In other words, God reveals himself in proliferating variety and there is no way for us to privilege some theophanic event or events once and for all. Contra Hegel, we are not the agents of our own destiny, we can only participate in our destiny. Openness requires submission to differentiating insight. If the "fact of revelation is its content," if the divine is what it shows itself to be in its eventuation, then we cannot look behind it—explain it or explain it away—but we must explain what it means to us, taking it, just as it shows itself to us, to be the reference against which our intellectual elaboration or explanation is to be judged. "All knowledge, including revealed knowledge, is human insofar as it is the knowledge of concrete men. But some knowledge is understood by the men to whom it befalls as stemming from a divine source. This formulation is not meant pseudopsychologically, because it does not dispute that the source is rightly diagnosed."[23]

Special moments for us will not be special for everyone. We cannot be certain how far they are universal for humanity. Even though they may be equivalent to experiences in other sectors of humanity, in touch with a universality apprehended in many ways by human beings under different conditions in different times and places, they cannot substitute for the others. Our experiences are thus universal in their *possibility* of equivalence to other experiences outside our local circumstances, from which we could also learn. Privilege for our experiences is largely a matter of familiarity with our own. As such, we can be satisfied with what we have, but we can have no basis for imputing superiority to our own. Even if we find it superior for us, we can neither expect nor demand outside confirmation. Is such confirmation really necessary? Perhaps not, but Christianity is then chastened in its claims against the world.[24]

---

beyond" can be "symbolized only by the myth," for "literalism as a social force endangers the humanity of the young, because it converts the real truth which the symbols of the myth have as the real expression of a real experience of real divine presence into the fictitious truth of human propositions about gods who are objects of cognition. Literalism splits the symbol from the experience by hypostatizing the symbol as a proposition on objects" (35–36). See also *Order and History*, vol. 5, *In Search of Order* (Baton Rouge: Louisiana State University Press, 1987). Almost the entire purpose of *In Search of Order* is to combat modernity's pervasive "literalism," its obsession with the "thingness" of reality.

23. Voegelin to Strauss, 22 April 1951.

24. The reader will note that there is a considerable difference between a

To Voegelin, the division of the experiential range between Hellenic philosophy and the Israelite-Jewish prophets is a mystery. We do not know why they came to the world separately. The sense of the mystery was maintained in the "generous openness" of Christianity from Paul to Nicaea,[25] but the subsequent doctrinization was a form of self-protection against the lingering multiplicity of experience in the "pagan" world, leading to "orthodoxy" and to organizational rigidity. For Voegelin this development increasingly threatened a perversion of both philosophy and revelation. This was particularly the case when the Augustinian preservation of the original tension, lasting from the fifth to the twelfth centuries, began to decline and to be supplanted by the flowering of monastic millennial speculations, later by the optimism of the humanist intellectuals, and eventually by Hegel's absolute science of history.

Voegelin presents us with a genealogy of decline into "ideological 'philosophies of history' as variations of the Pauline myth in the mode of deformation."[26] From the awareness of permanent situatedness in the *metaxy*, we fell into imagining a knowable beginning and end to human existence in history. The seeds of this lengthy decline in modernity were sewn in Paul's "inclination to abolish the tension between the eschatological *telos* of reality and the mystery of the transfiguration that is actually going on within historical reality."[27] The experience of spiritual transcendence henceforth was in continual danger of being transposed into a story of immanent achievement by autonomous human ingenuity.

Such expectations are hard, perhaps virtually impossible, to preclude. Thus Christianity cannot avoid responsibility for the derangements of modernity, even as it must be credited for deepening the insight into the spirit of man and making it accessible on an unprecedented scale.

From this point of view, Strauss correctly opposes the amalgamation of faith and philosophy in its form as the immanentist-revolutionary malaise of modern life. But Voegelin would want to say that this opposition rightly

universalizing but "chastened Christianity" and a philosophy that for fulfillment demands to remain tied to a polis or a nation. See "Jerusalem and Athens."

25. *The Ecumenic Age*, 259.

26. Ibid., 269. See also Voegelin's letter to Strauss, 4 December 1950.

27. *The Ecumenic Age*, 270. The term *metaxy* has been in Voegelin's technical terminology at least since *The New Science of Politics*. One excellent description is offered in "Gospel and Culture," but he repeatedly characterizes it, for instance, in volumes 4 and 5 of *Order and History*.

rejects the deformed version, not the thing itself. The alternative strategy to insisting on the unmediability of faith and philosophy is to recapture an understanding of the common character of both. The latter project would include the Christian insight, but not in the role of superseding and summing up all other insights.[28]

For Strauss, the safeguard against the modern derangements is the rigid separation of philosophy and religion, based on the truth of their incompatibility. He certainly knew that to characterize Western civilization as the permanent split of philosophy and religion was to offer a definition opposed by powerful alternatives covering the same empirical territory as his own.[29] To assert that philosophers *cannot* be men of faith or religiously committed may require that some significant thinkers (Voegelin?) be considered as either dissembling or self-deluding. At the very least one must question how far this can be shown to be understanding them as they understood themselves. Moreover, how far is this a strategic doctrine, arguable but indemonstrable, a protective measure against modern excesses?

Those who review the matter will have to go through these reflections, questioning both progress and this dichotomy as they begin the effort at recollection of the experiences of the ancients. Is it impossible that a Straussian beginning could reach a Voegelinian conclusion? Obviously, it need not. It is not apparent where such an inquiry must end. To claim to know would itself be unphilosophical. To have an inclination on the matter is not to bring the matter to a close.

For example, Voegelin's might be thought a superior position because it refers us back to the formative experiences prior to crystallization and doctrinization, breaking down the categories "philosophy-theology," "faith-reason," "reason-revelation." We would have to wonder if the whole

28. For a powerful analysis of the problem of Hegel for Christianity and for modern existence in general, one should consult Emil Fackenheim, *To Mend the World: Foundations of Future Jewish Thought* (New York: Schocken Books, 1982).

29. See Strauss's introduction to *Natural Right and History*, 8, where he acknowledges the prominence of the Thomistic solution among modern followers of Thomas Aquinas. Even so, in his letter to Voegelin of 9 May 1943, he refers to "Neo-Thomism" as, however laudable, at a "low level not worth considering." Voegelin's is, of course, *not* a Roman Catholic solution, despite the belief of some, particularly before the appearance of *The Ecumenic Age* in 1984, that it might be. How "Thomistic" it might be depends on the missing discussion of Thomas in the incomplete volume 5 of *Order and History*.

formulation in these terms is not already a falling away from the experiential basis of the question itself.[30]

Voegelin is well aware of the fact that Christianity does not prevent this deformation of faith and philosophy. Indeed, it lends itself to this after the period of its initial openness. Voegelin is defending a version of Christianity that is not Christianity as we ordinarily know it. It is strikingly enough different so that commentators have wondered and will wonder if it is Christianity. If it is Christianity, it must be ecumenical and philosophical, "unprogressive," Christianity.[31] Voegelin, throughout his writing, philosophizes. Christianity cannot "complete" philosophy. Philosophy must, by its presence, also offer Christianity liberation from its own worst tendencies.

The offer depends, however, on philosophy seeing itself as Voegelin sees it: as expanded by the Incarnation (properly, i.e., philosophically, understood). This may be too much for the Platonist and too little for the Christian. Undoubtedly, this is intentional on Voegelin's part; the cure for the Platonist and the Christian are the experiences of Plato and of, for instance, Paul.

Plato and Aristotle, for Voegelin, crystallize a tradition of inquiry that includes Heraclitus before and Paul after.[32] In saying this, Voegelin does not intend to diminish the centrality of the texts of the philosophers but rather, by recapturing their experiential bases, to heighten our awareness of their significance. For Voegelin this is what it means to understand past thinkers as they understood themselves.

Voegelin is a Christian thinker in the sense that his work began with Christian assumptions. Nevertheless, it has continually advanced by means of an effort of self-liberation from claims of the exclusive or necessarily superior character of the Christian experiences of theophany. Christianity is a crucial episode in man's implication in a much larger cosmic order that

30. See *The New Science of Politics*, 69–70, 79, where "revelation" is seen to be a reduction, when treated as an orthodoxy. See also page 80, note 7, where Voegelin sets out the arguments over the "superiority" of either Aristotelian or Christian metaphysics. Voegelin, in the final analysis, counsels us not to be content to set up the problem in this way.

31. Voegelin would not intend "philosophical" and "ecumenical" to mean Christianity should follow the contemporary trends of liberalizing-secularizing Protestantism or Catholic liberationism. These are forms of eschatological immanentism. Strauss would identify them as existentialist-historicist.

32. *The New Science of Politics*, 66.

necessarily must be apprehended by many in undergoing other theophanic experiences.

In all cases, there is an inevitable tension between emphasis on the human side of revelatory experience and emphasis on the divine side—who is doing what to whom? The philosopher's task is to maintain the appreciative balance that admits there is no resolving the tension. The tension is not a "problem" with a "solution"; it is the field of reality within which human consciousness comes to know itself and also the limits of its capacity for self-knowledge. The confrontation with the divine forces us to respond, but in terms we must devise for ourselves.[33]

Thus Voegelin frees himself also from Hegel, who carries forward the exclusivity of the Christian frame of mind as the medium of his progressive interpretation of history, transforming exclusivity into a claim of absolute knowledge about world history. Here Plato and undeformed Christianity share the "struggle against apocalyptic and Gnostic sectarians who want to find shortcuts to immortality" by separating "the pursuit of immortality from the Ananke of existence in the Metaxy."[34]

Voegelin learned this as much or more from Plato as from Christianity.[35] Christianity carries forward the Platonic insight, in some ways deepening it, but it is also prone to excessive or unrestrained eschatological formulations.[36] What Paul emphasized was the "exodus from structure" as opposed to the "cognition of structure." The Platonic and the Pauline together reveal "history in suspense between the Ananke of the cosmos and the freedom of eschatological movement."[37]

The danger of the Christian experience is that in its eschatological aspirations it will fall into despair of fulfillment and relapse into a search for immanent, this-worldly meaning to obtain "imaginary immortality through active participation in an imaginary process of history."[38]

33. Ibid., ch. 3. The awareness of our participation in response is the beginning of a cure for the peculiar use of this otherwise correct insight by Hegel.

34. *The Ecumenic Age*, 237.

35. This is evident in reading *In Search of Order*. As that is an unfinished work not included a projected analysis of Thomas Aquinas, it might have been intended as more of a balance between Platonism and Christianity, or between what Voegelin earlier referred to as the "anthropological" and the "soteriological" truths.

36. *The New Science of Politics*, 122–23, and *The Ecumenic Age*, passim.

37. *The Ecumenic Age*, 258.

38. *The New Science of Politics*, 122–23. This succinctly renders Voegelin's judgment on Hegel's philosophy of history.

The only plausible meaning of "progress," then, is one which undermines its modern political usage altogether: progress is the experience of deepening insight into the inexhaustible mystery of the human condition. One can progress but yet also regress. There is an ascending and descending experience, no perpetual progress or necessary forward movement. The *metaxy* is invulnerable to reshaping by human ingenuity. One can be in tune with or falling away from it—that is all. Awareness of cosmic order can be enhanced or diminished. When we are losing it, we can be anxious for "the vision of a divine intervention that will put an end to disorder in time for all time," genesis without perishing.[39]

Plato and Aristotle, and Christianity in its balanced form, recognize and take measures to circumvent this deformed condition of human understanding. Plato and Aristotle are "mystic philosophers."[40] In comparing the "noetic theophany" of Plato and Aristotle to the "pneumatic theophany" of Paul, Voegelin finds a common apprehension of the structure of birth-death-rebirth, but a divergence on where to place the interpretative emphasis. Hence in the aftermath of the experiences it is possible to construct doctrines that will be at odds with each other. The experiences are real, the doctrines are the aftermath and already a falling away from the experiences. A doctrine is hence not "progress" of understanding but an effort at recapturing or recollecting or reawakening the formative experience. That we must fall into the problem of loss and recovery, that we cannot simply possess and hold on to the formative experience, indicates that we are not dealing with a "progressive science" or an "academic field" but rather the "field of reality."[41]

39. *The Ecumenic Age*, 239ff. And: "Ontological knowledge emerges in the process of history and biographically in the process of the individual person's life under certain conditions of education, the social context, personal inclination, and spiritual conditioning. *Epistēmē* is not just a function of misunderstanding, it is also, in the Aristotelian sense, a dianoetic *aretē*" (Voegelin to Strauss, 2 January 1950). Such remarks obviously led Strauss to wonder if Voegelin had genuinely avoided historicism. Will this give pause to those who believe that Strauss is a historicist in disguise?

40. *The New Science of Politics*, 77. Here Strauss must dissent. If the disagreement of Strauss and Voegelin on this most basic point will not incite fresh reexamination of the issues posed by the ancients, it is hard to know what will.

41. Ibid., 67. Also, "the theophanic events do not occur in history; they constitute history together with its meaning" (*The Ecumenic Age*, 252). We participate in such events but distort them in trying to abstract them into objects of study or into formulized characterizations. This point is elaborated in *In Search of Order*.

Since "a theophanic event is a turbulence in reality,"[42] definitions come after and are arbitrarily fixed, having always to be reconnected to the turbulence whence they arose. Modern revolutionary-ideological politics are such attempts to induce the theophanic experience. Thus new "messiahs" appear to lead us into "immortality" in history.[43] They think that the divine truth is self-generated, whereas "the critique of society is not man himself but man in so far as through the differentiation of his psyche he has become representative of divine truth."[44] But unfortunately, "in the modern state of alienation, the enterprise of self-salvation dominates the concern with history and meaning."[45]

Obviously we cannot avoid the question, Who or what is doing the differentiating? Interpretation can go either in the direction of the divine irruption in human endeavor or in the direction of self-created human insight. There is no guaranteed method of insuring the balance through which human self-understanding is in balance with the balance of cosmic order to which it seeks to correspond. The philosopher cannot simply defeat the "philodoxer" (nor will distinguishing them from each other be an easy task), even if we insist that reality will defeat the latter (whoever it turns out to be). Neither philosophy nor faith is a savior in an activist, programmatic sense; they are the resources that keep alive the possibility of recollecting the truth of reality when efforts to overcome reality, and the empirical plausibility of progress, begin to fail. Strauss and Voegelin were each inclined to place the emphasis on different aspects of the reality they equally longed to know. This prompted their conversation that each saw was of necessity of the eternal things. We would do well to note that concern for the eternal things generates the human conversation, and that human conversation grounds humanity itself.

42. *The Ecumenic Age*, 252.
43. Ibid., 224–25.
44. *The New Science of Politics*, 68.
45. *The Ecumenic Age*, 255.

Medieval Rationalism or Mystic Philosophy? Reflections on the Strauss-Voegelin Correspondence

Ellis Sandoz

The fascinating correspondence between Leo Strauss and Eric Voegelin raises more questions than it answers, if merely taken by itself.[1] To be sure, a number of extremely valuable debates arise between the two writers, especially in the letters of 1949 through 1951. Often, however, the exchange gives only straws in the wind and a sense of agreements and disagreements, but much that unites and much that separates them ultimately remains obscure. To account adequately for everything would require a review of the correspondence in the context of the entire corpus of the technical writing and teaching of both men. That large task cannot be undertaken on this occasion, although some tentative suggestions will be ventured by way of conclusion. Since this correspondence is an exchange between the two giants of political philosophy of our time, there should be no doubt of its importance and great intrinsic interest.

1. As Ernest L. Fortin puts it: "What do we learn from the correspondence that we did not already know or could not know from other sources about Strauss's or Voegelin's thought? Not much, I suspect. Both authors have written extensively elsewhere on the subjects with which they deal here. There is nevertheless in the letters a certain bluntness or candor that would have been out of place in a piece written for publication. . . . Not surprisingly, neither one appears to have learned much from the other or to have budged in any way from his position" (Fortin, "Men of Letters: The Little-Known Correspondence between Leo Strauss and Eric Voegelin," *Crisis* [March 1991], 36).

The tone of the exchange, stretching over the three decades from 1934 to 1964, is respectful and even warm to the extent of polite friendliness. It is a bit stiff, formal and civil, thawing eventually to "Mr. Strauss" and "Mr. Voegelin," never to Leo and Eric, but this does not inhibit a lively and frank discussion. Most of the efforts to define the intellectual relationship between the two men are made by Strauss, and these almost always point up differences. It is of some moment that only five of the fifty-one surviving letters presented herein were written after Voegelin published the first three volumes of *Order and History* (1956 and 1957), perhaps a significant fact. Moreover, Strauss makes little or no comment to Voegelin about what he has written on the basis of a profound study of the Bible—specifically of the Hebrew Old Testament—in *Israel and Revelation*,[2] his meticulous interpretation of the pre-Socratics that displays a philosophical and theoretical mastery of the some fifty-five Greek authors considered in *The World of the Polis*, or about the close textual analysis and interpretation given of the principal political writings of Plato and Aristotle as powerfully presented in the third of these volumes. Of course, there are gaps from missing letters, but this is mainly a problem for the correspondence during the years down to 1953 or so; and it is extremely unlikely that a discussion of *Order and History* has disappeared.[3] There is the relocation (which could have played

2. There is mention by Voegelin in his letter of 10 June 1953, that he is "working on the Israelite chapter in [his] *History*" and "greatly regretted that [they] have no opportunity to speak occasionally." Strauss in his letter of 23 June 1953, responds that "the problem of history in the Old Testament" is "one of the most complex problems in intellectual history. . . . perhaps the utopian plan would be to devote about ten years to the solution of this problem." He says not a word in subsequent correspondence about the long book on the subject published in 1956 as *Israel and Revelation*. Voegelin's lamentation about his command of Hebrew in the June 10 letter seems to have been partly modesty, since W. F. Albright in reviewing *Israel and Revelation* makes a point of noting that "his use of Hebrew is almost impeccable" (*Theological Studies* 22 [1961]: 275; see also the review by James B. Pritchard in *The American Historical Review* 63 [1957–58]: 640–41).

3. I say this on the basis of Voegelin's careful habit of retaining carbon copies of his own letters and dutifully keeping a file of letters received. It is nearly inconceivable that an exchange with Strauss on *Order and History*, or any part of it, would have escaped this methodical practice. On the other hand, there appears to be no extant letter from Voegelin regarding Strauss's own Walgreen Lectures of 1949, *Natural Right and History* (Chicago: University of Chicago Press, 1953), after publication, despite a series of eager queries scattered through his earlier letters about when the book would appear. These materials now are organized in the Eric Voegelin Archive at Hoover Institution Library (box 38.34; on microfilm reel 37.1), the source of forty of the fifty-one letters

a part in disrupting the correspondence) as the Voegelins moved from Baton Rouge to Munich in 1958. There he began a new phase of his career in Germany by establishing the Political Science Institute through his appointment to the chair in that discipline left vacant at the University of Munich since the death of Max Weber.

But the silence is significant, no matter what allowances are made. And apart from rare occasions such as the present one, when the matter is directly raised (or the annual meetings of the Eric Voegelin Society when panels were devoted to the relationship in 1989 and 1990), the silence continues virtually into the present by latter-day Straussian scholars. Thus, a 1989 recall of critical exchanges with Strauss mentions Alexandre Kojève, C. B. Macpherson, Raymond Aron, Hans-Georg Gadamer, Karl Löwith, and Arnaldo Momigliana but passes over Voegelin—surely classified with Strauss as another "maverick" taking on the "authorities" and on much the same ground, i.e., an insistence of the indispensability of classical philosophy for a rational understanding of the human condition per se, not least of all of the contemporary world and its crisis.[4]

---

published in this collection. The two men continued to exchange publications, as can be seen from the very last letter (that of 7 September 1964) in which Voegelin thanks Strauss for his apparently having had his publisher send him a copy of *The City and Man* (Chicago: Rand McNally, 1964).

4. Thomas L. Pangle, ed., *The Rebirth of Classical Political Rationalism: An Introduction to the Thought of Leo Strauss; Essays and Lectures by Leo Strauss* (Chicago: University of Chicago Press, 1989), ix. Voegelin's name does not appear in the index to the volume. The only reference to Voegelin made by Strauss in print that I can think of is his comment that the former's 1949 review of the latter's study of Xenophon's *Hiero* was one of only two critiques from which "one could learn anything," the other being by Kojève. Voegelin then is identified as "one of the leading contemporary historians of political thought"—*not* as a *political philosopher*, a matter of consequence in the world of esoteric communication inhabited by such a careful writer as Strauss. See Strauss, "Restatement on Xenophon's *Hiero*," in *What Is Political Philosophy? And Other Studies* (Glencoe, Ill.: The Free Press, 1959), 96–103, on Voegelin at 96 [see pages 49–57 in this volume]; cf. Voegelin to Strauss, 14 January 1949, Letter 20; Strauss to Voegelin, 15 April 1949, Letter 25; Strauss to Voegelin, 8 August 1950, Letter 31; and Voegelin to Strauss, 21 August 1950, Letter 32, herein.

On exoteric and esoteric writing, see Strauss, *Persecution and the Art of Writing* (Glencoe, Ill.: The Free Press, 1952); see also Strauss, "Exoteric Teaching," *Interpretation: A Journal of Political Philosophy* 14 (1986): 51–59, reprinted in *The Rebirth of Classical Political Rationalism*, ed. Pangle, 63–71. Receipt of *Persecution and the Art of Writing* is acknowledged by Voegelin in his letter of 5 August 1952, and the subject matter is referred to subsequently; the article from which the book grew, published in

The silence may be the most important aspect for consideration. How is the silence to be interpreted? Perhaps these letters point toward an answer. A preliminary answer must be that Voegelin's publication of the initial volumes of *Order and History* finally put a period to the relationship that had been declining since his 1951 Walgreen Lectures at the University of Chicago, published as *The New Science of Politics.*[5] So, the further question to be wondered about is exactly *why*? To which the preliminary plausible answer must be that—from the perspectives of both men—persuasion had reached its limits, and there was little more to be said between them because of fundamental disagreement.

Social Research in 1941, was called to Voegelin's attention in Strauss's letter of 13 February 1943. There is no direct suggestion by Voegelin that Strauss himself engages in esoteric writing, but he shows interest in the subject and understands its ramifications, as hyperbolic remarks about John Locke intimate in his letter of 15 April 1953 (apparently never sent), and the letter of 20 April 1953, covering the same ground more circumspectly (see the editors' note to Letter 42). Strauss responds by commending Voegelin for his acuity regarding types of esotericism (letter of 29 April 1953, penultimate paragraph).

An evenhanded discussion of Strauss's own employment of this technique in his writing is given in Bernard Susser, "Leo Strauss: The Ancient as Modern," *Political Studies* 36 (1988): 497–514 at 509; contrast the scathing denunciation of Strauss's "secret art of writing" (among other things) by Stephen Holmes in "Truths for Philosophers Alone?" *Times Literary Supplement* (1–7 December 1989), 1319–20, 1322–24, ending in his declaration that Strauss "was no philosopher." Cf. the response by Thomas L. Pangle, ibid. (5–11 January 1990), 11.

5. Voegelin, *The New Science of Politics: An Introduction* (Chicago: University of Chicago Press, 1952); Voegelin, *Order and History*, vol. 1, *Israel and Revelation* (Baton Rouge: Louisiana State University Press, 1956), vols. 2 and 3, *The World of the Polis* and *Plato and Aristotle* (Baton Rouge: Louisiana State University Press, 1957). For a bibliography of Voegelin's publications through 1980, see Ellis Sandoz, *The Voegelinian Revolution: A Bibliographical Introduction* (Baton Rouge: Louisiana State University Press, 1981); also Peter J. Opitz and Gregor Sebba, eds., *The Philosophy of Order: Essays on History, Consciousness, and Politics* (Stuttgart: Klett-Cotta, 1980). The essay by Helmut R. Wagner in the latter volume is particularly pertinent for understanding the Strauss-Voegelin relationship and the debt of both men to Husserl, as discussed in Letters 6, 9, 10, and 11 herein; it is entitled "Agreement in Discord: Alfred Schütz and Eric Voegelin," 74–90. An irregularly updated *Bibliography of Works by and about Eric Voegelin* is published by the Eric Voegelin Institute for American Renaissance Studies at Louisiana State University.

I

The air of mutual respect that pervades the correspondence is founded partly on common civility and Old World manners and partly on a recognition of the seriousness of each other's scholarship, with a sense that their exchanges constitute a conversation between *spoudaioi*. There is strong general agreement about the defectiveness of modern philosophy and the science of man from Machiavelli and Hobbes onward. Both see this as requiring a return to the Greeks, and Strauss remarks that radical doubt of all of the dogmas of the past three or four centuries is the beginning of wisdom. Voegelin more often than not is conciliatory, obliging, even deferential, seemingly intent on coaxing as much candor and insight as he can from his guarded correspondent. Clearly enough, sparring is going on, as each writer tests the other in various ways. There is eagerness for rapport, especially from Voegelin's side, but caution, wariness, and dubiousness, especially from Strauss's side. Now and then an issue becomes transparent for disagreement, the debate is joined, and sparks fly.

Thus, with enthusiasm Voegelin embraces Strauss's principle of understanding a thinker as he understood himself. And how is that? Voegelin, in characteristic fashion, elaborates the principle to mean that the conscientious interpreter has "to restore the experiences that have led to the creation of certain concepts and symbols; or: [since symbols] have become opaque . . . they must be made luminous again by penetrating to the experiences they express." "We are in very much greater agreement . . . than I first supposed," Voegelin concludes.[6] Still, Strauss remains silent on the key question of how and in what sense philosophy can be said to be experientially anchored.

That silence, however, is broken by an alarmed and indignant outburst provoked by Voegelin's use of the term *existential* in the *Gorgias* essay. Strauss writes:

> In his critique of Plato, Heidegger tries to find the way by rejecting philosophy and metaphysics *as such* . . . [But] insofar as I am serious and there are questions, I look for *the* "objective" truth. The sophist is a man to whom truth does not matter. . . . The passion

6. Voegelin to Strauss, 12 March 1949.

> for *knowledge* that moves the Platonic dialogue, this highest *mania*, cannot be understood within Kierkegaard's concept of "existence," and [the attempt to do so] must be rejected as a radical illusion. . . . The question Plato *or* existentialism is today the ontological question—about "intellectuals" we (you and I) do not need to waste words, unless it were about how they finally have to be interpreted, namely, within Platonic or existentialist philosophy.[7]

Clearly, Voegelin struck a nerve. Strauss seems mollified by Voegelin's conciliatory explanation that existential*ism* (which he has no wish to defend) is not intended and that ontology is, indeed, centrally important. "I swear, I am not straying on existentialist paths; we are in agreement also on the question of ontology." However, Voegelin presses the point:

> The truth of ontology (including in particular philosophical anthropology) is not a datum that can be recognized by anyone at any time. Ontological knowledge emerges in the process of history and biographically in the process of the individual person's life under certain conditions of education, social context, personal inclination, and spiritual conditioning. *Epistēmē* is not just a function of understanding, it is also in the Aristotelian sense, a dianoetic *aretē*. For this *non*cognitive aspect of *epistēmē* I use the term "existential."
>
> . . . A history of political ideas, in particular, should investigate the process in which "truth" becomes socially effective or is hindered in such effectiveness. You see, it does not have to do with a negation or relativization of ontology, but rather with the correlation between perception in the cognitive and existential sense; this correlation is for me the theme of "history."[8]

To this Strauss responds with worries of why Voegelin puts "truth" in quotation marks. "Is truth only so-called truth, the illusion of a respective period?" The closest classical equivalent to existential he believes is *practical*, understood as the contradiction of *theoretical*. "If I am not totally mistaken," Strauss goes on, "the root of all modern darkness from the

7. Strauss to Voegelin, 17 December 1949. The essay in question is Voegelin's "The Philosophy of Existence," *Review of Politics* 11 (1949): 477–98; it is included in revised form in *Order and History*, vol. 3, ch. 2.

8. Voegelin to Strauss, 2 January 1950.

seventeenth century on is the obscuring of the difference between theory and praxis." An intervening letter from Voegelin is lost, but it apparently allayed Strauss's worst fears. He writes:

> The question is whether there is a pure grasp of truth as an *essential human possibility*, quite regardless of what the conditions and *actualization* of this possibility are, or whether there is *not* such a grasp as an essential possibility. When you say "only at such and such a time did that order of the soul emerge," you leave open the question whether this order of the soul is the natural telos of Man or a "coincidence"; that it also *could not* have emerged, does that deprive it of the status of a telos? However that may be, it seems to me, nonetheless, that we are in more fundamental agreement than I believed.[9]

Strauss's questions go unanswered in this context. At an earlier place, Strauss writes of "the science established by Plato and Aristotle: the postulate of an exact ethics and politics in Plato; Aristotle's adhering to the ideal of exactness despite the abandonment of its application to the human things; the necessarily higher ranking of physics over ethics and politics, at least for Aristotle and his successors."[10] Whether the exactness of the theoretical sciences, in contrast to the practical ones, equates with the pure grasp of truth as possibility for Strauss remains unclear, and he seems to leave it "open." At a later place, he speaks of his Walgreen Lectures, published as *Natural Right and History*, as presenting the "*problem* of natural right as an unsolved problem," thus holding out the conception of philosophy itself as "an uncompletable ascent." Philosophy on the classical model is disclosed as an unsuspected third way to the conventional alternatives of choosing between "positivism-relativism-pragmatism and Neo-Thomism," whereby it is shown that the consequences of one's ignorance is "that one must strive after knowledge."[11]

A not dissimilar third way is disclosed by Voegelin from his study of the same sources. The paradigm of true philosophy is provided by Plato and Aristotle. But underlying classical philosophy itself, by Voegelin's reading, is *faith* in the divine cosmos as the primal experience articulated in myth

9. Strauss to Voegelin, 10 April 1950.
10. Strauss to Voegelin, 24 November 1942.
11. Strauss to Voegelin, 10 December 1950.

and differentiated through *noēsis* in philosophy. It may be true that classical philosophy is "ahistorical" in that it is a loving search of the heights and depths of reality, to discern the process and structure of being, by the spiritually sensitive man who seeks abiding truth. But the modern derailment of philosophy from Descartes to Hegel (which Voegelin considers as a unit) deforms this questing dimension of philosophizing by transforming the uncompletable ascent described as the *love of wisdom* in Plato into the possession of exact truth as the *system of science*.[12] "I would permit myself a correction to your formulation," therefore, Voegelin writes,

> that "*all* earlier philosophy" was unhistorical. Philosophy [deformed into] the system, from Descartes to Hegel, seems to me to form a unity, insofar as the idea of a philosophical, closed "system" dominates. However, the idea of "system," of the possible exhaustive penetration of the mystery of the cosmos and its existence by the intellect, is itself a Gnostic phenomenon, a drawing in of eternity into the time of the individual thinker. I would therefore restrict your comment to philosophy in the Platonic-Aristotelian sense. . . .
>
> With regard to the "second thesis" of your letter, that philosophy is radically independent of faith, . . . I do not see how you get around the historical fact of the beginning of philosophy in the attitude of faith of Xenophanes, Heraclitus, and Parmenides.[13]

II

Now to the crux of the disagreement between the two writers: Strauss, in his letter of 25 August 1950, had written that this second thesis was "the

12. The contrast between love of wisdom as the form of classical philosophy and the system of science, with particular attention to Hegel, as a deformation of modern philosophy, commanded Voegelin's attention repeatedly throughout the rest of his life, one may note. See Voegelin, *The World of the Polis*, 16–19; Voegelin, "Hegel: A Study in Sorcery [1971]," in *The Collected Works of Eric Voegelin*, vol. 12, *Published Essays, 1966–1985*, ed. Ellis Sandoz (Baton Rouge: Louisiana State University Press, 1990), 213–55, and cf. 89–91, 300; and Voegelin, *Order and History*, vol. 5, *In Search of Order*, intro. by Ellis Sandoz (Baton Rouge: Louisiana State University Press, 1989), 48–70 and passim.

13. Voegelin to Strauss, 4 December 1950.

root of *our* disagreement," and in this he was not wrong. In response to Voegelin's asserted "historical fact," Strauss flatly denies it and adds: "Whatever *noein* might mean, it is certainly not *pistis* in some sense. On this point Heidegger . . . is simply right."[14] This becomes the "one point where our paths separate," Strauss states, although Voegelin reads *Philosophy and Law* (1935; English translation, 1987) and finds that Strauss had in that earlier book held a view much like his own. But this, too, Strauss denies. The "classics are the Greeks and not the Bible," he argues. "The classics demonstrated that truly human life is a life dedicated to science, knowledge, and the search for it." "I believe still today," writes Strauss, "that the *theioi nomoi* is the common ground of the Bible and philosophy—humanly speaking. But I would specify that, in any event, it is the problem of the multitude of *theioi nomoi* that leads to the diametrically opposed solutions of the Bible on the one hand and of philosophy on the other."[15]

The sharp contrast between a Middle Ages based on revelation and a classical antiquity not so grounded, according to Strauss, leads him to this further statement:

> There is a double reason not to obscure this essential difference in any way. First, it is in the interest of revelation, which is by no means merely natural knowledge. Secondly, for the sake of human knowledge, *epistēmē*. You yourself have said that science matters very much to you. For me, it matters a great deal to understand it as such. . . . The classics demonstrated that truly human life is a life dedicated to science, knowledge, and the search for it. . . . Every synthesis is actually an option either for Jerusalem or for Athens.
>
> Well, you speak of the religious foundation of classical philosophy. I would not do so.[16]

Of course, "religious foundation" was not part of Voegelin's speech either, but words put in his mouth by Strauss.[17] He passes over the matter,

14. Strauss to Voegelin, 10 December 1950.
15. Strauss to Voegelin, 25 February 1951.
16. Ibid.
17. On the point, see the instructive discussion of the transformation of the "living order of Israel" into "the 'religion of the book'" in Voegelin, *Order and History*

however, and his responsive analysis qualifies the sharp distinction between "human knowledge and revealed knowledge" by noticing that the latter *is* human insofar as it is the knowledge of concrete persons who experience it as stemming from a divine source and (while pointedly rejecting psychologizing explanations, i.e., Feuerbach's and Marx's), he arrives at the following important formulations.

> Revelation, then, is humanly debatable because it, like all knowledge, is human knowledge. . . . It distinguishes itself from "mere" human knowledge in that the experience of the contents of revealed knowledge is of "being addressed" by God. And through this experience of "being addressed," the essential contents of revealed knowledge are given: (1) a man who understands himself in his "mere" humanness in contrast to a transcendental being; (2) a world-transcendent Being who is experienced as the highest reality in contrast to all worldly being; (3) a Being who "addresses," and therefore is a person, namely, God; (4) a man who can be addressed by this Being and who thereby stands in a relation of openness to Him. In this sense I would venture the formulation: the fact of revelation is its content.[18]

This sense of revelation as the *experience of divine presence*[19] is shown to require the development of self-reflective consciousness whereby the man separates himself clearly from the divine, the movement from compactness toward differentiation, a "process in which man dedivinized himself and realized the humanity of his spiritual life."[20] This achievement of Greek philosophy is absorbed by Christianity in the early centuries. The erotic orientation toward divine Being of man in Plato meets with no response, however, in contrast with the *amicitia* of Thomas—a contrast familiar from the *New Science of Politics* but qualified by Voegelin in later work so as to

---

1:376–79; also 120, 288, 381; cf. ibid. 2:218–19. On *nous* and *pistis* in Plato's *Republic* see ibid. 3:113–14.

18. Voegelin to Strauss, 22 April 1951.

19. See the recent analysis of this defining theme by Paul Caringella, "Voegelin: Philosopher of Divine Presence," in Ellis Sandoz, ed., *Eric Voegelin's Significance for the Modern Mind* (Baton Rouge: Louisiana State University Press, 1991), 174–206.

20. Voegelin to Strauss, 22 April 1951.

take account of his subsequent understanding of both reason and revelation in Hellenic philosophy, as suggested below.[21]

Strauss's response is to appeal to Christian *dogma*, rather than enter into a discussion that appeals to experiential analysis, which Voegelin is steadily stressing. The former suggests that there may yet be a common ground between himself and Voegelin, if only the latter accepts dogma in the Catholic sense, "because [he writes] my distinction between revelation and human knowledge to which you object is in harmony with the Catholic teaching. But I do not believe that you accept the Catholic teaching."[22] By this is meant the clear doctrinal distinctions reflected by the dichotomies natural human knowledge and supernatural revelation, reason and faith, science and religion, in particular—and again Strauss is right. Because, just as Voegelin has here discerned the human element in revelation and the presence of revelatory experience (faith) as undergirding Greek philosophy from its pre-Socratic beginnings through its climax in Plato and Aristotle, so also he is moving in the direction that takes him, in the decades ahead, to an analysis of reason (*Nous* and *noēsis*) in classical philosophy that greatly widens our understanding of it and attributes the notion of merely "natural reason" to a misunderstanding fostered by the medieval Christian philosophers.[23] The human reality of philosophy no less than of Judaic and

21. Cf. Voegelin, *The New Science of Politics*, 76–80. For the later work, especially pertinent are the essays reprinted in *The Collected Works of Eric Voegelin*, vol. 12, *Published Essays, 1966–1985*, ed. Sandoz, including "Immortality: Experience and Symbol," 52–94 [reprinted in the present volume]; "Equivalences of Experience and Symbolization in History," 115–33; "Reason: The Classic Experience," 265–91; "Wisdom and the Magic of the Extreme: A Meditation," 315–75; and "Quod Deus Dicitur," 376–94. Of capital importance for the matters at hand also is Eric Voegelin, "The Beginning and the Beyond: A Meditation on Truth," in *The Collected Works of Eric Voegelin*, vol. 28, *What Is History: And Other Late Unpublished Writings*, eds. Thomas A. Hollweck and Paul Caringella (Baton Rouge: Louisiana State University Press, 1990), 173–232.

22. Strauss to Voegelin, 4 June 1951.

23. See the works cited in the previous note, especially Voegelin, "The Beginning and the Beyond," in *Collected Works* 28:210–11, for the present point. The relationship of *noesis* and *pistis* is analyzed in ibid. 12:273–74. That, and in what respects, Voegelin's position leaves him vulnerable on multiple grounds to being charged with the so-called "Modernist" heresy condemned by Roman Catholicism is observed and discussed by Fortin, "Men of Letters," *Crisis*, 34–35. Voegelin long ago understood this problem quite clearly himself, as is explicit in his letter to Alfred Schütz, 1 January 1953: "All that I have said about the problem of 'essential Christianity' is . . . untenable from the Catholic standpoint and would have to be classified as a variant of that Modernism

Christian revelation is the *metaxy* or participatory reality of the In-Between of divine-human encounter, to hint at the later formulations.

How closely faith and reason verge can instructively be seen from a passage from Voegelin's Candler Lectures of 1967, entitled "The Drama of Humanity," where he was able to enumerate ten meanings of Reason in Plato and Aristotle, as follows.

> Reason is:
>
> 1. the consciousness of existing from a Ground, an awareness filled with content and not empty. Reason is thereby the instrument for handling world-immanent reality. Rebellion against reason since the eighteenth century creates a void in this dimension that must then be filled by substitutes.
> 2. the transcendence of human existence, thereby establishing the poles of consciousness: immanent-transcendent.
> 3. the creative Ground of existence which attracts man to itself.
> 4. the sensorium whereby man understands himself to exist from a Ground.
> 5. the articulation of this understanding through universal ideas.
> 6. the perseverance through lifetime of concern about one's relation to the Ground, generative of existential virtue: *phronēsis* (wisdom, prudence), *philia* (friendship), and *athanatizein* (to immortalize human existence).
> 7. the effort to order existence by the insight gained through understanding the self to be existentially linked to the Ground and attuned to it: the major intellectual operation of so translating consequences of this insight as to form daily habits in accordance with it.
> 8. the persuasive effort to induce conscious participation of the self, and other men's conscious participation, in transcendent reason (Plato's *peitho*). The problem of communicating and propagating the truth of being.

---

which has been condemned as a heresy" (reprinted in Opitz and Sebba, eds., *The Philosophy of Order*, 457). On the meaning and extent of the heresy *Modernism*, see Richard P. McBrien, *Catholicism: Study Edition* (Minneapolis, Minn.: Winston Press, 1981), 55–56, 218–23, 644–55. On his concern for Christian orthodoxy, on the other hand, see Voegelin, "Response to Professor Altizer's 'A New History and a New but Ancient God?'" in *Collected Works* 12:292–95; also "Quod Deus Dicitur," ibid., 376–83.

9. the constituent of man through his participation in (the reason of) the Ground; or the constituent force in man *qua* human through participation in the divine *Nous* which is his specific essence.
10. the constituent of society as the *homonoia* or "like-mindedness" of Everyman in a community formed through recognition of the reason common to all men. In Aristotle, if love within the community is not based upon regard for the divinity of reason in the other man, then the political friendship (*philia politike*) on which a well-ordered community depends cannot exist. The source of the Christian notion of "human dignity" is the common divinity in all men. Nietzsche perceived that if that is surrendered then there is no reason to love anybody, one consequence of which is the loss of the sense and force of obligation in society and, hence, of its cohesiveness.

If any of the enumerated components of reason is lost, imbalanced constructions result which eventuate in psychological and social breakdowns and disintegrations. As is suggested by this listing of the meanings of reason in Plato and Aristotle, noetic reason is philosophic or scientific reason, an activity of the consciousness articulated out of experience in a variety of interrelated symbolisms and symbolic forms.[24]

In his Aquinas Lecture of 1975, entitled "The Beginning and the Beyond," Voegelin characterizes the relationships between philosophy and revelation in this way:

> The dichotomies of Faith and Reason, Religion and Philosophy, Theology and Metaphysics can no longer be used as ultimate terms of reference when we have to deal with experiences of divine

24. Quoted from Ellis Sandoz, "The Philosophical Science of Politics Beyond Behavioralism," in George J. Graham and George W. Carey, eds., *The Post Behavioral Era* (New York: McKay, 1972), 301–2. This same volume, interestingly enough, included Leo Strauss's essay entitled "Political Philosophy and the Crisis of Our Time," 217–42. The Candler Lectures remained otherwise unpublished, but Voegelin's work along the lines indicated by the enumeration of Nous's meaning in classical philosophy reached its finished form in the previously cited essay, "Reason: The Classic Experience," *Collected Works* 12:265–91.

> reality, with their rich diversification in the ethnic cultures of antiquity, with their interpretation in the cultures of the ecumenic empires, with the transition of consciousness from the truth of the intra-cosmic gods to the truth of the divine Beyond, with the contemporary expansion of the horizon to the global ecumene. We can no longer ignore that the symbols of "Faith" express the responsive quest of man just as much as the revelatory appeal, and that the symbols of "Philosophy" express the revelatory appeal just as much as the responsive quest. We must further acknowledge that the medieval tension between Faith and Reason derives from the origins of these symbols in the two different ethnic cultures of Israel and Hellas, that in the consciousness of Israelite prophets and Hellenic philosophers the differentiating experience of the divine Beyond was respectively focused on the revelatory appeal and the human quest, and that the two types of consciousness had to face new problems when the political events of the Ecumenic Age cut them loose from their moorings in the ethnic cultures and forced their confrontation under the multicivilizational conditions of an ecumenic empire.[25]

Had Leo Strauss lived to read these words, it seems likely that his reaction might have been much as it was in his ironic letter of 4 June 1951: "Said in one sentence—I believe that philosophy in the Platonic sense is possible and necessary—you believe that philosophy understood in this sense was made obsolete by revelation. God knows who is right."

III

One has the familiar sense of ships passing in the night, after this review of some of the salient passages in the correspondence. Is there more to it than that? What conclusions can be drawn, however tentatively?

The restraining sentiment to be remembered as a kind of motto of civility for whatever one concludes about the debate under consideration

25. Voegelin, *Collected Works* 28:210–11. For the references to "Ecumenic Age" and related matters, see Voegelin, *Order and History*, vol. 4, *The Ecumenic Age* (Baton Rouge: Louisiana State University Press, 1974), 114–70.

may be taken from a remark Strauss made to Voegelin: ". . . the agreement in our intentions . . . so long as we have to combat the presently reigning idiocy, is of greater significance than the differences [between us], which I also would not wish to deny."[26]

That said, some of the differences can be noted, on the assumption that the agreements have become clear enough by now. What lies behind the basic disagreement is expressed already in 1942 by Strauss and is accurate for the entire subsequent relationship with Voegelin: "The impossibility of grounding science on religious faith. . . . Now, you will say . . . that the Platonic-Aristotelian concept of science was put to rest through Christianity and the discovery of history. I am not quite persuaded of that."[27]

Behind these formulations stand two philosophers both victimized and appalled by the deculturation and banality of modernity, who devoted their lives to the recovery of true philosophy, Strauss on the basis of the medieval Arabic and Jewish philosophy of Averroës, Alfarabi, and Maimonides, Voegelin by a far-reaching critical revision of the medieval Christian philosophy of Augustine, Anselm, Aquinas, and Eckhart. This is not to question that from their divergent perspectives, both men took classical philosophy and the science of man and being it achieved with utmost seriousness, or that each deeply, even fervently, believed his interpretation to be both true to the texts and in accord with the "real" self-understanding Socrates, Plato, and Aristotle had of the philosopher's calling. It is entirely understandable that a "nonbeliever," as Strauss termed himself, and a mystic philosopher in the Christian tradition would not see eye to eye about ultimate things.

How, indeed, could it be otherwise? And both Strauss and Voegelin believed that they avoided religious dogma out of devotion to the quest for the truth of being, one in the name of ancient rationalism, the other in the name of the fundamental experiences and their noetic and pneumatic articulation through several modes of symbolization. Thus, to Voegelin the core problem of all philosophy was the problem of transcendence—meaning not the immanent transcendence of Husserl and of the nature-based philosophy of Strauss, but the transcendence of divine Being. His definition is given at the beginning of *Order and History* in the following words and are taken as true to philosophy as Plato perfected it:

26. Strauss to Voegelin, 17 March 1949.
27. Strauss to Voegelin, 24 November 1942.

> Philosophy is the love of being through love of divine Being as the source of its order. The Logos of being is the object proper of philosophical inquiry; and the search for truth concerning the order of being cannot be conducted without diagnosing the modes of existence in untruth. The truth of order has to be gained and regained in the perpetual struggle against the fall from it; and the movement toward truth starts from a man's awareness of his existence in untruth. The diagnostic and therapeutic functions are inseparable in philosophy as a form of existence. And ever since Plato, in the disorder of his time, discovered the connection, philosophical inquiry has been one of the means of establishing islands of order in the disorder of the age. *Order and History* is a philosophical inquiry concerning the order of human existence in society and history. Perhaps it will have its remedial effect—in the modest measure that, in the passionate course of events, is allowed to Philosophy.[28]

As one recent commentator has remarked after surveying the Voegelinian corpus, "Voegelin adumbrates a philosophy of spiritual ascent, of which there are famous examples, such as Plotinus, Plato, St. Bonaventura, and Meister Eckhart."[29] If the understanding of reason is so expanded as to reassert the participatory and intuitive dimensions of classical philosophy's Nous, the understanding of faith and revelation also is reevaluated—and it emphatically is *not* creedal, doctrinal, or dogmatic faith that is at issue in Voegelin's work. In reflectively groping toward his later (1975) formulation of the matter quoted at the end of the preceding section, he finds in Strauss's *Philosophy and Law* (1930) substantial agreement with his own understanding of the fundamental experience of the divine cosmos as the background of all experiences of order. "I have the impression that you have retreated from an understanding of the prophetic (religious) foundation of philosophizing (with which I would heartily agree) to a theory of

28. Voegelin, *Israel and Revelation*, xiv. For the express statement that transcendence is the "decisive problem of philosophy," see Eric Voegelin, *Anamnesis: Zur Theorie der Geschichte und Politik* (Munich: R. Piper Verlag, 1966), 36, 46–48; the first page references a line in Voegelin's letter to Alfred Schütz of 17–20 September 1943, which Voegelin invites Strauss to get from Schütz and read if he is interested and which Strauss, then, reads and reacts to (Letters 10 and 11, herein).

29. Paul G. Kuntz, "Voegelin's Experiences of Order Out of Disorder," in Sandoz, ed., *Eric Voegelin's Significance for the Modern Mind*, 138.

epistēmē, and that you refuse to see the problem of *epistēmē* in connection with experience, out of which it emerges." Almost sorrowfully, Voegelin continues, "Why you do this, I do not know. And how this position can work . . . I cannot predict."[30]

As noticed earlier, Strauss acknowledges that "the law has primacy" and that "I basically still stand on the same ground" as fifteen years before, but with deeper understanding. "I believe still today that the *theioi nomoi* is the common ground of the Bible and philosophy—humanly speaking." But the multitude of divine laws so confuse things as to lead to solutions diametrically opposed to one another in the Bible and in philosophy. He rejects any blending of the two, contending that every "synthesis is actually an option either for Jerusalem or for Athens."[31] For Voegelin, the theoretization of this problem by Augustine is essentially valid for an understanding of the relationship of science (especially metaphysics) and revelation.

> Revealed knowledge is, in the building of human knowledge, that knowledge of the pregivens of perception (*sapientia*, closely related to the Aristotelian *nous* as distinguished from *epistēmē*). To these pregivens belongs the experience of man of himself as *esse, nosse, velle*, the inseparable primal experience: I am a knowing and willing being; I know myself as being and willing; I will myself as a being and a knowing human. (For Augustine in the worldly sphere, the symbol of the trinity: the Father—Being; the Son—the recognizable order; the Spirit—the process of being in history). To these pregivens belongs further the being of God beyond time (in the just characterized dimensions of creation, order, and dynamic) and the human knowledge of this being through "revelation." Within this knowledge pregiven by *sapientia* stirs the philosophic *epistēmē*.[32]

Strauss remains adamant, however, in seeing this as a problem traditionally comprehensible in terms of faith and knowledge, but not of

30. Voegelin to Strauss, 21 February 1951, Letter 36. Thus, already in 1957 Voegelin wrote of the meaning of *Nous*: ". . . even in Aristotle it still has an amplitude of meaning from intellection to faith" (*Order and History*, vol. II, *Plato and Aristotle*, 208).

31. Strauss to Voegelin, 25 February 1951, Letter 37. The medieval roots of the primacy of law in Strauss's thought are carefully explored in Hillel Fradkin, "Philosophy and Law: Leo Strauss as a Student of Medieval Jewish Thought," *Review of Politics* 53 (Winter 1991): 40–52, esp. 49–52.

32. Voegelin to Strauss, 22 April 1951, Letter 38.

universal faith, and as a particularly Christian, and by extension, a Jewish, problem. Hence, the problem is not a universal-human one but "presupposes a *specific* faith, which philosophy as philosophy does not and cannot do. Here and here alone it seems to me lies the divergence between us—also in the mere historical."[33] The richness and subtlety of the debate does not lend itself to adequate summary. The prefiguration of the outcome is Strauss's early reaction: "What you wrote about Plato and Aristotle naturally interested me quite directly. . . . I do not hold this interpretation to be correct. But it is toweringly superior to nearly all that one gets to read about Plato and Aristotle."[34]

The gentleness and civility of Strauss himself, it must be said, is not always emulated by all who identify with his cause, and the silence that descended on these correspondents after publication of the initial volumes of *Order and History* was briefly if stridently shattered by a long essay in *The Review of Metaphysics* in which Voegelin's whole interpretation of Hellenic philosophy was resoundingly rejected (for, among other reasons) as existentialist, theologico-historicist, Christian, fideistic and not scientific, empiricist, mystical, Toynbeean, Thomistic, too concerned with experience and too little concerned with reason, theological, politically neglectful, egalitarian, liberal, reductionist in seeing Plato's myths as revelation, oblivious to the tension between theory and practice, inverting the classic philosophic theory of the relationship between being and history (historicism, again), blocking instead of fostering access to Greek philosophy because of Christian assumptions in quasi-Hegelian dress. "Voegelin is forced by his commitments both to reject Hellenism and at the same time to preserve it in unrecognizable form." "He excludes the possibility of a non-empiricist and non-mystical philosophy." "It is not easy," the author patronizingly sighs, "to make such a judgment of what may well be a devout man's life work."[35] After this blast, there was little more that could usefully be said. Silence reigned.

33. Strauss to Voegelin, 4 June 1951, Letter 39. For "mere historical," see Letter 35.

34. Strauss to Voegelin, 20 December 1942, Letter 5.

35. Stanley Rosen, "*Order and History*," *Review of Metaphysics* 12 (December 1958): 258, 268, 276, and passim. The reader is helpfully directed to "a definitive discussion [of the relation between religion and philosophy], with full references," namely Strauss's *Persecution and the Art of Writing* (ibid., 267n.).

IV

In modern philosophy the hard line drawn between religion and philosophy is exemplified in Spinoza's attitude as expressed in *Tractatus theologico-politicus* (1670) where the principle is laid down as follows: "Between faith or theology, and philosophy, there is no connection, nor affinity. I think no one will dispute the fact who has knowledge of the aim and foundations of the two subjects, for they are as wide apart as the poles.

"Philosophy has no end in view save truth; faith . . . looks for nothing but obedience and piety. Again, philosophy is based on axioms which must be sought from nature alone."[36] "The core of Strauss's thought is the famous 'theological-political problem,' a problem which he would say 'remained *the* theme of my studies' from a very early time."[37] Strauss's gloss on the quoted Spinoza passage suggests that the philosopher who knows truth must refrain from expressing it out of both convenience and, more so, duty. If truth requires one not to accommodate opinions to the Bible, piety requires the opposite, "i.e., that one should give one's own opinions a Biblical appearance. If true religion or faith, which according to him requires not so much true dogmas as pious ones, were endangered by his Biblical criticism, Spinoza would have decided to be absolutely silent about this subject." But, of course, to thicken this tangle, the rule of speaking "ad captum vulgi" means so as to satisfy the dominant opinion of the multitude, which in Spinoza's situation was that of a secularist Jew speaking to a Protestant Christian community.[38] It was Spinoza's intention to emancipate philosophy from its position as mere handmaid of scripture. "In his effort to emancipate philosophy from its ancillary position, he goes to

36. Benedict de Spinoza, *Writings on Political Philosophy*, ed. A.G.A. Balz, trans. R.H.M. Elwes (New York: Appleton-Century-Crofts, 1937), 16.

37. Steven B. Smith, "Leo Strauss: Between Athens and Jerusalem," *Review of Politics* 53 (Winter 1991): 78. Strauss's early study of Spinoza's *Tractatus* was written between 1925 and 1928 and published as *Die Religionskritik Spinozas als Grundlage seiner Bibelwissenschaft: Untersuchungen zu Spinozas Theologisch-Politischem Traktat* (Berlin: Akademie Verlag, 1930; English translation 1965). As he remarks to Voegelin, "Hula was telling me that you are interested in Arabic political philosophy. That was once my speciality" (20 February 1943, Letter 7). Strauss recurs to a comparison of Averroës with Husserl's treatment of Aristotle's *De Anima*, book 3, and to his medieval studies, including Maimonides and his "Essay on the Law of the *Kuzari*" on 11 October 1943, Letter 11.

38. Strauss, *Persecution and the Art of Writing*, 142–201 at 168, 178.

the very root of the problem—the belief in revelation. By denying revelation, he reduces Scripture to the status of the works of the Greek poets, and as a result of this he revives the classical conception of Greek philosophers as to the relation between popular beliefs and philosophic thought."[39]

Behind Spinoza and Strauss stand the great Spanish Islamic philosophers of the medieval period who insisted upon philosophy as a purely rational enterprise based on Aristotle and steering a middle way, one infected neither by dogmatic religion nor by traditional mysticism—to take the case of Averroës, the great twelfth-century *falasifa* Ibn Rushd. It may be useful to recall that Thomas Aquinas's *Summa Contra Gentiles* is the Western Christian "comprehensive systematic work against the Arabic-Aristotelian philosophy. In 1270, thirteen Averroistic propositions were condemned by Etienne Tempier, the bishop of Paris, and the year 1277 brought the sweeping condemnation of 219 propositions, including besides the Averroistic proper, several of Thomas Aquinas which seemed equally dangerous."[40] By the Averroist tradition, philosophy is considered to be "the systematic application of demonstrative reasoning to the world." Such philosophy starts from indubitable first principles and cannot be empirical, since philosophy is conceived as a demonstrative science and there can be no indubitable premises about any part of the world as experienced, much less about the whole cosmos.[41] Philosophers are capable of arriving at truth directly and, thus, at the highest level, have no need of scripture or revelation—a teaching that necessitates discretion in communication. As a thoroughly rationalistic enterprise, not mysticism but only philosophy allows union with the divine, since that union requires knowledge of the theoretical sciences.[42] There are levels of human nature and levels of discourse and truth to match. "For the natures of men are on different levels with respect to [their paths to] assent. One of them comes to assent through demonstration; another comes to assent through dialectical

39. Harry Austryn Wolfson, *Philo: Foundations of Religious Philosophy in Judaism, Christianity, and Islam* (Cambridge, Mass.: Harvard University Press, 1947), 1:163. For Spinoza's "grand assault on traditional philosophy," see ibid. 2:160–64. Cf. Strauss, *Persecution and the Art of Writing*, 188–91.

40. Voegelin, "Siger de Brabant," *Philosophy and Phenomenological Research* 4 (June 1944): 511.

41. George F. Hourani, *Averroës: On the Harmony of Religion and Philosophy* [a translation of Ibn Rushd's *Decisive Treatise*] (London: Luzac, 1961), 20–21.

42. Ibid., 27–28.

arguments, just as firmly as the demonstrative man through demonstration, since his nature does not contain any greater capacity; while another comes to assent through rhetorical arguments, again just as firmly as the demonstrative man through demonstrative arguments."[43] Ibn Rushd identifies the elite (philosophers) as those who are taught by demonstrative argument, the theologians (a mere subclass of the masses) as those suitable for dialectic, and the masses themselves as those who can understand only through imaginative and persuasive language. Farabi names only two classes, the elite and the masses.[44] This view, of course, requires secret or artful teaching and caution of philosophers. Thus, Farabi endorses Plato's techniques of concealment and Aristotle's methods. They "used different methods but had the same purpose of concealment; there is much abbreviation and omission in Aristotle's scientific works, and this is deliberate. . . . Different expressions of truth suit different levels of understanding. . . . Zeno said: 'My teacher Aristotle reported a saying of his teacher Plato: "The summit of knowledge is too lofty for every bird to fly to."'"[45] Finally, there is the agreement of the greatest Jewish philosopher, Maimonides, who writes of Genesis 1:1 ("In the beginning God created heaven and earth"): "It has been treated with metaphors in order that the uneducated may comprehend it according to the measure of their faculties and the feebleness of their apprehension, while educated persons may take it in a different sense."[46] Strauss's embrace of this paradigm of philosophy is stated in many ways, such as the following from his 1962 preface to the English translation of *Spinoza's Critique of Religion*: "I began . . . to wonder whether the self-destruction of reason was not the inevitable outcome of modern rationalism as distinguished from premodern rationalism, especially Jewish-medieval rationalism and its classical (Aristotelian and Platonic) foundation."[47]

43. Ibid., 49 [*The Decisive Treatise*, 6.17–21], cf. 92. In this work the judge and philosopher Averroës defends philosophy on the basis of Law, which is to say politically. Thus, "if teleological study of the world is philosophy, and if the Law commands such a study, then the Law commands philosophy," a sentence that stands as the summary of chapter 1 (ibid., 44; cf. 83 n. 7).

44. Ibid., 92.

45. Ibid., 106.

46. Moses Maimonides, *The Guide for the Perplexed*, trans. M. Friedlaender, 2d ed. (London: G. Routledge and Sons, 1904), 4.

47. Strauss, *Spinoza's Critique of Religion*, trans. E. M. Sinclair (New York:

Voegelin's attitude toward this model of philosophizing—and hence toward the Straussian approach to philosophy to the degree it is indebted to this model, a matter to be more fully ascertained than I can attempt here—is suggested by his study of Siger de Brabant, a Latin Averroist. The notions of the grades of human nature and levels of communication just noticed, Voegelin finds, show "the inclination to treat the non-philosophical man as an inferior brand and even to compare him to animals, an attitude which seems to crop up as soon as the Christian insight into the equal spiritual dignity of all men is abandoned." Along with the elitist idea, which may be confined to "the intellectual sphere of the *vita philosophi* . . . [comes also] the liberal idea of the educated man as a social type superior to the uneducated common man, the *vilis homo*. . . . The bourgeois implications are obvious, for the ideal of intellectual life is coupled with the idea that the man of substance is morally superior to the poor man."[48]

More generally, then, Voegelin remarks of the *falasifa* that "philosophy had become in the Arab environment, more so than it was with Aristotle, a form of life for an intellectual elite."[49]

> Philosophy did not mean for them a branch of science, but signified an integral attitude towards the world based on a "book," much as the integral attitude of the orthodox Muslim would be based on the Koran. The sectarian implication is beyond doubt; the *falasifa* represent a religious movement, differing in its social structure and content of doctrine from other Islamic sects, but substantially of the same type. . . . The great Arabic philosophical discussions did not center in the *Organon* or *Physics* of Aristotle, but were concerned with the twelfth book of *Metaphysics* and the third book of *De Anima* as transmitted by the Commentary of Alexander of Aphrodisias. . . . The keystone of the canon was the so-called *Theology of Aristotle*, an abridged paraphrase of the last three books of the *Enneads* of Plotinus. The Neo-Platonic mysticism and the Commentary of Alexander of Aphrodisias to *De Anima* were the dynamic center of Arabic philosophy, furnishing the principles of

Schocken, 1965), 31; also reprinted in Strauss, *Liberalism Ancient and Modern* (New York: Basic Books, 1968), 257.

48. Voegelin, "Siger de Brabant," 520.

49. Ibid., 512.

> interpretation for the comments on Aristotelian works proper. They made possible the evolution of the idea of the Active Intellect as an emanation from God arousing to activity the passive intellect of man. The aim of human life is in this system the achievement of the complete union, the *ittisal*, of the human intellect with the Active Intellect. Behind the dry technical formula of the oneness of the Active Intellect in all human beings, lie a mystical experience and a well-developed religious attitude giving their meaning to the theoretical issues. The clash between Faith and Reason in the thirteenth century is at bottom a clash between two religions, between Christianity and the intellectual mysticism of the *falasifa*.
>
> . . . It was this mythical Aristotle who dominated the *falasifa* and through their mediation became known to the West. It was not primarily the content of his work that created the disturbance; the Aristotelian results could be assimilated, as Albertus Magnus and Thomas Aquinas have demonstrated. The danger was the mythical Aristotle as a new spiritual authority of equal rank with the Christian revelation and tradition. The Aristotle who was a *regula in natura et exemplar* could be a model requiring the conformance of man in the same sense in which the Christ of St. Francis could be the standard of conformance for the Christian.[50]

The gulf that separates Eric Voegelin and Leo Strauss and some of the possible reasons for it by now have become more evident, even if the heart of their rival modes of philosophy remains to be explored. That is a task readers must undertake for themselves, if they are drawn to pursue the quest for truth in the loving search of the Ground called Philosophy.

50. Ibid., 514–16.

Platonic Political Science in Strauss and Voegelin

Thomas L. Pangle

In commenting on the correspondence between Leo Strauss and Eric Voegelin, I feel somewhat handicapped, I must confess, by my limited familiarity with Voegelin's works and by my still-imperfect grasp of Strauss's thought. These shortcomings are compounded by the fact that the letters represent an encounter between two immensely erudite and conceptually complex philosophic positions, neither of which is fully developed within the epistolary exchange. I therefore take my initial bearings from the most superficial surface. The title of Voegelin's great work is *Order and History*. Strauss for his part produced no single great work, but I believe that remarks in the present correspondence support the view that the book whose title most clearly captures the theme of his lifework is *Philosophy and Law*.[1] A comparison of the two titles seems to adumbrate the two thinkers' common ground (concern for order or law), and their decisive parting of the ways: over the estimation of the rank and relation, and hence the very definition, of history and philosophy, especially as correlated to law or lawful order.

1. See especially Strauss's letter to Voegelin, 25 February 1951.

The Common Ground

Both Strauss and Voegelin were abidingly preoccupied with the problematic character of the lawful ordering of human society—understood not merely as the effective regulation but above all as the moral direction and the spiritual ennobling of humanity's necessarily social or political existence. Both theorists were convinced that the modern West, especially in the twentieth century, suffered from an obscuring or distortion of the elemental moral and religious experiences (for example, the full demand of justice linked to divine law and the ordering of the soul, the at once undiminished and unexaggerated confrontation with death, the higher reaches of the bewitchment of love) that lie at the root of humanity's restless quest for truly satisfactory lawful order.

The cause of this obscuring or distortion Strauss and Voegelin both traced, to a large extent, to modern science and philosophy. They saw the minds of the inhabitants of the modern West to be deeply and thoroughly shaped from earliest youth by certain basic presuppositions shared by the various warring versions of modern thought. These presuppositions, regarding morality, divinity, nature, and human nature, are not simply or totally wrong but, insofar as they are correct, they are drastically incomplete, or in need of being integrated into a higher and fuller kind of self-knowledge. Yet these presuppositions are held in such a way as to mask their incompleteness. They thus constitute a veil between the mind and a clear view of itself and its own experiences. Modern science and philosophy permeate and structure the consciousness of contemporary humanity with such uncontested power as to make necessary enormous efforts of liberation if one is to achieve a view of life freed from, i.e., freed to question radically, these unquestioned ultimate presuppositions of modernity.

Both Strauss and Voegelin responded to their diagnoses of the moral and philosophic self-estrangement of modern man by turning to amazingly extensive, painstakingly meticulous, and radically unconventional or challengingly unorthodox reinterpretations of past thinkers and texts. They did so in order to disinter the authentic, lost or forgotten or misunderstood, spiritual wellsprings of the West.[2]

2. See Strauss's letter to Voegelin, 13 February 1943: "I share the enthusiasm about your essay [referring to a manuscript submitted to, but eventually not accepted for publication by, *Social Research*—a chapter entitled "The People of God," from

Voegelin's Philosophy of History

The divergence between Strauss and Voegelin begins to emerge from the observation that for Voegelin the study of history becomes or constitutes a philosophy of history. The history of order reveals the order of history: human experience is given its most important shaping by what is historically changing in humanity's consciousness, and in particular by the changing "myths" or "symbols" by which mankind orders and apprehends and thereby undergoes its most important (moral-religious) experience differently at different epochs. The doctrines and especially the "systems" of the "great" thinkers are misleading in their pretention to permanent or universal validity: "The motivation of ideas through sentiment is covered by the exigencies of immanent logical consistency." In fact, even the greatest thinkers achieve at best only "the approximately rational expression" of "the matrix of sentiments in which they are rooted." Even the very greatest thinkers of a very great era (e.g., Plato and Aristotle) were literally unable to think *decisive* insights or symbolic mediations of a later era (e.g., the Middle Ages); and this is *not* due simply or even chiefly to intervening, miraculous revelations (as thinkers like Maimonides and Thomas Aquinas, who were insufficient, from Voegelin's viewpoint, in their historical consciousness, have claimed). For Voegelin, this is due to the historical process:

Voegelin's unfinished history of ideas]. Above all, I completely agree, that the radical doubt about the dogmas of the last three or four centuries is the beginning of every pursuit of wisdom. The frankness with which you address this preliminary question is praiseworthy in the highest degree. Only I am not sure if you proceed far enough." And see Voegelin's letter to Strauss, 12 March 1949, reacting to Strauss's essay "Political Philosophy and History," *Journal of the History of Ideas* 10 (1949): 30–50, and republished in *What Is Political Philosophy?* (Glencoe, Ill.: The Free Press, 1959): "I have the impression, that we are in very much greater agreement than I first supposed in the direction of our work. Your main thesis—based on Hegel—that historical reflection is a peculiar requirement of modern philosophy seems completely right to me; and I view this motive also as the *raison d'etre* of my own historical studies. As I have only engaged myself with these questions in English, allow me my English formulation of the problem: To restore the experiences which have led to the creation of certain concepts and symbols; or: Symbols have become opaque; they must be made luminous again by penetrating to the experiences which they express.—Very fine too is your critique of the attitude that would understand the thinker better than he would understand himself; and your insistence that the purpose of historical analysis is the production of meaning, as it was intended by the author."

to the human condition as such, as the condition of a being whose conscious essence unfolds in history.[3]

Voegelin's philosophy of history is not in its intention relativistic. Reflecting upon our experience in the twentieth-century West, viewed in the comparative light of historical research, we can pronounce some epochs, such as our own, to be spiritually more impoverished or threatened than others, such as that of ancient Israel or Greece, or, above all, the Augustinian Christian period. An epoch such as ours has lost or is in danger of losing, on account of a pathological historical evolution, the ability to be guided by myths or symbols that play a soberly inspiring rather than a fanatically destructive or spiritually stultifying cultural and personal role. More specifically, historical epochs and epochal transformations may be judged and evaluated by the degree to which they preserve, in a "differentiated" experience, the awareness of the distance between mundane human existence and the realm of the divine, the realm of the ultimate end and purpose of all existence—to which Voegelin refers by using the Greek term *eschaton*. When correctly experienced and symbolized, the *eschaton* is not immanent in but is instead transcendent of, and thus limiting and humbling of, human action and nonsymbolic thinking. When pathologically or "gnostically" experienced and symbolized, the

3. The quotations are from *From Enlightenment to Revolution*, ed. John H. Hallowell (Durham, N.C.: Duke University Press, 1975), 68. As Voegelin makes clear on 116–17, his philosophy of history draws heavily on Schelling (especially *The Philosophy of Mythology and of Revelation*) and, for the political implications of this posture toward history, Bergson (especially *The Two Sources of Morality and Religion*)—who writes "strongly under the influence of Schelling." Yet in *The New Science of Politics: An Introduction* (Chicago: University of Chicago Press, 1952), 124, Voegelin classifies Schelling along with Hegel as attempting an illegitimate "contemplative gnosis" in "the form of speculative penetration of the mystery of creation and existence"; Voegelin must therefore be confident that his own philosophy of history avoids the overwhelming gravitational pull toward "gnostic" thinking that has tainted the historical philosophies of even his closest predecessors. For the importance, but also an indication of the gravely problematic character, of Bergson, see *The New Science of Politics*, 60–61 on the one hand and 79 on the other. In the correspondence, see especially Voegelin's letter of 9 December 1942, and Strauss's letters of 14 March and 10 April 1950. For the principles of Voegelin's philosophy of history, see also *The New Science of Politics*, 1 (first sentence), 78–79, 87–89, and especially the statement of principle on 125: "the substance of history is to be found on the level of experiences, not on the level of ideas" (in Strauss's annotated copy, this sentence is highlighted in the margin, with cross-references to the discussion of Augustine on 87 and 89).

eschaton is falsely believed to be "knowable," and, in the extreme cases, even attainable by human action in history.[4]

The Challenge for Voegelin

For Voegelin, then, philosophy in the highest sense is absorbed by historical philosophizing, guided and limited by faith or faithful intimation through symbolization of moral-religious experience. Now the great question or difficulty this raises is one that may be addressed to all positions resting on faith—but in the case of Voegelin the question becomes especially pointed because of the unorthodox character of Voegelin's historicized faith. The question is this: What is the precise nature and foundation of the normative standpoint from which Voegelin issues evaluations and judgments—the standpoint from which, indeed, he takes the bearings for his whole existence? The superiority of the Christian conception or symbolization of the soul and its experiences, in general—but even more in the specific, historicized, way in which the Christian conception is understood by Voegelin—does not seem to be *demonstrated* by Voegelin. It does not seem to be arrived at by reasoning from premises that are necessary, that are compelling, for all of us, or for all thinking human beings in all times and places. If Voegelin's Christian conception is an undemonstrated or indemonstrable presupposition of faith, what, if anything, makes it persuasive to those who do not share this faith? What ranks it above, or gives it more validity than, other faiths or interpretations of faith, Christian and non-Christian—with their often diametrically op-

4. See *The New Science of Politics*, ch. 4, "Gnosticism—the Nature of Modernity," on "the fallacious construction of history which characterizes modernity" (126), and also 79: "Theory is bound by history in the sense of differentiating experiences. Since the maximum of differentiation was achieved through Greek philosophy and Christianity, this means concretely that theory is bound to move within the historical horizon of classic and Christian experiences. To recede from the maximum differentiation is theoretical regression" (Strauss highlights the quoted passages in the margin of his annotated copy). In the correspondence, see Voegelin's letters to Strauss of 2 January and 4 December 1950, and his letter to Alfred Schütz of 17 September 1943. See also Voegelin's critique of Hannah Arendt's historicism, or loss of a normative concept of nature, in his review of *The Origins of Totalitarianism: Review of Politics* 15 (1953): 68–76, together with Arendt's response, ibid., 76–85.

posed moral and political commands? How does this faith provide an answer to the person who takes with utter seriousness the moral duty to do what is right in truth and not merely what one feels or believes to be right, or what some authority commands as right (without explaining why, or without justifying the right to issue such commands)? This question, and the moral need to answer this question, is manifestly imbedded in what is called duty. Surely Voegelin intends his Christian conception to be something more than a subjective presupposition of personal faith. But precisely how does Voegelin escape what Strauss refers to as "the desert of Kierkegaard's subjectivism?"[5]

The Dispute over the Status of Revelation

These challenges emerge most clearly in the correspondence when Voegelin responds to Strauss's having "quite rightly identified" the "problem of revelation" (along with "that of the Platonic dialogue") as "the cardinal points at which our views probably differ."[6] Strauss had insisted that "there is an essential distinction between the thinking of the Middle Ages based on revelation and the thinking of classical antiquity not based on revelation," and had furthermore insisted on the dual importance of "not obscuring this essential difference in any way":

> First, it is in the interest of revelation, which is by no means merely natural knowledge. Secondly, for the sake of human knowledge, *epistēmē*. You yourself have said that science matters very much to you. For me, it matters a great deal to understand it as such. Its classics are the Greeks and not the Bible. The classics demonstrated that truly human life is a life dedicated to science, knowledge, and the search for it. Coming from the Bible the *hen anagkaion* [one thing necessary] is something completely different. No justifiable purpose is served by obscuring this contradiction. . . . You speak of the religious foundation of classical philosophy. I would not do so. . . . One would have to elucidate further which *experiences* of the divine the philosophers recognized as genuine. Plato and

5. Strauss to Voegelin, 4 June 1951.
6. Voegelin to Strauss, 22 April 1951.

> Aristotle attained, after all, *proof* [*Beweis*: Strauss's italics] of the existence of gods not from experience and customs but rather from the analysis of motion.[7]

In his response (22 April 1951), Voegelin seems to wish to soften somewhat this sharp dichotomy between scientifically demonstrative philosophic knowledge and knowledge based on revelation; he seems to wish thereby to remove the challenge to faith-based thinking from scientific thinking. He tries to argue that *all* coherent thinking *must* be based in "revelation." He appeals to a revised Augustinian view, according to which "revealed knowledge [*das Offenbarungswissen*]" is "the knowledge of the pregivens of perception [*das Wissen um die Vorgegebenheiten der Erkenntnis*]." This is what Augustine calls "*sapientia*, closely related to the Aristotelian *nous* as distinguished from *epistēmē*." To these "pregivens" belong, Voegelin says, the experience of man himself as a being with will. But, "to these pregivens belongs further the being of God beyond time," in the dimension of "creation" as well as "order and dynamics," and in addition "the human knowledge of this being through 'revelation.' Within this knowledge pregiven by *sapientia* stirs the philosophic *epistēmē*," Voegelin concludes (para. 9). Voegelin can consequently dismiss as "pseudoproblems" (*Scheinproblemen*) all the agonizing issues concerning the ground of valid human consciousness over which Husserl struggled in the *Cartesian Meditations*: "Materialism and idealism disappear as philosophical problems when the order of being and its recognition belong to the pregivens" (para. 11).

This is doubtless true—all philosophizing is either rooted in acceptance of God the creator or it becomes otiose or delusionary—*if* the "pregivens" are indeed as rich as Voegelin claims. For then to deny the creator God is to deny the presuppositions manifestly underlying all human perception. But is there not an enormous difference between the status of the first sort of "pregiven" (man's awareness of himself as knowing and willing), and the rest (knowledge of God the Creator existing beyond time)? The first sort of "pregiven" is indeed given or available to all self-conscious human beings in all times and places; it is manifestly present in every self-conscious thought. Similarly, awareness that our duty to do what is right entails a duty to distinguish between what is truly right and what is merely commanded is present in or can be made intelligible to every reflective

7. Strauss to Voegelin, 25 February 1951.

moral sense.[8] Knowledge of God the Creator existing beyond time is, to say the least, rather more restricted in its availability and potentially compelling power. A few pages earlier, Voegelin had noted that Hesiod and Homer—two human beings whom no one would characterize as mentally defective or lacking in piety—quite lacked a notion of a transcendent God beyond time (not to mention God the Creator, who was unrecognized by Aristotle as well): "Revelation in the Jewish and Christian sense seems possible only when man historically developed a consciousness of his humanness, which clearly separates him from transcendence. Such consciousness is, for example, not yet given in Homer's polytheism or with Hesiod" (para. 8). Furthermore, Voegelin had also earlier in this letter declared that "the essential contents of revealed knowledge [*der wesentliche Inhalt des Offenbarungswissens*]" include not only a self-understanding of man as in contrast to a transcendental being who is understood as the highest reality, but also a knowledge of this transcendental being as one "who 'addresses,' and therefore is a person, namely God [*ein Sein, das 'anspricht', also Person ist, Gott*]" (para. 7). Such a God is of course not the *Nous* or the heavenly beings whose existence is acknowledged, because it has been scientifically demonstrated, by Aristotle and Plato's Athenian Stranger. As Voegelin himself puts it:

> In Plato, and even more clearly in Aristotle, the maximum closure of the soul [*das Maximum der Seelenschliessung*] seems to have been reached, in which the maximally concentrated soul comes to an understanding of transcendent Being, and orients itself 'erotically' to such Being, *but without finding a response* [my italics]. . . . Decisively in contrast to the Aristotelian *philia*, which is excluded between God and man, is the Thomistic *amicitia* between God and man. (para. 8; cf. *The New Science of Politics*, 77–78)

Voegelin here admits that the most important so-called pregiven knowledge within which the philosophic *epistēmē* stirs was in fact not given, pre- or post-, to even the wisest and noblest among the Greek philosophers, whose philosophic *epistēmē*, or science, and scientific conviction regarding the divine, was therefore completely independent of any such presuppositions.

8. Consider Sophocles, *Antigone*, and Genesis 18:23–33; see Strauss's *Natural Right and History* (Chicago: University of Chicago Press, 1953), 79–80 and ch. 3, "The Origin of the Idea of Natural Right."

Only that minority of human beings who share Voegelin's faith will share what he calls "the pregivens." This minority shrinks, and the danger of subjectivism in Voegelin's position becomes greater, when one notes, as Strauss insists on doing in his renewed challenge,[9] that Voegelin does not himself seem to follow faithfully Augustine and Thomas Aquinas, i.e., the twin pillars of the Christian tradition. In crucial respects, Strauss insists, his own philosophic position is closer to those pillars.

In the first place, the conception of the order of historical experiences of the soul that Voegelin sketches in his letter and elaborates in his great work, the conception leading from Homeric polytheism through Platonic "maximum closure of the soul" to Christianity, is drawn not from Augustine or any other traditional Christian authority but is strictly "Voegelinian." This modern historical philosophy does not supplement but in fact supplants the Augustinian historical teaching, which was a teaching about the history of the *cosmos.* "Now, is there no problem," Strauss writes in his response of June 4, "in your quietly replacing this teaching on the cosmos with a modern view of history (ascent from polytheism to monotheism and the like)?"

In the second place, while appeal to faith means an appeal to divine guidance, this divine guidance is known only through the formulations uttered or written by men, who *believe* they have such guidance. How does one judge which of them really do, and, of these, which have formulated their experiences properly? Which formulations of the divine commandments are valid and legitimate, which distorted or delusionary, and hence invalid? Either one is unable to judge between claims, "and then one ends up in the desert of Kierkegaard's subjectivism," or

> the human formulation is *not* radically problematic—that is to say, there are *criteria* that permit a distinction *between* illegitimate (heretical) and legitimate formulations. If I understand you correctly, the latter is your view. On the basis of the same, you accept Christian dogma. I do not know, however, if you do this in the Catholic sense. In case you did this, we would easily come to an understanding. Because my distinction between revelation and human knowledge to which you object is in harmony with the Catholic teaching. But I do not believe that you accept the

9. Strauss to Voegelin, 4 June 1951.

> Catholic teaching. Here a considerable difficulty could result, from your getting rid of the principle of tradition (in distinction from the principle of scripture), and Catholicism is most consistent in this respect.[10]

But the deepest and broadest question, Strauss goes on to indicate, is not how Voegelin legitimates his version of Christianity over and against others, and particularly traditional Catholicism; the deepest and broadest question is one that Strauss, on behalf of philosophy, addresses to Jew and Christian alike:

> It is with some reluctance that I as a non-Christian venture on this intra-Christian problem. But I can do so precisely because I can make it plain to myself that the problem, and the whole problem area, is, exactly, a Christian one and, through an appropriate extension, also a Jewish one; but then precisely it is not a "universal-human" one. That means that it presupposes a *specific* faith, which philosophy as philosophy does not and cannot do. Here and here alone it seems to me lies the divergence between us.[11]

The real issue is how any faith-grounded position establishes its *morally* as well as intellectually binding necessity in the face of philosophy that does not rest on faith or revelation but grounds all its beliefs, including its beliefs in justice and nobility (or virtue) and its beliefs in the divine, in

10. Ibid. See *From Enlightenment to Revolution*, 23: "man in search of authority cannot find it in the Church"; in the context, esp. 24–25, Voegelin shows his clear awareness of the traditional, Thomistic dichotomy between "natural reason" and "faith" or revelation. See also the characterization of "the essence of Christianity" as "uncertainty," in *The New Science of Politics*, 122. For a striking illustration of the distance between Voegelin's perspective on the problems and the perspective of St. Ambrose and St. Augustine—which in this crucial respect seems closer to that of Strauss—consider the following remark in *The New Science of Politics*, 87: "It is curious that both St. Ambrose and St. Augustine, while bitterly engaged in the struggle for the existential representation of Christianity, should have been almost completely blind to the nature of the issue. Nothing seemed [to them] to be at stake but the truth of Christianity versus the untruth of paganism." (This passage is highlighted in the margin of Strauss's annotated copy.)

11. Strauss to Voegelin, 4 June 1951.

demonstrative knowledge that starts from truly self-evident premises that must be granted by all thinking men (e.g., the existence of oneself as thinking and willing, the duty to do what is truly right, the visible motions, causality). The supreme version of such a philosophic position, Strauss never tires of insisting, is the Platonic-Socratic-Aristotelian.

The Dispute over the Meaning and Validity of Platonic Rationalist Philosophy

In the same few letters on which I have just been focusing, Voegelin and Strauss join issue also over the interpretation of Platonic-Socratic-Aristotelian philosophy. They begin from a very considerable range of agreement, often in opposition to all conventionally respectable contemporary approaches to the Platonic dialogues. Above all, both see a necessity for distinguishing between a public, "exoteric," political purpose or intention of the dialogues, and a partly hidden, private, "erotic," and "esoteric" intention. In Voegelin's words, which I believe Strauss largely endorses,

> the dialogue is no longer a political cult like the Aeschylean tragedy, but instead becomes an exoteric work of literature [*exoterisches Literaturwerke*] intended for every private person who may wish to listen. . . . When the conversation is carried on with success—in the Socratic-Platonic circle—then a further motive comes to light: the formation of the community through eros. This is the point that the members of the Stefan George Circle saw clearly. To see the image of the beautiful-good man (the *kalos k'agathos*) in the other, to awaken it and draw it out (complicated by the mystery that the image in the other is one's own image), is possible only through the eroticism of conversation. . . . what is involved in his philosophizing is not a "doctrine," but instead a dialogic awakening through the living word. (For the esoteric explanation of this awakening [*zur Esoterik dieser Erweckung*], it would be necessary to draw from the less-known *Theages*.) When this process is extended over the community of the spoken word,

> then the literary form of the dialogue (particularly, the factually resultless dialogue) seems to be again appropriate.[12]

Strauss responds: "You are quite right: Georg understood more of Plato than did Wilamowitz, Jaeger, and the whole gang." But, Strauss asks, "was that not a consequence of the fact that he did not think in biblical or secularized-biblical concepts?" Strauss goes on to put the disagreement in a nutshell:

> Said in one sentence—I believe that philosophy in the Platonic sense is possible and necessary—you believe that philosophy understood in this sense was made obsolete by revelation. God knows who is right. But: insofar as it concerns the interpretation of *Plato*, it appears one must, before criticizing Plato, understand Plato in the sense in which *he* wanted. And this was, from the first and to the last, philosophy. Only here can the key to the dialogue be found.
>
> Naturally, I do not say that someone who thinks in biblical concepts cannot understand Plato. I only say that one cannot understand Plato, if, in the undertaking of Platonic studies, one thinks in biblical concepts. In this sense the biblical question is to be separated from the philosophic one.[13]

What Strauss is objecting to here is the tendency he finds in Voegelin to try to disarm and hence avoid the challenge from Plato by interpreting Plato as fundamentally a "religious" thinker who, because he lived in a

12. Voegelin to Strauss, 22 April 1951, secs. 3 and 7 of the Plato discussion. It is especially striking to observe that Voegelin and Strauss agree on the importance of the *Theages* (and its indications about the "esoteric" dimensions of the "erotic" in Plato), since the *Theages* is a dialogue contemporary, conventionally respectable scholarship rejects as spurious (the dialogue was never questioned in antiquity, and was in fact regarded as perhaps the best introduction to the Platonic corpus as a whole; see Albinus's *Isagogē* [*Introduction to Plato*], sec. 6). For Strauss's understanding of the importance of the *Theages*, see his *Studies in Platonic Political Philosophy* (Chicago: University of Chicago Press, 1983), 46–47. For Voegelin's praise of *Persecution and the Art of Writing*, see his letter of 5 August 1952; for his approval of Strauss's interpretation of Locke, ascribing to Locke a covert teaching, see his letter of 15 April 1953; for Voegelin's ascription of "esotericism" to Voltaire, see *From Enlightenment to Revolution*, 29–30.

13. Strauss to Voegelin, 4 June 1951, near the end.

pre-Christian epoch, could find no satisfactory response to his "religious" longings or experiences. As Strauss had stressed in his letter of 25 February 1951, there is not even a word in ancient Greek for "religion" or "religious experience."

Voegelin's critical posture toward Plato and Aristotle, and the problem in that posture, emerges most clearly in his letter of 9 December 1942. "At the center of Platonic *political* thinking," Voegelin finds "the *fundamental experiences*, which are tied together with the person and death of Socrates—catharsis through consciousness of death and the enthusiasm of eros both pave the way for the right ordering of the soul (*Dike* [Justice])." Voegelin then adds that "the *theoretical* political-ethical achievement seems secondary to these fundamental experiences." But is this how it seems to *Plato*, or his *Socrates*? Does not Plato or his Socrates argue that the theoretical achievement in fact completes experience, or makes it truly human? That prior to this achievement life and life-experience is cavelike? "The unexamined life is not worth living for a human being" (*Apology* 38 a). Voegelin goes on to indicate that his perspective on Plato decisively breaks with Plato's own self-understanding: "I understand the theoretical-scientific achievement of Plato as founded in myth"; but "Plato orients his idea of science to the nonmythical, person-peripheral sphere of logic, mathematics, and dialectic." According to Voegelin, Plato thereby involves himself in "the problem of scientism"; Plato is at best guilty of a "neglect" that taints his whole theory of ideas; Plato surely sets in motion the scientistic distortion of the fundamental experiences, which can only properly be apprehended by the personal, the historically subjective, the mythic and symbolic:

> The problem of scientism in the science of man as spiritual being appears to me to have its roots in the fact that the idea of science that is ordered to the model of person-peripheral areas is transferred to the subject fields that have to substantiate their scientific meaning in the mythical order of the soul (in the case of Plato it has less to do with a transfer than with a neglect of differentiation; out of this problem then arises the difficulty that the "idea" of a triangle can also be of a biological genus or of the Good).

Aristotle's situation seems even worse, for he has lost "existential participation in the myth." As a result, he falls into the delusion that "the completely scientific-theoretical treatment of the political [is] possible."

Yet Voegelin seems to retract or qualify this on the next page, where he suggests that it is a "misunderstanding," born of the Renaissance, to suppose that the Greek thinkers ever intended a universal political science: "Precisely from the Hellenic position, a universal political science is radically impossible." Instead, it is "Christianity and historical consciousness" that lead to the "universalization of the image of man," and "that is the decisive reason for the superiority of the Christian anthropology over the Hellenic."

If I understand Voegelin aright, he suggests that Christianity achieves a "universal" image of man that is undistorting because it is a "differentiated" image of all men as distinct and unique individuals, with diverse sorts of symbolic access to the divine. The political reflection of this image would be some version of Bergson's mystically inspired "open society." I cannot help wondering how this interpretation of Christianity avoids becoming so open-ended or indiscriminating and formal as to lose all decisive content. In any case, it would appear that Plato and Aristotle are charged with profound confusion: on the one hand, they introduced the methods of logic, mathematics, and dialectic into the study of the fundamental human experiences, thereby beginning the obscuring of those experiences—which can be apprehended only through historically changing myths and symbols, interpreted by various individuals in more or less kindred but always distinct ways—and, on the other hand, they failed to grasp the true, if rather formalistic or vague, spiritual universality of mankind.

Strauss's criticism of Voegelin's interpretation of Plato is more than a dispute over the meaning of the dialogues. It is at the same time Strauss's intransigent defense of the propriety, consistency, and absolute moral necessity of the Platonic-Aristotelian use of universalizable logic and dialectic, inspired to some crucial degree by the model of mathematical knowledge, as *the* key to the fundamental human experiences. To see the implications, or what is at stake, one needs to recognize that the return to the fundamental experiences that Strauss seeks is different from the return sought by Voegelin, since Strauss sees those experiences differently. The difference is due ultimately to the fact that Strauss insists on the sovereign importance of one specific experience that he contends Voegelin fails to make room for or admit. Voegelin does not do justice to the experience of doubt: not the "feeling" or "sentiment" of doubt, not guilty doubt ("doubting Thomas"), but the erotic doubt of the scientist or philosopher such as that young Socrates who knew something about the criteria of validity or clarity, and whose soul was electrified by the recognition or admission of his overwhelming *certainty* that he did *not* know the answer to certain specific moral and human questions on which his whole life depended.[14]

It is this experience, in its compelling (if forgotten and obscured) necessity—it is this experience and all the wonderful consequences that follow in its train—to which Strauss returns and seeks to help others return. Strauss does seek a return to the experiences Voegelin mentions—but in their full, i.e., problematic, troubling, questionable character: "The question concerns the *beginning*; clarity about the fundamental questions and how they should be approached."[15] For the fundamental experiences Voegelin speaks of (justice, love, mortality) are not only ambiguous but *contradictory*. Their contradictoriness arises above all from the recognition that the *opinions* that are inseparable from—indeed lie at the heart of—the *meaning* of the experiences, the opinions reflected in the myths and symbols and commandments that loom as authoritative, *contradict* one another. The experience of justice, for example, as an experience of contradictory commands or laws, and, behind those commands or laws, of contradictory conceptions of the right society and ordering of the soul, compels the question, "What is justice?"—"What is the best regime?"

One might go so far as to say that Strauss seeks to return to precisely that Socratic moment in experience that Voegelin seems to wish to avoid or blur: the moment where one must *finally justify* to one's conscience or heart a fundamental choice between two contradictory, authoritative or compel-

14. On page 122 of *The New Science of Politics*, Voegelin asserts that "uncertainty is the essence of Christianity." The impressively eloquent description of the "uncertainty" he has in mind indicates how far it is from Socratic doubt, or how much the uncertainty presupposes faith: "The life of the soul in openness toward God, the waiting, the periods of aridity and dulness, guilt and despondency, contrition and repentence, forsakenness and hope against hope, the silent stirrings of love and grace, trembling on the verge of a certainty which if gained is lost." There is no word for "doubt" in the Old Testament; as for the New Testament, see especially Matthew 14:31, 21:21, and 28:17; Mark 11:23; Acts 10:20 and 11:12; Romans 4:20 and 14:23. It is illuminating to juxtapose these passages with the exhortation of Plato's Athenian Stranger, speaking as lawgiver, to the young atheist (Plato, *Laws* 888 a–d): "Lad, you are young. . . . If you should be persuaded by me, you'll wait until after you have a doctrine about these matters that is as clear as it can be, and meanwhile you'll investigate [*anaskopeō*] whether things are as we say or are otherwise, and you will inquire from others, and especially from the lawgiver. During this time you would not dare to do anything impious." Consider in this light Strauss's description of the "younger ones'" reaction to his Walgreen Lectures on natural right, in his letter to Voegelin, 10 December 1950.

15. Strauss to Voegelin, 9 May 1943.

ling, interpretations and two contradictory moral laws, or commandments, entailed in those interpretations (the moment when, for example, one must take a stand on the commandment that prohibits one from asking, "*quid sit deus?*").[16] *This* experience, of the contradictory character of reality as it manifests itself in our speech or opinion, i.e., in our only intelligible beginning point for the comprehension of reality, at the morally and humanly most serious moment of our existence, is what compels the beginning of rigorously logical, dialectical analysis of this and all fundamental opinions or experiences. This rigorously logical analysis, as a dialectical analysis, as an analysis that proceeds through Socratic dialogue or conversation, cannot of course copy, but it is surely inspired in part by, the procedure of the undialectical arts and especially of mathematics.[17] For it is in mathematics that we find the most undeniable and readily available experience of clarity and universalizability; it is there that we find or experience what, for Plato and Strauss at least, is a priceless model of clarity and universalizability—a model of what *epistēmē* can and ought to be. If or insofar as our knowledge falls short of this model, we have matter for grave reflection. This, I believe, is why Strauss states that he assigns a "much more serious and crucial meaning" than does Voegelin to "demonstrations of the existence of God."[18]

Strauss is well aware that the life of most, perhaps all, men who are not

16. Compare Strauss's *Spinoza's Critique of Religion* (New York: Schocken Books, 1965), 193ff.

17. Cf. Strauss's "Mutual Influence of Theology and Philosophy," *Independent Journal of Philosophy* 3 (1979): 112 [see page 219 here]:

> [The classical philosophers'] quest for the beginnings proceeds through sense perception, reasoning, and what they called *noēsis*, which is literally translated by "understanding" or "intellect," and which we can perhaps translate a little bit more cautiously by "awareness," an awareness with the mind's eye as distinguished from sensible awareness. But while this awareness has certainly its biblical equivalent and even its mystical equivalent, this equivalent in the philosophic context is never divorced from sense perception and reasoning based on sense perception. In other words, philosophy never becomes oblivious of its kinship with the arts and crafts, with the knowledge used by the artisan and with this humble but solid kind of knowledge.

For a most illuminating treatment of Strauss's understanding of the meaning of Socratic "dialectic," see Christopher Bruell, "Strauss on Xenophon's Socrates," *Political Science Reviewer* 14 (Fall 1984): 263–318.

18. Strauss to Voegelin, 11 October 1943.

truly philosophic in some degree is a life that tries to avoid or seek refuge from the initially painful confrontation with the fundamental problems. But he addresses Voegelin as one who can be brought to recognize the inescapability of the questions. In the course of a striking criticism of Voegelin's employment of the term "existential," Strauss writes:

> *If* one wants to use the Kierkegaardian expression, one has to say that for Socrates-Plato, "existential" and "theoretical" are the same: insofar as I am serious and there are questions, I look for *the* "objective" truth. The sophist is a man to whom the truth does not matter—but in this sense all men except for the *gnēsios philosophountes* [the ones genuinely philosophizing—see *Republic* 473 d, and cf. *Phaedo* 66 b] are sophists, especially the *polis* as *polis* (and not only the decadent ones). The passion for *knowledge* [*Erkenntnis*] that moves the Platonic dialogue, this highest *mania*, cannot be understood within Kierkegaard's concept of "existence" [*Existenz*], and [the attempt to do so] must be discarded as a radical illusion. This *mania*, from which Faust himself turns away, [is] in opposition to the creature in paradise, on the Isles of Blessed, or to the painstaking searches of Goethe himself.[19]

The "passion for knowledge" of how we *ought* to live, and hence of who or what we are as moral beings, seems to be understood by Strauss not only as a kind of burning, inescapable thirst but also as a reaching out for what is intrinsically attractive or lovable. Philosophy, he says in his letter of 11 November 1947, must be distinguished from art or poetry, "philosophy meaning *the* quest for *the* truth (a quest that, for everyone who understands what that means, is an erotic affair), and poetry meaning something else, i.e., at best the quest for a particular kind of truth." This may be the crucial difference between Platonic philosophizing, as Strauss understands it, and the form of philosophy he finds so beautifully expressed in Lucretius.[20] At the very least, I suspect Strauss would say, we find in Plato to a greater or more successful degree than we find in Lucretius an argument that demonstrates *dialectically* and hence conclusively the *naturalness* of the ascent from love or eros, as we experience it primarily, to love or eros for the truth as such: we find in the conversations presented in dialogues like

19. Strauss to Voegelin, 17 December 1949.
20. Strauss to Voegelin, 15 April 1949.

the *Phaedrus*, *Lysis*, and *Symposium* the irresistable charm or appeal (for those who will listen to and follow Socrates' dialectical arguments) of that ascent, and hence the irresistable charm or appeal of the love of truth seen not merely as the consolation but as a kind of completion of our primary natural longings. Despite all the towering barriers to the attainment of happiness, that attainment is possible and natural; the theoretical life is the life toward which our soul is naturally, essentially directed: "The classics *demonstrated* that truly human life is a life dedicated to science, knowledge, and the search for it."[21] One small but significant sign of the naturalness of philosophy is the naturalness of laughter. Voegelin characteristically stresses the link between the Platonic dialogues and tragedy, even Aeschylean tragedy; he goes so far as to interpret the *Apology* as "the tragedy of Socrates."[22] Strauss responds by noting, "You are silent about comedy, even though the dialogue just spoken about [Strauss had just spoken about the *Laws*] is a 'synthesis' of tragedy and comedy." Strauss proceeds to clarify the link between the Platonic dialogue and comedy: "On the basis of known statements of Plato one might say that tragedy and *polis* belong together—correspondingly comedy and doubt about the *polis* belong together. From the standpoint of the philosophers the decay of the *polis* is not simply the worst thing."[23] Laughter may be crude, but it may also be very fine; at its finest, laughter is the explosion of our natural pleasure at the sudden insight that liberates. Laughter of course marks only the starting points, not the core, of the philosophic experience, which moves beyond the moments of liberation, and comes to be animated by a more serene kind of passion. But tears, or a "tragic sense of life," is certainly alien to the philosophic experience as portrayed in the life of Socrates.

This is not to say that tragedy, tears, and a tragic sense of life are unnatural. In Strauss's understanding of Plato and Aristotle, tragedy belongs to the city or to political life, and man is by nature a political animal. In other words, man is not by nature simply or immediately or easily philosophic, because man's nature is dual, and the duality is to some extent a tension. The duality is traceable ultimately to the body, without which we could not think (sense perception), but which is not inclined to thinking (see above all Aristotle, *Nicomachean Ethics* 1154 b 22–35). The

21. Strauss to Voegelin, 25 February 1951 (my italics).

22. Voegelin to Strauss, 22 April 1951, sec. 1 of the Plato discussion; see also *The New Science of Politics*, 76–77.

23. Strauss to Voegelin, 4 June 1951.

city or political society attempts to mediate between the two poles of human nature, body and *nous*—animal and divine. But this mediation is of only limited success at best: the regime in the *Republic* demonstrates the limits by trying to force them. Voegelin, in Strauss's view, takes too unambiguously the proposition on which the conversation in the *Republic* is based, namely that there is a strict correlation between types of soul and types of society.[24] The true teaching at the heart of the *Republic* is an analysis of this proposition, and more broadly an analysis of the meaning of justice, which demonstrates dialectically that there is no empirical or possible political order that correlates with the philosophic soul. This same teaching is presented in a different way, on the basis of a more direct analysis of law, in the *Laws*, to which Strauss appeals for a vivid indication of the problem in Voegelin's thesis:

> You say that the order of the soul is a properly functioning conversational community. . . . [and] the proper order of the soul corresponds to the proper order of the *polis*. Can one call the proper order of this *polis* (in Plato's *Laws*) a *conversation*? Here [in the *polis* established in the *Laws*] exists domination by command and legend, but precisely no conversation, which as such is based on the fiction or the reality of *equality*. In the Platonic sense, there is no Socratic dialogue [in the city established in the *Laws*].[25]

This teaching entails very large consequences. To begin with, it means that philosophers are never at home in any political order. But therefore they are far more independent than they would otherwise be of every political order, and in particular of their own "historical situations," or the political order that surrounds them (hence Plato and Aristotle were far more independent of the *polis* than Voegelin perceives). What is more, it follows that Voegelin, in Strauss's view, exaggerates the degree to which Plato and Socrates are concerned with "the restoration of public order"; he exaggerates the degree to which they are hopeful about such restoration, and hence the degree to which they are disappointed and saddened or filled with a tragic sense at the spectacle of the decay of the *polis*. The political hopes and goals of Platonic philosophizing as Strauss conceives that

24. Voegelin to Strauss, 22 April 1951, sec. 2 of the Plato discussion; see also *The New Science of Politics*, 61–66.

25. Strauss to Voegelin, 4 June 1951.

philosophizing are much more sober and modest than appear in Voegelin's interpretation. By the same token, in Strauss's view Voegelin exaggerates the seriousness with which the Socratic dialogue, as a "weapon for the restoration of public order," depends, if it is to avoid becoming "a meaningless undertaking," on "the judgment of the dead" by an "other worldly leader of the dialogue" who "has healing and punishing sanctions at his disposal." Strauss certainly does agree with Voegelin when the latter says that "the problem of the Platonic myth" has "a close connection to the question of revelation." To the degree that the Platonic enterprise was a political enterprise, which depended on an otherworldly judgment in order to avoid becoming "meaningless," Voegelin would be right in his claim that Plato needs what he has not yet found, "the experience of a prophetic address from God."[26]

But for Plato and Aristotle, as Strauss reads them, there is a fundamental disjunction between theory, or the theoretical life, and practice, or the political life. The moral virtues, which enrich and adorn the life of action, are not the same as the intellectual virtues of the philosophic life; they are not even, strictly speaking, deducible from the philosophic virtues. Still, they are dependent on those philosophic virtues, and most obviously in the following way. The moral virtues are a product of common sense, which is rooted in the habits instilled by a decent upbringing. The practice of these moral virtues does not require knowledge of their foundations. But moral virtue, precisely because it is a matter of action and habit and practical wisdom rather than speculative inquiry, is threatened by challenges or questions that arise from such inquiry. Philosophy, which necessarily traffics in this kind of inquiry, is therefore under an obligation to protect the moral sphere from the possible, erroneously disturbing consequences of theorizing: philosophy does this by providing a quasi-theoretical defense of the moral virtues, such as will to some extent calm the waters philosophy inevitably has a hand in troubling. At the same time, the political philosopher, having listened with painstaking care to the most thoughtful opinions of the "most serious" practical men, brings an order, clarity, and awareness to the moral life that it would otherwise lack. The political philosopher even opens the moral man to the higher philosophic virtues—but in such a way as will do the least damage to the integrity of the moral virtues as they are known to and experienced by men of action. The supreme example of this activity of the political philosopher is Aristotle's *Nicomachean Ethics*, which is explicitly indebted to Plato's *Laws*.

26. Voegelin to Strauss, 22 April 1951, secs. 4–6 and 10 of the Plato discussion.

From this perspective, the modern attempt—from which Voegelin does not seem entirely to depart—to break down the distinction between theory and practice, to provide a philosophical ethics for the direct guidance of moral and political life, *or* to make practice an autonomous realm without any dependence whatsoever on theoretical defense, is a fundamental misstep. Strauss indicates that he suspects this to be the fundamental mistake of modernity altogether. To quote again from Strauss's criticism of Voegelin's employment of the concept "existential":

> The closest classical equivalent of "existential" is "practical," insofar as one understands "practical" in contradistinction to "theoretical." Existentialist philosophy will perhaps appear at some time in the future as the paradoxical effort to lead the thought of the praxis of the practical to its, in my mind, absurd last consequences. Under these conditions praxis ceases indeed to be actually praxis and transforms itself into "existence." If I am not totally mistaken, the root of all modern darkness from the seventeenth century on is obscuring of the difference between theory and praxis, an obscuring that first leads to a reduction of praxis to theory (this is the meaning of so-called rationalism) and then, in retaliation, to the rejection of theory in the name of a praxis that is no longer intelligible as praxis.[27]

The Challenge for Strauss

In contrast to Voegelin's faith-inspired historical philosophizing or philosophy of history, Strauss takes an intransigent stand for philosophy as rigorous science. Strauss does recognize the need, in our peculiarly alienated epoch, for the blazing of a new trail up to this original level of philosophizing. For Strauss, the study of the history of the West, and especially the study of the history of Western thought, is a temporary means—"a desperate remedy for a desperate situation"—to the recovery of a standpoint from which can be renewed an "ahistorical" philosophizing, in the sense intended but not entirely achieved by Husserl and achieved, at least in the decisive foundational sense, by Plato and Aristotle and

27. Strauss to Voegelin, 14 March 1950.

their greatest medieval students (the *falasifa*, especially Farabi and Maimonides).[28] Despite "the inadequacy of certain aspects or views that deform the surface of Husserl's thesis," which are largely "due to the situation in which Husserl started," Strauss holds that one should not, as does Voegelin in Strauss's opinion, lose sight of the heart of the Husserlian achievement.

> Husserl's phenomenological analysis ended in the radical analysis of the whole development of modern science (the essay in *Philosophia* and the essay on geometric evidence, as well as the great fragment on space consciousness in the Husserl Memorial Volume)—I know nothing in the literature of our century that would be comparable to this analysis in rigor, depth, and breadth. Husserl has seen with incomparable clarity that the restoration of philosophy or science—because he denies that that which today passes as science is genuine science—presupposes the restoration of the Platonic-Aristotelian level of questioning. His egology can be understood only as an answer to the Platonic-Aristotelian question regarding the *Nous*—and only on the level of this question is that answer to be discussed adequately.[29]

28. See Strauss's *Persecution and the Art of Writing* (Glencoe, Ill.: The Free Press, 1952), 154; see also the context, for a remarkable statement of Strauss's understanding of the "historical situation" of thought in our epoch. Cf. Strauss's letter to Voegelin, 10 December 1950. As Strauss repeatedly stresses, when these thinkers (Plato, Aristotle, Maimonides, or, for that matter, Thomas Aquinas) interpreted—as they constantly did—past thinkers, or when they discussed and analyzed historical events, persons, and societies, they did *not* do so as part of an enterprise that can be called "the history of philosophy" or that can be classified under the modern historical sciences and disciplines. To interpret old texts philosophically—that is, to confront and argue with them dialectically, in pursuit of *the* truth—is not to engage in a "historical" study. One could also say: dialectics in the Socratic sense does not presuppose essentially, but only "accidentally" (in our time and for the time being), historical dialectics (e.g., dialectics in the Hegelian sense). Strauss's own studies of past thinkers weave together, I believe, the historically dialectical (i.e., the preliminary or temporarily necessary) and the nonhistorically dialectical (i.e., the truly philosophic) modes of analysis of past philosophers. In some works, most notably *Natural Right and History*, the historical or preliminary mode tends to bulk large; in others, for example, *Thoughts on Machiavelli*, and to an even greater degree the late works on Socrates, the philosophic mode predominates.

29. Strauss to Voegelin, 9 May 1943.

> The decisive point in Husserl is the critique of modern science in the light of genuine science, that is to say, Platonic-Aristotelian. His work can only be understood in the light of the enormous difficulties in which Platonic-Aristotelian science culminated, the problem of the *nous*. Considering the enormous difficulties of understanding *De Anima* III, 5ff., Husserl's egological foundation of the ontologies is at least excusable.[30]

Strauss admits, then, that Platonic-Aristotelian science "culminated in enormous difficulties"—the problem of "the *nous*." These difficulties "excuse" Husserl's decisive departure from the highest doctrine or conclusion or proposition of the Platonic-Aristotelian science, whose "level of questioning" Husserl, and Husserl alone, sensed the need to return to. Husserl's departure from Plato and Aristotle, his "transcendental phenomenology" centered on the "egological analysis," apparently does *not*, then, *remedy* the "enormous difficulties" one encounters when one attains the Platonic-Aristotelian "level of questioning."

Elsewhere Strauss, following Farabi's lead, suggests that the classics were fully aware of these enormous difficulties—that they regarded their metaphysics or theology as tentative or incomplete, and, what is more, uncompletable: "Classical philosophy understands itself as the uncompletable ascent from *proteron pros hēmas* [what is first for us] to *proteron physei* [what is first by nature]." "Classical philosophy denies" that "the *hylē* [basic stuff, or matter, of the universe]" can "be resolved into intelligible relations or the like." "Classical philosophy is" the "*search* [my italics] for the *aie ōn* [that which exists always]." But "the decisive questions," the "fundamental questions—(1) the question of the *archē* or the *archai* [the fundamental cause or causes], (2) the question of the right life or the *aristē politeia* [best regime]"—"necessarily relate to the *aie ōn*."[31]

If knowledge of the first principles of the universe and of the relation between them and intelligence (*nous*) remains forever tentative or incomplete in critical respects, how can knowledge of the right way of life not remain in a similar condition? At first sight, the answer would seem to be that one may understand human nature without necessarily understanding

30. Strauss to Voegelin, 11 October 1943.

31. Strauss to Voegelin, 10 December 1950; see also *Xenophon's Socratic Discourse* (Ithaca: Cornell University Press, 1970), 147–50. The penultimate sentence of Farabi's most philosophic work, *The Philosophy of Plato and Aristotle*, includes the assertion that "we do not possess metaphysical science."

the nature of the whole of which human nature is a part or a derivative. Strauss sometimes gives this answer. But even as he gives it, he tends to note its provisional or soberly practical character. And in highly visible places—for example at the outset of *Natural Right and History*—Strauss draws attention to the inadequacy, in the final analysis, of this answer.[32] This answer neglects, above all, the challenge posed by faith-inspired theology. The answer to the question how one ought to live depends on the answer to the question about the first causes. For while classical moral teaching and the biblical teaching on justice agree on almost all points, they disagree on certain crucial points. Again, Strauss speaks of this fact in very prominent places—for example, at the dramatic beginning of the chapter on Machiavelli he wrote for the introductory textbook on the history of political philosophy (edited with Joseph Cropsey). There Strauss did not hesitate to draw the conclusion that is so problematic for philosophy as he understands philosophy:

> Who is right, the Greeks or the Jews? Athens or Jerusalem? And how to proceed in order to find out who is right? Must we not admit that human wisdom is unable to settle this question and that every answer is based on an act of faith? But does this not constitute the complete and final defeat of Athens? *For a philosophy based on faith is no longer philosophy* [emphasis added]. Perhaps it was this unresolved conflict which has prevented Western thought from ever coming to rest.[33]

According to Strauss, philosophy, in the sense that was discovered and defended by the Greek thinkers and their students, and partially resuscitated by Husserl, represents not only the ultimate or richest source for humanity's understanding of the principles of just and noble lawful ordering of society; philosophy as a way of life consumed by the unfinished quest for scientific or rational knowledge and self-knowledge (*epistēmē*) is demonstrably the summit of human existence and the highest, though of course by no means the only high, rationally demonstrable purpose of society.

32. *Natural Right and History*, 7–8; cf. "Social Science and Humanism," in T. L. Pangle, ed., *The Rebirth of Classical Political Rationalism: An Introduction to the Thought of Leo Strauss* (Chicago: University of Chicago Press, 1989), 7–8.

33. Leo Strauss and Joseph Cropsey, eds., *History of Political Philosophy*, 3d ed. (Chicago: University of Chicago Press, 1987), 296–97.

Insofar as a higher notion of contemplation and action than that known to the Greeks claims to make itself manifest in other climes and later times, that higher notion originates not from history or historical experience as such but only from the shattering interruption into history of an altogether unexpected and unprepared claim to divine revelation, as delivered in the scriptures. How does philosophy meet this claim? Certainly not by any sort of psychological reduction; certainly not by any claim to explain away revelation on the basis of some philosophic psychology—however subtle and comprehensive. Strauss joins Voegelin in rejecting any attempt to meet the issue on a psychological level (in the manner, for example, of Heidegger): "You are completely right when you assume that a 'psychologizing,' that is to say, atheistic interpretation of revelation leads to confusion. It is sufficient to remember the example of Heidegger, whose interpretation of conscience ends in the 'calling' being grasped as *Dasein* calling itself—here guilt, conscience, action, lose their meaning."[34] The reflection on the mutual challenge or debate between nonhistorical philosophy as rigorous science and nonhistorical theology as spokesman for the divine call is for Strauss the highest theme of essentially nonhistorical *political* philosophy. In our peculiar age, this highest theme must be prepared by a preliminary reflection on the mutual challenge or debate between nonhistorical and historical philosophizing (here again, Husserl at the end of his life took the first steps). *Political* philosophy understood in terms of these tasks is thus necessarily the first or most fundamental philosophy, the true or adequate fulfillment of that to which Husserl's phenomenology aspired, the philosophy that is essentially prior to and more fundamental than metaphysics or philosophic theology as well as psychology and physics.

But with what right does Strauss assign to *political* philosophy the supreme task? What makes political philosophy, and political philosophy alone, capable of this gravest responsibility? Political philosophy for Strauss means above all Socratic philosophy; and Socratic philosophy means above all dialectics, the art of friendly disputation. According to Aristotle, this art is used "in the philosophic sciences"

> with a view to the first premises in each science. For from its own first principles any given science is incapable of saying anything about them, since the first principles are the first of all; it is instead

34. Strauss to Voegelin, 4 June 1951; cf. Voegelin to Strauss, 22 April 1951.

> necessary to proceed by way of the generally accepted opinions concerning them. But this task is either uniquely or especially the province of dialectic. For to it, as the art capable of thorough scrutiny, belongs the path to the ultimate first principles of all paths of knowledge [*exetastikē gar ousa pros tas hapasōn tōn methodōn archas hodon echei*].[35]

What does Aristotle mean? Dialectics in its supreme form is the method exemplified in Socratic political philosophy. The theme of these dialectics would seem to be justice, or the just and noble things. How can a dialectical inquiry into this theme ground all the sciences? How can this dialectical inquiry dispose of the debate between the competing claims of reason and revelation? What is the relation between these two momentous tasks? How does Socratic political philosophy proceed in these tasks, according to Strauss? What, for Strauss, is political philosophy?

No one can say that Strauss failed to bring this question before his readers. But I at least have had some trouble finding, among his readers, friend or foe, people who can give me a satisfactory account of what Strauss's answer is. The Straussian answer one finds most frequently cited or referred to is a two-page answer that Strauss characterizes, in the midst of developing the answer, as "even the most provisional explanation of what political philosophy is." The book that includes this "most provisional explanation," the book whose title trumpets the question, takes its title from its opening chapter, a lecture on the question delivered in Jerusalem. The lecture, and hence the book, begins with a section entitled "The Problem of Political Philosophy," and opens with the following words:

> It is a great honor, and at the same time a challenge to accept a task of peculiar difficulty, to be asked to speak about political philosophy in Jerusalem. In this city, and in this land, the theme of political philosophy—"the city of righteousness, the faithful city"—has been taken more seriously than anywhere else on earth. Nowhere else has the longing for justice and the just city filled the purest hearts and the loftiest souls with such zeal as on this sacred soil. . . . I shall not for a moment forget what Jerusalem stands for.

35. *Topics* 101 a 37–b 4. I am indebted to David Bolotin for drawing my attention to this passage and its importance.

The taking seriously of justice is obviously a most important common ground between the Bible and Plato, especially Plato's *Republic.* In the same lecture, however, Strauss says that "the character of classical political philosophy appears with the greatest clarity from Plato's *Laws*, which is his political work *par excellence.*"[36]

This characterization of Plato's *Laws* is repeated at the beginning of the last book Strauss completed before he died, a commentary on Plato's *Laws.* For the epigraph to this commentary, Strauss made a literal translation from Arabic of a statement of Avicenna's to which Strauss had often referred previously, and which (as I understand) hit him, the first time he read it (when he was a young man in his thirties), as a bombshell: ". . . the treatment of prophecy and the Divine Law is contained in . . . the *Laws.*" The commentary is marked, as are all Strauss's commentaries, by a meticulousness as regards terminology: Strauss almost never expresses a thought of Plato's in language that is not capable of literal translation into Platonic Greek. There is one striking exception. Early on he characterizes a crucial step of Plato's Athenian Stranger as follows: "He appeals as it were from the accepted interpretation of revelation to revelation itself, which discloses its true meaning only to those who never forget that, being divine, it is supremely reasonable."[37] If this sentence is not Maimonidean, it surely recalls Maimonides. The sentence would seem to describe the start, though only the start, of the dialectic that is exemplified in the *Laws.* That dialectic, Strauss repeatedly indicates, is "sub-Socratic," even though the Athenian Stranger is himself Socratic. The dialectic of the *Laws* needs to be complemented or completed by the dialectic of the *Republic.* But it has this key advantage over that of the *Republic*: certain essential first principles that are taken for granted in the *Republic* are not taken for granted but are instead demonstrated dialectically in the *Laws*: "In the *Republic*, reason or intellect guides the foundation of the city from the beginning."[38] The *Laws*, it would seem, is understood by Strauss to exemplify the art of conversational examination by which one can ascend from the quarrel between reason and revelation to its resolution.

36. *What Is Political Philosophy?* 9–12, 29.

37. *The Argument and the Action of Plato's "Laws"* (Chicago: University of Chicago Press, 1975), 1, 7.

38. Ibid., 27 and 38; see also the comparisons between the *Republic* and the *Laws* drawn at 14, 31, 75, 113, and 128.

The Reason-Revelation Tension in Strauss and Voegelin

David Walsh

The publication of the previously little-known correspondence between Eric Voegelin and Leo Strauss is an event of considerable importance. It provides their readers and admirers with an opportunity to explore one of the questions that has enlivened political theory in the latter half of the twentieth century. What is the relationship between the work of these two giants of the discipline, Strauss and Voegelin? They are the acknowledged leaders in the restoration of classical political theory in the post-war period. As a result of their labors we have a discipline of political theory that has emerged from the wasteland of ideological debate, with a range and depth virtually unknown since the beginning of the modern world. Yet the precise nature of their individually different contributions to the common enterprise has nowhere been clearly delineated.

For despite the evident convergence of achievements, Voegelin and Strauss also exhibited a significant divergence of approaches. The best means of exploring such differences must remain their published works. It is in their writings that the most adequate exposition of their understanding is to be found. No unpublished or occasional writings will present their views better than the books into which they poured their efforts at communication. But there is something peculiarly valuable about the kinds of letters included within the present volume. What they lack in terms of comprehensive exposition they make up for in the specificity they give to particular questions. The authors are compelled to answer the questions they pose to one another and therefore to give shape to the relationship within which the work of each bears on that of the other.

This gives a concreteness and a concentration to the dialogue that is uniquely important. While one might wish that their correspondence had been marked by a more continuous flow (without some of the trifling interruptions of everyday life), the clarity of some of these pages in their mutually articulated relationship is striking. The letters mainly derive from the forties and fifties, when the nature of their agreements and disagreements was in the process of definition. Out of the very rich array of topics that emerge from this remarkable conversation I would like to focus on the one that seems to underlie many of the others. That is the divergence that characterized the approaches Strauss and Voegelin took to the tension between reason and revelation. I believe it is the thread that if followed out will be found to be at the root of their different approaches to epistemology, the Platonic dialogues, the nature of myth, and the various other points of contention.

Perhaps the first thing to notice is the importance both Voegelin and Strauss place on this question of reason and revelation. Strauss sees it as the tension at the heart of the vitality of Western civilization; Voegelin makes it central to his entire conception of the emergence of order in history. Unlike so many of their contemporaries they refuse to subscribe to the prevailing secularist prejudice. They are convinced that there is more to human life and knowledge than is available through the instrumentalized rationality of modern science. One cannot come away from reading them without a profound sense of their dedication to the rational articulation of order, paralleled by an equally profound reverence for the truth unfolded only within the context of revelation.

This persistent tension became one of the defining parameters of their work. Their different responses to it constituted much of the divergence of their approaches to the questions of political theory. Strauss sought to maintain the validity of both sides by preserving their separation. Voegelin undertook an accommodation between reason and revelation that was intended to establish their continuity. Each could accuse the other of misunderstanding the nature of revelation in a world that was defined by reason, but neither could accuse the other of being motivated other than by a concern with revelatory truth as well as rationality. They exhibit no lack of respect for the revelatory traditions of Judaism and Christianity.

Of the two, Strauss speaks more self-consciously out of a revelatory tradition. He is not just ethnically or culturally Jewish, but spiritually Jewish as well. I am not referring to his own religious practices, but to his understanding of the nature of Judaism and of the Mosaic revelation. He provides as clearheaded an analysis of the situation of Jews in the modern world as can be found. The strength of his analysis arises from his penetration of the spiritual nature of Judaism, the unwavering insight into the revelatory events that constituted it. One could scarcely find a more acute understanding of the contradictions of Zionism than in Strauss's remark that "when religious Zionism understands itself, it is in the first place Jewish faith and only secondarily Zionism. It must regard as blasphemous the notion of a human solution to the Jewish problem."[1]

To this clear-mindedness might be added an equally searing analysis of the spiritual condition of the modern world. In this, Strauss relies on Nietzsche, but takes from him a depth of insight that all too few readers have been able to absorb. "Nietzsche's criticism," Strauss observes, "can be reduced to one proposition: modern man has been trying to preserve Biblical morality while abandoning Biblical faith. That is impossible. If the Biblical faith goes, Biblical morality must go too, and a radically different morality must be accepted. The term which Nietzsche used is 'the will to power.'"[2] Voegelin shared this critique of the modern world's lack of foundation and of the political movements that came to dominate it. And more recently this Nietzsche insight seems to have gained wider currency. But neither Nietzsche nor Strauss, Voegelin, or any of the others, seems to have followed out the implication contained within the critique. That is, that if the spiritual crisis of modernity is rooted in the turning away from revelation, the crisis will only be overcome by a return to the sources of revelation.[3]

Such an implication is contained in the title of Strauss's essay "Progress

1. Strauss, "Preface to Spinoza's Critique of Religion," *Liberalism Ancient and Modern* (Ithaca, N.Y.: Cornell University Press, 1989), 230. There is also a fascinating defense of Judaism in an unpublished manuscript of a talk given by Strauss on "Freud on Moses and Monotheism." (I am grateful to Ronald Angres for sharing a copy of this with me.)

2. Strauss, "Progress or Return?" *The Rebirth of Classical Political Rationalism,* ed. Thomas L. Pangle (Chicago: University of Chicago Press, 1989), 240. Voegelin's parallel analysis of Nietzsche is to be found in *Science, Politics, and Gnosticism* (Chicago: Regnery, 1968).

3. I have tried to explore this issue more extensively in *After Ideology: Recovering the Spiritual Foundations of Freedom* (San Francisco: HarperCollins, 1990).

or Return" and in Voegelin's "Gospel and Culture," and they do seem to flirt with that consequence.[4] Yet in the last analysis each comes down on the side of philosophy as the way out of our troubles. This is all the more remarkable as each acknowledges that philosophy is a symbolism or a way of life for an elite. It is incapable of forming the spiritual and moral order for society as a whole. No historical political society has existed on the basis of classical political philosophy. Revelation, which is in principle less political, directed as it is toward man's transcendent fulfillment, has nevertheless proved capable of ordering the souls of human beings within concrete political existence.

Despite the enormous sympathy for the revelatory tradition evinced by Voegelin and Strauss, they leave the impression that there are still dimensions to the tension with reason that remain to be explored. They have both been in the forefront of the contemporary search for a modus vivendi between reason and revelation—Voegelin, in particular, has done more than any other twentieth-century thinker to uncover the common ground between the two great symbolisms of Western order—so the achievements and limits of their meditations are among the most instructive starting points for any sober assessment of the state of the question. Their fascinating engagement with the relationship, both individually and dialogically, leads to the borders of a mystery that Strauss rightly suspects to be central to Western civilization and Voegelin goes on to regard as the core of human history.

Strauss provides the most evenhanded summation of the conventional understanding of reason and revelation as utterly distinct modes of knowledge. Reason is the exercise of the human capacity for rational inquiry into the nature of reality and the exploration of how humans ought to live. It arises because of the need to "find one's bearings independently of the ancestral," and especially within the context of confusion generated by the multiplicity of divine laws. The scientific or philosophic investigation of nature is an attempt to uncover the rational order of the cosmos and of human life within it. The traditional understanding of the divine law, "where it is a code traced to a personal God, is replaced by a natural order,

4. Voegelin, "The Gospel and Culture," in *The Collected Works of Eric Voegelin,* vol. 12, *Published Essays, 1966–1985,* ed. Ellis Sandoz (Baton Rouge: Louisiana State University Press, 1990), 172–212. [Reprinted in this volume.]

which may even be called, as it was later to be called, a natural law—or at any rate, to use a wider term, a natural morality."[5]

Revelation, according to Strauss, is rooted in obedience to the message received from the transcendent God, who is omnipotent and unknowable apart from revelation itself. The truth of revelation is vouchsafed, not by the independent authority of human reason, but by the transcendent authority of the personal God who reveals himself to human beings. In response to the question of how such a God can be trusted, Strauss answers: "only because of the covenant. God has freely bound himself, but all trust depends on trust in God's word, in God's promise; there is no necessary and therefore intelligible relation; and, needless to say, this covenant is not a free covenant, freely entered into by originally independent partners; it is a covenant which, according to the Bible, God commanded man to perform." The search for understanding is still compatible with biblical revelation, but only so long as it continues to be in the service of God. Once it becomes an independent quest for the truth, it is no longer subservient to the service of God. "This emancipation is the origin of philosophy or science from the Biblical point of view."[6]

Philosophy establishes itself as an independent tribunal and cannot therefore submit to revelation without surrendering its claim to authority. From the viewpoint of philosophy, revelation is either a "brute fact" without any universal significance, or it is a "product of reason" and therefore suitable for judgment by the criteria of philosophy. What philosophy cannot do is assent to revelation as revelation. It cannot acknowledge that there is a higher authority than reason or that there is a truth beyond the philosophic quest for wisdom. Strauss summarizes their opposition in a memorable passage.

> Philosophy demands that revelation should establish its claim before the tribunal of human reason, but revelation as such refuses to acknowledge that tribunal. In other words, philosophy recognizes only such experiences as can be had by all men at all times in broad daylight. But God has said or decided that he wants to dwell in mist. Philosophy is victorious as long as it limits itself to repelling the attack which theologians make on philosophy with the weapons of philosophy. But philosophy in its turn suffers a defeat as soon as

5. Strauss, *Rebirth of Classical Political Rationalism,* 255, 256.
6. Ibid., 256, 258.

> it starts an offensive of its own, as soon as it tries to refute, not necessarily inadequate proofs of revelation, but revelation itself."[7]

Strauss is also strikingly clear on the limitations of the philosophic way of life that devolves into "the self-admiration of the virtuous man." The Greek emphasis on contemplation, rather than action, as the goal of human striving "necessarily tends to weaken the majesty of the moral demands, whereas humility, a sense of guilt, repentance, and faith in divine mercy, which complete morality according to the Bible, necessarily strengthen the majesty of the moral demands." Moreover, the rejection of revelation by philosophy is irrational, since it is "without sufficient grounds."[8] Yet Strauss finally comes down on the side of philosophy because, he argues, philosophy is itself not a position or a doctrine but a way of life. It is the way of life that is defined by the search for "knowledge of the most important thing." I assume he means that philosophy is to be preferred because it is the symbolism that remains most open to possible understanding of the whole.

This preference does not in any way mitigate the respect Strauss holds for revelation. He is scrupulously fair in his balancing of the two symbolisms. For just as revelation cannot establish its superiority to philosophy, being unable to render a rational and necessary account of its knowledge, so philosophy is likewise unable to prevail in its claims against revelation, since it is not in possession of the comprehensive knowledge of all things that would supercede revelation. The latter was the task attempted by Spinoza, whom Strauss regards as the most formidable opponent of orthodox revelation. Spinoza's inability to realize his objective of necessary comprehensive knowledge of the whole is a crucial demonstration of the precariousness of the situation of philosophy. Unable to establish its faith in the order of the whole or to reinforce its rejection of revelation, philosophy remains an ungrounded preference for rational inquiry.

Strauss's last word, however, is that philosophy and theology ought to coexist side by side as the source of the continuing "vitality" of the West. Neither one can refute the other, and it has been the unending series of attempts to resolve this conflict that has been the source of the fecundity of Western civilization. He emphasizes the extent to which it has been the

7. Ibid., 265–66.
8. Ibid., 250, 259.

tension between two codes that has been the life of Western civilization. "No one can be both a philosopher and a theologian, nor, for that matter, some possibility which transcends the conflict between philosophy and theology, or pretends to be a synthesis of both. But every one of us can be and ought to be either one or the other, the philosopher open to the challenge of theology or the theologian open to the challenge of philosophy."[9] In many respects Strauss is himself a powerful embodiment of that tension, a student of classical philosophy who cannot forget that he also lives within the tradition of Judaic revelation.

The difficulty is that his heightening and dramatizing of the tension may have the unintended consequence of suggesting that it is a fruitless opposition. The further exploration of these questions has, for example, not been much pursued by followers of Strauss. Revelation can more easily be dismissed as irrelevant to philosophy. This, as I understand it, was not Strauss's position or intention. On the contrary, he sought to emphasize that revelation is the great challenge to philosophy, calling it to acknowledge that "the quest for evident knowledge rests itself on an unevident premise."[10] But without a continuing effort to enlarge and elaborate their common ground there is a perennial danger of the tension degenerating into sterility.

Strauss's position runs the risk of encouraging a wall of separation between theology and philosophy, rather than the mutual recognition he wishes to promote. If reason and revelation are irreducible forms of knowledge, then we might be inclined to regard them as mutually irrelevant. This, by the way, is not the Catholic position that acknowledges their separation but ultimately looks toward their continuity.[11] It is best reflected in Aquinas's principle that grace does not abolish nature but brings it to perfection. Strauss's identification is more properly with part of the Catholic position. One might characterize his achievement as an evenhanded acknowledgment of what is due to each side of the tension. In many ways Strauss's contribution has heightened the distinction between reason and revelation, thereby better preserving the integrity of the two traditions.

Voegelin, by contrast, is more absorbed with the other side of the

9. Ibid., 270.

10. Ibid., 269.

11. Strauss suggests in the correspondence that his "distinction between revelation and human knowledge to which you [Voegelin] object is in harmony with the Catholic teaching" (Strauss to Voegelin, 4 June 1951, Letter 39).

Catholic position, which looks toward the movement from reason to revelation. It is an emphasis that eventually led him to declare the untenability of the reason-revelation distinction, as it had been derived from the efforts of the Church Fathers to demonstrate the superiority of Christianity to Greek philosophy. This realization was part of the larger discovery Voegelin made in the 1940s of the secondary nature of all doctrinal or conceptual formulations. He abandoned the largely completed project of a "History of Political Ideas" when "it dawned on me that the conception of a history of ideas was an ideological deformation of reality. There were no ideas unless there were symbols of immediate experience."[12] A distinction such as the long-standing separation between reason and revelation did not necessarily reflect the situation in reality; it was simply an intellectual construction that had been overlaid on a concrete situation of much greater fluidity and mystery.

"Reason," Voegelin discovered, did not mean the utterly independent light of human intellect, nor did "revelation" mean the totally arbitrary obedience of the human soul. Such are merely the caricatures of reason and revelation that developed in the history of philosophy as a result of an all-too-ready acceptance of the divorce between the two. Moreover, the division between reason and revelation asserted by the Fathers had more than its share of ironic consequences. For the distinction was made in order to assert the superiority of revelation over Greek philosophy, and it reached a precarious balance in St. Thomas's synthesis of the two, only to fall completely apart again when the modern world turned the tables by insisting on the superior authority of reason.

> Christian theology has denatured the Platonic *Nous* by degrading it imaginatively to a "natural reason," a source of truth subsidiary to the over-riding source of revelation; by an act of imaginative oblivion the revelatory tension in Plato's vision of the *Nous* as the "third god" was eclipsed, in order to gain for the Church a monopoly on revelation. But history has taken its revenge. The nonrevelatory reason, imagined by the theologians as a servant, has become a self-assertive master.[13]

12. Voegelin, *Autobiographical Reflections*, ed. Ellis Sandoz (Baton Rouge: Louisiana State University Press, 1989), 63.

13. Voegelin, *Order and History*, vol. 5, *In Search of Order* (Baton Rouge: Louisiana State University Press, 1987), 43.

Perhaps nowhere is this more clearly seen than in John Locke's assertion that revelation must submit to the judgment of reason before it is permitted to speak. To a certain extent it might be said that Strauss's position merely perpetuates this distortion.

What made it possible for Voegelin to go some distance in unraveling the confusion was his momentous discovery that behind the ideas lay another and more fundamental level of living experiences and symbols. They too could be investigated by a scholar, since they had been given linguistic expression. By retracing the process of discovery one could get back to the preanalytic experiences and the symbols in which they had been most directly expressed. This made it possible to deal with problems as they existed in immediate reality, before they had been distorted through the lens of conceptual debates. When this was done, Voegelin discovered, the so-called problems frequently disappeared. The reason-revelation dichotomy was a dogmatic imposition on a more complex living reality that was in no way structured by such an awareness.

The classical philosophers did not assume that they were only using their unaided "natural" reason. On the contrary, they identified *Nous* as a divine reality in which the human *nous* participates and knows through participation. Voegelin for a long time still retained the fundamental distinction between revelation and philosophy as, along with myth, the three irreducible symbolic forms. But in *The Ecumenic Age* he abandoned the distinction because, as he explained, philosophy was itself a mode of revelation. Consciousness of divine reality occurs in the two fundamental modes of the immediate awareness of divine presence, drawing the soul from the Platonic Beyond (*epekeina, Republic* 509 b), and the mediated experience of divine presence ordering the cosmos from the Genesis Beginning (*bereshit, Genesis* 1:1). Revelation and myth now become the irreducible symbolic forms. On Voegelin's view there would be no knowledge of divine Being unless God had revealed himself to man; there would not even be a search for the divine ground if the ground itself were not already present in the soul as the source of its movement. At the same time, advances in man's consciousness of divine reality do not provide any comprehensive illumination of the order of the whole. There still remains a need to symbolize the divine ordering of the cosmos in accordance with the divinity disclosed within the soul. Revelation never dispenses with the need for a form of cosmogonic myth, and much of what we understand by the content of the Judaic and Christian revelations consists of such an extrapolation to the order of the whole.[14]

In what way then do Greek philosophy and the revelation of Judaism and Christianity differ? Voegelin's answer seems to be to deny any qualitative difference; they are both forms of theophany, revelations of the "fullness of divine reality" (*theotes*, Col. 2:9), and are to be distinguished primarily by the directions pursued in elaborating their experiences and by the degrees of differentiation in the correlative myths that arise from them. Voegelin's clearest statement on the relationship between philosophy and revelation is to be found in his chapter on St. Paul, where he draws attention to the parallels between the philosophers and the apostle. "That is to be expected," he remarks, "since both the saint and the philosophers articulate the order constituted by man's response to a theophany. The accent, however, has shifted decisively from the divinely noetic order incarnate in the world to the divinely pneumatic salvation from its disorder, from the paradox of reality to the abolition of the paradox, from the experience of the directional movement to its consummation."[15] He distinguishes them as noetic and pneumatic theophanies, depending on which dimension of the experience is emphasized. Philosophy unfolds the noetic or rational order that emanates from its pneumatic contact with the divine; revelation looks toward the consummation of its pneumatic experience but also remains aware of the requirement for a noetic ordering of the community.

On this view the two symbolisms are correlative. Judaism and Christianity provide a greater differentiation of the transcendent divine *pneuma* that reveals itself within history as the Redeemer of mankind. Philosophy contains greater noetic precision and the rational categories so essential to the creation of individual and social order within history. Far from being opposed, they are derived from a common source in the illuminative experience of theophany, and their elaboration unfolds between the poles of the struggle to realize order in existence and the pull toward the eternal order beyond all struggle with existence. On any basis this is a daring

14. Voegelin, *Order and History,* vol. 4, *The Ecumenic Age* (Baton Rouge: Louisiana State University Press, 1974), 7–11; "The Beginning and the Beyond: A Meditation on Truth," in *The Collected Works of Eric Voegelin,* vol. 28, *What Is History? And Other Late Unpublished Writings,* ed. Thomas A. Hollweck and Paul Caringella (Baton Rouge: Louisiana State University Press, 1990), 173–232.

15. Voegelin, *The Ecumenic Age,* 241.

reconsideration of one of the long-standing disputes of Western civilization. It is replete with consequences for all areas of human life and it may well be Voegelin's greatest theoretical achievement. But is it a satisfactory way of conceiving the reason-revelation distinction?

There is probably no better test than to juxtapose Voegelin's correlation to the heightened opposition between philosophy and theology articulated by Strauss. Drawing on their own epistolary dialogue on this question and extending it by means of their writings, it should be possible to probe the relationship between Athens and Jerusalem a little further. Strauss has provided the most forceful expression of the conventional distinction between them, and Voegelin has developed the most profound reconciliation of them since Hegel. The question is, does Voegelin provide a means of resolving the disjunctions that Strauss regards as ultimate? Can he demonstrate, not only that one can, but that one ought to be both a believer and a philosopher?

The first disjunction to be overcome is that which regards their different conceptions of morality as determinative. Strauss seems to be conceding this in his identification of morality as the common ground between philosophy and revelation. He even goes on to acknowledge the extent to which revelation, with its emphasis on humility and obedience to the divine will, offers a stronger moral foundation than the philosophic reliance on magnanimous man's sense of self-worth and superiority to all wrongdoing. But why should these be exclusive possibilities? Is it not possible that magnanimous man might recognize that a truer sense of self-worth is to be acquired when reflecting on the self in light of the redemptive divine love? Perhaps this might spark the Augustinian insight that the human soul that relies exclusively on its own strength eventually collapses into the abyss of pride. What is needed is some means of understanding the process as a movement from a more compact morality to a more differentiated one. In some sense this is already implied in Strauss's own recognition that the revelatory morality is superior—which means that "reason" and "revelation" are commensurable, not simply irreconcilable.

To pursue this further it would be necessary to overcome the second opposition that Strauss identifies between intellectual obedience to God and the free pursuit of rational inquiry. They are irresolvable only if the rational pursuit of truth necessarily requires disobedience to divine reality. What about the possibility that rationality is to be acquired only by participation in the luminous order of the divine source? A major consequence of Voegelin's work, it seems to me, has been to demonstrate that the classical understanding of *nous* is rooted in participation in the divine *Nous*. There is no rationality, Voegelin insists, apart from the ordering of human reason toward the divine. This would seem to carry the further implication that the unfolding of reason outside of the Greek context would also involve fidelity to the pattern of the differentiating revelation of God within history. This is surely the major thesis of *Order and History.*[16]

Voegelin has been able to undertake such an exploration of the revelatory grounding of order because he has been able to overcome the third fundamental dichotomy concerning the interpretation of symbols. Strauss, while he acknowledges that they cannot be shown not to have come from God, not to be an expression of divine revelation, insists that neither can they be positively demonstrated to have a transcendent origin. The best that can be said for them is that they are "a human interpretation of God's actions."[17] But there is a third possibility between the alternatives of divine or human origination, that they are divine-human symbols created through the mutual participation of divine and human reality within the revelatory encounter. They are neither strictly divine nor strictly human but partake of both sides. How then do we recognize them as such? Voegelin's answer, I believe, is that by reconstructing the experiences behind them and recognizing or failing to recognize the authoritative divine presence, we already "know" within our own souls.

There is a strong prima facie case to be made that the "conflicts" between reason and revelation dissolve when they are viewed within the movement of grace perfecting nature. But this does not answer Strauss's fundamental concern, which is the concern of secular science in general,

16. Voegelin formulated it in the Walgreen Lectures as "the principle that a theory of human existence in society must operate within the medium of experiences which have differentiated historically. There is a strict correlation between the theory of human existence and the historical differentiation of experiences in which this existence has gained its self-understanding. Neither is the theorist permitted to disregard any part of this experience for one reason or another; nor can he take his position at an Archimedean point outside the substance of history. Theory is bound by history in the sense of the differentiating experiences. Since the maximum of differentiation was achieved through Greek philosophy and Christianity, this means concretely that theory is bound to move within the historical horizon of classical and Christian experiences" (*The New Science of Politics* [Chicago: University of Chicago Press, 1952], 79).

17. Strauss, *Rebirth of Classical Political Rationalism*, 261.

that by adopting this perspective we abandon reason to faith. Strauss is concerned that the acknowledgment of the "suprarationality" of revelation is tantamount to succumbing to the darkness of irrationality.[18] He may be willing to grant the possibility of grace perfecting nature, but from the side of nature it still looks like the abolition of reason. A leap of faith is required before all is made clear to us again, and it is precisely that leap that is without foundation. Voegelin seems to have been aware of Strauss's concern within their dialogue and recognized this as a core difficulty that his work would have to overcome. The depth of his penetration of this issue alone would make his efforts worthy of attention. His work might be read as an extended reply to the objections inconclusively raised in the letters with Strauss.

But the letters provide an important starting point, in particular, the two most substantial letters in the collection, Letters 38 and 39. In the first of them Voegelin insists on rejecting the premise from which Strauss begins, that we can distinguish a priori between reason and revelation. "The contrast between human knowledge and revealed knowledge can, therefore, not be set up without qualification." His point is that the characterization of revealed knowledge as different already puts in question the authenticity of its source. When we go beyond that to identify it as knowledge that human beings claim to have received from God, then "not only is the content of revelation psychologized, but also its presumed source, namely God, is denied." Voegelin's position is that the problem of revelation is "inseparable from the problem of recognizing revelation as such."[19] How is it possible to determine what is and what is not revelation if we do not already possess some implicit criterion of what revelation is. That is, we must already know what revelation is.

This, Voegelin emphasizes, is what revelation has always been about. There has been a process of sifting through the claims to revelation to distinguish the genuine from the spurious, and this has been done on the basis of the community tradition that is grounded in the living experience of revelation. The passage in which Voegelin develops his position is sufficiently valuable to be worth quoting in full.

> These formulations seem to be necessary so as to understand certain historical facts appropriately, as, for example, the problem of levels

18. Ibid., 264–65.
19. Voegelin to Strauss, 22 April 1951.

> of clarity of the revelation, which is suggested by the Pauline series of nature, law, and spirit. Knowledge can be revealed knowledge even when it is not understood as such as, for example, "natural" law. Thereto belongs also Clement of Alexandria's conception that Greek philosophy is the "old testament" of the heathens, or the patristic theory of the *anima naturaliter Christiana.* And above all the factum of the *doctrina Christiana,* understood as a two-thousand-year development of revelation, belongs here. The "word" of God is not a word that can be pronounced, but is instead a meaning that can be articulated in a very "free" interpretation that legitimates itself from the presence of the spirit in the historical community.[20]

Without this more expansive notion of revelation, then, we will be unable to account for the process by which its interpretation is progressively refined and clarified over time. We will even be unable to explain how we are able to recognize revelation.

Indeed, without such an intuitive understanding of revelation we will run the danger of unraveling the whole of human knowledge. Even the distinction of "natural" or merely "human" knowledge is derived from the awareness of its not being divine knowledge. Without the openness to revelation, then, human knowledge finds itself compelled to establish the "pregivens" of the order in which it finds itself, only now out of the resources of its own ego. The tortuous reflections of modern epistemology from Descartes to Husserl constitute an extensive illustration of the difficulties. Voegelin is surely correct in maintaining that the relationship of the 'I' to the world, the reliance on the intelligibility and order of reality, and the recognition of the being of God beyond time are more properly established through an articulation of the "pregivens" of consciousness. This is the knowledge of revelation, whether in its self-conscious differentiation of Judaism and Christianity or in its implicit presence in the law of God written in the human heart.

In this sense Strauss is correct in complaining "that all alleged refutations of revelation presuppose unbelief in revelation, and all alleged refutations of philosophy presuppose faith in revelation."[21] But the point is not to regard this lack of agreement on presuppositions as the last word. It is only the first word in a conversation that ought to raise the question of

20. Ibid.
21. Strauss, *Rebirth,* 269.

which set of presuppositions is the more inclusive. If philosophy, modern examples notwithstanding, is based on the presupposition of openness to the divine, then it is irrelevant that revelation is itself based on a similar expectation of divine presence. The question to be asked therefore is to what extent philosophy is itself rooted in and expressive of the movement that unfolds into revelation.

Strauss himself understandably provides confirmation for this connection. Philosophy is the quest for knowledge of essence, for the nature of reality as it is in itself and apart from appearances and conventions. It aims ultimately at a comprehensive knowledge of the whole in which it finds itself and for this reason comes into competition with the comprehensive knowledge of God. But philosophy need not lose itself in the futile Promethean hubris of an effort that reached its first complete expression in Spinoza. In many ways Spinoza represents the failure of philosophy when it sets out on the basis of a categorical opposition to revelation. It was a failure that was inherent in the project from the start because "God's perfection implies that he is incomprehensible."[22] A more reasonable and more fruitful approach would be to pursue the wisdom, concerning the whole, that is available to a human being. This would entail the Socratic recognition that the god alone is wise and that human wisdom consists in following the divine wisdom.

The quest for form would unfold into the meditative pursuit of the divine ground that is the formative source of all. It would begin, as Voegelin has shown of the philosophic experience, in a state of restless ignorance, of awareness of not being the origin and end of all things and of erotic longing for what is the ground of all that exists. When this unfolds into the search for that which it knows as present in the search as the object of its quest, it arrives eventually at the Platonic vision of the Good that is beyond being in dignity and power. It is at that point of touching the divine, the Beyond, that the human nous participates in the divine *Nous* and apprehends the meaning of all things in their proper measure.[23] This is the comprehensive

22. Ibid., 267.

23. "The consciousness of questioning unrest in a state of ignorance becomes luminous to itself as a movement in the psyche toward the ground that is present in the psyche as its mover. . . . There would be no existential unrest moving toward the quest of the ground unless the unrest was already man's knowledge of his existence from a ground that he is not himself. The movements of the divine-human encounter are understood to form an intelligible unit of meaning, noetic in both substance and structure" (Voegelin, "Reason: The Classic Experience," *Published Essays,* 272–73).

knowledge that is available to human beings. Philosophic wisdom is a participation in the divine wisdom.[24]

Through this process of meditative actualization of what it knows, philosophy has reached the threshold of revelation. Whether revelation occurs is of course not simply a function of the human agent. What is essential is that the constitution of human consciousness through the tension toward the divine ground has become transparent. The unfolding has reached the point of confirming or validating the faith with which the quest began. Strauss regards this dependency on faith as a vulnerability of philosophy, that "it is incapable of giving an account of its own necessity."[25] But this is not the same as admitting that the quest is groundless. On the contrary, the pursuit of truth in the most comprehensive sense can be shown to be most reliable by following out the meditative quest for the divine ground of existence. Through the process in which the search becomes transparent for the tension of attraction and being drawn, ignorance and knowledge, the ground that is the source of the trust becomes present. Philosophy may not be able to validate its own faith, but it is capable of articulating it to the point where the divine reality that underlies it becomes transparent.

This means that philosophy does not operate within a context of radical ignorance. Strauss seems to suggest such a position when he observes that "the right way of life cannot be fully established except by an understanding of the nature of man, and the nature of man cannot be fully clarified except by an understanding of the nature of the whole," and draws from it the conclusion "that the right way of life remains questionable."[26] His characterization of our "ignorance concerning the most important thing" is valid only if knowledge is defined as discursive, necessary knowledge. It is not valid if we accept as knowledge the very faith on which philosophy itself rests, and which is capable of articulation into the kind of concrete

24. In this sense Hegel may be a more instructive example than Spinoza, because he understood more clearly that the human and divine wisdom could become coincident only when they had transcended their separate identities. *The Phenomenology of Spirit* was "the ladder" that showed the individual the way toward this absolute knowledge of science. It had become possible only because the historical process had reached the culmination in which the separation between human and divine had been overcome within the self-consciousness of absolute Spirit. This is why Hegel claimed to have gone beyond the love of wisdom to its actual possession.

25. Strauss, *Rebirth*, 270.

26. Ibid., 260.

experience of order described above. Strauss's reluctance to accept this possibility together with his insistence on necessary knowledge of the whole is perhaps the ultimate point of division with Voegelin.

Yet they may not be as far apart as they appear. For Strauss, the most crucial consideration on this topic is to recall his recommendation to live within the tension of Jerusalem and Athens. As a philosopher he feels compelled to reject the authority of revelation; otherwise he cannot be free to pursue necessary knowledge of the whole. But as a Jew he cannot forget the revelatory truth that constitutes his own community; otherwise he ceases to be a Jew except in name. There is a remarkable passage in his "Preface to Spinoza's Critique of Religion" in which his closeness to Voegelin on these matters becomes apparent. Discussing the skeptical critique of religious knowledge, he dismisses them as without foundation.

> God's revealing Himself to man, His addressing man, is not merely known through traditions going back to the remote past and is therefore now "merely believed" but is genuinely known through present experience which every human being can have if he does not refuse himself to it. This experience is not a kind of self-experience, of the actualization of a human potentiality, of the human mind coming into its own, into what it desires or is naturally inclined to, but of something undesired, coming from the outside, going against man's grain; it is the only awareness of something absolute which cannot be relativized in any way as everything else, rational or nonrational, can; it is the experience of God as the Thou, the father and king of all men; it is the experience of an unequivocal command addressed to me here and now as distinguished from general laws or ideas which are always disputable and permitting of exceptions; only by surrendering to God's experienced call which calls for one's loving Him with all one's heart, with all one's soul and with all one's might can one come to see the other human being as his brother and love him as himself.[27]

It would be hard to improve on this statement as an account and a defense of the validity of religious knowledge. Accepting that it is the same form of knowledge that is the source of the faith from which philosophy springs,

27. Strauss, *Liberalism Ancient and Modern*, 232–33.

one can only wonder why Strauss could not recognize this experiential knowledge as the bridge that unites the poles of faith and reason.

Voegelin's genius was to have understood the continuity between them. He saw that reason and revelation are one in the experiential openness to the divine ground from which both philosophy and religion spring. The great difficulty for him was to overcome the charge Strauss leveled at all such efforts, that "every synthesis is actually an option either for Jerusalem or for Athens."[28] Clearly Jerusalem had not been given priority, despite the charge that Voegelin had made the acceptance of revelation a condition of philosophizing, since the synthesis had largely been accomplished by recasting the revelatory events within the language of philosophical reflection. The most telling objection has been that Voegelin introduces a *sub rosa* option for Athens. Has Voegelin reduced the word of God to the *logos* of the philosophers?

This of course is the charge that has been confronted by all such efforts of synthesis back to the Patres, and often with justification. Discovering the right balance in the unity of reason and revelation has not been easy over the past two millennia. Voegelin too has come under suspicion, particularly in light of his later work, of turning the historical uniqueness of Christianity into the immanent dynamics of consciousness. Such criticisms may have a surface plausibility, but when examined more deeply turn out to be wide of the mark. Indeed, the extent to which Voegelin has succeeded in reaching a synthesis that preserves the identity of all sides is demonstrated by this objection.

Voegelin's integration of reason and revelation has been achieved, not by reducing the biblical experience to the level of philosophy, but by raising the philosophical explorations up to the level of the revelatory events. Instead of looking toward a least common denominator of the two, he has sought to relate them as levels or strata that reach back in depth to the primary experiences of the human race. He expressed it best in the context of a discussion of how Aquinas's principle, that Christ is the head of all human beings, applies today. "In practice," Voegelin explained, "this means that one has to recognize, and make intelligible, the presence of Christ in a Babylonian hymn, or a Taoist speculation, or a Platonic dialogue, just as much as in a Gospel."[29] It is not that the Christian

28. Strauss to Voegelin, 25 February 1951.

29. Voegelin, "Response to Professor Altizer's 'A New History and a New but Ancient God?'" *Published Essays*, 294.

revelation is made to conform to the other traditions, but that they are in some sense raised up to the Christian level. Besides being understood on their own terms, the hymn, the speculation, and the dialogue can also be read as prefigurations of the truth attained within revelation. Rather than a reduction to a homogeneous medium Voegelin presents an opening to the mystery of the partnership of human beings in the search for truth.

The unity between reason and revelation and between all the symbolic forms of human history can be articulated through a theory of equivalences of compactness and differentiation. It enables us to understand how one symbolism emerges from another, for example philosophy from the world of the myth. How could it emerge if it were not already in some way implicitly present within the earlier form? And if it did emerge, how was it recognized as superior to the preceding symbolism if it did not constitute an advance in articulating what was already known? At the same time, compactness and differentiation constitute a theoretical approach that preserves the validity of all the historical symbolizations of order.[30] Differentiation occurs within a context structured by the earlier more compact symbolic forms. The later developments do not render the earlier obsolete, they are differentiations only of a part of the whole. Symbolizations of the whole, of the cosmos, remain the same as far back as we care to trace them.[31]

The relationship between philosophy and revelation is not of course simply an advance from compactness to differentiation, since philosophy is in some respects more differentiated than revelation and in some ways less. They are more properly characterized as parallel differentiations that struggle with their own surrounding compactness. But even where they are not parallel and apparently opposed, as in regard to the creation of the world, the necessity of divine redemption, or the incarnation of God in human nature, they are not necessarily in conflict. The differences can be

30. Voegelin, "Equivalences of Experience and Symbolization in History," *Published Essays*, 115–33.

31. It is part of the mystery of the process of history that the earlier symbolic forms do not simply disappear but continue to exist alongside the new symbolizations that have emerged from them. This is surely a reflection of the wholeness of the traditional symbolisms that they retain their validity even when they are succeeded by more differentiated expressions. Judaism and Christianity are a particularly clear example of this process of succession without obsolescence. Nothing is to be gained from juxtaposing them as alternatives of truth or falsity, or by lapsing into a confused subjective indifference. Only an approach that is willing to acknowledge distinctions without asserting definitive superiority or inferiority fits the situation.

resolved in light of the movement from compact cosmological formulations to the more differentiated transcendent horizon. If this were not the case, how else could one account for the ability of a rather limited religious movement within Judaism to persuade the world civilized by Greek philosophy that it represented the more adequate account of the order of reality?

Even further, the question becomes whether reason and revelation ultimately serve the one truth. If truth is one, however dimly perceived it may be by contingent human beings, then we must preserve the faith that reason and revelation are united. To do this we must take seriously the task of exploring their continuity to the fullest extent available to us. Strauss's tension between Athens and Jerusalem defines the impasse better than it has been expressed in recent times. Voegelin's theory of equivalences of compactness and differentiation provides the most convincing means of overcoming it in the contemporary world. It is intriguing to consider that it may well have been their epistolary dialogue that provided some of the impetus for articulating their respective positions.